BELINsup

Langues

The English of Law: England and Wales

Jean-Éric BRANAA, ANNE BRUNON-ERNST, NICKI CHAUDOIR, CHARLES DAVEY,

SÉVERINE LETALLEUR, JENNIFER MERCHANT, YASMINE MOHAMMEDI,

FRÉDÉRIQUE PODOLIN, YVONNE-MARIE ROGEZ, WILLIAM YEAGO

Belin: 8, rue Férou 75278 Paris cedex 06
www.editions-belin.com

Sommaire

Pour les enseignants :
Vous trouverez des informations complémentaires sur cet ouvrage sur notre site
(www.editions-belin.com) dans l'espace enseignants.

Avant-propos

Cet ouvrage, rédigé en anglais, est le fruit de la collaboration d'enseignants d'anglais juridique de l'Université Panthéon Assas (Paris II) et de Charles Davey, avocat britannique.

Ce livre est à la fois un manuel d'apprentissage de l'anglais juridique dans l'enseignement supérieur et un « livre ressource » où enseignants, étudiants et professionnels pourront trouver des informations précises correspondant à leurs besoins. Par conséquent, l'ouvrage se destine aux étudiants de droit, d'autres disciplines (études anglophones, sciences politiques, économie, histoire), aux professionnels (juristes, avocats, chercheurs en droit) et à tous ceux qui visent à améliorer leurs connaissances dans le domaine de l'anglais appliqué au droit anglais.

Ce manuel comporte 11 chapitres de difficulté croissante qui permettent d'aborder les grands thèmes nécessaires à la connaissance du système juridique britannique (chapitres 1 à 5) ainsi que celle de branches spécialisées répondant aux attentes d'un public désireux d'approfondir certains domaines du droit anglais (chapitres 6 à 11). Au sein de chaque chapitre, le lecteur retrouvera six sections cohérentes permettant un repérage aisé de son contenu.

Cet ouvrage intègre pour la première fois des volets juridiques absents jusquelà des ouvrages du même type. Il offre aussi un choix de textes récents, allant des parties écrites par les auteurs jusqu'aux documents authentiques (articles de presse et de recherche, extraits de manuels de droit anglais, décisions de justice, articles de loi, documents juridiques et professionnels, etc.).

L'anglais juridique étant indissociable de la culture et de l'histoire du Royaume-Uni, l'enseignement de la langue de spécialité ne peut faire l'économie du contexte propre aux institutions et au droit anglais. Ainsi, la première partie de chaque chapitre, *Fundamentals*, est une présentation complète et accessible des notions nécessaires à la compréhension du point de droit abordé. Définitions, questions de compréhension et exercices sur les notions participent à la maîtrise des concepts. La seconde partie, *More about…*, apporte un complément d'information sur les points évoqués auparavant. Des activités sont proposées à l'apprenant pour utiliser ses connaissances. La troisième partie, *Off the presses*, se compose d'un ou plusieurs articles d'actualité et d'exercices qui offrent une activité complète sur le thème du chapitre. La quatrième partie, *Food for thought*, est une section de niveau avancé, destinée à développer la capacité des étudiants à aborder des textes de longueur et de difficulté plus importantes, tout en exigeant un travail de recherche faisant appel aux compétences acquises. Une attention toute particulière est attachée à la compréhension orale dans *Listening*, la cinquième partie des chapitres, qui s'accompagne d'un CD-audio. La sixième partie, *Grammar practice*, s'inscrit dans l'objectif d'améliorer la maîtrise de la langue anglaise. La présence de divers index à la fin du livre permet un repérage facile et transversal.

L'un des buts de cet ouvrage (ainsi que du deuxième volume, *The English of law and politics: the USA*, à paraître en 2007) est d'adapter l'enseignement de l'anglais juridique aux exigences de la réforme LMD qui requiert la connaissance d'au moins une langue étrangère. Les cinq compétences détaillées par le Conseil de l'Europe (compréhension écrite, expression écrite, compréhension orale, expression orale en continu, expression orale en interaction)[1] sont abordées. Selon la classification établie par la grille de référence du Conseil de l'Europe, ce livre correspond à un niveau progressant de B1 à C1/C2, c'est-à-dire de la première année de Licence jusqu'au Master 2, voire aux études doctorales.

Bien que ce volume n'ait pas pour objet d'être un manuel de préparation à une certification universitaire, nationale ou européenne, il constitue une parfaite référence pour un travail éventuel de préparation. Il peut aussi servir de complément à d'autres ouvrages ou programmes qui préparent à des certificats internationaux d'anglais juridique.

Les Auteurs

---

1. Le Conseil de l'Europe a défini plusieurs niveaux de maîtrise des compétences, mais il importe de souligner qu'une certification en anglais de spécialité en deçà du niveau B2 ne saurait être acceptable pour un employeur qui, dans ses critères de recrutement, accorde une place importante à la maîtrise d'une langue étrangère de spécialité. Voir le site du Conseil de l'Europe pour plus d'informations : www.culture2.coe.int/portfolio/ inc.asp?L=E&M=$t/208-1-0-1/main_pages/welcome.html.

Chapter 1

Origins and development of English law

1. Fundamentals

Europe uses two major systems of law that have developed from each country's specific history and customs: the Roman system (otherwise known as codified law, applied from the 7th century onwards) and the English **common law** system. The Roman system was adopted in France and remains the basis of many other modern systems, notably in continental Europe but also in Quebec (Canada), Louisiana (United States of America), Japan, Latin America and most former colonies of continental European countries. Other countries, including the United States of America, Canada and Australia, have adopted the common law system. The English legal system is in force in England and Wales. The administrative entity of England and Wales is not to be mistaken for **Great Britain** (GB), **the United Kingdom** (UK) or the **British Isles**.

Two kinds of law

England is often referred to as a common law country whereas continental legal systems are described as **civil law** systems. One author has used the story of Brutus stealing Caesar's marble to turn it into a statue to explain the differences between the two systems (cf. P. Fitgerald & G. Kewley, *This Law of Ours*, Sidney: Prentice Hall, 1978, pp. 35-6). Once the marble has been made into a statue, can Caesar get his marble back?

Law professors of continental legal systems, influenced by Roman law, would approach this question from an academic perspective and raise questions of **rights** and **duties**, such as, "Who should own the statue, the person who owned the raw material or the person who transformed it into a work of art?"

In contrast, judges of common law countries would work from a practical perspective and focus on concrete **remedies**. "Can Caesar take the statue? Can Brutus keep the statue? Can Brutus pay the cost of the raw material to Caesar?"

The common law countries' approach is different from that of Roman law countries. The reason for this difference lies in the history the British Isles. Although the Romans briefly conquered England and Wales, Roman law did not have the lasting influence there that it had on the Continent. The roots of the English legal system grew after the Norman invasion.

Common law can be defined in two different manners : 1) as the legal system in England and Wales in its historical development; 2) as the general system of law, its sources and its particular set of rules established within the United Kingdom. There are four sources of English law: custom, case law, UK legislation and EU legislation.

Custom

The historical origins of custom

Custom law first took hold during the Anglo-Saxon period when local customs determined most laws affecting family rights, ownership and inheritance, contracts and personal violence. The Norman Conquest of England, begun with the Battle of Hastings in 1066 won by William the Conqueror, laid the foundations for the English legal system. Before 1066 there was no unified body of law in the country. Local unwritten **customs** were used to oversee, compensate and punish members of the community.

From custom law to common law

The Norman conquerors sought to establish their rule in England by introducing their methods of administration. William I appointed **itinerant justices** to examine different local practices dealing with disputes and crimes, with the goal of rejecting the less pragmatic and reasonable ones and founding a set of regulations to be applied uniformly throughout the country. The King sent itinerant commissioners out to different parts of the country to carry out varied tasks which became increasingly judicial in nature. Common law was built up from both custom and judge-made law. This did not mean that the custom automatically obtained the status of law. What was a practice among the judges became a system thanks to the principle of *stare decisis*, whereby judges should follow decisions taken by their predecessors. The law was created by the decisions of judges in recognising some customs and not others.

Custom today

Today, custom consists of established patterns of behaviour that can be verified objectively within a particular social setting. Custom has the status of law when a particular practice is followed and relevant actors consider it to be law. Hence, in the UK system, it is always possible for any individual to plead custom, as long as he or she complies with the requirements for it to be law . A given custom must meet several conditions to be legally enforceable. It must be:

1) reasonable;

2) in existence since "time immemorial" (fixed by statute in 1275 as meaning since at least 1189). In practice today, claimants seek to establish that a custom has the force of law by proving that the custom has existed as far back as living memory can go, thus turning to the oldest inhabitant as a witness. For example, in a dispute over the right to use local land, if the other side could prove that the land was under water until the 17th or 18th century, the right could not have existed before 1189;

3) clear and certain;

4) specific to a particular geographical region;

5) uninterrupted;

6) exercised in a peaceful manner, and with the permission of someone else;

7) consistent with other local customs;

8) in conformity with existing statutes.

Examples of enforceable customs are found in Chapter 9 (Employment law). Today, the conditions are so stringent that the latest case to prove custom failed: *Beckett Ltd v Lyons* [1967] 1 All ER 833. Indeed, custom is seldom involved in litigation.

Case law

Common law and its developments

Over the centuries, common law developed as a system that had its shortcomings. Firstly, it was a rigid system, especially because it was based on a system of **writs**. The **maxim** "*ubi remedies ubi ius*" stated that a **remedy** at common law existed only if there was a procedure to enforce it. Procedures were started with writs. There were several writs available, but only a limited number. The **plaintiff** (now also known as the **claimant**) needed to select the appropriate writ to start his action. If there was no writ corresponding to his case, the claimant had neither claim nor remedy. Secondly, in some cases the remedies awarded by the courts were inadequate. Except in real actions, at common law, the plaintiff could only be granted **damages** for a civil wrong. Thirdly, the common law only recognised certain rights. For instance, it did not acknowledge the concept of **trust**, which was already commonly used at the time in the management of estates. As **litigants** grew dissatisfied with the rigidity, costs and delays of the common law, the practice grew of petitioning the King for redress. Successive monarchs gradually handed over the management of petitions to the **Lord Chancellor**. On hearing the petitions, the Lord Chancellor took decisions based on what he deemed fair or equitable.

The difference between common law and equity

Hence **equity** was born. It developed through a certain number of doctrines. For example, in equity a judge will consider what ought to have been done and not what was actually done. It is also important to remember the following maxim: "He who comes to equity must come with clean hands," which means that an equitable remedy is at the **discretion** of the court. Equity recognises rights that the common law does not, such as the **equity of redemption** and the rights of a **beneficiary** under a trust. Equity grants numerous remedies which are still available today, such as **injunction**, **specific performance** and **rescission**.

If, at the beginning, equity was meant to supplement the common law and not to challenge it – hence the maxim "equity follows the law" – in the long term, equity conflicted with common law. Moreover, although equity was created to remedy the deficiencies of common law, it was not without its own problems. Lord Eldon comments on one of the shortcomings of equity in *Gee v Prichard* (1818): "The equity of this court varies like the Chancellor's foot." As a consequence, in the 19th century, the administration of equity and common law were substantially amended in the wake of the reform of the justice system (see Chapter 4, The court system). Nowadays, equity and common law are administered alongside each other. S.25 of the Judicature Act 1873 provides that if a conflict appears between common law and equity, the latter will prevail. This is reasserted under s.49 of the Supreme Court Act 1981. Nonetheless, the basic principles of both equity and the common law remain the same: if the claimant can substantiate his or her claim, he or she has a right to a common law remedy, whereas equitable remedies remain discretionary.

The doctrine of precedent

Case law is often also referred to as "judge-made law", though the present-day role of judges as lawmakers is much reduced compared to the past. Whilst the common law is constantly developing, most new law in England and Wales is **statute** law. Even here, however, judges play an important role in the shaping of English law by deciding upon cases and by interpreting primary and secondary legislation. The body of their decisions is thus known as **case** law, i.e. legal decisions that interpret prior decisions, statutes and other legal texts. These decisions are systematically collected and assembled into volumes of reported cases, **law reports**, probably the most important source of law for the legal profession.

The basis of the system of **precedent** is known as the principle of *stare decisis* ("stand by what has previously been decided in a similar case"). A statement of law by a judge in a case can become **binding** on judges of inferior courts in similar cases. This means that 1) inferior judges may not arrive at a different conclusion in a similar case, and therefore must adopt the argument or arguments put forth in the previous ruling, which is referred to as a precedent, and,

2) that the court hierarchy is important in defining which court ruling is binding. Generally speaking, higher court decisions are binding upon lower courts. The Supreme Court (formerly known as the House of Lords, or, to give it its full name, the Appellate Committee of the House of Lords) sits at the apex of the court structure. Its decisions are binding on all lower courts. In order to allow for a more flexible system, the House of Lords is no longer bound by its previous rulings (as explained in the 1966 Practice Statement), though it is reluctant to depart from them and only rarely does so.

A judicial decision will include a statement of the **material** facts, a statement of legal principles material to the decision (the *ratio decidendi*, i.e. the reasoning behind the decision) and the court's decision or ruling. Decisions frequently contain other statements about legal points raised in the case that are not material to the decision. The latter are referred to as *obiter dicta*, i.e. statements about the law made "by the way" and thus not strictly necessary for the legal basis of the decision. Only the *ratio decidendi* is subsequently binding upon lower courts; the *obiter dicta* are not binding but, if made by a higher court, are of "persuasive authority". Persuasive authority also includes decisions emanating from equivalent or lower courts, from the Judicial Committee of the Privy Council, from the courts of Commonwealth countries, from the European Court of Human Rights, from legal textbooks or periodicals, from conventions, etc.

The doctrine of precedent governs the development of case law: a later judge will have to determine 1) what pronouncements of earlier decisions are relevant to the present case, and 2) what parts of the earlier decisions are binding.

Thanks to the judicial tools of **overruling**, **distinguishing** and **departing**, the doctrine of precedent is rather more flexible than might at first appear. A higher court can overrule the decision of a lower court. A judge who thinks that there are material differences between his or her case and an apparently binding precedent may be able to distinguish the case before him from the precedent, entitling him to apply different principles. The Court of Appeal, however, is normally bound by its own decisions, though it can depart from them in limited circumstances as when a previous decision was given *per incuriam*, i.e. in ignorance of a statute or an earlier case that should have led the court to have made a different decision. The House of Lords can depart from its own previous decisions, but is reluctant to and rarely does so.

UK legislation

As previously mentioned, the major source of UK law is statute law, otherwise known as legislation. Legislation can be either primary or secondary. The British

Parliament at Westminster (London) enacts **primary legislation** (see Chapter 2, Modern political institutions), in the form of **Acts of Parliament**. Government ministers are empowered by Parliament to introduce a great volume of legislation known as **secondary legislation** or **delegated legislation**. Such legislation is issued in the form of **statutory instruments** (approximately three thousand per year), otherwise known as **orders** or **regulations**.

European Union legislation

The United Kingdom is a member of the European Union, hence European Union legislation is also a source of English law. The interaction between EU law and national law covers those areas where the two systems complement each other. In cases of conflict between UK and EU legislation, EU law takes precedence. However, European Union legislation contains no specific provision stating that European Community law overrides or is subordinate to national law. Nevertheless, the principle of the primacy of European Community law over national law was pronounced by the European Court of Justice in the case *Costa v ENEL* (1964).

EU legislation is having an increasing effect on all aspects of life in the United Kingdom, ranging from health, education and safety to movement of goods.

EU law consists of Treaty Articles, regulations and directives, decisions and recommendations (see Chapter 11, EU law).

Emphasis must be placed on the role of the European Court of Justice and the Court of First Instance. The main mission of the latter, established in 1989 to ease the load of the former, is to guarantee that EU law is observed and correctly applied among Member States and to strengthen the protection of individual interests.

The responsibilities and powers of the Court of Justice revolve around issuing opinions on international agreements and addressing disputes:
- between Member States;
- between the EU and Member States;
- between institutions;
- between individuals and the EU;
- between individuals and Member States

One cannot underestimate the importance of decisions and rulings in the uniform interpretation of European Community law. The Court also issues rulings on breaches of Community law by the Member States. As a result of the Amsterdam Treaty, the Court has been granted more power in cases of infringement of European Union legislation.

The European Convention on Human Rights

Most of the European Convention on Human Rights has now been "incorporated" into English law by virtue of the Human Rights Act 1998. The articles incorporated are listed in Schedule 1 to the Act. Section 3 provides that all legislation passed by the United Kingdom Parliament must be interpreted in such a way as to make it compatible with the articles of the Convention listed in Schedule 1. If this is not possible, then a higher court (High Court, Court of Appeal or House of Lords) can make a declaration of incompatibility. This does *not* give precedence to the articles of the Convention, but allows Parliament to amend English law to make it compatible with the Convention, which it can do using a special "fast track" procedure.

Parliament is not obliged to make any changes to domestic law, and accordingly remains supreme in this area.

Definitions in context and key words

Act of Parliament: a law passed by Parliament and having received the Royal Assent.

beneficiary: a person meant to receive something, to benefit or gain profit from something.

binding: requiring lower courts to follow earlier decisions.

British Isles: a group of islands in Western Europe comprising Great Britain, Ireland and adjacent islands.

case law: the corpus of judicial decisions.

civil law: the general system of law based on the *Corpus Juris Civilis* and prevalent in continental Europe and Scotland, Central and South America, and is to be distinguished from the common law system.

claimant: the person who first lodges a complaint in a civil case.

common law: the general system of law, its sources and its particular set of rules established in England and Wales.

custom, customs: established patterns of behaviour established as the norm within a particular social setting.

damages: monetary compensation.

delegated legislation (see secondary legislation).

depart *(v.)* from: refuse to follow (a previous decision of the same court).

discretion: prudence; ability to adapt action to circumstance. (The exercise of discretion by judges is an inherent aspect of judicial independence under the doctrine of the separation of powers.)

distinguish *(v.)*: apply different principles to (a decision), when the judge decides that there are material differences between his or her case and a precedent.

duty: obligation.

equity: a part of the common law system that provides remedies other than damages.

equity of redemption: a right to redeem or recover property in certain circumstances.

Great Britain: island in Western Europe comprising England, Scotland, and Wales.

injunction: an equitable remedy in the form of a court order that (usually) prohibits a party from doing or continuing to do something.

itinerant justices: (historical) a group of judges who travelled throughout England to examine local practices and deal with disputes and crimes.

Law reports: volumes containing previous decisions.

litigant: a person engaged in a lawsuit.

Lord Chancellor: (historical) important adviser and minister of the monarch.

material: tangible, concrete (facts or elements of a case).

maxim: a general rule of conduct.

obiter dictum: comment in a judicial decision that says something "by the way" about the law or the facts of the case and is thus not necessary for the legal basis of the decision.

order: delegated legislation in the form of a statutory instrument, rule or regulation.

overrule *(v.)*: rule against, cancel or reverse (a previous decision).

per incuriam: (literal translation) "through want of care", (referring to a court decision) taken without reference to a statutory provision or earlier judgment which would have been relevant.

plaintiff: (see the more recent term, **claimant**).

precedent: a previous judicial decision that has a subsequent binding effect.

primary legislation: laws passed by the UK Parliament.

ratio decidendi: the core reasoning within a judicial decision.

regulation: rule.

remedy: solution, compensation for a claimant.

rescission: an equitable remedy of the court which consists in the cancellation of a contract between the parties.

right: the power or liberty to which a person or a group is justly entitled or to which they have a moral or legal claim.

secondary legislation: laws passed by government bodies empowered to do so by Parliament.

specific performance: an equitable remedy in the form of a court order requiring a party to perform a specific act.

stare decisis: the principle of standing by what has previously been decided in a similar case.

statute: a law passed by Parliament, then received the Royal Assent, and now in the Statute Book.

statutory instrument: delegated or secondary legislation inroduced by Government ministers, exercising legislative powers delegated to them by an Act of Parliament.

trust: a property interest held by one person on behalf of another.

United Kingdom (or **United Kingdom of Great Britain and Northern Ireland**): country in Western Europe comprising Great Britain and Northern Ireland.

writ: a formal written order issued by an administrative or juridical authority.

Exercises

1 Write the question that corresponds to each of the following answers.

1. The general system of law, its sources and particular set of rules established in England and Wales.

2. When judges follow decisions taken by their predecessors.

3. In existence since "time immemorial".

4. The person who first lodges a complaint.

5. Injunctions, specific performance, rescission.
6. Where case law is recorded.
7. The core legal reasoning of a judicial decision.
8. A form of persuasive authority.
9. Two forms of legislation.
10. The case that defined the primacy of European Community law over national law.
11. That which obliges a judge in an inferior court to follow the reasoning in a similar previous case.

2 **Answer the following questions in no more than three sentences.**

1. What is the main difference between the Roman legal system and the English common law system?
2. Why was equity developed?
3. Describe the hierarchical application of the doctrine of precedent.

3 **Discuss. Using the information provided in "Fundamentals", carry out the following tasks.**

1. In a short speech (five minutes) and in your own words, present the main points raised in this section.
2. Two students or two class groups : choose sides (English system versus the legal system in your home country) and debate the merits and drawbacks of both systems from the standpoint of the ordinary citizen.

2. More about...

A. A very short history of the English legal system before 1900

From the reign of Alfred the Great until the arrival of William the Conqueror in 1066, the people of England lived under a local form of feudalism. The lords, called *thegns*, administered justice to their tenants. Since land was often given to the church, many churchmen became lords, and these literate people were often familiar with Old Testament and Roman law. They codified elements of civil and criminal law in their Germanic dialect. Clans were organised in "hundreds" (100 families) and subunits called *tithings* (10 families); clan assemblies, presided over by ecclesiastics, served as courts of justice to settle disputes. Each side in a conflict would pronounce an oath and provide *compurgators* to support their declarations. Trials by contest or by test (ordeal) were the rule.

After the Norman Conquest, William I reinforced and centralised the feudal system from continental Europe by requiring lords to swear loyalty to him as vassals. Among his advisers were the Chancellor – a churchman and scholarly authority – and the first "lawyers" on English soil; his men replaced some of the ecclesiastics in county "courts". The law administered now derived from a combination of practices – Anglo-Saxon, Norman, Roman and canon. William had all the lands and properties surveyed and listed in the Domesday Book to organise taxation. Henry I continued the task by setting up an advisory group, the Exchequer, to deal with the finances of the realm.

What came to be known as the common law, because it was common to all of England, developed significantly under Henry II. He appointed judges to travel on circuits and hold court sessions across the land, replacing some of the lords' courts. A grand jury of twelve would establish the accusation, a petit jury of twelve would seek the facts of the case, and the rule of law would finally be pronounced. Meanwhile, separate ecclesiastical courts developed to handle church-related matters. The bitter conflict over who would try priests for crimes saw the King opposed by the Archbishop of Canterbury, Thomas à Becket, who was then murdered by four unthinking knights loyal to the monarch. This damaged the King's cause, so Henry had to let the church retain the right to judge its clerics, which it did with great leniency.

During Henry II's reign, a new royal court – later to be called the Court of Common Pleas – was set up at Westminster, while the financial committee became the Court of the Exchequer. The monarch's Chief Justician, Ranulf de Glanville, wrote a treatise explaining the system of writs as established under the Norman kings. A person of rank brought an action, or lawsuit, by paying for a writ to be issued, usually by the Chancellor. This type of official document had already been used in other legal systems, and here each new writ served to describe a particular kind of complaint. Once a "writ of debt", for example, had been created for a case, any subsequent demand for payment of debt required a copy of that original writ. As new situations arose, writs increased in number.

Despotic King John was unable to maintain full authority. His plotting caused him to lose Normandy and Brittany to Philippe Auguste; his refusal to appoint the papal choice as Archbishop of Canterbury infuriated the Pope, who excommunicated him until he accepted submission; his treatment of English barons led them to revolt, forcing him to sign their Magna Carta to protect their rights.

John's son Henry III seemed to further the cause of justice by creating the Court of King's Bench, but he ignored the rights formerly granted to the barons, who revolted once more. In 1265 he was obliged to accept the terms of Magna Carta and set up a "parlement" of barons and prelates at Westminster that could petition the King for action. A few years later Henry de Bracton, a judge, finished his work, *De Legibus Angliae*, which set down the cases making up the common law of the time and incorporated principles of Romanesque law. Henry III's successor, Edward I, had a wholly different relationship with the nobles of the land and took initiatives that made him popular. He conquered Wales (but not Scotland), partly reorganised the judicial system and started a yearbook to record new legal cases. Guilds of lawyers would soon begin the first law schools and prepare their own law reports. In 1295 Edward I set up a Model Parliament, which now included knights and burgesses, often descendants of lords; this sub-group would later become the House of Commons. A body of legislation began to grow, with statutes that codified existing rules and created new law. The power of the church was diminished in England and titles to land, if proved, were recorded in the Hundred Rolls.

The long reign of Edward III was marked by the beginning of the Hundred Years War in 1339. The King needed substantial funds for battle and could enact laws only with the full consent of Parliament, now clearly consisting of lords on one side and "commoners" on the other. At the same time, the feudal system was declining: after the Black Death, which killed over half of the population in 1349-50, the labour shortage led to more wage offers; commerce was now developing more quickly than ever. In 1362 Parliament changed the official language of the courts of law from the mixture of approximate Latin and Old Norman French to vernacular English, which would finally enable all parties to understand legal arguments, but it took over a century for the transition to take place.

The Plantagenet kings that followed also dealt with a strong Parliament, and at the same time their rival families fought the War of the Roses. When the Pope refused to allow the second Tudor king, Henry VIII, to divorce his wife Catherine, Henry summoned Parliament to extend his powers, establishing the Church of England and making him its Supreme Head in 1534, validating his divorce and remarriage, and declaring that any opponents were guilty of high treason. His Chancellor, Sir Thomas More, decided to resign in protest and was beheaded the following year. The study of canon law was now prohibited in England, but not that of Roman law, whose principles were a major contribution to the development of law in 16th century Scotland.

At the end of the Tudor dynasty, the judicial system still condoned harsh treatment of criminal defendants: torture, long imprisonment before trial, refusal of access to counsel. However, the rules of trial by jury were well established and did provide some protection.

The House of Stuart made final attempts to rule without the consent of Parliament. James I, after the Gunpowder Plot involving Catholic conspirators was uncovered in 1605, could not impose law bestowing tithes on the Church of England. He was obliged to grant members of Parliament freedom of speech so that they could express dissenting opinions. Charles I faced even more pressure, being forced to sign the Petition of Right before trying to dispense with Parliament altogether, which led to civil war and his own execution in 1649.

The Commonwealth was then established under the leadership of Oliver Cromwell, a Puritan. He managed to govern with Parliament, giving himself the title of Protector, until his death. His son proved unable to maintain the power, and the throne was restored to Charles II, who had grown up in France at the court of Louis XIV. He agreed to cooperate with Parliament and signed the Habeas Corpus Act in 1679. Under his reign the first political parties, the Whigs and the Tories, were established.

James II attempted to restore Catholicism in England, but was forced out; Parliament called upon Mary and her husband William of Orange to take the throne. At the start of the 18th century, the Act of Settlement (1701) and the Act of Union (1705) established the rules of succession and finalised the union of England, Wales and Scotland as Great Britain.

George I came from Germany and spoke no English. As he was not interested in becoming involved in the detail of running his British possession, a new executive power was finally granted to the first Prime Minister, Robert Walpole, in 1721. George II had a similar opinion and spent most of his time on the Continent. The long reign of George III was full of conflict, covering the period of the American Revolution, the Napoleonic Wars, and a second war against the US in 1812. In 1800, Ireland became a part of Great Britain. England then had a population of eight million, although only 160,000 people had the right to vote. By the end of George III's life, all chances of recovering absolute power were lost.

The judicial system in the early 19th century still needed considerable improvement. There still existed two hundred crimes – including chopping down certain trees –for which the sentence could be the death penalty. Political and legal philosophers such as Adam Smith, Jeremy Bentham and John Austin contributed to the call for reform to protect workers, women and citizens in general.

Queen Victoria's reign – the longest in British history – was a period of enormous change. The British Empire grew and thrived. The last public hanging took place in 1868. At the same time, public education was becoming available to all children. The nation's population grew from twenty million in 1851 to forty million at the turn of the 20th century. Thanks to a series of electoral reforms, four million citizens had the right to vote by the 1880s. By this time, most of the political power was in the hands of the Prime Minister and his cabinet along with the House of Commons.

In the early years of the 20th century, the House of Lords, still composed mainly of hereditary aristocrats, lost most of its legislative power. However, it retained its role as the highest court of appeal with specially appointed judges, the Law Lords.

B. Timeline

55 + 54 B.C.	Julius Caesar and his army in Britain (peopled by the Celts); no occupation
43 A.D.	Roman invasion and occupation of Britain
after 400 A.D.	withdrawal of Roman forces from Britain
c. 450	beginning of German barbarian invasions: Angles, Saxons, Jutes
597	St. Augustine's arrival in Britain to begin conversion of the people to Christianity
827-839	*Egbert*, Saxon of Wessex, the first English "king"
866	successful invasion of part of Britain by Danish Vikings
871-899	*Alfred the Great*, Saxon of the Wessex dynasty, set up a decentralized feudal system
1016-1035	*Canute the Dane* established Viking power for two decades
1042-1066	*Edward the Confessor* restored the House of Wessex
1066	*Harold II*, elected by the *Witan* (great council) to succeed Edward
1066	Battle of Hastings: William of Normandy defeated Harold (who died in battle)

Normans

1066-1087	*William I (The Conqueror)*
1087-1100	*William II Rufus*
1100-1135	*Henry I*
1135-1154	*Stephen*

Plantagenets

1154-1189	*Henry II*
1167	Oxford University founded
1189-1199	*Richard I The Lionheart*
1199-1216	*John*
1215	Magna Carta
1216-1272	*Henry III*
1272-1307	*Edward I*
1307-1327	*Edward II* (deposed)
1327-1377	*Edward III*
1377-1399	*Richard II* (deposed)

Plantagenets, House of Lancaster

1399-1413	*Henry IV*
1413-1422	*Henry V*
1422-1461	*Henry VI* (deposed)
1453	end of Hundred Years' War, of Byzantine Empire

Plantagenets, House of York

1461-1483	*Edward IV*
1476	Caxton's printing press at Westminster
1483	*Edward V*
1483-1485	*Richard III*

Tudors

1485-1509	*Henry VII*
1509-1547	*Henry VIII*
1547-1553	*Edward VI*
(1553	*Lady Jane Grey)*
1553-1558	*Mary I*
1558	French recovered Calais from English
1558-1603	*Elizabeth I*
1591	first performance of a play by Shakespeare
1600	East India Company established; British population > 4 million

Stuarts, first monarchs of Britain

1603-1625	*James I (James VI of Scotland)*
1603	union of English and Scottish Crowns
1605	Gunpowder Plot (Catholics)
1606	Union Flag adopted
1607	Jamestown colony founded
1620	*Mayflower* colonists landed in America
1625-1649	*Charles I* (beheaded)
1628	Petition of Right
1629-1640	Parliament dissolved; persecution of Puritans begun
1642-1648	Civil War

The Commonwealth

1649-58	*Oliver Cromwell*
1652	tea first imported into Great Britain
1658-1659	*Richard Cromwell*

Stuarts, restored

1660-85	*Charles II*
1664-1665	Great Plague and Great Fire of London
1679	Habeas Corpus Act
1685-1688	*James II (James VII of Scotland)* (deposed)
1688	Glorious Revolution
1688-1689	*interregnum*

1689	Bill of Rights
1689-1702	*William III (of Orange) and Mary II*
1701	Act of Settlement
1702-1714	*Anne*
1705	Act of Union, end of Scottish independence

Hanoverians

1714-1727	*George I*
1721-1742	Sir Robert Walpole, first Prime Minister
1727-1760	*George II*
1760-1820	*George III*
1807	abolition of the slave trade
1820-1830	*George IV*
1833	abolition of slavery in the colonies
1834	Poor Laws
1830-1837	*William IV*
1837-1901	*Victoria*
1876	Judicature Act

(House of Saxe-Coburg)

| 1901-1910 | *Edward VII* |

(House of Saxe-Coburg) renamed Windsor

1910-1936	*George V*
1911	Parliament Act
1931	Stature of Westminster, established the Commonwealth
1936	*Edward VIII* abdicated to marry an American divorcee
1936-1951	*George VI*
1937	Ministers and Crown Act
1949	Parliament Act
1952-	*Elizabeth II*
1963	Peerage Act
1968	Race Relations Act
1972	European Communities Act
1997	Devolution Act
1999	House of Lords Act

C. The British Constitution

A. V. Dicey in *An Introduction to the Study of the Law of the Constitution* (1885) wrote: "Constitutional law, as the term is used in England, appears to include all rules which directly or indirectly affect the distribution of the exercise of the sovereign power in the state." Contrary to widespread belief, the UK has a Constitution, but it is not a single formal document. Rather it is made up of the following sources:

1. Legal rules – statutes, Acts of Parliament (e.g. Magna Carta, the Bill of Rights, the Parliament Act, the European Communities Act, the Human Rights Act, etc.) and case law (decisions of judges in leading cases).

2. Non-legal rules – rules of parliamentary and constitutional conventions (e.g. the role of the Queen, collective and individual ministerial responsibility, parliamentary privileges, and to some extent the opinions of famous jurists such as Blackstone and Dicey).

The Habeas Corpus Act, 1679

II. For the prevention whereof, and the more speedy relief of all persons imprisoned for any such criminal or supposed criminal matters; (2) be it enacted by the King's most excellent majesty, by and with the advice and consent of the lords spiritual and temporal, and commons, in this present parliament assembled, and by the authority thereof. That whensoever any person or persons shall bring any *habeas corpus* directed unto any sheriff or sheriffs, gaoler, minister or other person whatsoever, for any person in his or their custody, and the said writ shall be served upon the said officer, or left at the gaol or prison with any of the under-officers, under-keepers or deputy of the said officers or keepers, that the said officer or officers, his or their under-officers, under-keepers or deputies, shall within three days after the service thereof as aforesaid (unless the commitment aforesaid were for treason or felony, plainly and specially expressed in the warrant of commitment) upon payment or tender of the charges of bringing the said prisoner, to be ascertained by the judge or court that awarded the same, and endorsed upon the said writ, not exceeding twelve pence per mile, and upon security given by his own bond to pay the charges of carrying back the prisoner, if he shall be remanded by the court or judge to which he shall be brought according to the true intent of this present act, and that he will not make any escape by the way, make return of such writ; (3) and bring or cause to be brought the body of the party so committed or restrained, unto or before the lord chancellor, or lord keeper of the great seal of *England* for the time being, or the judges or barons of the said court from which the said writ shall issue, or unto and before such other person or persons before whom the said writ is made returnable, according to the command thereof; (4) and shall then likewise certify the true causes of his detainer or imprisonment, unless the commitment of the said party be in any place beyond the distance of twenty miles from the place or places where such court or person is or shall be residing; and if beyond the distance of twenty miles, and not above one hundred miles, then within the space of ten days, and if beyond the distance of one hundred miles, then within the space of twenty days, after such delivery aforesaid, and not longer.

The Bill of Rights, 1689

[...] That the pretended power of suspending the laws or the execution of laws by regal authority without consent of Parliament is illegal;

That the pretended power of dispensing with laws or the execution of laws by regal authority, as it hath been assumed and exercised of late, is illegal;

That the commission for erecting the late Court of Commissioners for Ecclesiastical Causes, and all other commissions and courts of like nature, are illegal and pernicious;

That levying money for or to the use of the Crown by pretence of prerogative, without grant of Parliament, for longer time, or in other manner than the same is or shall be granted, is illegal;

That it is the right of the subjects to petition the king, and all commitments and prosecutions for such petitioning are illegal;

That the raising or keeping a standing army within the kingdom in time of peace, unless it be with consent of Parliament, is against law;

That the subjects which are Protestants may have arms for their defence suitable to their conditions and as allowed by law;

That election of members of Parliament ought to be free;

That the freedom of speech and debates or proceedings in Parliament ought not to be impeached or questioned in any court or place out of Parliament;

That excessive bail ought not to be required, nor excessive fines imposed, nor cruel and unusual punishments inflicted;

That jurors ought to be duly impanelled and returned, and jurors which pass upon men in trials for high treason ought to be freeholders;

That all grants and promises of fines and forfeitures of particular persons before conviction are illegal and void;

And that for redress of all grievances, and for the amending, strengthening and preserving of the laws, Parliaments ought to be held frequently.

And they do claim, demand and insist upon all and singular the premises as their undoubted rights and liberties, and that no declarations, judgments, doings or proceedings to the prejudice of the people in any of the said premises ought in any wise to be drawn hereafter into consequence or example; to which demand of their rights they are particularly encouraged by the declaration of his Highness the prince of Orange as being the only means for obtaining a full redress and remedy therein.

The European Communities Act, 1972

2. - (1) All such rights, powers, liabilities, obligations and restrictions from time to time created or arising by or under the Treaties, and all such remedies and procedures from time to time provided for by or under the Treaties, as in accordance with the Treaties are without further enactment to be given legal effect or used in the United Kingdom shall be recognised and available in law, and be enforced, allowed and followed accordingly; and the expression "enforceable Community right" and similar expressions shall be read as referring to one to which this subsection applies.

(2) Subject to Schedule 2 to this Act, at any time after its passing Her Majesty may by Order in Council, and any designated Minister or department may by regulations, make provision

(*a*) for the purpose of implementing any Community obligation of the United Kingdom, or enabling any such obligation to be implemented, or of enabling any rights enjoyed or to be enjoyed by the United Kingdom under or by virtue of the Treaties to be exercised; or

(*b*) for the purpose of dealing with matters arising out of or related to any such obligation or rights or the coming into force, or the operation from time to time, of subsection (1) above; and in the exercise of any statutory power or duty, including any power to give directions or to legislate by means of orders, rules, regulations or other subordinate instrument, the person entrusted with the power or duty may have regard to the objects of the Communities and to any such obligation or rights as aforesaid.

The Human Rights Act, 1998

Interpretation of legislation.

3. - (1) So far as it is possible to do so, primary legislation and subordinate legislation must be read and given effect in a way which is compatible with the Convention rights.

(2) This section

(a) applies to primary legislation and subordinate legislation whenever enacted;

(b) does not affect the validity, continuing operation or enforcement of any incompatible primary legislation; and

(c) does not affect the validity, continuing operation or enforcement of any incompatible subordinate legislation if (disregarding any possibility of revocation) primary legislation prevents removal of the incompatibility.

Declaration of incompatibility.

4. - (1) Subsection (2) applies in any proceedings in which a court determines whether a provision of primary legislation is compatible with a Convention right.

(2) If the court is satisfied that the provision is incompatible with a Convention right, it may make a declaration of that incompatibility.

(3) Subsection (4) applies in any proceedings in which a court determines whether a provision of subordinate legislation, made in the exercise of a power conferred by primary legislation, is compatible with a Convention right.

(4) If the court is satisfied

(a) that the provision is incompatible with a Convention right, and

(b) that (disregarding any possibility of revocation) the primary legislation concerned prevents removal of the incompatibility [...]

10. - (1) This section applies if

(a) a provision of legislation has been declared under section 4 to be incompatible with a Convention right and, if an appeal lies

(i) all persons who may appeal have stated in writing that they do not intend to do so;

(ii) the time for bringing an appeal has expired and no appeal has been brought within that time; or

(iii) an appeal brought within that time has been determined or abandoned; or

(b) it appears to a Minister of the Crown or Her Majesty in Council that, having regard to a finding of the European Court of Human Rights made after the coming into force of this section in proceedings against the United Kingdom, a provision of legislation is incompatible with an obligation of the United Kingdom arising from the Convention.

(2) If a Minister of the Crown considers that there are compelling reasons for proceeding under this section, he may by order make such amendments to the legislation as he considers necessary to remove the incompatibility.

(3) If, in the case of subordinate legislation, a Minister of the Crown considers

(a) that it is necessary to amend the primary legislation under which the subordinate legislation in question was made, in order to enable the incompatibility to be removed, and

(b) that there are compelling reasons for proceeding under this section, he may by order make such amendments to the primary legislation as he considers necessary.

(4) This section also applies where the provision in question is in subordinate legislation and has been quashed, or declared invalid, by reason of incompatibility with a Convention right and the Minister proposes to proceed under paragraph 2(b) of Schedule 2.

(5) If the legislation is an Order in Council, the power conferred by subsection (2) or (3) is exercisable by Her Majesty in Council.

Exercises

1 Answer the following questions.

1. Read "A very short history of the English legal system before 1900" and use the timeline to present the major events of British history.

2. Write five sentences using the information in the timeline, using in each sentence the following link words: "since, for, until, between, ago, before, after, in".

3. What are the rights that the four previous documents guarantee to the individual?

2 Discuss.

1. Do you think the documents provide for these rights to be effectively protected?

2. Are these rights also protected in your home country? If so, how?

3. Off the presses

A brief history of habeas corpus

Habeas corpus is under attack, say critics of the government's anti-terror bill. But what is it and why is it so cherished?

Habeas corpus (ad subjiciendum) is Latin for "you may have the body" (subject to examination). It is a writ which requires a person detained by the authorities be brought before a court of law so that the legality of the detention may be examined.

The name is taken from the opening words of the **writ** in medieval times.

Although rarely used nowadays, it can theoretically be demanded by anyone who believes they are unlawfully detained and it is issued by a **judge**.

It does not determine **guilt** or innocence, merely whether the person is legally imprisoned. It may also be writ against a private individual detaining another.

[...]

The *Habeas Corpus* Act passed by Parliament in 1679 guaranteed this right in law, although its origins go back much further, probably to Anglo-Saxon times.

Sir William Blackstone, who wrote his famous Commentaries on the Laws of England in the 18th century, recorded the first use of *habeas corpus* in 1305. But other writs with the same effect were used in the 12th century, so it appears to have preceded Magna Carta in 1215.

Its original use was more straightforward – a writ to bring a prisoner into court to bear witness in court in a pending trial. But what began as a weapon for the king and the courts became – as the political climate changed – protection for the individual against arbitrary detention by the state.

It is thought to have been common law by the time of Magna Carta, which says in Article 39: "No freeman shall be taken or imprisoned or disseised or exiled or in any way destroyed, nor will we go upon him nor will we send upon him except upon the lawful judgement of his peers or the law of the land."

Over the next few hundred years, concern grew that kings would whimsically intervene on matters of detention, so it was enshrined in law in 1679.

In 1772, there was a landmark case in which it was invoked. James Somersett, a black slave brought back to the UK from Jamaica, was freed after a debate sparked by his demand for *habeas corpus*. Lord Mansfield successfully argued for his release.

These days it is rarely used, although it has greater effect in the US, where its most common use is by prisoners after **conviction**.

Michael Zander QC, Emeritus Professor of Law at the London School of Economics, says: "*Habeas corpus* has a mythical status in the country's psyche. In reality it is no longer of great practical significance as there are today very few *habeas corpus* applications, but it still represents the fundamental principle that unlawful detention can be challenged by immediate access to a judge – even by telephone in the middle of the night."

"It no longer plays a role in regard to detention by the police as it has been superseded by the much more detailed and workable provisions of the Police and Criminal Evidence Act 1984, which lays down precise rules about the length of pre-charge detention," he adds.

But there have been occasions when the British Parliament has suspended it, usually in times of social unrest.

William Pitt, startled by the success of the French Revolution, did so after France declared war on Britain in 1793, to arrest parliamentary reformers. This was repeated by Lord Liverpool's government against the same movement in 1817.

War was a particularly fraught time for individual liberty. The Defence of the Realm Act 1914 meant the Home Secretary could intern residents and it was used against people of German descent, and Irish suspected of involvement in the Easter Uprising.

These powers were reinstated in World War II to detain those of German background, including Jewish refugees, as well as those with known fascist sympathies, such as Oswald Mosley. At the same time, the US authorities interned more than 110,000 Japanese-Americans.

But the most recent example happened in 1971, when the British Government introduced the internment of hundreds of republican suspects in an attempt to shut down the IRA. The tactic was abandoned four years later and is thought to have increased support for the IRA.

Whether the anti-terror **bill** is the latest chapter in the history of *habeas corpus* is a matter of debate. Boris Johnson MP said earlier in the week that Tony Blair is the first peacetime prime minister to curtail the right to *habeas corpus*.

Since then, the Lords appears to have won a concession that all the control orders issued against terror suspects be made by judges, not by ministers. And Home Secretary Charles Clarke insists there is no plan to detain anyone under the new laws.

Mr Zander says: "The Anti-terrorism, Crime and Security Act 2001 passed in the aftermath of 9/11 set aside *habeas corpus* in regard to terrorism suspects who cannot be prosecuted. The Prevention of Terrorism Bill now before Parliament would broaden the ways in which terrorism suspects can be dealt with without being charged or prosecuted."

But the Home Office denies its plans amount to *habeas corpus* suspension. A spokesman said: "We are not removing *habeas corpus* rights. Everyone has a **right** to *habeas corpus* and that will remain the case."

http://news.bbc.co.uk, 9/3/2005.

1 Meanings.

Find the meanings of the words in bold type. They are defined in the other chapters of the book.

2 Recap.

Summarise the various developments of *habeas corpus*.

Research tasks.

1. Find information on William Blackstone, Lord Mansfield, William Pitt, Lord Liverpool and Oswald Mosley. Present brief biographies.
2. Find information on the Easter Uprising. Write a short summary explaining what it was.
3. What are the provisions of the Police and Criminal Evidence Act 1984 and the Anti-terrorism, Crime and Security Act 2001? Highlight them in a short memo.

4. Food for thought

The separation of power in historical perspective

In England power started with the Crown. Power was not conferred through the force of a revolutionary constitutional document on three institutions separate but equal, as happened in the United States at its founding at the end of the eighteenth century. Rather, power emerged. By the beginning of what historians refer to as the early modern period, power was vested in the Crown. In the Tudor period (1485-1603) great monarchs ruled England. This was the grand, flamboyant, and self-confident time of Henri VIII and Elizabeth I. England was proud, protestant, and powerful. For England, it was a time of intellectual and cultural development, of commercial success, and of military domination. At the centre of everything – the social, the religious, the legal, and the political – was the **Crown**. This was an age when the Crown did not merely **reign**: it **ruled**. Parliaments were **summoned**, and **dissolved**, at the Crown's will. When they met their task was not so much to make the law as to offer guidance and support, especially financial support, to the **sovereign**. The administration of justice likewise fell under the authority, and the control of the Crown.

Even by this early stage, however, the Crown's power was not absolute. Three hundred years before the Tudors came to power King John had been required by his barons to accede to the terms and conditions of Magna Carta. This document, first drawn up in 1215 and reconfirmed on numerous occasions since, marked the first great attempt to limit the power of the Crown, which had grown steadily since the Norman conquest of 1066. Magna Carta provided a series of liberties to be enjoyed by English freemen: rights which the people would hold as against the Crown. A small number of Magna Carta's provisions remain on the **statute book** to this day, and are indeed still relied on from time to time in modern day **case law**. The most important of these is contained in cap. 29, which provides that "no freeman shall be taken or imprisoned [...] or exiled [...] but by [...] the law of the land". More significantly for present purposes, however, Magna Carta also contained a number of provisions limiting the powers of the Crown to raise various forms of revenue, both through its powers over land and through taxation. While the great fame of Magna Carta, both in England and perhaps even more in the United States, derives from its somewhat mythological status as the source of such basic rights as **trial** by **jury** and *habeas corpus*, from the sense that it was the first great Bill of Rights, its constitutional significance actually lies less in what it says about liberty and more in what it says about the Crown.

Magna Carta was not alone. Similar charters were drawn up elsewhere in Europe during the thirteenth century. In two respects, however, Magna Carta was special. First, consider its target. Whereas the continental charters were aimed at safeguarding municipal independence or the privileged position of the aristocracy, Magna Carta was aimed instead at the control and subjection of the Crown. It was based on the emerging political theory of "monarchical responsibility and communal participation in government"[1]. Secondly, its drafting was such that Magna Carta was framed not as a document of force, but as one of law. Even though the political circumstances in which Magna Carta was drawn up were of political crisis and indeed civil war, both the King and the baronage appeared eager to conceal this. The reality was that Magna Carta represented a series of concessions and promises which had to be squeezed out of the King by force and might – it was not until after King John lost effective power of London that he eventually agreed, at Runnymede, to its terms. But the presentation was that Magna Carta was a freely given grant in perpetuity of the liberties of freemen. Legally, Magna Carta was a mix of the old, the new, and the wishful: "sometimes Magna Carta stated law. Sometimes it stated what its supporters hoped would become law. Sometimes it stated what they pretended was law"[2]. Constitutionally, however, what turned out to be its central claim was its extension and reinforcement of the notion that the Crown is not to levy certain forms of taxation "except by the common counsel of our realm"[3].

Who would give this common counsel or consent? At the time of Magna Carta there was no **Parliament**. The Crown through the *Curia Regis*, the members of which were supplied from among the baronage. Parliament emerged during the course of the thirteenth century out of these medieval institutions, the greater barons forming what became the **House of Lords** and, with the lesser barons emerging as the **House of Commons** slightly later. Only

---

1. See J. Holt, *Magna Carta*, 2nd Edition, Cambridge University Press, 1999, at 29.
2. *Ibid*, at 300.
3. *Magna Carta*, 1212, cap. 12.

by the middle of the fourteenth century had a settled bicameral Parliament been established. The constitutional role of this Parliament was to be the vehicle through which the Crown would consult. If the Crown needed revenue, as it frequently did – the process of governing is expensive enough in peacetime but it is exorbitant in war – it was to Parliament that it would turn. The Crown ruled, but Parliament held the purse strings.

Magna Carta did not establish this doctrine, but it rapidly became and long remained the most important constitutional document in which the doctrine was set out. On the basis of the terms laid down by Magna Carta, Parliament during the fourteenth and fifteenth centuries established three principles: first, that all taxation without consent of Parliament is illegal; secondly, that the consent of both Houses of Parliament is required for the passage of legislation; and thirdly, that the Commons has the right to inquire into and to amend the abuses of the Crown's administration. These are the principles of what had become known as the ancient constitution. Under the ancient constitution power started with the Crown, but its power was checked by Parliament. Now, this division of power, with the Crown on one side and Parliament on the other, clearly looks rather different from the principle of separation of powers which was considered above. Here there is no division into legislative, executive, and judicial, with each function neatly distinguished from others and each being performed by separate constitutional actors. Instead, the separation of powers in the ancient constitution is an institutional divide. Power resides in the authority of the Crown, save for that which has been specifically forced from it by Parliament.

The doctrines of the ancient constitution have not gone unchallenged since medieval times. The most significant threat to them was posed by the Stuart kings in the seventeenth century. The Tudor line came to an end with the death of Elizabeth I in 1603. The throne passed to James Stuart, King James VI of Scotland, who became James I of England. Neither James nor his son and successor, Charles I (1625-1646), found it at all easy to accommodate themselves to the doctrines of the ancient constitution. The Stuarts were advocates of an altogether different theory of kingship, the divine right theory. This view supposed that the Kings were God's representatives, and were accountable only to God, and not such earthly authorities as Parliament. Under the ancient constitution, not all the powers of the Crown had to be shared with Parliament: in areas such as foreign affairs, the army and navy, and coinage, the Crown reigned supreme. James and Charles sought to extend these limited spheres of absolute power to embrace all areas of domestic policy. James fixed new, higher, levels of indirect taxation such as import duties [...] without parliamentary assent. Charles could not make do with the levels of revenue available to him through indirect taxation, and imposed a forced loan, again, without parliamentary assent. When faced with opposition in the House of Commons Charles had his opponent MPs arrested and they were incarcerated in the Tower of London. After dissolving Parliament in 1629 Charles ruled without it for eleven years – the period known as the personal rule. But the Crown was short of revenue throughout the 1630s and was required to impose even more imaginative forms of taxation on its subjects – always without parliamentary sanction, of course [...]. All of these royal acts were challenged in court, but in every case unsuccessfully. In a series of controversial, and critical, cases, the judges offered support to the Crown, even when the weight of precedents was against them.

By the 1640s the ancient constitution could take the strain no longer, and it collapsed as England descended into civil war. The constitutional disagreements between the parliamentarians and the royalists were not the only causes of the English civil war – religion too played a significant role – but they were a central aspect to it. War engulfed England, and spread to Scotland and Ireland, between 1642 and 1648. The war was soon won by the parliamentarians, led by the end of the decade by Oliver Cromwell. In 1649 Charles I was executed and between 1649 and 1660 England was, for its only time in its history, a nation without a Crown. Together with the monarchy the House of Lords was also abolished, leaving the House of Commons, along with Cromwell's new model army, to rule. But the republic did not last. Cromwell died in 1658, and within two years of his death the Stuart dynasty had been restored to the throne, Charles II becoming king. However, while the Stuarts were returned, this was no restoration of divine right or of absolute monarchy. Parliament allowed Charles II to enjoy neither the religious, the military, nor the political powers which his father had assumed.

The restoration, however, settled the constitutional disagreements of the seventeenth century only temporarily. On the death of Charles II in 1685 the throne passed to his (Catholic) brother, James II, and, once again, England rapidly descended into political and religious crisis as the new king, with a fixed design to make himself an absolute monarch, attempted to subvert the established church; radically augmented the size of the standing army; procured a judgment from the courts affirming its prerogative power to dispense with the observance of the law; and generally made it clear that constitutional limitations would not longer be suffered to stand in the way of his despotic designs. Three years after having come to power, James was overthrown, as Parliament offered the Crown to William of Orange, the protestant husband of James' daughter Mary. In 1688-1689, unlike in 1660, Parliament took no chances, and passed into law arguably the most important single document of England's unwritten constitution, the Bill of Rights.

The Bill of Rights 1689 lays down the circumstances under which the Crown may exercise its power. The "rights" of the Bill of Rights are those enjoyed by Parliament. It is thus a document which governs the constitutional relationship between Parliament and the Crown. Its central provisions are still in force, and form the key pillar of the contemporary constitution. Its effects include the following: the prerogative power of dispensing with the law is abolished (Article 1); "levying money for or to the use of the Crown by pretence of prerogative, without grant of Parliament […] is illegal" (Article 4); no standing army may be kept in peacetime other than with the consent of Parliament (Article 6); and the "freedom of speech, and debates or proceedings in Parliament ought not to be impeached or questioned in any court or place out of Parliament" (Article 9). While the Bill of Rights established that Parliament could lay down the terms and conditions on which England was to continue as a monarchy, the Act of Settlement, which followed in 1701, established that Parliament could also control the very identity of the monarch, by altering, if it wished, the line of succession. The combined effect of these constitutional statutes is that monarchs reign in England not because they have a divine right to do so, but because Parliament has permitted it. Power started with the Crown, but it continues to vest in the Crown only because, and for only as long as, Parliament continues to wish it.

Adam Tomkins, *Public Law*, Oxford University Press, 2003, pp. 39-44.

Exercises

1 Meanings.

Find the meanings of the words in bold type. They are defined in the chapters of the book.

2 Use of the article.

1. Note the use of the article with the following nouns: Magna Carta, House of Lords, House of Commons, Parliament, England, King, *habeas corpus*.
2. Write a sentence using each of these terms.

3 Explanations.

1. Explain the historical origin and the development of Parliament in England.
2. Explain what the ancient constitution is.

4 Research task.

1. Find information in textbooks or on the internet about the English Civil War, the republican era and the Restoration.
2. Present the information orally.

3. Take notes on the oral presentations.

4. Compare your notes with the information given in the presentations.

5. Assess the reasons why there are discrepancies.

5 **Discuss.**

Is there a separation of powers in England?

5. Listening

Exercises

1 🔘 **Listen to the interview with Matt Ronson of the Disability Rights Commission who talks about Rachel McKee's discrimination case against her employer, and complete the extract with the missing words.**

MATT RONSON: I think this ...... establishes a number of things. The first ...... that the case set was that ...., which happens when the employee leaves their job due to the employer's behaviour, is covered by the .... Interestingly, since that decision, the ...... amended the DDA to ...... a clear definition of what constructive dismissal was, but at the time Rachel brought her ...... , she was in a position where her constant ...... to get the ...... she needed had led her to resign and it wasn't clear whether the DDA gave her any .... So we were quite anxious to see that employees, who have to ...... as a result of the treatment they experience, can find a remedy through a DDA claim and the .... did find that. But as I said the law's ...... been amended. The second precedent the case set is that while Rachel was ...... waiting for adjustments to be made, her employer considered she was sick, reduced her sick pay and finally stopped paying her. So what Rachel and the Disability Rights Commission ...... is that she wasn't sick at all, she was perfectly capable of ...... her job providing simple adjustments had been made. Consequently, if the employer had broken the ...... and .... her by not making the necessary adjustments, she should then be ...... to full pay while she was off and the .... agreed on that point.

2 **Answer the following questions.**

1. Who is Rachel McKee? What was her claim?

2. What piece of legislation was relevant to her case?

3. What does the expression 'make adjustments' mean?

4. What are the two precedents that Rachel's case established?

5. What new measure was introduced in December 2005?

3 **Discuss.**

1. From what you heard in the audio recording, what is the relationship between case law, policy-making and legislation passed in Parliament?
2. Should the law force employers to make adjustments in order to enable disabled people to work?

6. Grammar practice

Exercises

1 **Expressing anonymity. In English, there are different ways of expressing anonymity, i.e. the action of an unknown individual or that of an indistinct group of people. Using the following list of sentences, say how anonymity may be expressed and in what case this or that form would be more appropriate.**

1. Today, then, one may say that custom or customary law consists of established patterns of behaviour.
2. Equity will consider what ought to have been done and not what was actually done.
3. In England, they have adopted the Common law system, whereas in France, we have adopted the Roman system.
4. From the reign of Alfred the Great until the arrival of William the Conqueror in 1066, people lived under a local form of feudalism.
5. EU regulations are said to have "general application and are binding in their entirety and directly applicable in all Member States".
6. In the UK system, it is always possible for anyone to plead custom, as long as s/he complies with the requirements for it to be law.
7. One should not underestimate the importance of decisions and rulings in the uniform interpretation of European Community law.
8. Someone tried to help the prisoner escape.
9. *Habeas corpus (ad subjiciendum)* is Latin for "you may have the body" (subject to examination).
10. Contrary to widespread belief, the UK has a Constitution, but it is not a single formal document.

2 **Tenses. Put the verbs in brackets into the correct tense, bearing in mind that you may have to use a passive form.**

When what was later to be called the Court of Common Pleas ...... (set up) in

Westminster, the financial committee ...... (become) the Court of the Exchequer. At the time, the monarch, Henry II, ... (conflict) with the Archbishop of Canterbury over who ...... (try) priests for crimes. This ...... (lead) to the unfortunate assassination of Archbishop Thomas Becket.

In those days, a person of rank ...... (bring) an action by ...... (pay) for a writ to be issued by the Chancellor. Once a writ ...... (issue), any demand for payment of debt ...... (require) a copy of that original writ. Because of the variety of cases ...... (arise), the number of writs ...... (keep/increase).

Over a hundred years after Henry II's death, the Black Death ...... (sweep over) England ...... (kill) every other person in the realm. Consequently, land ...... (go out) of cultivation and prices ...... (rise). Meanwhile, discontent ...... (start/grow) against the corrupted Church, not so much against the poor and humble parish priests but against the wanton monks and friars who ...... (live) in luxury. The people's anger ...... (pave) the way to the Reformation. Two centuries later, Henry VIII ...... (establish) the Church of England. His daughter, Elizabeth I ...... (aim) at a compromise between Catholics and Protestants in order to unite as many of her people as possible. Her reign ...... (embody) a golden era in the history of England. A nice but probably apocryphal story ...... (say) that Queen Elizabeth ...... (try/distract) Shakespeare while he ...... (play) the role of a king by ...... (shake) her handkerchief on the stage at his feet. Without ...... (miss) a beat, he ...... (spring) from his seat, ... (strike) one of the play's courtiers and ...... (order) him to "Take up our sister's handkerchief."

3 Nominalised adjectives. Transform the underlined words in order to obtain nominalised adjectives.

1. Members of the Tudor family ruled until the year 1603.
2. The Gunpowder Plot was fomented by members of the Catholic Church.
3. Members of the Tory party still sit in Parliament today.
4. Subjects who are members of the Protestant Church may have arms for their defence suitable to their conditions and as allowed by law.
5. There were a few Irish persons who moved to London.
6. The Norman conquerors sought to establish their rule in England by introducing their methods of administration.
7. It is now acknowledged that the State should assume responsibility for the poor and needy people in the community, but also for those who are jobless, homeless, disabled and elderly.
8. The British royal family is extremely wealthy.
9. British monarchs are now rich and famous members of the jet set.
10. Indian people obtained their independence after World War II.

4 Translate the following sentences into English.

1. Il s'était écoulé à peine deux ans après la mort d'Oliver Cromwell lorsque la monarchie fut restaurée.

2. Henry VIII fit exécuter Thomas More parce que ce dernier s'opposait à son divorce.

3. Charles II avait passé des années à la cour de Louis XIV avant de régner sur l'Angleterre.

4. Il est grand temps que la monarchie soit abolie !

5. Depuis combien de temps régnait la reine Victoria lorsqu'elle mourut ?

6. Peu de choses ont changé à Buckingham Palace depuis que la reine a été couronnée.

7. La liberté d'expression est garantie depuis 1689.

8. De nos jours, on peut dire que la reine règne mais ne gouverne pas.

9. Le droit anglais est fondé sur le précédent, on parle de droit jurisprudentiel.

5 **Articles. Complete the sentences with *a*, *an*, *the* or *ø* (zero article).**

1. …… implementation of …… case law can be summarised by …… term ……
"doctrine of precedent", i.e. …… fact that …… later judge will have to determine 1°
what …… pronouncements of …… earlier decisions are relevant to …… present
case ; and 2° what …… parts of …… latter are binding.

2. …… United Kingdom is a member of …… European Union, hence ……
European Union legislation is also …… source of …… English law.

3. In cases of …… conflict between …… UK and …… EU legislation, …… EU law
takes …… precedence. Nevertheless, …… principle of …… primacy of ……
European Community law over …… national law was pronounced by ……
European Court of Justice in the case *Costa v ENEL*.

4. Even though …… Sir Thomas More was …… much-hailed chancellor, he was
beheaded. He is also known for being …… author of *Utopia*.

5. At …… end of …… Tudor dynasty, …… judicial system still condoned …… harsh
treatment of …… criminal defendants: …… torture, …… long imprisonment before
…… trial, …… refusal of access to counsel. However, …… rules of trial by …… jury
were well established and did provide some protection.

6. At …… beginning of …… Hundred Years War in 1339. …… King Edward III
needed …… substantial funds for …… war and could enact …… laws only with
…… full consent of …… Parliament, now clearly consisting of …… lords on ……
one hand and …… "commoners" on …… other.

7. …… Elizabethan period was …… time of …… intellectual and …… cultural
development, of commercial success, and of …… military domination, …… age
when …… Crown actually ruled.

6. **Wishes and regrets. Transform the following sentences so as to express regret.**

1. Henry II had Thomas Becket executed because the latter had opposed him.

2. Henry III ignored the rights formerly granted to the barons, who revolted once
more.

3. The king needs substantial funds to wage war against the French.

4. The Pope excommunicated Henry VIII because he had divorced Catherine of Aragon.

5. Despotic King John's plotting caused him to lose Normandy and Brittany to Philippe-Auguste.

6. In 1971, the British Government introduced the internment of hundreds of Republican suspects in an attempt to shut down the IRA. The tactic is thought to have increased support for the IRA.

7. Mr Zander said that the Anti-Terrorism, Crime and Security Act 2001, passed in the aftermath of 9/11, set aside *habeas corpus*.

Chapter 2

Modern political institutions in the United Kingdom

1. Fundamentals

Power in the United Kingdom is not constitutionally structured into three separate branches as in the United States, for example. The interactions between the powers are numerous, such as those between Parliament and the Executive. The presence of the monarch, however symbolic and limited, also still pervades the institutions. Recent constitutional reforms, however, have emphasised the need to establish a clearer division between the judicial and the legislative power, especially by creating a Supreme Court of the United Kingdom (in operation from October 2008) and by reviewing the functions of the Lord Chancellor. More information about the Supreme Court can be found in Chapter 4 (The court system and the personnel of the courts), which focuses on the Judiciary.

The British monarchy

The British monarch or sovereign is the Head of State of the United Kingdom and British territories and some Commonwealth countries. Known as the **royal prerogatives**, the powers of the monarchy are essentially symbolic and are not usually exercised by the monarch but by ministers acting on his or her behalf. For example, the royal prerogative of patronage is exercised by the Prime Minister. Some major powers, like the power to dissolve Parliament, are exercised personally by the monarch, albeit on the advice of the Prime Minister and Cabinet, according to constitutional convention.

Political power is exercised by the Parliament of the United Kingdom, of which the Sovereign is a non-partisan component, and by the Prime Minister and Cabinet. In the modern British constitutional monarchy, the Sovereign's role is limited in practice to ceremonial functions. Famous 19th century journalist and thinker Walter Bagehot identified the monarchy as the "dignified part" rather than the "efficient part" of government in *The English Constitution* (first published in 1867).

Functions of the monarchy

The present Sovereign (at the time of writing) is Queen Elizabeth II, who has reigned since February 6, 1952. The heir apparent is her eldest son, Prince Charles, Prince of Wales and Duke of Rothesay.

The sovereign has to remain politically impartial and it is his or her duty to ask the leader of the majority party in the House of Commons to become Prime Minister and to form a government. The monarch and the Prime Minister (PM) meet on a weekly basis after Cabinet meetings but what is said remains private. Through these meetings, the monarch may advise the PM on policy matters.

The concept of the **King/Queen in Parliament** refers to the role of the sovereign as part of the legislature. These legislative functions involve royal interventions at each crucial stage of Parliament's activities. The monarch delivers a speech known as the King's or Queen's Speech (or Speech from the Throne) at the State Opening of Parliament, and he or she summons Parliament for each new session and prorogues it at the end of a session. Another aspect of the monarch's legislative role is the **Royal Assent** whereby a bill becomes an Act of Parliament. It is given at the end of the law-making process. Theoretically, the sovereign may grant Royal Assent or withhold Royal Assent (veto the bill). However, under modern notions of a constitutional monarchy the sovereign always grants Royal Assent.

As Head of State, the monarch symbolises the sovereignty of the State. One of his or her functions in this capacity consists in representing Britain when foreign officials visit the country.

He or she is Commander in Chief of the Armed Forces and grants civilian and military honours on the advice of the PM.

The sovereign is also the Supreme Governor of the established Church of England, but in practice the spiritual leadership of the Church is the responsibility of the **Archbishop of Canterbury**.

Finally, the British monarch is also Head of the **Commonwealth**, an association of 53 sovereign and independent nations, which were formerly part of the British Empire and comprise 1.8 billion people (in 2006).

The sovereign's official expenditure is controlled by Parliament through the **Civil List** which establishes a budget. It has been fixed at £7.9 million per year until 2011. It should be added that Her Majesty has paid income tax on her personal income since 1993.

The executive branch

The Government performs the executive functions of the United Kingdom and defines the policies that determine how the country is run. The Government is divided between specialised Departments of State and is headed by the Prime Minister, who is by convention the Member of the House of Commons most likely to form a government after a general election. The Prime Minister establishes the number and the nature of government departments and selects the Ministers from among Members of the House of Commons and House of Lords pursuant to constitutional convention. As the executive is drawn from Parliament, it is also accountable to it. In practice, Members of Parliament of the major parties vote according to party policy. Thus, a government backed by a large majority is seldom defeated in Parliament. On the other hand, a government with a small majority or a coalition government may be much more vulnerable and easily lose votes if a few of its **backbenchers** vote against its proposals.

The Cabinet

The key decision-making body in government is the **Cabinet**, which is made up of about twenty of the most senior government ministers. Cabinet members traditionally include the Lord Chancellor (see Chapter 1, Origins and developments of English law) and Secretary of State for Constitutional Affairs, the **Chancellor of the Exchequer** (in charge of HM Treasury), the Home Secretary, the Secretary of State for Foreign and Commonwealth Affairs, the Education Secretary, the **Lord Privy Seal** (a Minister without Portfolio who is often the Leader of the House of Commons), etc. The Prime Minister exercises his or her power of patronage to appoint and dismiss members of the Cabinet, although each new appointment requires the monarch's formal approval. The PM may constitute the Cabinet by drawing from both Houses of Parliament, but recent custom favours members of the House of Commons, who are directly elected by the people. The Cabinet meetings are held and policies are discussed in the Cabinet room at 10 Downing Street, the PM's headquarters and residence. The Cabinet relies on the work of various specialised committees to efficiently handle the current political issues. The Cabinet members have **collective responsibility** to Parliament: they are bound to support Cabinet decisions even if they were absent or if they disagreed. If they break this rule, they have to resign.

The **Opposition** organises its highest-ranking members into a **Shadow Cabinet**. Each Shadow member is a counterpart of a Cabinet member. Shadow ministers thus sit on the **front benches** of the Opposition in Parliament.

Government departments

Ministerial departments are headed by a Secretary of State (Government Minister), who is usually assisted by junior ministers, and managed by a civil servant called the Permanent Secretary, who handles administrative tasks. The **Civil Service** constitutes a major part of the Government. Each department is indeed staffed by civil servants, who are unelected, permanent and non-political officials and whose expertise is crucial.

The Treasury, the Department for Constitutional Affairs, the Home Office and the Foreign Office are generally considered as the most important of the government departments. The Department for Constitutional Affairs was created in 2003 to replace the Lord Chancellor's Department, which formerly handled the administration of justice. The new department is responsible for upholding justice and deals with electoral and constitutional issues. At its head, the Secretary of State for Constitutional Affairs also holds the title of Lord Chancellor, although PM Tony Blair's administration has proposed to abolish this latter office.

Government departments are supplemented by various **executive agencies** to which specific tasks are delegated, such as Her Majesty's Court Service, which is an executive agency of the Department for Constitutional Affairs and is charged with responsibility for the administration of courts in England and Wales.

Parliament

The Parliament of the United Kingdom of Great Britain and Northern Ireland is one of the oldest representative assemblies in the world. It is the supreme legislative institution in the UK. It is a bicameral **legislature** which includes an upper house, called the House of Lords, and a lower house, called the House of Commons. Members of the **House of Lords** are at present not elected by universal suffrage whereas Members of the **House of Commons** are democratically elected. The members of the United Kingdom Parliament come from England, Scotland, Wales and Northern Ireland. The House of Lords and the House of Commons meet in separate chambers in the Palace of Westminster in London (commonly known as the Houses of Parliament). The legislative process involves three components, namely both Houses of Parliament and the Monarch. The supremacy of the House of Commons was clearly established during the 20th century through various Acts of Parliament which deprived the upper house of much of its power.

1. Composition

The British Sovereign plays an essentially ceremonial role at the head of Parliament. The modern House of Lords is mostly made up of members called Lords of Parliament who are not elected but appointed. The Lords Spiritual are clergymen of the Church of England and the Lords Temporal are Peers of the Realm.

In the past the Lords Spiritual included all of the senior clergymen of the Church of England. Today, twenty-six Lords Spiritual remain, including the Archbishop of Canterbury, the Archbishop of York, the Bishop of London, the Bishop of Durham and the Bishop of Winchester.

The Lords Temporal are members of the Peerage. Formerly, they included hereditary **peers**, of the ranks of Duke, Marquess, Earl, Viscount and Baron. The House of Lords Act 1999 abolished hereditary peerage, stating that only life peerage dignities (which cannot be inherited) give their holders the right to sit in the House of Lords. Pursuant to the Act, ninety-two of all the hereditary peers, who used to constitute the major part of the House, were elected by their peers to retain their seats in the Chamber while the others had to leave office. The Act provides for a gradual removal of hereditary peers from the Upper House. Today, Lords Temporal are therefore mostly made up of life peers, appointed for life by the Prime Minister.

The Lords Spiritual and Temporal sit, debate and vote together.

In addition to Lords Temporal and Lords Spiritual, the twelve Law Lords who sit as judges of the highest court in the UK (the House of Lords in its judicial capacity) will remain full members of the House of Lords until the Supreme Court of the UK is set up. Nonetheless they are expected to abstain from taking part in controversial legislative issues. It should also be noted that the Government is considering further reform of the Upper House.

The House of Commons consists of 646 members. Each MP represents a single **constituency**. MPs are elected according to the **First-Past-The-Post** electoral system (FPTP). Universal adult suffrage exists for all citizens aged 18 and over. The term of the Members of the House of Commons lasts five years maximum. A general election, in which all the seats are contested, takes place once it has been decided to dissolve Parliament.

No individual may be a part of more than one component of Parliament. Lords of Parliament are not allowed to vote in elections for Members of the House of Commons; furthermore, by convention the Sovereign does not vote.

2. Speakers

Each of the two Houses of Parliament is presided over by a **Speaker**. The Lord Chancellor was formerly the *ex officio* Speaker in the House of Lords in addition to being the head of the judiciary in England and Wales and a Cabinet minister. A new office of Speaker of the House of Lords was created under the Constitutional Reform Act 2005 to endow the Upper House with a full-time speaker with no ties with the other branches of power. The House of Commons elects its own Speaker whose powers are far broader than those of the Lord Speaker.

While speeches in the House of Lords are addressed to the House (using the words "My Lords"), those in the House of Commons are addressed to the Speaker alone (using the words "Mr Speaker" or "Madam Speaker").

Both Houses may decide questions with voice voting: MPs shout out "Aye" and "No" and peers "Content" and "Not-Content". If the pronouncement of the Lord Speaker or Speaker of the Commons is challenged, a recorded vote (known as a division) may be requested. The Speaker of the House of Commons, who is not supposed to take sides, does not cast a vote except in the case of a **tie**.

3. Legislative functions

Laws are generally introduced by a Minister of the Crown in **draft** form known as **bills**. Most bills involving the general public are called "Public Bills". A bill aiming at granting special rights to an individual or small group of individuals is called a "Private Bill". "Hybrid Bills" are Private Bills which deal with larger issues.

Bills go through several stages in both Houses. The first stage, or first reading, is a formality.

During the second reading, the general principles of the bill are debated and the House at that stage may vote to reject the bill.

After the second reading, the bill is sent to a committee. In the House of Lords, the Committee of the Whole House, consisting of all members of the House, is used. In the House of Commons, the bill is usually committed to a **standing committee**, made up of between sixteen and fifty members. The **Committee of the Whole House** may also be used when important legislation is being debated. A committee considers the bill clause by clause, and proposes its amendments to the entire House.

The third reading follows the committee stage. In the House of Commons, no further amendments may then be added, and the passage of the motion "That the Bill be now read a third time" amounts to passage of the whole bill. In the House of Lords, however, further amendments to the bill may be made. Once passed by one House, the bill is sent to the other House. If the two Houses do not pass the same amendments and do not resolve their dis-agreements, the bill fails. If passed in identical form by both Houses, it may be presented for the Sovereign's Assent.

The power of the House of Lords to reject bills passed by the House of Commons has been restricted by Parliament Acts 1911 and 1949, the Salisbury convention, etc. If the House of Commons passes a public bill in two successive sessions, and the House of Lords rejects them both times, the bill may never-theless be presented to the Sovereign for his/her Assent. Money bills concern national taxation or public funds and are dealt with according to a special proce-dure decided by the Speaker of the House of Commons. If the House of Lords fails to pass a money bill within one month of its passage in the House of Commons, the Lower House may decide that the bill be submitted for the Sovereign's Assent immediately.

The last stage of a bill involves the granting of the Royal Assent.

4. Relationship with the Government

Governments can exercise a tremendous influence on Parliament by using their inbuilt majority in the House of Commons, and by appointing supportive life peers in the Lords. Governments can pass any legislation they wish in the Commons, unless there is major dissent by MPs in the governing party, in which case dissenting MPs may be able to extract concessions.

Parliament controls the Executive. It passes or rejects its bills and obliges Ministers of the Crown to answer for their actions, at **Question Time** or during meetings of the parliamentary committees. While the House of Lords cannot bring about the end of a Government, the Lower House may indicate its lack of support by rejecting a Motion of Confidence or by passing a Motion of No Confidence. Confidence Motions generally originate in the Government and are intended to reinforce its support in the House. The Opposition introduces No Confidence Motions.

Important bills that form part of the Government's agenda and are stated in the Speech from the Throne are generally considered matters of confidence. If such a bill is defeated in the House of Commons, the Government has lost the confidence of that House and the Prime Minister has either to resign or ask for the dissolution of Parliament.

A new general election is then held but the Sovereign can theoretically reject the dissolution, forcing the PM's resignation and allowing the Leader of the Opposition to be asked to form a new government.

5. Sovereignty

Parliament's power has often been undermined by its own Acts. Its sovereignty has been restricted by the United Kingdom's membership of the European Union. European law is **enforceable** in each member state. Parliament has also created national devolved assemblies which have legislative authority in Scotland, Wales and Northern Ireland. However, authority has been conceded by Act of Parliament, and may be taken back in the same manner. Parliament may abolish the devolution of power to Scotland, Wales and Northern Ireland or leave the European Union.

6. Privileges

Each House of Parliament preserves various ancient privileges. The most notable is that of freedom of speech in debate. Nothing said in either House may be challenged in any court of law or other institution outside Parliament.

Freedom from arrest except in case of high **treason, felony** or **breach of the peace** constitutes another of those privileges. Members of both Houses are also excused from jury duty.

Devolution

The United Kingdom is said to have a unitary state with a **devolved system of government**. This contrasts with a **federal system**, in which sub-parliaments or state legislatures have a clearly defined constitutional right to exist, to exercise certain constitutionally defined functions, and cannot be unilaterally abolished by acts of a central parliament.

In addition to the House of Commons, Scotland now has its own unicameral parliament established by the Scotland Act 1998, and Wales and Northern Ireland have assemblies. England, however, has no devolved government, following the failure of proposals for regional assemblies. This has led to the formation of democratic reform groups such as the Campaign for an English Parliament. Some members of the devolved bodies are elected by a form of proportional representation. The new devolved parliament and assemblies have limited powers, substantially fewer than those of the UK Parliament. There are also fundamental differences between them. For example, the Scottish Parliament has the power to legislate, whereas the Welsh Assembly only has the power to spend the budget formerly allocated to a Government department known as the Welsh Office. In addition, as devolved systems of government, they have no constitutional right to exist and can have their powers broadened, narrowed or changed by an Act of the UK Parliament.

The present policy of the UK Government is to increase national and regional **devolution**. The opportunity to elect a regional level of elected government, which was to be offered to some of the regions of England, was accepted by referendum in London, but was rejected in a referendum in north-east England and is now less likely to be offered elsewhere. A movement to obtain some degree of home rule also exists in Cornwall where a petition of over 50,000 signatures endorsed the call for a Cornish Assembly. However, the UK Government does not appear to be considering any form of devolution for Cornwall.

Local government

The UK is divided into a variety of different types of local authorities, with different functions and responsibilities, which are further subdivided – in rural areas and some urban areas – into **parishes**.

Local authorities are responsible for such matters as administering education, public transport and managing public spaces. They are often engaged in community politics. In England most counties, cities and towns each have their own councils, as do parishes at a local level, consisting of councillors elected by local people.

There are two common systems of local government in the UK: the old-style two-tier and the newer single-tier system. The older (and far more complex) two-tier system consists of District Councils and County Councils. The District Councils are responsible for rubbish collection, planning permission and council housing. County Councils are responsible for education, social services, some public transport, etc.

Unitary Authorities, which are in use throughout the whole of Scotland, Wales and Northern Ireland and in some areas in England, have a single tier of local government and combine District and County Council functions into one body.

In Greater London, a unique two-tier system exists, with power shared between the London Borough Councils and the Greater London Authority, which is headed by an elected mayor.

Definitions in context and key words

Archbishop of Canterbury: the main religious figure in the Church of England, also head of the worldwide Anglican community, and one of the Lords Spiritual.

backbencher: a Member of Parliament who is not a member of the Government, or in the case of opposition parties, does not shadow a government minister.

bill: a parliamentary proposal which becomes an Act of Parliament if it is passed by both Houses and receives the Royal Assent.

breach of the peace: behaviour harming or likely to harm a person or his property or likely to provoke violence in others.

Cabinet: a group of senior government ministers appointed by the Prime Minister, responsible for much of the Government's policy-making, and collectively answerable to Parliament.

Chancellor of the Exchequer: a Secretary of State responsible for the Treasury.

Civil List: the budget for the Sovereign's official expenditures.

Civil Service: the body of non-political public servants.

Committee of the Whole House: the entire House of Commons instead of a standing committee – meeting to examine and discuss a bill in detail.

Commonwealth: former British colonies now mostly forming an association of 53 sovereign and independent nations.

constituency: a geographical area for European, parliamentary or local elections.

draft: an attempt at a legal document that has yet to be approved.

devolution: the delegation of powers from a central government to regional or local government.

devolved system of government: a system wherein certain limited powers are exercised by locally elected bodies.

enforceable: that has to be obeyed.

executive agency: a public body in charge of a specific administrative task.

federal system: a system wherein limited powers exercised by regional and locally elected bodies are constitutionally defined.

felony: a serious offence.

First-Past-The-Post system (FPTP): a system in which the election of the Member of Parliament for each constituency is determined by which candidate has the most votes cast in a single vote in that constituency, irrespective of whether he has a majority of the votes cast.

front bench: the bench occupied by Government ministers, known as frontbenchers or, on the other side, the bench where Shadow ministers sit.

House of Commons: the lower house of Parliament.

House of Lords: the upper house of Parliament.

King/Queen in Parliament: the role of the sovereign as part of the legislative branch.

legislature: a State body empowered to make law.

Opposition: the minority party or coalition that sits in Parliament.

Lord Privy Seal: leader of the House of Commons; also a minister but without a portfolio.

parish: a local government unit acting as local authority.

peer/peeress: a Member of the House of Lords.

Question Time: a regular period set aside for ministers to respond to questions from MPs.

collective reponsibility: a principle whereby all Cabinet members are collectively responsible to Parliament for the decisions taken.

Royal Assent: the monarch's formal approval of a bill passed by Parliament.

royal prerogatives: the collective powers of the monarchy.

tie: an equal number of votes.

treason: violation of allegiance to sovereign or State.

Shadow Cabinet: counterpart Cabinet set up by the Opposition mirroring the Cabinet in power.

Speaker(s): the presiding member(s) of the House of Commons and the House of Lords.

standing committee: a group of MPs who analyse and review bills.

1 **Find the words corresponding to the following definitions.**
1. The monarch's formal approval of a bill.
2. The powers of the monarchy.
3. The group made up of the most important government ministers.
4. Non-political government staff.
5. A senior minister at the head of a Department of State.
6. Members of the British Parliament who represent the clergy.
7. An elected representative who sits in the House of Commons.
8. A bill of general interest and applicability.
9. A voting district.
10. A member of the Upper House who inherited his/her title.

2 **a. Classify the following twenty terms into relevant categories. Some terms may fall within more than one category.**

Royal Assent	10 Downing Street	Westminster
Whitehall	Cabinet	Church of England
MPs	treason	back bench
bill	patronage	prerogative
motion	Commonwealth	Speech from the Throne
peers	Lord Chancellor	Chancellor of the Exchequer
committee	Speaker	

b. Now write five sentences, each incorporating two of the terms listed above.

3 **Answer the following questions.**
1. What are the functions of the monarch?
2. What are the three branches of Parliament? What are the powers of each component?
3. Summarise the reforms that have affected the legislative system since the early 20th century.
4. What is the difference between the British system of devolution and a federal system of government?
5. What is a constitutional convention?

4 **Research task.**
1. Find more about the role of the monarch.
2. Further describe how the Cabinet works.
3. Find the list of Government departments in the present Government.
4. Find information about the House of Commons select committees.

2. More about...

A. The politics of the United Kingdom

1. Electoral system

The UK is divided into 646 parliamentary constituencies, each of which elects a Member of Parliament to the House of Commons. There is almost always a party with a majority of MPs in the House. Since 1964, all Prime Ministers and leaders of the Opposition have been drawn from the Commons, not the Lords.

The system used for general elections and local government elections in England and Wales is a relative majority system called First-Past-The-Post.

No government has won an absolute majority of the popular vote since the National Government of Stanley Baldwin in 1935. Indeed, on two occasions since World War II the party with fewer popular votes has obtained the larger number of seats in the House of Commons (in 1951 when the Conservative Party under Winston Churchill won with fewer votes than the Labour Party led by Clement Attlee, and in February 1974). Although the First-Past-the-Post system has contributed to a political landscape dominated by a two-party division, it has also enabled smaller parties to win constituencies with less than 50% of the vote.

Other systems are also in use for different types of ballots. For example, European Parliamentary elections are organised according to the party list system, in which voters choose a list and seats are allocated proportionally to the number of votes.

Although electoral reform has been considered for general elections many times, it is highly unlikely that anything will happen unless there is a significant change in the balance of power.

Low turnout has become a major concern, as the percentage of the electorate who voted in the 2005 general election was only 61%.

2. Political parties in the UK

1. Small parties and independents

The Green Party and the United Kingdom Independence Party have no seats in Parliament but are represented in the European Parliament.

A number of other parties only have local councillors such as the Liberal Party (in Kidderminster), Mebyon Kernow (the Cornish Nationalist Party) in Cornwall, the Scottish Socialist Party in Glasgow and the Communist Left

Alliance in Fife. The far-right British National Party (BNP) has councillors in a number of towns and obtained 5% of the national vote in the 2004 European Elections.

Yet, some regionally-based parties, advocating independence for their country or region, are represented in Parliament. In the 2005 general election, the Northern Ireland parties Sinn Fein, the Democratic Unionist Party and the Ulster Unionist Party all returned Members of Parliament to Westminster. In the same election, the Scottish National Party and Plaid Cymru (the Welsh Nationalist Party) also obtained representation.

There are a few independent politicians with no party allegiance in Parliament. This usually occurs when an MP decides to split from his party in mid-session. Since the Second World War, only three MPs have been elected as real independents, though others have been (re-)elected after breaking away from their party.

2. The Liberal Democratic Party

The following summarises the beliefs of the Liberal Democratic Party, as stated on their website homepage: "The Liberal Democrats exist to build and safeguard a fair, free and open society, in which we seek to balance the fundamental values of liberty, equality and community, and in which no-one shall be enslaved by poverty, ignorance or conformity [...]" (http://www.libdems.org.uk).

The Liberal Party was founded in 1859, although liberal political thought in England goes back further. Parliamentary groups began to form in the 18th century. The Tories supported the Crown and the Anglican Church while the Whigs were inspired by the Glorious Revolution of 1688, which established the supremacy of Parliament over the monarchy. The American War of Independence and the French Revolution revived the debate on government and a Whig government passed the Great Reform Act of 1832, which extended the franchise (the right to vote) and therefore the need to appeal to a wider electorate. This turning point is known as the birth of modern politics in England.

In 1981, the Social Democratic Party was formed to "get away from the politics of out-dated dogmatism and class confrontation". After alliances with the Liberal Party failed to yield satisfactory results, the two parties merged. In recent times the Liberal Democrats have gained momentum and in the 2005 General Election the "Lib Dems" obtained 62 seats in the Commons.

3. The Conservative Party

It is the oldest party in the world and dates back to the Tory Party of the 18th and 19th centuries. Its members are still very often referred to as Tories. It is the most successful party if one considers election victories.

The Tories formed many governments from 1760 (accession of King George III) up to the Great Reform Act of 1832, but the Conservative Party as such was founded in 1835. With the widening of the franchise in the 19th century, the party, which was rooted in the aristocracy, was forced to popularise its approach, and did so under the influence of Benjamin Disraeli, who was Prime Minister in 1868 and from 1874 to 1880.

It dominated the political scene during World War I, the inter-war period and World War II with Winston Churchill as Prime Minister. In the 1945 general election, however, the Conservative Party lost power in a landslide victory for the Labour Party.

The Heath government (1970-1974) took Britain into the EEC. In 1975 Margaret Thatcher became leader of the Conservatives and Prime Minister in 1979. The party adopted a free market policy, embarked on a vigorous privatisation of the public sector and won elections in 1983 and 1987.

John Major replaced Mrs Thatcher in 1992. His government was defeated in 1997 because of growing unemployment and media accusations of sleaze. In late 2005, the Conservatives chose David Cameron to replace Michael Howard as the head of the party. Young and charismatic, Cameron is expected to bring about a revival of the party's fortunes by modernising its old-fashioned image.

As a general rule, Conservative Party policies support reduced government intervention, particularly in the economic domain. Tories defend traditional family values and restrictions on immigration. They are generally known to be "Eurosceptics" and are opposed to the European single currency. They do not defend devolution, preferring a unitary centralised state.

4. The Labour Party

The Labour Party has been the main left-wing party in the UK since the beginning of the 20th century. It emerged from the 19th century trade union movement and socialist parties when there was an increasing need felt for a political party which would represent the interests and needs of the large working class of that period.

Labour formed its first government in January 1924 with Ramsay MacDonald as Prime Minister. Two decades later, after WWII, Labour won a landslide victory against Churchill's Conservatives. Clement Attlee remained Prime Minister from 1945 to 1951 and set up the National Health Service, amongst other social measures.

Labour returned to government from 1964 until 1970, and again from 1974 to 1979 year of the electoral victory of the Conservatives led by Margaret Thatcher.

Labour won the 1997, 2001 and 2005 elections with Tony Blair as party leader. After seeking to retain much of the laissez-faire capitalism of the

Thatcherite era and initally keeping its promise to restrict its spending plans, the party has substantially increased public spending, especially on the National Health Service and education.

Exercises

1 Answer the following questions.

1. What period in the history of England is often referred to as the beginning of modern politics?
2. Comment upon the British two-party political system.
3. Compare British politics with the political landscape in your home country.

2 Research tasks.

1. Find out about the results of the latest general election in the UK.
2. Find out which party won the 1974 elections.
3. Find more about the differences between Labour and the Conservatives.

B. The role of the Speaker of the House of Lords

Title
The usual title of the office is "Lord Speaker".

Length of appointment
The Lord Speaker is elected for five years. No Lord Speaker may serve for more than two terms.

Role in the Chamber of the House of Lords
The Lord Speaker will enter the Chamber in procession at the start of each sitting. A report published in 2006 by the Procedure Committee of the House of Lords provides the following description of the Lord Speaker's role in the Chamber:

(1) The primary role of the Speaker is to preside over proceedings in the Chamber, including the Committee of the whole House. The Speaker seeks the leave of the House for any necessary absence of a full sitting of a day or more.

(2) The Speaker has no power to act in the House without the consent of the House.

(3) The role of assisting the House at question time rests with the Leader of the House, not the Speaker.

(4) At other times of day the Lord on the Woolsack or in the Chair may assist the House by reminding members of the relevant parts of the *Companion*. Such assistance is limited to procedural advice and is usually given at the start of the business in hand, for example how time is to be divided between the front and back benches in response to a statement, the correct procedure at Report stage, the handling of grouped amendments, and the procedure to be followed in the case of amendments to amendments. Assistance may be helpful at other stages when procedural problems arise.

(5) The Government Chief Whip advises the House on speaking times in debates. Enforcing such time limits is handled by the front benches rather than the Speaker. Timed debates are brought to an end (if necessary) by the Speaker on an indication from the Table.

(6) Interventions, in particular those calling attention to the failure of an individual Member to comply with the rules, may come from the front benches or other Members. This would be the case, for example, when arguments deployed in committee were repeated at length on report. Such interventions would not normally come from the Speaker.

(7) The Speaker observes the same formalities as any other Member of the House. He addresses the House as a whole, and not an individual Member. He does not intervene when a Member is on his feet. His function is to assist, and not to rule. The House does not recognise points of order. Any advice or assistance given by the Speaker is subject to the view of the House as a whole.

It is expected that the Lord Speaker will occupy the Woolsack, or the Chair when the House is in Committee, usually for not less than three hours per sitting day except when other commitments as Speaker make that impossible. The Chairman of Committees or a member of the panel of Deputies would preside at other times, and in Grand Committee.

Role outside the Chamber

Private Notice Questions

Private Notice Questions will be submitted in the first instance to the Lord Speaker before 12 noon (or before 10 am when the House sits in the morning). The decision whether the question is of sufficient urgency and importance to justify an immediate reply will rest in the first place with the Lord Speaker, after consultation, and ultimately with the general sense of the House.

Emergency recall

The Lord Speaker will have the role of authorising the recall of the House during a recess (under Standing Order 17), subject to consultation with Her Majesty's Government.

Matters *sub judice*
The Lord Speaker will have the role (previously carried out by the Leader of the House) of determining whether the *sub judice* rule may be overridden.

Select Committees
The Lord Speaker will chair the House Committee and be a member of the Procedure Committee.

The Palace of Westminster
The Lord Speaker will have formal responsibility for the security of the Lords part of the Parliamentary estate. The Lord Speaker will be one of the three "keyholders" of Westminster Hall, together with the Speaker of the House of Commons and the Lord Great Chamberlain.

Ceremonial occasions
The Lord Speaker will take over the Lord Chancellor's role of speaking for the House on ceremonial occasions, such as the presentation of Addresses to Her Majesty the Queen.

Representational role
The Lord Speaker is expected to have a strong representational role acting as non-political spokesman for the House at home and abroad. The Lord Speaker will also have an important educational role making sure that the public understand the significance of the work of the House.
The Lord Speaker will represent the House at international Speakers' conferences and entertain visiting Speakers and parliamentarians from abroad.

Miscellaneous statutory functions
Schedule 6 to the Constitutional Reform Act 2005 confers on the Lord Speaker the following functions previously undertaken by the Lord Chancellor:
• under the Clerk of the Parliaments Act 1824, the power to appoint, subject to approval by the House, clerks officiating at the Table other than the Clerk of the Parliaments;
• under the Parliamentary Papers Act 1840, the role (held concurrently with the Clerk of the Parliaments) of certifying that papers have been published by order of the House;
• under the Church of England (Assembly) Powers Act 1919, the appointment of the Lords members of the Ecclesiastical Committee;
• under the Statutory Instruments Act 1946 and the Laying of Documents before Parliament (Interpretation) Act 1948, the role of receiving notifications in cases where a statutory instrument comes into operation before being laid;
• under the Consolidation of Enactments (Procedure) Act 1949, certain functions in relation to the parliamentary scrutiny of consolidation bills which incorporate "corrections and minor improvements";

• under the Exchequer and Audit Departments Act 1957, the giving of authority for an authorised officer to perform functions of the Comptroller and
Auditor General;
• under the Ministerial and other Salaries Act 1975, the power to determine
who is the Leader of the Opposition in the House.
In addition the following functions are expected to be transferred to the Lord
Speaker by an Order subject to approval by both Houses:
• under the Civil Contingencies Act 2004, the duty of recalling the House if
emergency regulations are made during an adjournment ending more than five
days later;
• under the Statutory Instruments Regulations 1947, the function, jointly with
the Speaker of the House of Commons, of nominating the members, and
establishing the quorum, of the Statutory Instruments Reference Committee.

Salary and expenses
The Lord Speaker's annual salary (subject to approval of the necessary Order by
both Houses) will be £102,685 from 5 July 2006 (the day after appointment),
and £103,701 from 1 November 2006. In addition, the Lord Speaker will be
entitled to an office-holder's allowance, currently £33,990 (220 times the
overnight subsistence allowance for backbench Members) or a London
Supplement of £1,667.
A former Minister or MP in receipt of a Parliamentary pension would not
receive that pension while holding office. It is expected that other public service
pensions would not be affected, but prospective candidates should consult their
pension provider.
The Lord Speaker will be able to recover the same expenses as other office-
holders, namely:
• Secretarial expenses incurred in respect of Parliamentary duties (subject to an
annual limit of £5,025);
• Travelling expenses from home to the House of Lords;
• Expenses of a spouse or civil partner and dependent children travelling to a
parliamentary occasion in London (subject to a maximum of 15 return trips per
person per annum).

Political activity
The Lord Speaker will be expected to lay aside any party or group affiliation on
appointment, and to refrain from political activity, including voting in the House.

Outside interests
The Lord Speaker will be expected to lay aside financial interests in the following categories, based on paragraph 12 of the House's Code of Conduct:
    (a) any consultancy agreement to provide parliamentary advice or services;

(b) employment or any other financial interest in businesses involved in parliamentary lobbying on behalf of clients, including public relations and law firms;

(c) any remunerated service provided by virtue of his or her position as a member of Parliament;

(d) employment as a non-parliamentary consultant;

(e) remunerated directorships;

(f) remunerated employment (including occasional income from speeches, lecturing, broadcasting and journalism);

(g) provision by an outside body of secretarial and research assistance;

(h) visits with costs paid in the United Kingdom and overseas, made as a member of Parliament, except any visits paid for from public funds, and except for minor hospitality.

There is no requirement to lay aside shareholdings, and there are no special requirements in relation to the interests of a spouse, relative or friend.

The Registrar of Lords' Interests will be available to advise. The Registrar shall consult the Sub-Committee on Lords' Interests of the Committee for Privileges when necessary. A Lord Speaker who acts on the advice of the Registrar will satisfy these requirements fully.

Accommodation and support

The Lord Speaker will occupy the office currently occupied by the Clerk of the Crown in Chancery on the Principal Floor and will be supported by a Private Secretary and a Personal Secretary. In addition the Reading Clerk will move to an office close to the Lord Speaker's.

Dress

The Lord Speaker will wear a gown when in the Chamber, like that worn by Clerks at the Table and QCs. Under the gown, and for other official duties outside the Chamber when a gown would not be suitable, it is expected that the Speaker will wear court dress.

For State occasions and similar ceremonies outside the Chamber, when Parliamentary robes might be unsuitable, the Lord Speaker will wear a black and gold robe (without a train).

The role of the Speaker of the House of Lords, Clerk of the Parliaments' Office, 10/5/2006.

1 True or false? Correct the statements that are wrong.

1. The House of Lords has always had a Speaker.

2. The Speaker's role in the Chamber is to conduct debates in whatever way he sees fit.

3. The Speaker must submit to the same rules as the other Members.
4. The Speaker's functions are limited to what happens in the Chamber.
5. The Speaker's presence in the UK is required at all times.

2 **Research task.**

Browse the UK Parliament's website and find out who sat on the Woolsack previously and what distinguishes the Speakership of the House of Commons from the Speakership of the House of Lords.

3. Off the presses

> ### Lords block right to die Bill
>
> The Lords tonight blocked a bid to allow terminally ill patients the right to end their lives, despite widespread public support for a change in the law.
>
> After an impassioned seven-hour debate, peers voted by 148 to 100 to delay the Assisted Dying for the Terminally Ill Bill's second reading for six months. The move further reduces the bill's chances of making its way through parliament.
>
> Crossbencher Lord Joffe's third attempt to enshrine in law the right-to-die aroused strong opposition from the medical profession and from church leaders, including the Archbishop of Canterbury Dr Rowan Williams.
>
> A YouGov poll commissioned by *Dignity in Dying*, the lobby group campaigning for a change in the law, meanwhile showed overall public support for right to die legislation.
>
> Lords turned out in force to debate the controversial issue, with 80 peers lined up to speak.
>
> The proposals would have allowed doctors the right to prescribe drugs that a terminally ill patient, in the final stages of life and suffering terrible pain, could take to end his or her own life.
>
> Opening the debate earlier today, Lord Joffe said: "As a caring society we cannot sit back and complacently accept that terminally ill patients suffering unbearably should just continue to suffer for the good of society as a whole. We must find a solution to the unbearable suffering of patients whose needs cannot be met by palliative care. This bill provides that solution in the absence of any other."
>
> He insisted the Bill would "not impose anything on anybody and only provides an additional end of life option for terminally ill patients which they are free to accept or reject as they and only they decide".

Opponents argued that the bill did not include safeguards to protect people suffering from depression, and could put pressure on the terminally ill to end their lives prematurely.

Archbishop Rowan Williams warned that the legislative proposals would "jeopardise the security of the vulnerable by radically changing the relationship between patient and physicians".

He said: "Whether or not you believe that God enters into the consideration, it remains true that to specify even in the fairly broad terms of this bill, conditions under which it would be both reasonable and legal to end your life, is to say that certain kinds of life are not worth living."

Outside the debating chamber, disabled opponents launched the *Not Dead Yet* campaign in protest at the proposals, while supporters of the Catholic church-backed *Care Not Killing* also held a protest.

Care Not Killing, which represents more than 30 charities and healthcare groups, warned that the Joffe bill would put the old and sick under intolerable pressure to end their lives, not least because of severe pressures on health and long-term care services.

Despite the vocal protests, a YouGov survey published today for the *Dignity In Dying* group found three-quarters of people in favour of the right-to-die bill.

More than half (59%) said there was good care for people in the later stages of a terminal illness, yet 76% were in favour of assisted dying as long as there were safeguards in place.

Of the 1,770 people questioned, 13% were opposed to the idea, while 11% said they did not know, and 39% said they had experienced hospice or palliative care either directly or though a loved one.

Deborah Annetts, chief executive of *Dignity In Dying*, said: "It is clear that the public truly appreciates the scope of the problem. Even with the high quality of our palliative care, some people will still want this option."

The government had resisted taking a position on the controversial proposals, citing a position of "neutrality". A Department of Health spokeswoman said it would "wait and see" what happens in the Lords before deciding whether to back the Bill's passage through the Commons.

Earlier today, the archbishop denied that opponents of the bill were trying to impose their religious beliefs on the general population, many of whom did not share their faith.

He told BBC Radio 4's *Today* programme that a "diverse range of groups" was opposed to the Bill and not just those "enslaved by so-called clerical superstition", including the Royal College of Psychiatrists and the Disability Rights Commission.

"[Opposition] comes from a number of people who are very close to the hardest of practical decisions who still say the costs of voting this through is disproportionately high to the benefit for certain individuals."

Hélène Mulholland and agencies,
Guardian Unlimited (http://politics.guardian.co.uk), 12/5/2006.

Exercises

1 Answer the following questions.

1. What is the purpose of the bill the article deals with?

2. Summarise the various steps the bill must have gone through by this point, drawing from the text and using your knowledge of the law-making process.

3. Classify the various organisations mentioned in the article, based on the orientation of their message (for or against?).

4. Summarise the arguments on both sides.

2 Discuss.

Which of these arguments are convincing, in your opinion? What would your position be over this issue?

3 Research task.

Find out whether the Bill eventually made it through Parliament and what the current state of the law is in the UK on the topic of assisted suicide for terminally ill patients.

4. Food for thought

The constitutional crisis we face when the Queen is gone

Read the coronation service and it's clear this framework of monarchy and established church cannot outlive Elizabeth.

There have been the official 80th photographs, the 80 facts for an 80-year-old monarch issued by Buckingham Palace, a respectful television programme on her extraordinary life and long reign. There will be plenty more celebrations come the official birthday in June, but as the Queen finally celebrates her landmark day, there's a thought that, however inappropriate, can't but rear its head: what happens to a monarchy that has become so profoundly associated with one particular person? Is the institution robust enough to survive its passage to a new incumbent?

So much of our understanding of the monarchy has been bound up with the character of Elizabeth Windsor; her combination of reserve, sense of duty and that quintessential English upper-class lifestyle of frugal and rural. The kilts, the corgis, the cereal-box Tupperware, the request to servants not to walk down the middle of carpets to prevent wear: all are redolent of an upbringing in the first half of the 20th century and its discipline of iron self-restraint and small indulgences. No one accuses the Queen of celebrity-style extravagance, of too many exotic holidays, house makeovers and absurd wardrobes of clothes. On the contrary, she is a woman of grimly determined duty and her face as often as not indicates the huge sacrifice of a woman who would probably have been far happier living in the obscurity of a large landed estate, breeding horses.

What is often missed out of the puzzling phenomenon of this woman's life is her religious faith. It is what makes her devotion to duty and self-sacrifice explicable. While the church over which she presides has faced dwindling congregations, her Christmas Day speeches and addresses to the Church of England Synod have often been remarkably religious. It's hard to think of a recent predecessor – let alone a likely successor – of a comparable sincerity of belief, and it has been vital in sustaining the establishment of the Church of England. It would be quite possible to make the claim that Elizabeth Windsor has become one of the nation's most articulate religious leaders – but that says as much about the timidity of the competition as it does about her.

Her belief explains much about how she has understood her position and her responsibilities, and about how she has developed a contemporary monarchy; it helps explain the ultimately ill-fated invention of the royal family just as the permissive 60s gathered pace – an alternative model of conjugal commitment and family responsibility – which foundered in the marital troubles of her offspring. It also helps explain why this is a woman who is extremely unlikely to abdicate, rather as Pope John Paul II soldiered on to the bitter end, driven by a sense that he had been chosen and consecrated by God to fulfil his earthly role.

If this sounds a bit far-fetched applied to the Queen, look at the order of service of the 1953 coronation: it makes explicit that she was chosen by God to be queen of England and anointed by the Holy Spirit with the wisdom and other blessings required for the job. If you believe that, retirement is not really an option.

All of which raises the question of how the idiosyncratic and delicate framework of the monarchy, the establishment of the Church of England and the state, which the Queen has managed to hold together despite the dramatic decline in Christianity, would survive her demise. It may be a tactless time to raise the question when celebrating an 80th birthday – it may also, given her mother's longevity, be a good 20 years off – but this framework will be suddenly exposed in all its glorious anachronisms come the next coronation.

There has been some speculation about how the coronation oath might have to be rejigged with some hasty legislation – four out of the five questions in the oath relate to the upholding of Christianity, three specifically to the upholding of the Church of England. How will that go down in a country where the number regularly attending Anglican services is roughly matched by the number of British Muslims? There has also been speculation about a tweaking of the official title to defender of faiths. But this is fiddling round the edges compared to the actual coronation service. This ceremony at the crux of the British constitution is a ritual steeped in the history of a millennium of European Christianity. It blows apart completely the fiction that we live in a secular state.

The nub of the ceremony is the anointing by the Archbishop of Canterbury of the monarch on the palms, chest and head. This is a sacrament; not just symbolic, it actually transforms the recipient. As the Bishop of Salisbury, David Stancliffe, puts it: "It marks an outpouring of the Holy Spirit with gifts of grace to sanctify the person, it marks the choice of God of this person to be king or queen and starts a process which will be fulfilled in the course of their reign."

After the anointing, the monarch dons robe royal, orb, sceptre, rod and crown – all symbols of the divine grace being poured on to the new sovereign – while the archbishop incants prayers such as "may you continue steadfastly as the defender of Christ's religion". He concludes in a benediction: "The Lord who hath made you [king or queen] over these peoples give you increase of grace, honour and happiness in this world and make you partake of his eternal felicity in the world to come."

The monarch is accountable to God for their rule, and the prayer is that they will eventually come to enjoy eternal life. (There are echoes here of Tony Blair's own admission recently that he would be accountable to God for his decision to go to war in Iraq; while he may have horrified secularists, he was, in fact, only articulating the spirit of the British constitution.)

Eternal life, divine grace, sacrament, anointing: it's hard to imagine, come the next coronation, a BBC commentator like Andrew Marr providing explanations that could satisfy secular Britain. Will a coronation be justified as a "heritage opportunity" marketed to tourists to enjoy some British pomp, or will this Charlemagne-derived event finally prompt the determination to update Britain's quaint constitution? It's hard to head off the latter with a discreet revamp of the ceremony ahead of time. That leaves a constitutional crisis waiting to happen: the relationship between sovereign, church and state, which the

Queen has managed to largely steer clear of public debate, would come under the bewildered glare of the global media, and who knows how it would fall apart under that kind of scrutiny?

Madeleine Bunting,
The Guardian (http://www.guardian.co.uk), 21/4/2006.

Definitions in context

dwindle (v.) : become smaller and smaller

idiosyncratic: related to unusual or original habits and ways

demise: the end or death of something

quaint: old-fashioned

bewildered: confused

Exercises

1 Answer the following questions.

1. What is said of the Queen's relationship with religion?
2. What is the place of religion in the British Constitution?
3. What will be the legacy of Queen Elizabeth II?
4. What questions does her succession raise?

2 Discuss.

1. What do you think could be the future of the British monarchy?
2. What constitutional changes are to be expected in your opinion?

5. Listening

Exercises

1 Listen to Part 1 of a passage about select committees and complete the extract with the missing words.

Part 1. Select committee set-up

.... Michael Jopling once declared that "select committees are giving ...... teeth with which to challenge the executive".

The function of Parliament's select committees is to ...... various aspects of .... and society. They have contributed significantly to the ...... of the role of Parliament.

As part of their work, committees call ...... with expertise and experience in the ...... of the inquiry. They may also produce ....

Select committees play a crucial role in the scrutiny of government and their ...... can lead to major reform.

The .... – around a horse-shoe shaped table – are at the heart of committee inquiries and can cause even the most senior government ministers to squirm in their ....

There is great ....on the more important committees and it's up to the Committee of Selection to select their make-up.

Non-departmental select committees date back to ...... , when the Public Accounts Committee was established. Most of them were known as "committees of the House". In July 2005, the Administration Committee replaced the five ...... house committees which were concerned with the administration of the House of Commons – ...... & works, administration, ... , catering, information.

The current system of departmental select committees was set up in ...... to shadow and report on the work of government departments.

The ...... original departmental committees have increased under the ...... that each department of state should have a committee shadowing it.

The size of committees varies but most have 11 members. They ...... the relative party sizes in the Commons.

2 **Say whether the following statements are true or false.**

1. Select committees carry very little weight compared to the Government.
2. Even senior ministers can experience embarrassment during select committee sessions.
3. There are currently five committees dealing with the management of the House of Commons.
4. There is a committee for each government department.
5. Frontbenchers often sit on select committees.
6. Joint committees are committees representing parliamentary parties.

3 💿 **Listen to Part 2 of the recording and use the context to determine which definitions match the terms below.**

1. *a one-off evidence session:*
    a) a session which is repeated on a regular basis
    b) a single session which is not part of a long process
2. *rebuff* (v.)
    a) acclaim
    b) reject or dismiss

3. *accountability*
   a) the obligation to answer for one's acts
   b) bureaucratic supervision of expenses

4 **Listen to Part 2 again and answer the following questions.**

1. What type of evidence does a committee work with?
2. Who is David Blunkett?
3. What is pre-legislative scrutiny? What does the year 1997 have to do with this notion?
4. What is the "biannual scrutiny" of the Liaison Committee?

6. Grammar practice

`Exercises`

1 **Interrogatives. Complete each sentence with one of the following question word(s).**

how much	*how many*	*how long*	*whose*
how often	*who*	*whom*	*what*

1. ...... does the PM keep informed on a weekly basis?
2. ...... money is the Queen given by Parliament for her annual official expenditure?
3. ...... privileges do MPs enjoy?
4. ...... constituencies is Britain divided into?
5. ...... do parliaments generally last?
6. ...... assent is necessary for a bill to become an Act?
7. ...... are general elections held?
8. By ...... are peers appointed?

2 **Prepositions. Complete each sentence with the missing preposition.**

1. Councils are responsible ...... such things as rubbish collection.
2. The Sovereign's duty consists ...... representing the country.
3. ...... the State Opening of Parliament the Monarch delivers a speech defining the political agenda of the Government.
4. The PM chooses Cabinet members ...... the most senior officials of the Government.
5. Members of Parliament generally vote according ...... party policy.
6. The newly elected MP does not know much ...... devolution.
7. The twelve Law Lords abstain ...... taking part ...... crucial legislative issues.

8. Parliament is made ...... two houses which sit in separate chambers and pass laws in compliance ...... very similar procedures.

3 **Complete each sentence with for, since or ago.**

1. Queen Elizabeth II has been reigning ...... 1952.

2. Tony Blair was first elected nine years ....

3. The House of Lords has had a Speaker ...... the Constitutional Reform Act 2005.

4. A few years ...... , automatic access to the House of Lords by hereditary peers was abolished and ...... then only 92 chosen hereditary peers have been allowed to go on sitting.

5. ...... the beginning of the 20th century the House of Lords' power to reject laws has been very much curtailed.

6. The issue of euthanasia has been debated ...... decades and in 2006 the House of Lords delayed the Assisted Dying for the Terminally Ill Bill's second reading ...... six months.

4 **Articles. Complete each sentence with a, the or ø.**

1. ...... UK has got ...... bicameral parliamentary system which has been very much imitated throughout ...... world.

2. ...... universal suffrage exists for ...... British citizens who are 18 and over.

3. ...... Queen started paying ...... income tax in 1993.

4. ...... two Houses of ...... Parliament function in ...... very similar way. ...... bills go through ...... different stages before being given ...... Royal Assent.

5. ...... Green Party has got no seat in ...... Parliament but has got ...... few MEPs in ...... European Parliament.

6. ...... Queen Elizabeth's parents are remembered for their courage during ...... World War II.

7. ...... important issues such as ...... EU currency have divided ...... political parties for decades.

8. ...... local authorities are very much involved in ...... people's daily life.

Chapter 3

The English legal professions

1. Fundamentals

Since the 14th century, the legal profession in England and Wales has been divided into two main branches: solicitors and barristers. Solicitors advise their clients on legal matters whereas barristers represent their clients in higher courts. A parallel is often drawn with the medical profession, with solicitors being compared to general practitioners (GPs) and barristers to consultants or specialists. Though solicitors and barristers are both lawyers, there are significant differences in training and practice between the two branches.

Solicitors

Solicitors' firms can be found on any High Street. People may require a solicitor for many reasons, e.g. to buy a house, adopt a child, get a divorce, settle a legal dispute or plan the distribution of their property after death.

Prospective solicitors need to achieve excellent **A-level** grades. They must then work towards either a **qualifying law degree** or a degree in any other subject.[1] In both cases, students generally need a 2.1 grade at least. An LLB (Bachelor of Laws) is obtained after a three-year university course based on the seven core subjects in law[2]. Non-law graduates must successfully complete a CPE/GDL course (Common Professional Examination/Graduate Diploma in Law) which is a one-year conversion programme.

After that academic stage of training, graduates with an LLB or GDL move on to the vocational stage, which begins with the one-year Legal Practice Course (LPC). Offered at over thirty universities and specialised institutions and designed

1. Non-graduate legal executives may take the Legal Practice Course without holding a law degree provided that they meet the academic requirements set by ILEX, their governing body.
2. Constitutional (Public) Law, Criminal Law, Tort, Land Law, Contract, European Law & Equity.

to teach students the skills to become lawyers, the LPC covers a common curriculum set by the **Law Society,** the body that regulates the profession of solicitors. On completion of the course, candidates enter a two-year training contract with a law **firm** and are called **trainee solicitors,** still sometimes referred to as "articled clerks". This experience enables them to qualify as solicitors: they are admitted to the roll, i.e. their names are entered on the Law Society's official list of solicitors. To obtain their annual practising certificate, they pay a **fee** to the Law Society.

Fully qualified solicitors may work as **sole practitioners** or join a firm; they may deal with all aspects of the law or concentrate on a particular field. The working environment of family solicitors in a small town stands in sharp contrast to that of **partners** in a City firm employing hundreds of **salaried solicitors.** Solicitors can also work in the legal departments of companies, NGOs and government services. The most common activities of a solicitors' firm are providing general legal advice, preparing documents, advising on **litigation** and **briefing barristers.**

1. Legal advice

Someone seeking legal advice generally turns to a solicitor in private practice or at a Citizens' Advice Bureau. For a person who wants to buy a house, adopt a child, get a divorce or set up a company, solicitors are the best advisors.

2. Legal documents

Solicitors may be consulted to prepare legal documents, e.g. to draw up **contracts, wills, leases, conveyances** or **mortgages,** and to ensure their execution, as in **probate.**

3. Litigation

Solicitors advise clients involved in litigation; they prepare cases for trial. Until fairly recently they could only appear as advocates in the lower courts. The Courts and Legal Services Act 1990 gave them the opportunity to obtain higher courts qualifications allowing them to present cases before the higher courts as **solicitor advocates.**

4. Briefing barristers

Before the above-mentioned Act, only barristers could appear in the higher courts, and they continue to do so in most instances. Barristers are instructed by solicitors. This means that the solicitor presents a client's case to the barrister in a document called a **brief,** and that the barrister represents the client in court.

Barristers

Like specialists in the medical profession, barristers (also called **counsel**) could not until recently be approached directly by members of the public. This is now possible under certain rules, but barristers still concentrate very much on providing specialist legal advice, drafting court documents and **pleading,** i.e. representing parties in court.

As for a solicitor, either the LLB or a non-law degree followed by the GDL is needed to become a barrister. Excellent results are required at all levels of study. After obtaining the required academic qualifications, future barristers must attend a school of law at one of the several (currently eight) accredited institutions, taking the competitive one-year Bar Vocational Course (BVC), during which they receive training in the drafting of legal documents and in **advocacy** skills. To register at a law school, they must first be admitted to one of the four **Inns of Court** in London.

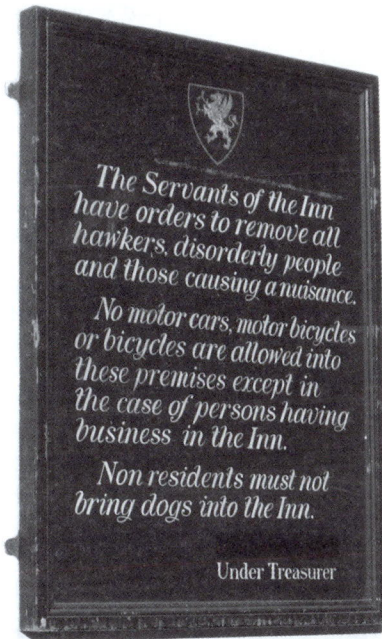

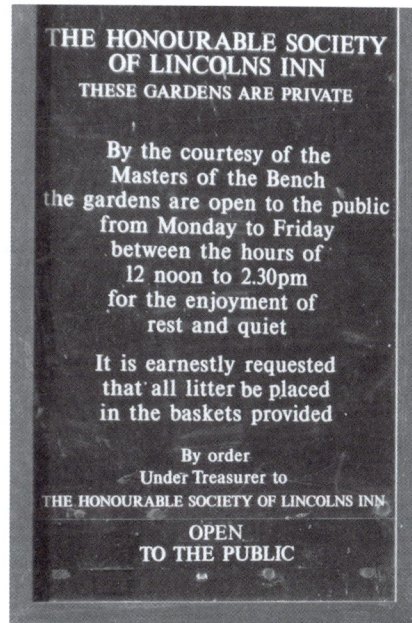

The Inns of Court can be very protective of their privacy…

The Inns of Court (Lincoln's Inn, Gray's Inn, Middle Temple, Inner Temple) date back to medieval times, and each has its own traditions. They are non-academic societies that provide collegiate and educational activities and support for barristers and student barristers. Students from all BVC centres must obtain twelve qualifying units by attending a number of Inn events and dinners; this requirement is called **keeping terms**. These occasions provide students with opportunities to meet practising barristers, seek their advice and learn from their professional experience.

After completing the Bar Vocational Course, a prospective barrister must undertake **pupillage**, a one-year apprenticeship under an established barrister acting as a **pupil supervisor**. Following this period, the student barrister is entitled to apply to sets of **chambers** in the hope of being offered a **tenancy**, i.e. a permanent place. **Pupil barristers** who have been awarded tenancy become qualified barristers when they are **called to the Bar** by their Inns of Court and the regulatory body for barristers, the **Bar Council**.

Barristers stand at the centre of the litigation process. They are specialised in civil or criminal cases. A good barrister must be persuasive in court and an effective advocate. The main activities of barristers are advocacy, providing written **opinions** on points of law and evidence for solicitors and drawing up documents. Some barristers (for example, those specialising in crime) spend nearly all of their time representing clients in court, whereas others have primarily paper practices and seldom leave their chambers.

1. Litigation

Since barristers plead in higher courts, they are more likely to act as advocates for big businesses and for individuals charged with serious criminal offences.

In chambers, clerks manage the practices of the members. They are contacted by solicitors who seek to instruct a barrister in order to advise or draft **pleadings** or who wish to brief a barrister for a court hearing. In theory, barristers are not permitted to refuse to take on a case, according to the **cab-rank rule**. However, they are under a duty to refuse to take on a case that is not within their experience or capability, and they may decline a brief or an instruction where the fee is insufficient. When briefed, they are paid by the solicitors on behalf of the clients. Though clients are represented by barristers, they do not necessarily meet each other. Barristers have both a relationship of confidence with their clients and, as officers of the courts, a duty not to mislead the courts. They must ensure that all information that should be disclosed is indeed disclosed, in accordance with the ethics of the profession.

2. Opinions

As barristers are specialists in their field, they can be asked to give advice on a particular point of law. Members of other professions (e.g. architects, conveyancers, **auctioneers** and **accountants**) have for some time been entitled to instruct barristers without the help of solicitors.

Queen's Counsel

Barristers and solicitor advocates who have made names for themselves and who have acquired the necessary experience and knowledge may apply to become **Queen's Counsel** (QCs), or senior counsel. The Commission for Judicial Appointments then selects the best candidates to be QCs. When they become senior counsel, it is said that they **take silk**, as the gowns they then wear are made of silk. Hence they are often referred to as "silks". QCs concentrate primarily on advocacy and deal with the most difficult cases. Generally a junior barrister (a barrister who is not a QC) will carry out the preparatory work for a QC. Being Queen's Counsel is often considered a first step to becoming a judge in the highest courts (see chapter 4, The court system and the personnel of the courts).

Reform

The English legal system is constantly under review. In theory it adapts to the changing needs of society. Reforms are often determined by different governments' political ideologies and by the need to comply with European Union law.

There has been a tendency in recent years for sole practitioners and small practices of solicitors to go out of business or be absorbed into larger firms. Increasingly, firms are specialising in particular areas of law, and one further recent development is the recruiting of barristers by a small number of firms to act as **in-house** counsel providing advice, drafting pleadings and appearing in court. Multi-disciplined practices may be putting an end to the traditional division in the legal profession between general practitioners and specialists.

As previously mentioned, barristers no longer have a monopoly on conducting litigation before the higher courts. Thanks to the Courts and Legal Services Act 1990, solicitors who have met the training requirements and obtained the Higher Courts Qualification have **rights of audience** before all courts in England and Wales.

Solicitors recently lost their monopoly on **conveyancing,** through the Administration of Justice Act 1985, which established the new professional category of licensed conveyancers.

Apart from solicitors and barristers, other members of the legal profession include legal executives, patent agents, coroners, licensed conveyancers and notaries public.

Definitions in context and key words

accountant: a person whose job it is to keep or check financial accounts.

auctioneer: a person whose job it is to direct an auction and sell goods by inviting people to make bids (offers).

advocacy *(uncountable)* : the work of lawyers consisting in pleading in court.

3. The term refers to the final two years of secondary schooling in the United Kingdom.

A-levels: final examinations that 6th-form[3] pupils take on a restricted range of chosen subjects at the end of their secondary education.

Bar Council: the body that regulates the profession of barristers.

brief: a document in which a solicitor sets out the facts of a case for the barrister who is to represent a client in court.

brief *(v.)* **a barrister**: instruct a barrister to represent a client in court by sending him or her a brief along with documents needed for the court hearing.

cab-rank rule: the principle by which a barrister should accept any case within his or her specialised field when briefed by a solicitor.

be called to the Bar: be given the title of barrister by the Bar Council, in a ceremony at an Inn of Court, after completing qualification.

chambers: offices from where self-employed barristers carry on their practices.

contract: an agreement between two or more parties to create legally enforceable obligations between them.

conveyance: a document used to effect a property transfer.

conveyancing *(uncountable)*: the legal process of transferring property from one person to another.

counsel: a barrister, barristers.

fee: an amount of money paid to a professional for his or her services.

firm: a business organisation, usually a partnership; a company.

in-house: employed by a firm or company for exclusive service within its domain of activity.

Inns of Court: the four legal centres in London in which barristers train and practice.

keep *(v.)* **terms**: attend training and/or social events, generally organised by a student barrister's Inn, to obtain the twelve qualifying units required to be eligible to be called to the Bar.

Law Society: the professional body, founded in 1825, that regulates the profession of solicitors.

lease: a contract between a tenant and a landlord for the letting of property.

litigation *(uncountable)*: the judicial process of solving a dispute between two parties, from legal advice to trial.

mortgage: a contract in which property being purchased (e.g. a house) is used to guarantee repayment of a loan.

opinion (of a barrister): a barrister's advice on a precise point of law needed by solicitors, other professionals or lay (non-professional) clients.

partner: a person who shares the ownership of a firm.

plead *(v.)* : represent a client in court.

pleadings: written statements setting out a party's legal and factual assertions about a case and filed at the court.

probate *(uncountable)* : 1. the process of proving a will and distributing a dead person's estate. 2. the area of the law dealing with the handling of estates.

pupil barrister: a law graduate who has completed the Bar Vocational Course and is carrying out a training period under a pupil supervisor.

pupil supervisor: from 2004, the name given to the experienced barrister (previously called a pupil master/mistress) who trains a pupil barrister.

pupillage: a period of apprenticeship required to practise as a barrister, which a pupil barrister must carry out under a pupil supervisor.

qualifying law degree: a university qualification in law (LLB or CPE/GDL), recognised by the Law Society and the

Bar Council, which enables the law student to complete the first stage of training to become a solicitor or a barrister, i.e. to gain access to the Legal Practice Course or the Bar Vocational Course.

Queen's Counsel[4] or, when the ruling monarch is a king, **King's Counsel (QC, KC)**: a barrister who has been appointed counsel to the Crown, and who specialises primarily in advocacy and pleads in the higher courts.

right of audience: the right of a solicitor or a barrister to appear on behalf of a client before a court.

salaried solicitor: a solicitor who is employed by a firm of solicitors but is not a partner.

4. Note that the full term does not generally take an "s" in the plural, whereas the abbreviation does.

sole practitioner: a solicitor who works on his or her own in a one-person law practice.

solicitor advocate: a solicitor who has completed further training in advocacy and thus obtained a higher courts qualification, enabling him or her to appear in all courts.

take silk: become a senior barrister (since the gowns worn by QCs are made of silk).

tenancy: a permanent place for a barrister in a set of chambers.

trainee solicitor: a law graduate who has completed the LPC and is carrying out a training period under the supervision of an experienced solicitor.

will (last will and testament): a legal declaration specifying the manner in which a person wishes his or her property to be disposed of when he or she dies.

Exercises

1 Using the information in the text, decide whether the following statements are true or false.

1. Today in England and Wales, you need a law degree to become a solicitor or a barrister.

2. In the past, solicitors could not appear in the higher courts, but they now have rights of audience in all courts.

3. When briefing a barrister, the solicitor does the background work for the barrister.

4. Solicitors can only work in private practice.

5. The Inns of Court are the only specialist institutions where a student can take the BVC.

6. If you have a problem and you need legal advice, you had better consult a barrister.

7. Only solicitors can handle conveyancing.

8. It is necessary to join an Inn of Court if you want to become a barrister.

9. After a few years a barrister automatically becomes Queen's Counsel.

10. Solicitors are sometimes compared to general practitioners.

2 Match each verb (1-8) with a relevant noun (A-H).

1. draft	**A.** a solicitor
2. draw up	**B.** a contract
3. represent	**C.** a law degree
4. approach	**D.** a barrister
5. work in	**E.** a client
6. complete	**F.** a will
7. enter	**G.** a solicitor
8. instruct	**H.** chambers

3 Find a term synonymous with each of the following.

1. law degree   **2.** conversion course   **3.** articled clerk   **4.** established solicitor   **5.** the solicitors' regulatory body   **6.** advocacy   **7.** probate   **8.** apprenticeship **9.** counsel   **10.** senior counsel   **11.** the barristers' regulatory body   **12.** one-man practice

4 What does each of the following Abbreviations stand for?

1. KC   **2.** LLB   **3.** BVC   **4.** CPE   **5.** GDL   **6.** QC   **7.** LPC   **8.** GP

5 Should the following terms be associated with barristers, with solicitors or with both categories?

1. Bar Council   **2.** client   **3.** A-levels   **4.** keep terms   **5.** LLB   **6.** trainee   **7.** BVC **8.** Inns of Court   **9.** LPC   **10.** GDL   **11.** CPE   **12.** the roll   **13.** chambers   **14.** pupil **15.** partner   **16.** tenancy   **17.** sole practitioner   **18.** Law Society   **19.** brief *(v.)* **20.** probate   **21.** conveyancing   **22.** pleading   **23.** contract   **24.** advocacy **25.** lease   **26.** will   **27.** mortgage   **28.** divorce   **29.** brief *(n.)*   **30.** QC

6 Tick the boxes in each list if you think they apply to you and find out which profession you would be better at. Score 1 point for each tick.

Could I be a solicitor?

1.	I have an excellent academic background.	☐
2.	My written and verbal communication skills are good.	☐
3.	My commercial awareness is up to scratch.	☐
4.	I get on well and confidently with a wide variety of people.	☐
5.	I can work effectively under pressure.	☐
6.	I enjoy working in a team.	☐
7.	My computer skills are up-to-date.	☐
8.	I have a reasonable level of numeracy.	☐
9.	I can organise my time effectively.	☐
10.	I pay sufficient attention to detail.	☐
11.	I am keen on taking personal responsibility.	☐

12. I can effectively organise and prioritise my own workload. ☐
13. I have plenty of initiative and enjoy solving problems. ☐
14. I thrive under pressure. ☐
15. I can think quickly. ☐
16. I have strong stamina. ☐
17. I have some foreign language skills. ☐
18. I have a healthy sense of humour. ☐

Could I be a barrister?

1. I have excellent communication skills, both oral and written. ☐
2. I am very persuasive. ☐
3. I take a keen interest in business affairs. ☐
4. I am flexible and readily adapt to changing situations. ☐
5. I am computer literate. ☐
6. I can easily put people at ease. ☐
7. I can act in a professional manner. ☐
8. I am someone who others would describe as confident and self-assured. ☐
9. I am independently minded. ☐
10. I take great pride in being well prepared with high standards
of attention to detail. ☐
11. I am highly self-motivated and determined. ☐
12. I can remain calm under extreme pressure. ☐
13. I have plenty of stamina to cope with long working hours. ☐
14. I am practical and realistic in my approach. ☐
15. I can effectively organise my own workload. ☐
16. I am quite smart. ☐
17. I can keep a sense of humour in times of great stress. ☐
18. I have great integrity and concern for justice. ☐

My score

• Qualities needed to be a solicitor ☐
• Qualities needed to be a barrister ☐

7 Discuss.

1. Using the list of skills and qualities needed by a solicitor and by a barrister, explain to your fellow students why you would be a successful solicitor or barrister.
2. Why is a good sense of humour important to be a talented barrister or solicitor? Give your opinion to the rest of the class.

8 Giving information.

Stephen and Emily are 16-year-old twins. They are studying for their A-levels. They are contemplating careers in law. Stephen would like to be a solicitor, and Emily a barrister.

1. Explain what Stephen needs to know to become a solicitor.

2. Describe how Emily can become a barrister.

3. What effect could the recent changes in the structure of the legal profession have upon Stephen's and Emily's prospective careers.

2. More about...

A. The practice of solicitors and barristers

1. The Law Society

The Law Society is the regulatory and representative body for 116,000 solicitors in England and Wales. It was established in 1825 as "The Society of Attorneys, Solicitors, Proctors and others not being Barristers, practising in the Courts of Law and Equity in the United Kingdom" to raise the reputation of the profession by setting high standards of practice. It became colloquially known as "The Law Society" and officially adopted this title in 1903.

How the Law Society regulates solicitors:
- We set the standards for qualifying as a solicitor.
- We set the rules of professional conduct.
- We provide guidance on professional conduct.
- We set requirements for continuing professional development.
- We monitor solicitors to make sure they comply with the rules.
- We deal with complaints about solicitors and help to resolve them.
- We investigate and, if necessary, discipline solicitors who don't meet the standards.

One important aspect of our representative work is to negotiate fair rates of pay for solicitors undertaking publicly-funded work. The Law Society is keen to ensure that sufficient solicitors are encouraged, through fair remuneration, to continue to do this work in the interests of securing access to justice for the most needy.

http://www.lawsociety.org.uk

2. The Bar Council

The General Council of the Bar (known as the Bar Council) was founded in 1894 to represent the interests of barristers.

The Bar Council's principal objectives are:

- To represent the Bar as a modern and forward looking profession which seeks to maintain and improve the quality and standard of service to all clients;
- To maintain and enhance professional standards;
- To maintain effective complaints and disciplinary procedures;
- To develop an effective, fair and affordable system for recruiting, and of regulating entry to the profession;
- To regulate education and training for the profession;
- To combat discrimination and disadvantage at the Bar;
- To develop and promote the work of the Bar;
- To conduct research and promote the Bar's views on matters affecting the administration of justice, including substantive law reform;
- To provide services for members of the Bar, eg Fees Collection, publications, conferences, guidance on practice management and development;
- To promote the Bar's interests with Government, the EC, the Law Society, International Bars and other organisations with common interests

http://access.barcouncil.org.uk

3. Codes of conduct

Both solicitors and barristers work within rigorously enforced codes of professional conduct.

Excerpt from the Code of Conduct of the Bar:

A barrister has an overriding duty to the Court to act with independence in the interests of justice: he must assist the Court in the administration of justice and must not deceive or knowingly or recklessly mislead the Court.

A barrister must promote and protect fearlessly and by all proper and lawful means the lay client's best interests and do so without regard to his own interests or to any consequences to himself or to any other person (including any professional client or other intermediary or another barrister)."

http://www.barcouncil.org.uk.

Excerpt from the Guide to the Professional Conduct of Solicitors:

"A solicitor shall not do anything in the course of practising as a solicitor, or permit another person to do anything on his or her behalf, which compromises or impairs or is likely to compromise or impair any of the following:

(a) the solicitor's independence or integrity;

(b) a person's freedom to instruct a solicitor of his or her choice;

(c) the solicitor's duty to act in the best interests of the client;

(d) the good repute of the solicitor or of the solicitor's profession;

(e) the solicitor's proper standard of work;

(f) the solicitor's duty to the Court."

http://www.lawsociety.org.uk

4. Liability

Both solicitors and barristers are liable for negligence, but only solicitors are liable in contract. Clients who are dissatisfied with a lawyer's services may lodge a complaint with the Law Society, the Council of the Bar or the Legal Services Ombudsman (LSO). Thirty office staff including a team of investigating officers work for the LSO. If there are sufficient grounds for the complaint, disciplinary action is taken against the negligent solicitor or barrister. Barristers' immunity from claims in negligence was withdrawn with the case *Hall v Simons* [2000]:

LORD STEYN [...] For more than two centuries barristers have enjoyed an immunity from actions in negligence. The reasons for this immunity were various. It included the dignity of the Bar, the "cab rank" principle, the assumption that barristers may not sue for their fees, the undesirability of relitigating cases decided or settled, and the duty of a barrister to the court [...]. There would be benefits to be gained from the ending of immunity. First, and most importantly, it will bring to an end an anomalous exception to the basic premise that there should be a remedy for a wrong. [...] That brings me to the argument that the ending of the immunity, if it is to be undertaken, is a matter for Parliament. This argument is founded on section 62 of the Courts and Legal Services Act 1990. It reads as follows:

"(1) A person – a) who is not a barrister; but (1) who lawfully provides any legal services in relation to any proceedings, shall have the same immunity from liability for negligence in respect of his acts or omissions as he would have if he were a barrister lawfully providing those services. (2) No act or omission on the part of any barrister or other person which is accorded immunity from liability for negligence shall give rise to an action for breach of any contract relating to the provision by him of the legal services in question."

The background to this provision is, of course, the judicially created immunity of barristers, which in 1967 (*Rondel v Worsley*) was held by the House to be founded on public policy. [...] Section 62 is clear. It provides that solicitor advocates will have the same immunity as barristers have. [...] Section 62 did not either expressly or by implication give Parliamentary endorsement to the immunity of barristers. In these circumstances the argument that it is beyond the power of the House of Lords, which created the immunity spelt out in *Rondel v Worsley*, to reverse that decision in changed circumstances involving a different balance of policy considerations is not right. Should the House as a matter of discretion leave it to Parliament? This issue is more finely balanced. It would certainly be the easy route for the House to say "let us leave it to Parliament." On balance my view is that it would be an abdication of our responsibilities with the unfortunate consequence of plunging both branches of the legal profession in England into a state of uncertainty over a prolonged period. That would be a disservice to the public interest. [...] My Lords, [...] I would rule that there is no longer any such immunity in criminal and civil cases. In doing so I am quite confident that the legal profession does not need the immunity.

http://www.parliament.the-stationery-office.co.uk

Exercise

Role play

A is a trainee solicitor completing his/her traineeship at B's law firm. C is another partner of the firm.
1. B summons A to his/her office to assess his/her work. He/she makes both positive and negative remarks, and formulates advice.
2. A responds (apologies, thanks, justifications...).
3. C tempers the conversation. Think of specific examples.

B. Other branches of the legal profession and their governing bodies

1. Legal executives

Legal Executives are qualified lawyers specialising in a particular area of law. They will have passed the ILEX Professional Qualification in Law in an area of legal practice to the same level as that required of solicitors.
They will have at least five years experience of working under the supervision of a solicitor in legal practice or the legal department of a private company or local/national government.
Fellows are issued with an annual practising certificate, and only Fellows of ILEX may describe themselves as "Legal Executives".

Specialising in a particular area of law, their day-to-day work is similar to that of a solicitor.

They cannot appear, however, as advocates in court.

Legal Executives are fee earners – in private practice their work is charged directly to clients – making a direct contribution to the income of a law firm.

http://www.ilex.org.uk

2. Patent agents

The Charted Institute of Patent Agents (CIPA) is the professional and examining body for patent agents (also known as patent attorneys) in the United Kingdom. It represents virtually all the registered patent attorneys in the United Kingdom, whether they practise in industry or in private practice.

Despite the historic name of the Institute, patent attorneys have always been qualified to advise on trade marks, designs and copyright as well as patents (collectively known as intellectual property).

http://www.cipa.org.uk

3. Coroners

The coronership at present responds to and investigates those deaths which have been referred to it for a wide variety of reasons (just over one third of all deaths in England and Wales at the present time), rather than pro-actively screening all deaths that occur, whether in the community or in hospital, and then determining which ones should be subjected to further scrutiny.

http://www.coroner.org.uk

4. Licensed conveyancers

The Council for Licensed Conveyancers (CLC) is the regulatory body for Licensed Conveyancers who are qualified specialist property lawyers. All conveyancing – essentially the legal processes involved in transferring buildings and/or land from one owner to another and dealing with the financial transactions – was the sole responsibility of solicitors until 1987.

Under current legislation, it is now possible for other people to become conveyancers, known as Licensed conveyancers. Banks, lenders, property developers and solicitors employ Licensed conveyancers.

http://www.theclc.gov.uk

Exercises

1 **Research tasks.**

1. Find the official websites for the different organisations mentioned in the texts above (Law Society, Bar Council, Legal Services Ombudsman, Office of Coroners, ILEX, CIPA, CLC).
2. Find the number of members registered in each body.

2 **Writing.**

For each of the organisations mentioned in the previous task, imagine a situation in which their services would be required.

C. Free legal advice and legal aid

1. Citizens Advice Bureau

The Citizens Advice service helps people resolve their legal, money and other problems by providing free information and advice from nearly 3,400 locations and by influencing policymakers.

Citizens Advice and each Citizens Advice Bureau are registered charities reliant on volunteers and need to raise funds to provide these vital services. The majority of their advisers are trained volunteers, helping people to resolve nearly 5.3 million problems every year.

All Citizens Advice Bureaux in England, Wales and Northern Ireland are members of Citizens Advice, the national charity which sets standards for advice and equal opportunities and supports bureaux with an information system, training and other services.

http://www.citizensadvice.org.uk

2. Legal Services Commission

The Legal Services Commission is an executive non-departmental public body. We are sponsored by the Department for Constitutional Affairs (DCA) and our work is overseen by a board of independent Commissioners.

We look after legal aid in England and Wales.

We're also responsible for ensuring that people get the information, advice and legal help they need to deal with a wide range of everyday problems.

Through the Community Legal Service (CLS) we help people who are eligible for legal aid to protect their rights.

We fund a network of Quality Marked solicitors, Citizens Advice Bureaux and other advice providers to help people who need advice about relationship breakdown or problems with debt, housing, domestic violence and benefits. Help is also available about asylum and immigration, education, employment, mental health and community care issues.

This type of help varies from information leaflets and directing people to other services, to specialist advice and taking cases to court where necessary.

The Criminal Defence Service (CDS) helps people who are under investigation or facing criminal charges. By ensuring that people accused of crimes have access to legal advice and representation, the CDS also helps the police and courts operate fairly and efficiently.

http://www.legalservices.gov.uk

Exercise

Internet research activity
1. What are the main areas in which a CAB may provide help? How many volunteers work for CABs?
2. Find out who is eligible for legal aid.

3. Off the presses

Solicitors, the new superheroes

No caped crusaders they say, just neatly-coiffed figures in pinstripe suits and freshly laundered shirts.

But that has not stopped the Law Society from spending tens of thousands of pounds to convince us that, however unlikely it may seem, the latest heroes for these unheroic times are solicitors.

"My hero – my solicitor" is the slogan to be unveiled to commuters in a Law Society poster campaign designed to persuade people going through life crises that a solicitor is just the person to ride to their rescue.

Posters will appear over the next five weeks at Newcastle, York and Leamington railway stations, and Euston and London Bridge tube stations in London. The series of four posters illustrates hypothetical cases - in which solicitors sorted out the problems of an employee with job difficulties, a trader whose business hit the rocks, a father denied contact with his children, and a sick mother-of-three threatened with losing her home.

The pressure group *Fathers 4 Justice* would no doubt point out that the scenario involving the dad who manages to see his children every other weekend after being denied access for three years plays down the serious problems in the family justice system.

These have provoked high-profile protests from fathers and even calls for radical change from senior judges.

"Hero" may not be a word uttered much these days, at least without irony. But in market testing, 73% of people in London described the ads as "believable"; 70% also said they were helpful in telling people how to find a solicitor, by consulting the Law Society's website.

Janet Paraskeva, the society's chief executive, said: "In a market where legal services are increasingly available from unqualified people, we want to remind the public about the benefits of using a solicitor.

"All solicitors are highly trained, properly qualified and insured, so clients know they are protected if things go wrong."

The campaign comes as new rules allow the public to consult barristers direct – without going through a solicitor – though the Bar has not publicised the change widely.

Curiously, although the typical solicitor is still a white male, there are none featured in the posters.

Of some 92,000 practising solicitors, around 36,000 are women and 7,000 come from ethnic minorities. Yet three out of four of the poster solicitors – represented by models – belong to ethnic minorities, and half are women.

A spokesman for the society said: "Nearly 8% of the profession is made up of people from ethnic minorities, which reflects society at large. Recent surveys show that about 20% of young people entering the profession are from ethnic minorities."

The poster campaign follows an ICM survey of 1,000 people two years ago, commissioned by RAC Legal Services, which found that nearly half those questioned believed solicitors were arrogant, slow and incompetent, and a quarter thought them "positively untrustworthy".

However, while solicitors as a class generally do poorly in opinion polls, most clients rate their own solicitors highly in surveys.

Clare Dyer, legal correspondent, *The Guardian*, 6/9/2004 (http://www.guardian.co.uk).

The poster mentioned in the article from *The Guardian*.

Exercises

1 **Answer these questions on the previous article.**

1. List the different terms used to describe the traditional image of the solicitor throughout the text.

2. What are the different means used to change that image?

3. Why does this image need to be changed?

4. What problem are they trying to solve?

2 **Picture analysis.**

1. Who is the person in the poster?

2. What is the Law Society trying to portray her as?

3. What do you think of the words used on the poster?

4. Write a few lines on the message that the poster conveys. How does it fit with the article from *The Guardian*?

3 **According to the article, are the following statements true or false?**

1. The Law Society has spent a lot of money on a campaign to convince the public that solicitors always wear pinstripe suits and freshly laundered shirts.

2. The pictures portray real people who need their problems sorted out by a solicitor.

3. According to *Fathers 4 Justice*, the family justice system does not function as efficiently as the poster implies

4. Solicitors are threatened by the fact that the public can now consult barristers directly.

5. The campaign is a very faithful image of the profession.

6. The percentage of solicitors who come from ethnic minorities corresponds to their percentage in society at large.

7. The Bar Council found out that solicitors were believed to be arrogant and incompetent.

8. People have a good opinion of the profession in general but have a very bad feeling about their own solicitor.

4. Food for thought

Silk Cut*

Are Queen's Counsel necessary?

State patronage

The great expense of legal proceedings, whether civil or criminal, is a constant target of criticism. Lawyers' charges are a major element of the price paid when using the courts. Of these, extremely high and disproportionate fees paid to Queen's Counsel often amaze the public, dismay litigants and attract judicial comment.

* The title is playing on the fact that Silk Cut is a well-known brand of cigarette.

Queen's Counsel belong to a small and privileged group of barristers who benefit from state patronage. Apart from an increase in earning power they form a pool from which members of the higher judiciary are selected.

Any assessment of the value of Queen's Counsel to the legal system must begin with an examination of the method of appointment. Conducted in secrecy there is no means of knowing whether this process leads to promotion of the most competent practitioners.

Even more disturbing is the evident restriction upon the number appointed each year. With the consequent lack of true competition a high level of fees is maintained. Prevailing rates are grossly in excess of those paid to barrister and solicitor advocates who are not Queen's Counsel.

Confidence in our legal system is being damaged by the constant revelation of the high cost of proceedings. The part played by Queen's Counsel in raising charges to inordinate levels has been exposed over many years. Even if excessive fees can be reigned in it must still be asked whether the office itself is really necessary.

History

Among historians it is generally accepted that Queen's Counsel first appeared as a recognised office at the end of the sixteenth century. They assisted the law officers of the Crown in conducting prosecutions and were described as "the Queen's Learned Counsel".

For some time after the Revolution of 1688 the office existed only as a dignity without meaning or function. Then it apparently evolved slowly to become a more prominent feature of the Bar. It was not until the second half of the 19th Century that the initials QC or KC appeared in law reports and it took another 30 years for the practice to become universal.

With diminishing official duties their last functional connection with the Crown was removed in 1920. Until that date King's Counsel, as they were then called, required a licence to represent a defendant in an action brought by the Crown.

With an increasing number of appointments their position as an elite class of counsel was firmly established.

Confusing title

Among lawyers, Queen's Counsel are usually called "silk". This odd description, first used in about 1810, is derived from the shiny appearance of the gown they wear. Although the title Queen's Counsel is merely a historical survival it serves to enhance both the income and prestige of the holder. Inevitably but incorrectly the impression is given that it is similar in nature to a Royal Warrant.

The Lord Chancellor uses the term "silk" in documents accompanying application forms for appointment to the office. Although not to be found in the Code of Conduct of the Bar of England and Wales, the description "silk" appears throughout the *Report of the Working Party Established by the Bar Council on the Appointment of Queen's Counsel* published in June 1994 (the Kalisher Report). Following this established custom Queen's Counsel will in this survey be referred to as "silk".

Appointment

Selected candidates for the office are recommended to the Queen by the Lord Chancellor and appointed by letters patent. This arrangement was instituted about a century ago. With a small practising Bar of about 1000 at the time about a dozen members or so applied for silk annually. Most of the candidates would have been known to the Lord Chancellor individually. Now, with between 450 and 500 candidates annually, the process of selection has, through sheer numbers, lost this personal element. It has become the practice to create a few honorary silk – there were six in the 1997 list. They are selected solely by the Lord Chancellor and not by application. Maundy Thursday is usually associated with the symbolic giving of alms by the Queen. Every year on this day a very different act is performed by the Lord Chancellor. He then announces the names of those who have been chosen to join the privileged ranks of silk. So far as barristers are concerned the recipients of this coveted accolade enjoy an immediate elevation of status and remarkable increase in earning power. It was only in 1995 that solicitors were invited to apply for appointment as practising silk. This was a radical innovation. It may, in time, weaken the present rigid division of the profession into solicitors and barristers. At present a client can instruct a solicitor silk direct. When employing a barrister, with a few exceptions, instructions must be given through a solicitor. This is just one of the anomalies which will arise when a significant number of solicitors become silk.

Investiture

Those selected to become silk soon become aware of the special attention they can expect for the rest of their careers. They are summoned to what can be described as an investiture at the House of Lords. Ceremonial dress is worn, which makes no concession to modernity and provides a photo opportunity for the media. The outfit consists of buckled patent leather shoes, silk stockings, breeches, a gown, lace around the wrist, white gloves and a shoulder length bell bottomed wig.

The Lord Chancellor gives an address to the assembled gathering and presents each counsel with a grand patent of precedence as one of Her Majesty's Counsel. In keeping with tradition this announces in archaic style,

"To all to whom these presents shall come Greeting Know Ye that We of Our especial grace have constituted ordained and appointed our trusty and well beloved…" then follows the name of the fortunate individual as being "one of our Counsel learned in the Law."

Rank

In contact with the public, the letters QC are used and displayed to distinguish the holder as possessing a superior rank in the legal profession. They are to be found outside barristers' chambers, in practice brochures and advertisements. No doubt to give authority to views being expressed, media interviewers will often introduce an individual as a QC as if this were a form of legal knighthood.

Emphasising a lower rank, the customary title "junior" is used officially to describe all practising barristers who are not silk. For the public the term is misleading and cannot be taken as an indication of ability or seniority. It embraces all counsel from the novice to senior experienced practitioners. The latter maybe equally competent as silk.

Traditional descriptions in the law are often archaic and bear no relation to their modern function. A solicitor, for instance, was at one time employed to tout for business and bribe court officials. The Master of the Rolls was keeper of records and assistant to the Lord Chancellor. Despite acquiring judicial authority in the 13th century, the ancient title persists.

Elitism

The survival of silk as an elite group stems from the rigid division of the legal profession into solicitors and barristers. Separation arose from a determination on the part of barristers to preserve their social position and sectional interests. The creation of what are now two legal professions was completed with the foundation of the Law Society in 1845 as the professional body of solicitors and other legal functionaries. Barristers remained separate and with their monopoly of advocacy in the higher courts retained, until recently, the sole privilege of appointment as silk.

With solicitors consolidating their position the Bar, governed by the four Inns of Court, organised collectively by forming the Bar Committee in 1883, later to be replaced by the General Council of the Bar in 1895 (the Bar Council). Constituted as an elected body, the Bar Council derived its authority from general meetings. Under the Courts and the Legal Services Act 1990 solicitors were granted rights of audience before all courts. On achieving parity with the Bar they became eligible to serve as silk.

Peter Reeve, The Adam Smith Institute, 1998.

Discuss.

1. In your opinion, isn't the QC system an out-of-date heritage from the past?
2. What are the advantages of having QCs?
3. What are the flaws?

5. Listening

1 🔘 **Listen to the interview with a young woman who talks about her job as a lawyer and complete the extract with the missing words. The interviewee is played by an actor, but the words are those of a real lawyer.**

INTERVIEWER: What is your worst memory as a lawyer?

LAWYER: It would have to be my first day as a ...... when my ...... asked me to do a "cheque req". I spent hours ...... what I thought was a complex legal ...... only to find out that he had simply asked me to raise a cheque. It was really embarrassing.

INTERVIEWER: Who has been the most influential person in your professional life?

LAWYER: It would be the ...... who handled the fascinating .... I'm dealing with now before she went on maternity leave. I was her trainee and she was a wonderful supervisor. She is one of the best lawyers I have ever worked with.

INTERVIEWER: What are the main ...... in dealing with such discrimination cases as the one you're dealing with now?

LAWYER: I cannot ...... on this particular case given that proceedings are ongoing and there has been an application to appeal the decision of the Employment Appeal Tribunal. However, it has been interesting to see things from the other side as my firm usually represents law firms or employers rather than claimants. Usually, the main challenge in discrimination cases, depending on which side I am on, is establishing whether or not the discriminatory behaviour happened.

INTERVIEWER: Why did you become a lawyer?

LAWYER: I come from an Asian background and my parents wanted me to become a lawyer or a doctor or a dentist. I was terrible at the sciences, so lawyer it was.

INTERVIEWER: What would your advice be to anyone who wants to make a legal career?

2 **Answer the following questions.**

1. Present the person who is interviewed in a few words.
2. How much does she say about the case she's working on?

3. Why did she choose to become a lawyer?

4. What is the advice that she gives to students who want to make a career in law?

5. What other career would she have been attracted to?

3 **Discuss.**

1. How would you describe this woman's experience of her job?

2. Does it seem typical of a lawyer's routine?

6. Grammar practice

Exercises

1 **Compounds.**

a. Make a list of all the compound words in the article "My hero, my solicitor". What different ways of constructing compound nouns do they illustrate? What other compound nouns do you know?

b. Complete each sentence with a compound adjective which begins with "well-" and uses a keyword already mentioned, as in the example, where the keyword is underlined.

Example : He <u>prepared</u> for the defence very thoroughy. He had a *well-prepared* case.

1. Our solicitor is most polite. He has beautiful manners. He is a ...... man.

2. A barrister has to be extremely knowledgeable. He has to have read a great deal about many different subjects. He has to be ......

3. It is important for Queen's Counsel to be able to speak with clarity, ease and elegance. They have to be ......

4. Since barristers pay a percentage of their fees to their senior clerks, the job of Senior Clerk may be considered to be ......

5. She has travelled far and wide for business and leisure. She is very ......

6. At the end of his course, he had a good grounding in common law. He was ...... in common law.

2 **Plural/singular. The following words are all plural. Give their singular form.**

1. heroes **2.** crises **3.** people **4.** series **5.** women **6.** cases **7.** difficulties **8.** children **9.** these **10.** minorities **11.** means

3 **Tenses. Complete the text by putting the verbs in brackets in the correct form.**

A young barrister's career, step by step

Jonathan Baker ...... (take) a Qualifying Law Degree in 1999. In order to obtain this diploma, he ...... (spend) three years ...... (study) at Lancashire Law School in Preston, where he ...... (meet) some of his future colleagues. Before that, he ...... (attend) Saint Paul's school in London where he ...... (achieve) excellent A-level grades as a 6th-former. Once he ...... (complete) his law degree, he ...... (join) the Middle Temple, one of London's four Inns of Court, in order to complete his Bar Vocational Course. After ...... (complete) the twelve qualifying sessions required, he ...... (be) eventually ...... (call) to the Bar. But before actually ...... (become) a junior barrister, he ...... (embark on) the required one-year pupillage. In 2002, he was lucky enough to be ...... (take on) by Kings Chambers, a set of chambers located in Leeds that ...... (accept) him as a tenant. There, he now ...... (specialise) in planning and environmental law as well as general common law. Deep down, he ...... (love) to become a senior counsel and perhaps ...... (join) the "privileged ranks of silk"; in which case he ...... (need) to apply for an appointment as practising silk in a few years.

4 **Articles. Complete the passage with a, an, the or ø.**

In ...... UK, ... appointment of ...... judges has often been criticised. For this reason ...... Bar Council is aiming at more ...... transparency. ...... lawyers are divided into ...... solicitors and ...... barristers; both usually hold ...... university degree in law or in some other subject. ...... solicitors, who used to be ...... generalists of ...... legal profession, have become more and more specialised. They still carry out a lot of ...... paper work though: they draw up ...... wills, brief barristers and, until recently, had ...... monopoly in ...... conveyancing. ...... barristers used to be ...... legal profession's specialists. It is worth noting that ...... latter usually do not discuss ...... fees with their clients. It is ...... clerk of ...... set of chambers that has taken them on who is in charge of negotiating ...... fees with lay clients. ...... barristers who plead in ...... superior courts can only be ...... practising barristers. One should always bear in mind that ...... barrister's main duty is to plead in ...... court. Contrary to ...... solicitors, ... barristers never have ...... direct contact with their clients. Indeed, most people can only approach ...... barrister through ...... solicitor; it is therefore often ...... solicitor who chooses ...... barrister for his client. ...... monopoly on advocacy enjoyed by ...... barristers was abolished in 1990. ...... solicitors who have trained in ...... advocacy may qualify for ...... right of audience; they are called ...... solicitors advocate.

5 **Link words. Complete the sentences using the words and expressions from the list. Use each expression only once.**

unless	owing to	whereas	although
because of	despite	unlike	instead of
after	since	provided	when

1. ...... solicitors, barristers have unlimited rights of audience.

2. ...... the growing number of solicitors in the UK, competition within the profession has increased.

3. A barrister must be contacted through a solicitor ...... a solicitor can be consulted directly.

4. ...... barristers are more prestigious than solicitors, they do not necessarily make a fortune right away.

5. Many young solicitors choose a career in the Crown Prosecution Service ...... joining a private practice.

6. ...... recent efforts to make the legal professions attractive to minorities, diversity could still be improved among solicitors and barristers.

7. You cannot become a solicitor ...... you are willing to put in a considerable amount of work.

8. ...... completing their pupillage, students become fully qualified barristers.

9. ...... the Courts and Legal Services Act 1990, solicitors have been able to appear in higher courts ...... they have acquired the requisite additional training.

10. ...... a barrister becomes Queen's Counsel he is said to take silk.

11. ...... all the reforms which have been implemented, the separation between the two professions is not as clear cut as before.

6 **Translate the following sentences into English.**

1. Depuis quand les *solicitors* ont-ils le droit de plaider en Grande-Bretagne?

2. Le système juridique anglais ne cesse de changer, notamment du fait qu'il doit s'adapter au droit de l'Union européenne.

3. « Allô, Mathilda ? C'est Rob. Cela fait une heure que j'attends John Richardson, le *solicitor* que tu m'as conseillé de contacter. » « Je crois qu'il est en retard car on lui a volé sa voiture. »

4. Pour être nommé *Queen's Counsel*, un *barrister* doit avoir beaucoup d'expérience, une solide réputation mais aussi et surtout un brin de chance.

Chapter 4

The court system and the personnel of the courts

1. Fundamentals

There are different ways of presenting the British court structure. One approach is to distinguish between courts of **first instance** and those with **appellate jurisdiction**. Another common division classifies courts as either civil or criminal. This chapter adopts the hierarchical approach, beginning with the inferior courts and then moving on to the superior courts, terminating with the House of Lords (soon to be renamed the Supreme Court of the United Kingdom).

A. Inferior courts

1. Magistrates' courts

Pursuant to the Courts Act 2003, which came into force in April 2005, the administration of all magistrates' courts in England and Wales was centralised under the authority of Her Majesty's Courts Service (**HMCS**) with a view to delivering better services to the community.

Jurisdiction

Magistrates' courts deal with around 95% of criminal cases in England and Wales, either in the adult court or in the **youth court**. They have been the cornerstone of the criminal justice system for over eight hundred years. The bulk of their work consists in deciding **bail** applications, trying criminal cases and imposing appropriate **sentences** on **offenders**. Minor criminal cases such as motoring offences and common assaults, also known as **summary** or **non-indictable offences,** are tried at the local level in magistrates' courts.

Most criminal cases start in a magistrates' court. The more serious crimes, or **indictable offences**, are committed – i.e. transferred – to the Crown Court, where the defendant, if he pleads not guilty, will be tried by a **judge** and **jury**.

There is an intermediate category of crimes: **either-way offences**, such as **theft**. They may either be committed to the Crown Court or heard in a magistrates' court.

In addition to their responsibilities in the area of criminal law, magistrates' courts handle a limited number of civil matters involving family issues such as adoption proceedings, applications for residence and contact orders, maintenance relating to spouses and children, and personal protection orders in cases of matrimonial violence. Their civil jurisdiction also includes the enforcement of financial penalties ordered in higher courts, licensing appeals from local authorities and the payment of council tax.

Personnel

Cases are either heard by a **panel** of two or three **lay magistrates** or by a single **district judge (magistrates' court)**. The former are unpaid volunteers and are referred to simply as **magistrates**, or sometimes as **justices of the peace** (JPs). They are assisted by legally-qualified **court clerks** who are trained solicitors or barristers. Clerks provide legal and procedural advice and carry out administrative work. Lay magistrates are members of the community and do not have any legal qualifications. They are required to undergo regular training sessions and are expected to sit for a minimum of 35 half-days each year. In the magistrates' courts of larger cities, district judges (magistrates' court) are full-time paid solicitors or barristers.

Decisions

Magistrates and District Judges have a range of sentences available to them, as defined by the Criminal Justice Act 1991 and the Powers of the Criminal Courts (Sentencing) Act 2000. There are statutory limits on sentencing in the magistrates' courts. S.154 of the Criminal Justice Act 2003 has increased sentencing powers to 12 months for a single offence and 65 weeks for two or more offences. Magistrates cannot impose **fines** above £5,000 on individuals and £20,000 on businesses. In fixing the amount of a convicted defendant's fine, magistrates take their income into account. They may pronounce an absolute discharge, a conditional discharge, **community rehabilitation orders** or **community punishment orders**. Compensation to an injured party may also be ordered against the defendant. In either-way cases tried in the magistrates' court, the offender may be committed to the Crown Court for sentencing if a more severe sentence is thought necessary (for example, after the magistrates have been informed of a defendant's previous convictions).

2. The county courts

Civil cases in England and Wales may be heard either in county courts or in the High Court, depending on the value and the nature of the claim.

Jurisdiction

There are 218 county courts with first instance jurisdiction for civil actions. County courts have jurisdiction to hear and determine *any* action founded in contract or tort. **Personal injury** claims where the claimant does not expect to recover more than £50,000, and money claims where the claimant does not expect to recover more than £15,000, *must* be started in a county court, whereas larger claims can be started or determined in either the county court or the High Court.

County courts deal mainly with personal injury, negligence and contract claims, matters involving equity such as trusts or mortgages, cases for the recovery of land, **bankruptcy** and some family proceedings including matrimonial finance and disputes over custody of and access to children.

Following the Civil Procedure Act 1997 and the Civil Procedure Rules 1998, claims in the county court are allocated to one of three tracks, according to the amount at stake. The small claims track is the normal track for claims with a value of no more than £5,000 and for personal injury claims in which the claim for damages for pain and suffering is unlikely to exceed £1,000. The fast track is the normal track for claims in which the value is between £5,000 and £15,000 and personal injury claims in which damages for pain and suffering are likely to exceed £1,000. The multi-track procedure applies when the value of the claim is higher, or the issues are complex. Case management is designed to ensure that the time and resources spent on each case are appropriate and proportional to the value and importance of the claim.

Personnel

Circuit judges, recorders, and district judges sit in county courts. Circuit judges are assigned to an administrative division, called a **circuit**, and are entitled to sit at the Crown Court or county courts on that circuit. District judges are also appointed to a particular circuit and may sit at any of the county courts or district registries of the High Court in that circuit. District registries, which deal with High Court family and civil business, are often located in the same building as county courts. Recorders work as part-time judges in the Crown Court and county courts, though some sit only in county courts. They will generally handle the less complex matters coming before the court. In claims for defamation, malicious prosecution and false imprisonment, either party has the right to a jury trial. The jury consists of eight members. As in a criminal case, the jury decides issues of fact, but must accept the judge's direction as to the law.

Decisions

The judge's decision is set out in an order, also called a judgment. Monetary compensation is the common remedy awarded by county courts. They may also grant equitable remedies such as injunctions, orders of specific performance, rectification and rescission of a contract. The successful party usually can expect to recover some of their costs, i.e. court fees, solicitor's fees, and experts' fees, from the unsuccessful party.

B. Superior or higher courts

1. The Crown Court

The Crown Court was created by the Courts Act 1971. Before then, serious criminal cases were heard by High Court judges who went round the country holding assize courts and quarter sessions, which were held four times a year. The Crown Court is a unified institution with 78 centres across England and Wales divided into six circuits for administrative convenience. In central London, the Crown Court centre is the Central Criminal Court, otherwise known as the Old Bailey.

The Crown Court is both a first instance and an appellate criminal court. There is no longer any right of appeal to the Crown Court for licensing applications.

Jurisdiction

The Crown Court has first instance jurisdiction in cases involving indictable offences, and in either-way offences committed by the magistrates' courts. Indictable offences are serious offences that must be tried before a judge and a jury. They include such offences as treason, murder, manslaughter, rape, robbery and causing grievous bodily harm. The Crown Court also hears appeals by defendants convicted in the magistrates' courts. In an appeal against **conviction**, the Crown Court retries the case, but without a jury. Two to four magistrates sit with the circuit judge (or recorder) to determine the appeal.

Personnel

The Crown Court is presided over by a professional judge. In the most serious cases, the judge is likely to be a High Court judge (from the Queen's Bench Division) also known as a **puisne judge**. Other cases are heard by a circuit judge or a recorder.

Decisions

Although the jury decides on the facts whether the defendant is guilty or not, the judge hands down the sentence. In Crown Court there is a wide range of possible sentences: community service, restraining orders, fines, imprisonment, etc. The judge has the power to impose any sentence up to the legal maximum for the offence. In cases of murder, life imprisonment is currently mandatory, though there are calls from many quarters for the law to be changed to allow for more flexibility. The death penalty was abolished in 1965 for most or all crimes, except for high treason for which it was finally abolished in 1998 with the Crime and Disorder Act.

2. The High Court

The High Court hears civil cases in England and Wales. The High Court sits at the Royal Courts of Justice in London and also in 26 cities across the country. It is organised into three divisions: the Queen's Bench Division (QBD), the Chancery Division and the Family Division. Each division includes a court of appeal called Divisional Court, in which two or three judges (usually a Lord Justice of Appeal sitting with one or two High Court judges) hear certain appeals from other courts and **tribunals**. To be appointed a High Court judge, candidates must be barristers or solicitor advocates with at least ten years' experience in the High Court or two years' experience as a circuit judge. Appointments are made by the monarch on the advice of the Lord Chancellor. The Constitutional Reform Act 2005 provided for the creation of a Judicial Appointments Commission to make recommendations to the Lord Chancellor.

1. The Queen's Bench Division (or the King's Bench Division)

Jurisdiction

The Queen's Bench Division (QBD) is the civil division with the heaviest workload. It has limited criminal jurisdiction and it has criminal and civil appellate jurisdiction.

It determines tort and contract cases where the damages claimed are substantial or the issues concerned are particularly complex, or of public importance (above a certain amount: £50,000 for contracts and torts and £30,000 for mortgages and trusts). There are also various specialised courts within the QBD: the Commercial Court (banking and insurance-related litigation), the Admiralty Court (shipping-related litigation), the Technology and Construction Court (computer and engineering-related litigation) and the Administrative Court (dealing with claims for **judicial review**).

The Divisional Court of the QBD has both criminal and civil appellate jurisdiction. It hears **appeals by way of case stated** from the magistrates' courts. In this procedure magistrates refer a statement of the facts and a question of law to the Divisional Court for a ruling. This court also hears applications for *habeas corpus*, in which applicants claim they are unlawfully detained, be it in a police station, a hospital, a prison or by any person, and demand to be set free. Lastly, it exercises judicial review of decisions made by government bodies, inferior courts and tribunals when two or three judges are required instead of the Administrative Court judge sitting alone.

Personnel

The QBD is headed by the Lord Chief Justice and has about 110 judges. The judge, also called a puisne judge, sits alone. In certain cases – non-complex **fraud, defamation (libel** and **slander**), **malicious prosecution** and false imprisonment – either party has a right to a jury trial. The jury consists of ten members. As in a criminal case, they decide on issues of fact, but must accept the judge's rulings as to issue of law.

Decisions

Remedies in civil cases are similar to those of lower courts. Nevertheless, the amounts involved are significantly higher. When it exercises its power of judicial review, the Administrative Court (often sitting as a Divisional Court) can rectify a procedural irregularity or an error of law by quashing a decision and remitting the case back to the relevant governmental body or lower court for it to reach its decision in accordance with the law. It can award damages. It can also quash orders and order injunctions against officers of the Crown.

2. The Chancery Division

Pursuant to the Judicature Acts 1873-1875, the High Court of Chancery, which had exclusive jurisdiction over equitable matters, was replaced by the Chancery Division of the High Court. Since then, equitable remedies have been administered alongside common law remedies by all three divisions of the High Court, but the Chancery Division has retained special authority over certain equitable matters.

Jurisdiction

The Chancery Division deals with civil cases of disputed wills, the administration of estates, the appointment of a **guardian** for the estate of an under-age child, **trusts**, the rectification of **deeds**, land and **mortgage** actions, partnerships, company law, bankruptcy, **patents**, trademarks, copyrights and revenue law.

There are also various specialised courts within the Chancery Division: the Patents Courts which deals with patent-related disputes, and the Court of Protection, which hears cases where the persons involved are unable to continue to manage their own affairs.

The Divisional Court hears appeals on taxation, land registration and bankruptcy matters.

Personnel

This division is presided over by the Lord Chancellor and has a bench of about 17 judges. Juries are never used in the Chancery Division.

Decisions

Although the Chancery Division no longer has a monopoly over equitable remedies, it still deals with matters involving such relief as equity provides. For example, a trust-related claim may result in the Chancery Division issuing an injunction against the unsuccessful party.

3. The Family Division

Jurisdiction

This civil division hears cases relating to minors, **defended divorce**, **wardship**, adoption, legitimacy, wills and declarations in medical treatment cases. It also has a

Divisional Court that hears appeals from magistrates' courts and county courts on family matters.

Personnel
It is headed by the President of the Family Division and has a bench of about 17 judges.

Decisions
The Family Division can issue adoption, guardianship and custody orders. The Divisional Court may affirm or reverse orders concerning financial provisions made by the lower courts.

3. The Court of Appeal

The Court of Appeal is divided into two branches: the Civil Division and the Criminal Division. There are 37 Lords and Ladies Justices of Appeal who usually sit in panels of three. Many of them also preside over cases in the Divisional Courts, sitting with one or two High Court judges. The Court of Appeal sits in up to 12 courts in the Royal Courts of Justice. The Court of Appeal considers the **evidence** that was presented to the trial court. Since it has no original jurisdiction, it does not determine disputed issues of fact. Accordingly, a jury is never required.

1. Civil Division

Jurisdiction
This court hears appeals from the High Court, in certain county court cases, from certain tribunals such as the Employment Appeal Tribunal, the Immigration Appeal Tribunal and the Lands Tribunal and of decisions of the Social Security Commissioners. This still accounts for a substantial volume of the work of the Court of Appeal and includes appeals from all judgments in multi-track cases, and second appeals from judgments in non-multi-track cases.

The **appellant** needs leave to appeal either from the lower court (i.e. the High Court or the county court) or from the Court of Appeal.

Personnel
The Master of the Rolls is the president of this division. He is also the head of the civil justice system. The other judges are the Lords and Ladies Justices of Appeal. These judges are chosen from among High Court judges with at least two years' experience, or advocates who have had a minimum of 10 years' experience. Appointments are usually from the ranks of experienced High Court Judges.

Decisions
Decisions are taken by a majority. The Civil Division hears appeals on questions of law and, in certain circumstances, on issues of fact. The Court of Appeal will seldom

interfere with a trial judge's findings of fact. If the appeal is accepted, the first decision can be **reversed**, affirmed or **amended,** or a new trial can be ordered.

2. Criminal Division

Jurisdiction
This court hears appeals against sentences and convictions in the Crown Court. The appeals are usually filed by defendants who were convicted on **indictment**.

Personnel
The Lord Chief Justice of England and Wales is the head of the criminal justice system and presides over this division. He is assisted by a Lord Justice of Appeal with the title of Vice-President of the Criminal Division. The judges who sit in this court are Lords and Ladies Justice of Appeal but some High Court judges and some circuit judges are authorised to sit in the Court of Appeal.

Decisions
The Criminal Division can **dismiss** appeals. It can also **quash** previous convictions and order **retrials**.

4. The Supreme Court of the United Kingdom

The Supreme Court of the United Kingdom is at the apex of the British court system. Formerly, this court was called the Appellate Committee of the House of Lords though it was generally known simply as "The House of Lords". It sits in Middlesex Guildhall, London (after 2009). It stands at the centre of the constitutional reform started in 2003.

Jurisdiction
This Court hears appeals on points of law of public importance. In both criminal and civil cases, appeal lies from the Court of Appeal and in exceptional circumstances from the Crown Court through a leapfrog procedure. The Court also hears appeals from the Court of Session in Scotland and the Court of Appeal in Northern Ireland. In criminal cases, appeal lies from the Court of Appeal, the Court of Criminal Appeal in Northern Ireland and from the Courts Martial Appeal Court. It has no jurisdiction in Scottish criminal cases following the Scotland Act 1998. The Supreme Court also acts as a court of appeal to resolve questions raised about the functions and the authority of the institutions (legislative and/or executive) under the UK devolution statutes of 1998.

Personnel
The 12 Justices of the Supreme Court who sit in the Supreme Court of the United Kingdom were previously called Lords of Appeal in Ordinary or Law Lords. As provided by the Constitutional Reform Act 2005, the Court is headed by a President and a Deputy President. Qualifications for office are at

least two years of high judicial office or a minimum of fifteen years as a qualified practitioner. In practice, Law Lords are generally appointed from among the most respected judges of the Court of Appeal in England and Wales, the Court of Session in Scotland, or the Court of Appeal in Northern Ireland. Supreme Court justices sit in panels of five and occasionally of seven.

Decisions

Decisions are taken by majority. Each justice may give a separate argued judgment or express his or her agreement with the judgment of one of the other members of the court. The Court can affirm or reverse a decision of the Court of Appeal, and has the power to overrule its own previous decisions, though this power is seldom used.

5. Judicial Committee of the Privy Council

Known as the Privy Council for short, this is the oldest institution in existence in the United Kingdom and performs a number of judicial functions, in addition to its executive role of advising the sovereign on policy.

Jurisdiction

The Judicial Committee of the Privy Council sits as a final court of appeal for the UK Overseas Territories and Crown Dependencies and for a number of Commonwealth countries which decided to keep this method of appeal after their independence (Antigua and Barbuda, Bahamas, Barbados, Belize, Grenada, Jamaica, St Christopher and Nevis, Saint Lucia, Saint Vincent and the Grenadines and Tuvalu).

It also has domestic jurisdiction, principally concerned with final appeals in matters relating to professional discipline for medical practitioners, dentists, opticians, veterinary surgeons, osteopaths, and chiropractors.

Personnel

The Judicial Committee of the Privy Council is made up of high level judges, and its members are the Lord Chancellor and past Lord Chancellors; the Lords of Appeal in Ordinary and former Lords of Appeal in Ordinary; other Lords of Appeal; Privy Counsellors who hold or have held high judicial office and Privy Counsellors who are judges of certain superior courts in other Commonwealth countries.

Five judges normally sit to hear Commonwealth appeals and three for other matters.

Decisions

The Privy Council is a consultative body but it still has great authority since under s.4 of the Judicial Committee Act 1833: "the Queen must refer any matter to it for an advisory opinion." For professional matters, it is still a final court of appeal and its decisions are enforceable.

Diagram of the court structure

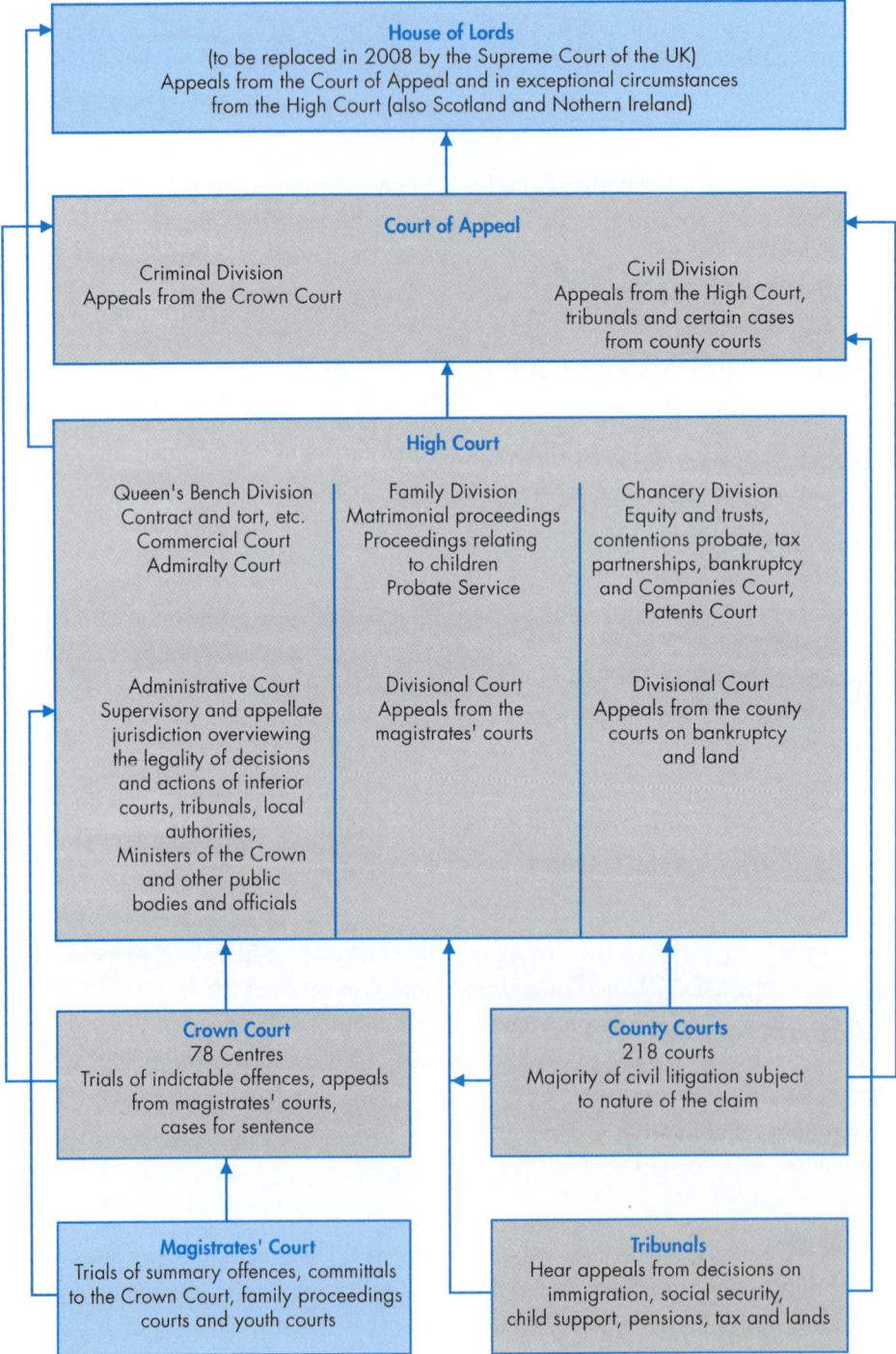

House of Lords
(to be replaced in 2008 by the Supreme Court of the UK)
Appeals from the Court of Appeal and in exceptional circumstances
from the High Court (also Scotland and Nothern Ireland)

Court of Appeal

Criminal Division
Appeals from the Crown Court

Civil Division
Appeals from the High Court,
tribunals and certain cases
from county courts

High Court

Queen's Bench Division
Contract and tort, etc.
Commercial Court
Admiralty Court

Family Division
Matrimonial proceedings
Proceedings relating
to children
Probate Service

Chancery Division
Equity and trusts,
contentions probate, tax
partnerships, bankruptcy
and Companies Court,
Patents Court

Administrative Court
Supervisory and appellate
jurisdiction overviewing
the legality of decisions
and actions of inferior
courts, tribunals, local
authorities,
Ministers of the Crown
and other public
bodies and officials

Divisional Court
Appeals from the
magistrates' courts

Divisional Court
Appeals from the county
courts on bankruptcy
and land

Crown Court
78 Centres
Trials of indictable offences, appeals
from magistrates' courts,
cases for sentence

County Courts
218 courts
Majority of civil litigation subject
to nature of the claim

Magistrates' Court
Trials of summary offences, committals
to the Crown Court, family proceedings
courts and youth courts

Tribunals
Hear appeals from decisions on
immigration, social security,
child support, pensions, tax and lands

Definitions in context and key words

amend *(v.)*: alter a written or oral statement by correcting or adding changes to it.

appeal by way of case stated: a procedure whereby a lower court issues a statement in writing of facts agreed upon during the first instance trial and formulates a question to a higher court seeking its opinion on the legal points raised.

appellant: a person who files an appeal against a court decision.

appellate jurisdiction: authority of a court or tribunal to determine appeals from lower courts.

bail: release from custody on a promise to return for the next stage of a criminal case.

bankruptcy: the condition in which an individual cannot meet his/her debt obligations, the court appoints a trustee in bankruptcy to control and distribute the bankrupt's assets among his creditors.

circuit: one of the six judicial and administrative divisions of England and Wales (Northern, North-Eastern, Midland and Oxford, Wales and Chester, South-Eastern, and Western circuits).

community punishment order: a sentence requiring an offender to complete a number of hours of unpaid work in the interest of the community.

community rehabilitation order: a sentence aimed at helping offenders towards rehabilitation through compulsory work with a supervising officer; this may include an obligation to undergo treatment or attend a training programme.

conviction: a court decision stating that someone is guilty of a crime.

court clerk: in the magistrates' court, a barrister or solicitor working as legal advisor to lay magistrates.

deed: a legal document which transfers goods and property from one individual to another.

defamation: tort of injuring a person's reputation by making false statement of fact.

defended divorce: a divorce where one party does not agree to the divorce.

district judge (magistrates' court): a professional judge appointed to sit full-time at a magistrates' court.

dismiss *(v.)*: stop a court case from continuing.

(triable-)either-way offence: an offence that can either be tried before a magistrates' court without a jury or with a jury in a Crown Court.

evidence *(uncountable)*: oral statements, written witness statements, affidavits, and various kinds of exhibits that are used in a trial.

fine: a financial penalty which may be imposed in a criminal case.

first instance jurisdiction: authority of a court or tribunal in which cases are first tried.

fraud: criminal or civil wrong involving the intentional deception of other persons in order to gain material advantage or injure their interests.

guardian: a person legally in charge of a child in the absence or death of the parents.

habeas corpus: a civil proceeding used to determine whether the imprisonment of a person is legal.

HMCS: an executive agency of the Department for Constitutional Affairs, called Her Majesty's Court Service.

indictable offence: a serious offence which can only be tried in a Crown Court with a jury.

indictment: an official written statement which charges someone with a criminal offence.

judge: a legally trained professional arbitrator appointed to settle disputes according to the law.

judicial review: the examination by judges of the legality and correctness of decisions emanating from lower courts or actions taken by government bodies. It is a procedure that should usually only be invoked when there is no further right of appeal from that decision or action.

jury: a group of 12 men and women selected at random from the electoral register and sworn in to decide the guilt or innocence of a person accused of a criminal offence and who is being tried in the Crown Court. Jurors are also called upon to sit on certain civil cases when they sit as a jury of 8 for trials in the County Court, and as a jury of 10 for trials in the High Court (on the conviction or liability of a defendant in court). The role of a jury in a civil case is to determine factual issues between the parties, and to determine the appropriate award of damages.

justice of the peace: see magistrate.

lay magistrate: see magistrate.

libel: the tort of publishing a false statement in some permanent form that is likely to injure a person's reputation in the opinion of others, or which makes him look ridiculous. It is a criminal offence to publish a libel maliciously, i.e. knowing it to be untrue.

magistrate: an unpaid member of the community without any legal qualification who volunteers and is appointed to sit for a set number of days per year in magistrates' courts to judge minor civil and criminal cases.

malicious prosecution: tort of instituting or pursuing civil or criminal legal action without probable cause and in bad faith.

mortgage: a legal document pledging property to the lender as security for payment of a debt.

non-indictable offence: see summary offence.

offender: a person who has been convicted of an offence.

panel: a group of people, often with specialist knowledge, chosen to give advice or take decisions.

patent: the registration of an invention, which gives the patentee the right to a short term monopoly on the production and sale of his or her invention.

personal injury: a wrong occurring when a person is physically or mentally injured as a result of another person's actions or omissions.

puisne judge: a judge who sits on the High Court.

quash *(v.)*: officially state that a legal decision is no longer valid.

retrial: the process of judging a case anew.

reverse *(v.)*: change a decision so that it is the opposite of what it was.

sentence: a punishment given by a judge to someone who is guilty of a crime.

slander: tort of making a false oral statement against a living person.

summary offence: an offence which can only be tried without a jury in a Magistrates' Court.

theft: an offence consisting in dishonestly appropriating property belonging to another person with the intention of permanently depriving the other of it.

tribunal: a body appointed to adjudicate or arbitrate on a disputed question.

trust: an entity created to hold goods and property for the benefit of certain persons, charities or companies, where a trustee manages the trust and often holds property titles on behalf of the trust, for the beneficiaries.

wardship: the fact of legally being in charge of a person, especially a child, called a ward.

youth court: a court held at a magistrates' court, hearing cases in which children between ten and seventeen have been charged with an offence.

Exercises

1 **Choose the correct ending for each sentence.**

1. Crown Courts hear appeals from
   a. county courts.
   b. magistrates' Courts.
   c. the High Court.
2. Crown Courts hold trial by jury for
   a. the more serious crimes.
   b. the less serious crimes.
   c. indicative offences.
3. The QBD is
   a. a civil court.
   b. a criminal court.
   c. both a criminal and a civil court.
4. Divisional courts are
   a. courts of judicial review.
   b. courts of appeal.
   c. courts of first instance.
5. In High Court cases
   a. there is a jury.
   b. there is no jury.
   c. there is a jury only in certain civil cases.
6. An appeal may lie from the High Court
   a. to a county court.
   b. to the Court of Appeal.
   c. to the Crown Court.

7. The Supreme Court used to be called
    a. the Appellate Committee of the Privy Council.
    b. the House of Commons.
    c. the Appellate Committee of the House of Lords.

8. Recorders are
    a. part-time judges.
    b. full-time judges.
    c. lay magistrates.

9. Magistrates may sentence offenders to
    a. a prison term of up to one year.
    b. a prison term of up to five years.
    c. life imprisonment.

10. In the magistrates' court, lay magistrates are advised by
    a. a district judge.
    b. a legally qualified court clerk.
    c. a justice of the peace.

11. County courts have
    a. no criminal jurisdiction.
    b. limited criminal jurisdiction.
    c. only criminal jurisdiction.

12. District judges in magistrates' courts are
    a. part-time volunteers.
    b. part-time recorders.
    c. fully qualified judges.

13. Family law is dealt with
    a. in the Crown Court.
    b. in the Privy Council.
    c. in the High Court.

14. Community orders are an alternative to
    a. imprisonment.
    b. fines.
    c. bail.

15. The Lord Chief Justice presides over
    a. the Supreme Court.
    b. the Family Division of the High Court.
    c. the Criminal Division of the Court of Appeal.

16. Magistrates receive
    a. no stipend for their role in the judicial system.
    b. a salary for their role in the judicial system.
    c. travelling and subsistence expenses for their role in the judicial system.

17. A High Court judge is also called
   a. a puisne judge.
   b. a penny judge.
   c. a circus judge.
18. In England and Wales the death penalty
   a. can be given for terrorism charges.
   b. has been abolished.
   c. can be given for high treason.
19. A recorder sits
   a. in a magistrates' court.
   b. in the Court of Appeal.
   c. in a county court.
20. A small claim is a civil dispute involving
   a. more than £1,000.
   b. less than £15,000.
   c. up to £5,000.

2 Complete the text with the words from the list below.

business	Family Division	assize	division
Chancery	sittings	unity	

It will be remembered that the High Court was formerly divided into the ...... , the Queen's Bench and the Probate, Divorce and Admiralty Divisions. The Administration of Justice Act 1970 abolished the last of these divisions and its jurisdiction was transferred partly to the newly created ...... and partly to the other two divisions. Moreover the Courts Act 1971 effected a radical change by abolishing the time-hallowed "......" system and making it possible for ...... of the High Court to take place anywhere is England or Wales according to convenience.

Any matter may be determined in any ...... of the High Court (even though it be assigned by any enactment to some other division). Thus the conception of the ...... of the High Court is preserved. But normally each division keeps to its special ...... : so that the three divisions will require separate consideration.

Philip S. James in *Introduction to English Law*, 12th ed., Butterworths, pp. 33-34.

3 Do the following situations fall under the categories of summary, indictable or (triable-) either-way offences?

1. Gerry Smith stabbed his neighbour Tony Johnson because he was too noisy.
2. John Mervin took two books and a box of chocolates from a supermarket without paying for them.
3. Eve Taylor drove 10mph over the limit and refused to stop when asked to do so by the police.

4. In the course of a demonstration, Mr Sam Jones participated in the destruction of a shop, causing damage valued at £15,000.

5. At a football match, Peter Philips punched Jeremy Williams in the nose because he was cheering for the other team.

6. Kevin Roberts was found sleeping in the gutter after drinking too many beers.

7. Jack Strummer sexually assaulted Angela Marks.

8. Diana Martin insulted a policeman because he wanted to give her a parking ticket.

9. Edward Roger borrowed John Fairbrother's car without his consent.

10. Alexander Burke got on the number 15 bus and did not pay the fare.

4 **Say which court(s) would have jurisdiction in the following situations.**

1. Mr Peters beat up Mr Mukherjee, a shopkeeper, and took 13 bottles of whisky without paying.

2. Brenda Davis administered a lethal dose of poison to her ex-husband.

3. John Smith was seriously injured in a car accident resulting from the incompetent repairs on his vehicle by mechanic Ben Roberts.

4. Tom Wealthy's son challenges the validity of his deceased father's will.

5. Ann Brown has a claim against a builder who failed to complete the work she paid for in advance.

6. A man was arrested whilst driving under the influence of alcohol.

7. A woman is suing her neighbour for damage to her property amounting to £500.

8. A couple is fighting over custody of their children.

9. Social services are recommending the temporary placement of a child.

10. An angry customer is seeking compensation for an injury resulting from the use of a faulty toaster.

5 **Discuss.**

1. Discuss the advantages and disadvantages of using lay personnel instead of employing professional judges.

2. How would you explain the difference between appeal and judicial review?

2. More about...

A. Tribunals

Tribunals are specialist courts that are outside the main court structure. However, certain appeals from tribunals may lie to one of the superior courts. (For example an Employment Tribunal is an inferior court of record for the purposes of the law of contempt of court.) In the absence of a specific appellate court, the only remedy from a decision of a tribunal may be by way of judicial review to the High Court.

The Tribunals Service is a new government agency within the Department for Constitutional Affairs which was launched in April 2006 to provide common administrative support for the main central government tribunals. Each tribunal has a tribunal chairman (who has previously been a lawyer for at least 7 years) who will normally sit with two other tribunal members.

Some of the tribunals

Asylum and Immigration Tribunal

The Asylum and Immigration Tribunal is the successor to the Immigration Appellate Authority and the Immigration Appeals Tribunal. The Tribunal was set up under the Asylum and Immigration (Treatment of Claimants etc.) Act 2004 and came into being on 4th April 2005. The purpose of the Tribunal is to hear and decide appeals against decisions made by the Home Office in matters of asylum, immigration and nationality.

Immigration Services Tribunal

This tribunal hears appeals against decisions made by the Office of the Immigration Services Commissioner and considers disciplinary charges brought against immigration advisors by the Commissioner.

Finance and Tax Tribunals

A group of four tribunals (Special Commissioners Tribunal, VAT and Duties Tribunal, Financial Services and Markets Tribunal and Pensions Regulator Tribunal) for those wishing to appeal against decisions of HM Customs & Excise and the Inland Revenue or to refer matters relating to certain decisions of the Financial Services Authority or the Pensions Regulator.

Gender Recognition Panel

The gender recognition panel assesses applications from transsexual people for legal recognition of the gender in which they now live. The panel was set up under the Gender Recognition Act 2004 and ensures that transsexual people can enjoy the rights and responsibilities appropriate to their acquired gender.

Information Tribunal

The remit of the Tribunal is to hear appeals by data controllers against notices issued by the Information Commissioner under the Data Protection Act 1998, usually enforcement notices. The Tribunal can now also hear appeals against enforcement notices or information notices issued by the Commissioner in regard to publication schemes under the Freedom of Information Act 2000.

Lands Tribunal

Determines questions of disputed compensation arising out of the compulsory acquisition of land, decides rating appeals, exercises jurisdiction under section 84 of the Law of Property Act 1925 (discharge and modification of restrictive covenants), and acts as arbitrator under references by consent. Rates are a local tax on commercial property.

Social Security and Child Support Appeals Tribunal

Hears appeals on decisions on: social security, child support, housing benefit, council tax benefit, vaccine damage, tax credit and compensation recovery.

Social Security and Child Support Commissioners

Decide appeals on points of law from appeals tribunals in social security, tax credit, child support, housing benefit and council tax benefit cases. They also decide compensation recovery cases which have been referred to them under the Forfeiture Act 1982.

Transport Tribunal

Hears appeals against decisions of Traffic Commissioners in connection with the Heavy Goods Vehicles & Public Service Vehicles Operators Licensing Systems, appeals against decisions of the Registrar of Approved Driving Instructors and is able to resolve disputes under the Postal Services Act 2000.

Employment tribunals

Resolve disputes between employers and employees over employment rights.

Employment Appeal Tribunal

A superior court of record dealing with appeals from the decisions of the employment tribunals.

Special Educational Needs and Disability Tribunal

Parents whose children have special educational needs can appeal to the Tribunal against decisions made by **local education authorities** in England and Wales about their children's education.

B. Judicial appointments

1. Eligibility

Who is eligible to become a judge or tribunal chairman?

The minimum eligibility requirements for most judicial offices are laid down in the Courts and Legal Services Act 1990. For salaried or fee-paid appointments as District Judge, Master or Registrar of the Supreme Court, District Judge (Magistrates' Courts) or (in most cases) tribunal chairman, candidates must have been qualified as a lawyer for at least seven years. Circuit Judges and Recorders must have been qualified for at least ten years, although three years' service in certain other full-time judicial posts (for example District Judge) is allowed instead for applicants to the Circuit Bench. High Court Judges and Lords Justices of Appeal must have been qualified as lawyers for at least ten years, although in practice only High Court Judges are appointed as Lords Justices of Appeal. A Circuit Judge of two years' experience can also become a High Court Judge. Lords of Appeal in Ordinary from England and Wales must have been qualified for at least 15 years. [...] The Constitutional Reform Act 2005 will in due course establish a new Supreme Court.

In July 2005 the Lord Chancellor and Secretary of State announced his intention to broaden the statutory eligibility requirements to make Fellows of the Institute of Legal Executives and registered Patents Agents and Trade Mark Attorneys eligible for some appointments, and to reduce the length of time an individual is required to have been qualified before becoming eligible for appointment. These changes require primary legislation.

Under the terms of the Judicial Pensions and Retirement Act 1993 all salaried and fee-paid judicial office holders appointed for the first time after 31 March 1995 must retire on their 70th birthday. For those appointed before that date different ages of retirement apply depending on the type of judicial office held.

2. How to become a magistrate

The local advisory committees who advise the Lord Chancellor on the appointment of magistrates in England and Wales welcome applications from people in all walks of life who have the qualities and the time to serve as magistrates. Individuals may put themselves forward for consideration or any person or organisation may recommend a candidate for appointment. Please note that non-British and Commonwealth residents of the United Kingdom can be appointed as JPs. Before making an application you are strongly advised to visit your local magistrates' court to observe a court in action.

Bench requirements

A balanced bench

The Lord Chancellor requires that each bench should broadly reflect the community it serves in terms of gender, ethnic origin, geographical spread, occupation and political affiliation. Achieving a balance is, however, a secondary consideration to the essential and pre-eminent requirement that a candidate must be personally suitable for appointment, possessing the qualities required in a magistrate.

Age

The retirement age for magistrates is 70 (Justices of the Peace Act 1997, s.7(2). Anyone 18 and over can apply to become a magistrate though in reality, due to the training during the first two years, it is unlikely that anyone over 65 would be appointed.

Gender

Each bench should have a roughly equal number of men and women. There should be sufficient magistrates of each sex who are eligible to sit in the family proceedings and youth courts, which must be made up of three magistrates and include a man and a woman, unless this is impractical.

Ethnic origin

Advisory committees are making strenuous efforts to recruit suitable candidates from the ethnic minorities. Advisory committees should be aware of the ethnic composition of the area for which they are responsible and seek to recruit sufficient numbers from the ethnic minorities to reflect that composition.

Geographical spread

Advisory committees should aim to recommend candidates proportionally from the areas for which they are responsible but ensure that there are not too many magistrates on any one bench from the same village, neighbourhood or street.

Occupation

Advisory committees should seek to recommend for appointment, candidates from a broad spectrum of occupations. No more than 15% of the magistrates on a bench should be from the same occupational group.

Membership of clubs/organisations including freemasonry

It is important that there are not too many magistrates on the bench from the same clubs or organisations. Candidates for the magistracy are specifically asked on the new application form if they are freemasons. If a candidate has completed the old form, they should be asked at interview if they are freemasons. Those recommended for appointment will be required to inform the chairman of the bench or the clerk to the justices if they subsequently become a freemason.

The Magistrates' Association

C. Reform

1. Explanatory notes to the Constitutional Reform Act 2005

Constitutional Reform Act 2005

The Constitutional Reform Act modifies the office of Lord Chancellor and makes changes to the way in which some of the functions vested in that office are to be exercised. The Act also creates the Supreme Court of the United Kingdom and abolishes the appellate jurisdiction of the House of Lords. It creates the Judicial Appointments Commission to select people for judicial appointments in England and Wales, and provides for judicial discipline in England and Wales. The Act modifies the jurisdiction of the Judicial Committee of the Privy Council and removes the right of the Lord President of the Council to sit judicially.

Part 1: The rule of law

Part 1: Provides that the Act does not adversely affect the Rule of Law or the Lord Chancellor's role in relation to that principle.

Part 2: Arrangements to modify the office of Lord Chancellor

Part 2: Makes provision for modifying the office of Lord Chancellor so that the office-holder is no longer a judge nor exercises any judicial functions. It also sets out the qualifications for appointment to the office of Lord Chancellor. This Part also deals with functions relating to the judiciary and courts so that they are appropriately shared between the reformed ministerial office of Lord Chancellor and the Lord Chief Justice (and/or other senior members of the judiciary as appropriate). It also provides a guarantee of continued judicial independence. There are provisions in relation to the Speakership of the House of Lords. There are also provisions for the modification, abolition or transfer of other existing functions of the Lord Chancellor and provision that certain functions cannot be transferred from the Lord Chancellor to other Ministers by a Transfer of Functions Order under the Ministers of the Crown Act 1975.

Part 3: The Supreme Court

Part 3: Makes provisions for a Supreme Court to replace the existing system of Law Lords operating as a committee of the House of Lords. It provides for the appointment of judges to the new Court, the Court's jurisdiction, its procedures, resources (including accommodation) and other matters.

Part 4: Judicial appointments and discipline

Part 4: Makes provision for a Judicial Appointments Commission to be responsible for recruiting and selecting judges for the Courts of England and Wales and members of certain tribunals, and makes special arrangements for the appointment of the Lord Chief Justice and other Heads of Division and of the Lords Justices of Appeal. It provides for the Commission to report to the Lord Chancellor on who has been selected, and for the Lord Chancellor to make the appointment or the recommendation for appointment to The Queen. It also makes provision for a Judicial Appointments and Conduct Ombudsman, and for judicial discipline. [...]

2. Supreme Court to replace House of Lords

The following text is the February 9, 2004 debate in the House of Lords about the Constitutional Reform Act 2005.

3.11 p.m.

The Secretary of State for Constitutional Affairs and Lord Chancellor (Lord Falconer of Thoroton): My Lords, with the leave of the House, I should like to make a Statement on the proposed new United Kingdom Supreme Court.

[...] Today, I am setting out our plans – a key element of our comprehensive programme of constitutional modernisation and reform, aimed at enhancing the credibility and effectiveness of public institutions and increasing trust and accountability.

Just as our proposals on the judicial functions of the office of Lord Chancellor rest on the separation of powers between the judiciary and the executive, so too with our court system: we believe that the time has come to make a clear and transparent separation between the judiciary and the legislature. By creating a Supreme Court, we will separate fully the final court of appeal from Parliament. [...]

The Government's view is that, as part of our plans to sustain and enhance the vital independence of the judiciary, the present position is no longer sustainable. The time has come for the United Kingdom's highest court to move out from under the shadow of the legislature. [...]

We will bring forward legislation to create a Supreme Court. Under our proposals the Supreme Court for the United Kingdom will replace the existing system whereby the Law Lords operate as a committee of this House. The Supreme Court will exercise the same appellate jurisdiction as the Appellate Committee presently exercises, in terms both of the courts from which appeals may lie and reviews by appellate petition. There will be no changes to the rules governing leave to appeal. The Supreme Court will also take over the jurisdiction of the Judicial Committee of the Privy Council in respect of devolution issues under the Scotland Act 1998, the Government of Wales Act 1998 and the Northern Ireland Act 1998.

[...] As the key objective is to achieve a full and transparent separation between the judiciary and the legislature, it follows that Justices of the Supreme Court, other holders of full-time judicial office, or retired justices of the Supreme Court who continue to sit, will no longer be entitled to sit or to vote in the House of Lords, or to participate in the work of Parliament for as long as they hold their judicial appointment. [...]

Appointments will be made on the recommendation of a new Supreme Court Appointments Commission to be convened when there is an actual or impending vacancy. The composition of the commission, consisting of members of the Appointments Commission from across the United Kingdom – with Members of Parliament and the Government ineligible for membership – guarantees nominations free from political influence. The president of the Supreme Court will chair the Appointments Commission, and the deputy president will also be an ex officio member. That will ensure a proper balance of lay and judicial input to its deliberations. The commission will consider candidates eligible for appointment by reference to criteria that have been approved by Parliament, subject to the overriding principle of merit. It will have a duty each time it meets to survey the field of all eligible candidates across the three jurisdictions and to focus on the most meritorious.

The commission will recommend to the Secretary of State a minimum of two and a maximum of five candidates for each vacancy. On receipt of the nominations, the Secretary of State will be under a statutory duty to ensure that the court has among its members sufficient knowledge and experience of the law in each United Kingdom jurisdiction. In doing so he will be required to consult the senior judiciary in the three jurisdictions. The Secretary of State will then submit a name from the shortlist to the Prime Minister, who will make a recommendation to Her Majesty accordingly. [...]

3.20 p.m.

Lord Kingsland: [...] As the noble and learned Lord is well aware, the Opposition believe that the real motive behind the Government's proposed

Bill, of which today's Statement will form a part, is to weaken the judicial arm of the constitution.

[...] Finally, I turn to the proposals for a Supreme Court Law Commission to select new justices of the Supreme Court. The noble and learned Lord has said that the appropriate standard will be based wholly and solely on merit, which I welcome very much indeed. He has said that, invariably, a recommendation will be made to the Secretary of State for Constitutional Affairs of between two and five members. The noble and learned Lord has also informed us that the Secretary of State for Constitutional Affairs will select the final name to propose to the Prime Minister only after the senior judges in all the jurisdictions of the United Kingdom and the First Ministers of Scotland, Wales and Northern Ireland have been consulted.

While that is all well and good, what is to happen if, as a result of these conversations, irreconcilable differences emerge about who should be the proposed candidate? Although the noble and learned Lord did not say so, I assume that the Secretary of State for Constitutional Affairs must also make the final selection on merit, as must the Supreme Court Law Commission. I also understand that, in future, the Secretary of State for Constitutional Affairs is likely to be an elected politician, usually a non-lawyer, in another place [= *The House of Commons*]. However, if the Secretary of State for Constitutional Affairs is under an obligation to select on merit one of the proposed five, what qualifications does he have to do so? Does this not mean that, in effect, the Secretary of State for Constitutional Affairs will have to be someone like the Lord Chancellor?

3.28 p.m.

Lord Goodhart: My Lords, Members on these Benches support the creation of a Supreme Court separate from your Lordships' House and, indeed, we advocated that proposal long before the Government became converted to it. We disagree strongly with the view put forward by the noble Lord, Lord Kingsland, that the Government's aim is to weaken the role of the judiciary and the constitution. On the contrary, taken as a whole, the Government's reforms will substantially strengthen the role of the judiciary and therefore we welcome much of the Statement.

[...] I turn now to an issue of concern with which, on this occasion, I very much agree with the noble Lord, Lord Kingsland. I refer to the method of appointment of Supreme Court justices. We agree that there should be a Supreme Court appointments commission consisting of members of the Judicial Appointments Commission for England, Scotland and Northern Ireland. [...]

We believe that the system should follow the system already recommended for the appointment of judges in England and Wales, which is that one name should be recommended by the appointments commission. The Prime Minister should have power to reject the nominee, or to ask for reconsideration, but only for reasons. If two names have to be submitted, it could lead to a situation in which, although the appointments commission believes that there is an outstanding candidate, that candidate may have made himself or herself unpopular with the Government. If another name has to be submitted as well, the Prime Minister can appoint the second name without giving reasons for rejecting the first. The reasons given in the Statement for requiring two names are unconvincing. The Statement says that "it will be necessary for the Secretary of State to consult on a wider range of candidates"– because– "the Court must always contain the necessary breadth of experience of each constituent jurisdiction". That is surely what the appointments commission is for. Why should the Secretary of State need to carry out further consultations? Unless there are real grounds for rejecting a nominee, we believe that the Prime Minister should be required to accept the nominations from the appointments commission. [...]

3.35 p.m.

Lord Falconer of Thoroton: My Lords, I am grateful to the noble Lord, Lord Goodhart, for his welcome in principle to the Statement. [...]

He said that it was a scheme intended to undermine the independence of the judiciary. He is the only one who has made such a suggestion, and it is completely wrong. The proposal to create the Supreme Court is a view shared by the current senior Law Lord and a number of other Law Lords. The senior Law Lord said that it was the mark of an independent, liberal democracy to have a Supreme Court separate from Parliament. That shows that it is a sensible proposal.

http://www.parliament.the-stationery-office.co.uk

Exercise

Research tasks.

1. Look up the names and biographical details of the 12 Justices of the Supreme Court of the UK.

2. Present your findings in written or oral form.

3. Comment upon the diversity of background of Justices in the Supreme Court of the United Kingdom.

4. Compare the Supreme Court of the UK with the US Supreme Court.

3. Off the presses

Diversity on the Bench

Solicitors, women and minorities – step up to the Bench

The Lord Chancellor wants to open up places in the judiciary to a much wider group of people

This week a huge recruitment drive gets under way for more judges. The Lord Chancellor's officials will be holding events in London and Birmingham to boost the numbers of applicants from among solicitors, women and ethnic minorities.

Lord Falconer of Thoroton believes that there is a "huge untapped pool of talent" and he is concerned that the judiciary – while "first class" – must diversify. He told the House of Lords' constitutional committee last week: "If, as time goes on, you don't diversify, you lose talent."

The most obvious need is for more women, he said. "We have a very, very small percentage of women on the Bench… and over time, if the group of people who are judges are 50 per cent men, 50 per cent women, that will have a significant effect on the sort of discretionary decisions judges make all the time."

The problem was starkly highlighted at a recent conference in London held by the independent Commission for Judicial Appointments, the watchdog on how judges are chosen. Only 26.3 per cent of judges are women and fewer than 5 per cent from ethnic minorities (8 per cent in the population).

He rules out quotas and the sacrosanct touchstone of "merit" will remain. But he wants to demolish the myth that being a judge is "for other people and more specifically for other barristers". Nor is merit "immutable", Lord Falconer added; it had to be worked at. Merit without maintenance would decay – it needed renewal.

"A country where you are much more likely to become a judge if you are a man rather than a woman is losing out on a whole range of people who, without doubt, have the merit to be judges." The same applied to ethnic minority groups: "If an excellent black solicitor thinks being a judge is for 'other people', then our judiciary is all the weaker for it."

He is right to be worried. The proportions are rising: in 2000, 19.8 per cent of judges were women, rising to 26.3 per cent in 2003-04. Ethnic minority judges rose from 3.14 per cent in 2000 to 7.21 per cent in 2003-04. But despite efforts to improve numbers further – and last year's promotion of Baroness Hale of Richmond as the first woman Law Lord – many solicitors, women and ethnic minorities, do not see judging as a career for them.

Stuart Popham, senior partner of Clifford Chance, said: "The idea of being a judge just never occurs to lots of lawyers because of its links with the

Bar and with advocacy. The general perception is that it is still something to do with being a senior barrister. If we can move away from that, it's more likely that a wider range of experience will be brought to the judiciary."

Another problem is that senior women are dropping out of legal practice just when they might think of the Bench. Mrs Justice Cox, one of ten woman out of 104 High Court judges and president of the Association of Women Barristers (AWB), expresses concern about the Bar drop-out. The Bar is potentially a good career to combine a profession and family, she says. "It should be of concern to everyone that increasing numbers of women may be finding the demands made of them in practice incompatible with family life or indeed with 'a life'."

So can being a judge be made more attractive? The way they are chosen still deters some: Lord Falconer came under fire from the Judicial Appointments Commission over one appointment in which he vetoed a candidate from his selection panel, substituting his own. But from next April, that involvement ceases and the new Judicial Appointments Commission under Baroness Ushar Prashar takes over. The process should be more transparent and objective.

Other measures are proposed: career breaks for judges; a change to allow judges to return to legal practice – even advertising themselves as "former judges"; allowing solicitors to notch up compulsory training points when shadowing a judge; and a pilot scheme in the North East with circuit judges mentoring district judges. Finally, letters will go to every lawyer when eligible for appointment.

The steps have been welcomed. Jane Hoyal, vice-president of the AWB, said: "I am all for changing the system to make it less of an old-boy network and if it gives solicitors a fair chance."

In five years Lord Falconer wants "every under-represented group apply-ing in proportion to its presence in the pool. At every level. In our tribunals and in our courts, progressing from post to post, according to ability."

Ambitious words – but not just for political correctness. He is aware that if the judiciary stays in its present image, judges will not command the public confidence so crucial to the justice system.

Frances Gibb, *The Times*, 15/11/2005 (http://www.timesonline.co.uk).

Definitions in context

notch up: achieve a particular total or number of points.

maintenance (uncountable): the steps that need to be carried out to keep something in good condition.

sacrosanct: sacred.

watchdog: a person or group of persons who insures that nothing illegal or harmful is done.

1 Are the following statements are true or false?

1. The Bench is generally perceived by solicitors as inaccessible.
2. A reform coming into force in 2006 increases the role of the Lord Chancellor in the area of judicial appointments.
3. Lawyers who join the Bench cannot return to legal practice.
4. Solicitors may ask to observe a judge's professional practice.
5. The first woman Law Lord was appointed in 2003.
6. Judges are always very transparent and open about the decisions they make.
7. Mrs Justice Cox tends to think that it is very easy to combine the Bench with having a family.
8. The lack of transparency in judicial appointments is what makes the profession unattractive.
9. A lawyer needs to express the desire to be a judge before he can be eligible for appointment.
10. The justice system needs to change because the public no longer trusts it.

2 Complete the second sentence so that it has a similar meaning to the first.

1. If, as time goes on, you don't diversify, you lose talent. (Unless...)
2. Can being a judge be made more attractive? (Can anything...)
3. Despite efforts to improve numbers further, many solicitors, women and ethnic minorities do not see judging as a career for them. (Although...)
4. The problem was starkly highlighted at a conference in London held by the independent Commission for Judicial Appointments. (The independent CJA held a conference...)

3 Find the synonym for each word or expression, according to its meaning in the article.

1. *rule out*	a. exclude	b. favour	c. consider
2. *untapped*	a. incompetent	b. not used	c. convenient
3. *decay*	a. thrive	b. deteriorate	c. disappear
4. *deter*	a. encourage	b. dissuade	c. convince
5. *come under fire*	a. be criticized	b. be praised	c. protect

4 Discuss.

1. Using information from the text and in your own opinion, answer the question: "Can being a judge be made more attractive?"
2. How do you understand the statement: "Merit without maintenance would decay – it needed renewal"?
3. Why has it become so important for the judiciary to become representative of the population?

4. Food for thought

Hobson v Gledhill **[1978] 1 All ER 945**

QUEEN'S BENCH DIVISION
LORD WIDGERY CJ, CANTLEY AND PETER PAIN JJ

12 OCTOBER 1977

Animal – Guard dog – Control by handler – Dog secured so that it is not at liberty to go freely about the premises – Handler not present on premises – Whether necessary that handler should be on premises while dog is secured – Guard Dogs Act 1975, s 1(1).

On the true construction of s 1(1)[a] of the Guard Dogs Act 1975 (which forbids a person to use or permit the use of a guard dog unless a dog handler is on the premises and the dog is under the handler's control 'except while the dog is secured so that it is not at liberty to go freely about the premises'), the exception applies to the requirement that a handler should be on the premises as well as to the requirement that the dog should be under his control, and therefore it is not necessary that a handler should be on the premises while the dog is secured (see p 947 *c* and *g h*, post).

[a] Section 1(1) is set out at p 946 e, post

Whether a dog which is secured by a length of chain is 'secured so that it is not at liberty to go freely about the premises', within s 1(1), is a question of degree depending on the facts of the individual case (see p 947 *d* to *h*, post).

Notes
For control of guard dogs, see Supplement to 2 *Halsbury's Laws* (4th Edn) para 368A.

For the Guard Dogs Act 1975, s 1, see 45 *Halsbury's Statutes* (3rd Edn) 27.

Case cited
Cummings v Granger (sued as Grainger) [1977] 1 All ER 104 [1977] QB 397, CA.

Case stated
On 7 May 1976 three informations* were preferred by the appellant, James Hobson, against the respondent, Norman Gledhill, alleging that on 27

* "informations": Note that the word in its countable form is a legal term referring to a formal accusation of a crime and should not be confused with its more common non-countable form "information".

March 1976 at Huddersfield, the respondent had used a guard dog at premises in George Street, Milnsbridge, when no person who was capable of controlling the dog was present on the premises and the dog was not under the control of a handler at all times while it was being used, the dog not being secured so that it was not at liberty to go freely about the premises, contrary to s 1(1) of the Guard Dogs Act 1975. On 21 July 1976 the justices for Huddersfield, sitting as a magistrates' court at Huddersfield dismissed the information. At the request of the appellant the justices stated a case for the opinion of the High Court. The facts are set out in the judgment of Peter Pain J.

Robert Taylor for the appellant.
Gordon Lakin for the respondent.

12 October 1977. The following judgments were delivered.

PETER PAIN J

delivered the first judgment at the request of Lord Widgery CJ. This is an appeal by way of case stated by the Huddersfield justices in respect of informations which they heard on 21 July 1976. There were three charges, all of them similar in nature, that on 27 March 1976 at Huddersfield the respondent did use a guard dog at premises in Milnsbridge when no person who was capable of controlling the dog was present on the said premises and the dog was not under the control of the handler at all times while it was being used, the said dog not being secured so that it was not at liberty to go freely about the said premises. There were in fact three similar charges because there were three Alsatian dogs.

One only has to read the charge with the several negatives in it to see how it can give rise to difficulties of construction. The court is told that the true meaning of s 1(1) of the Guard Dogs Act 1975 is a matter that has been of some concern to the authorities who are responsible for enforcing it, and there has as yet been no decision on it. The authorities are anxious for the ambiguity which appears to arise on the section to be disposed of by this court.

Before I come to read the section, I will deal with the short facts as found by the justices. They found that on 27 March 1976 the respondent was the owner of premises consisting of a yard and buildings situate at George Street, Milnsbridge, Huddersfield. On that date the respondent used three Alsatian dogs as guard dogs at the premises.

The dogs were secured in the following manner, that is they were fastened independently on chains 12 feet, 12 feet and 13 feet long respectively and were unable to reach the gates by at least two feet. Two of the chains were securely anchored to the ground on either side of the main gates which were locked. The third chain was secured at a point set back from the main gates.

They also found that the dogs were not able to go into every part of the premises, and that at the time no person was present on the premises of the respondent. But they did not make any finding as to the extent of the premises, though one supposes from the fact that there was a yard and buildings that they must have been a good deal more extensive than the 12 feet chains by which the dogs were held.

Section 1(1) of the 1975 Act provides:

'A person shall not use or permit the use of a guard dog at any premises unless a person ("the handler") who is capable of controlling the dog is present on the premises and the dog is under the control of the handler at all times while it is being so used except while it is secured so that it is not at liberty to go freely about the premises.'

The section clearly is ambiguous, and one asks oneself: does the exception which applies while the dog is secured so that it is not at liberty to go freely about the premises apply to the whole previous sentence, or does it apply only to the latter part of the sentence, which would be the time when the dog might be out of the control of the handler who is nonetheless on the premises? Or, to put it another way, does the section, and this is the important point, require a person who uses a guard dog to have a handler on the premises all the time the dog is there, and when the dog is not under the immediate control of the handler to tie him up, or does it require the person using the guard dog either to have a handler on the premises under whose immediate control the dog is or to tie the dog up? If it be the latter, then the handler can leave the premises leaving the dog secured.

Realising this ambiguity, one comes to the rule that a penal statute where there is an ambiguity should always be construed in favour of the citizen who may find himself the subject of the penalty.

That was the first point which was put before us by counsel for the appellant and, applying that principle, it would seem clear that the more restricted duty should be placed on the citizen, that is to say that to use a guard dog either he must have a handler on the premises with the dog under his control or he must have the dog secured. For myself, it seems to me also that, if that be done, it does meet the mischief which Parliament was seeking to provide against because, provided the dog is properly secured, the person who may come on the premises whether lawfully or not is in a position to remove himself from the ambit of the dog's teeth.

One also does have the point that, although there is no finding on this, one can probably take judicial notice of the fact that a number of fairly small premises do protect themselves by the use of guard dogs. If a handler always had to be on the premises with the guard dogs, the economic burden on a person's using those premises would be very heavy indeed.

One does ask oneself, as Lord Widgery CJ asked in the course of the argument, would it satisfy s 1 if the handler just tied the dog up and went away and left it indefinitely. On the construction which I favour there would, I think, be no offence under s 1. But it has to be remembered that there are several other sections in the Act providing for the licensing of kennels used for guard dogs by the local authority, and it is to be assumed that the local authority in imposing conditions and the like in respect of those licences will take proper steps to see that dogs are properly treated and cared for as they should be and are not abused.

Coming, therefore, to the questions propounded by the justices, the first question they ask is:

> 'Whether by virtue of s 1(1) of the Guard Dogs Act 1975 where a guard dog is used on premises it is necessary for a person capable of controlling the dog to be present on the premises at all times whilst the dog is being so used notwithstanding that the dog is secured so that it is not at liberty to go freely about the premises.'

The answer that I give to that is that it is not necessary.

They ask a second question: 'whether a dog secured on a chain 12 feet in length can be regarded as "not at liberty to go freely about the premises".' This is a question which I feel unable to answer at large. Whether it is able to go freely about the premises must depend on the size of the premises. If it is a small workshop it might despite the chain be able to go freely about the premises; it would be quite wrong for this court to attempt to give any sort of guidance as to the appropriate length of chain for a dog because it must depend on all the circumstances, bearing in mind of course the purpose of the chain, which is to enable the person, even though he may be a trespasser or burglar, to be able to remove himself from the dog's range. That would always have to be borne in mind in considering the length of chain provided. But, subject to that, this must be a question of degree depending on the facts of the individual case.

The justices having in this case dismissed the information, I would dismiss the appeal.

CANTLEY J.

I agree. I must confess that my initial impression on reading s 1(1) was that the exception applied only to the phrase 'the dog is under the control of the handler at all times while it is being so used' and not to the entire paragraph. But I am persuaded that the ambiguity to which Peter Pain J has referred does exist, and accordingly I agree that the section should be construed in this way, it being a penal section.

LORD WIDGERY CJ.

I agree with all the propositions put forward so clearly by Peter Pain J. One thing is clear to me, and that is that since the passing of the Guard Dogs Act 1975 one can no longer have a guard dog roaming at large on premises with no handler in control of it. That has gone once and for all.

I think there is a good deal for saying that it would be desirable to take the reform further and to abolish for all time the conception of a dog alone on the premises, even when it is tied up. But for the reasons which have been given, I am quite unable to say which of the solutions canvassed was the intention of Parliament, and the right course in those circumstances is to favour the citizen. I would do so, as have already the other members of the court.

If we are wrong, and if we have chosen a solution which is contrary to the wishes of Parliament, it will not be very difficult for Parliament to put it right in a suitable statute hereafter. The appeal is, therefore, dismissed.

Appeal dismissed.
Solicitors: Hewitt, Woollacott & Chown agents for M D Shaffner, Wakefield (for the appellant). Drabble & Co, Huddersfield (for the respondent).
N P Metcalfe Esq Barrister.

http://www.lexisnexis.co.uk

Exercise

Answer the following questions.

1. In which court was this case heard?
2. List the facts of the case.
3. What is the point of law at stake?
4. Describe the type of appellate procedure involved.
5. What are the judges' opinions?

5. Listening

Exercises

1 Listen to an interview with John Gallagher, a representative of *Fathers 4 Justice*, a pressure group challenging family law, and complete the following extract.

INTERVIEWER: John and his ...... run *Fathers 4 Justice* .... this room. The ...... for information has increased dramatically, especially since ......flour bombed the Prime Minister last month, which generated a .... in Parliament.

GALLAGHER: The Labour Party was forged in the fires of .... I find it amazing that the party has forgotten their ....

INTERVIEWER: Any regrets about that?

GALLAGHER: Absolutely not. At *Fathers 4 Justice*, we always claim and account for our actions. There's always a bit of ...... in our actions. There have been condoms for obvious reasons, self-raising flour, again for obvious reasons. It got them off their feet any way.

INTERVIEWER: What you did is against the law though.

GALLAGHER: It is in the very nature of this organisation to explore the .... of the law. We break the law deliberately and we expect to be held ...... for that. Whether or not we're right, we'll let ...... be our judge.

INTERVIEWER: Back at the office, they're fine-tuning the ..... . *Fathers 4 Justice* says it's choosing music for superhero dads ready for the .... in London. But are all the fathers who've been denied contact really superheroes or do some represent a ...... to women and children? Women's groups are saying in the vast majority of cases when women are denying contact, they're doing it because the men are dangerous.

GALLAGHER: That's not borne out in any way, shape or form. This is about children and about good, loving parents.

INTERVIEWER: What is your view regarding cases when there is .... of domestic violence in the family perpetrated by the man? Do you think for example, for argument's sake, that contact should be automatically ...... by the court, or that it should be ...... ?

GALLAGHER: I'm not here to talk about domestic violence, I'm here to talk about family law. Let's be very clear about the .... If your purpose is to talk about domestic violence then you should do a programme about that. Our position is that if the child's at risk from any parent, ...

2 Answer the following questions.

1. Does John Gallagher think that abusive fathers should have access to their children?

2. What is his opinion of the way politicians deal with this issue?

3. What are the suggestions of the campaigners interviewed during the London rally to improve family law?

4. What is "plan zero"?

3 Discuss.

1. Is civil disobedience a good way to have the law changed?

2. Do you think men have fewer rights than women in divorce cases?

3. Can a pressure group influence the way judges decide their cases?

6. Grammar practice

1 **Pronunciation. Look up the phonetic transcription of the following words in your dictionary. Try to say in what way their pronunciation differs from what you would expect.**

debt	clerk	puisne	Privy Council
libel	jurisdiction	indictment	chiropractor
patentee	nominee	appointee	sacrosanct
fastened	premises	whilst	covenant
construed	pseudo		

2 **Spelling. For each of the following words, circle the letter(s) that differ from the French spelling. Look up the words in a dictionary to check if the English meaning is different from the French one.**

independence	responsible	functions	correspondence
recruitment	recommendation	current	particular
sacrosanct	professional	clerk	committee
discharge	respondent	spouse	engineer

3 **Prepositions. Match each verb with an appropriate preposition. Look up the words in your dictionary in case there might be several possibilities and write down the meanings.**

1. meet	A. from
2. relate	B. about
3. cope	C. between
4. consist	D. by
5. deal	E. upon
6. lie	F. to
7. comment	G. for
8. compensate	H. on
9. depend	I. in
10. agree	J. with
11. result	
12. distinguish	
13. account	
14. abide	
15. suffer	
16. worry	

4 **The passive. Put the following sentences in the passive form.**

1. The victim laid an information with the police against the alleged rapist.

2. The Queen appoints High Court judges.

3. The Crown Court hears serious criminal cases.

4. In appeals by way of case stated, a lower court issues a statement in writing of facts agreed upon during the first instance trial.

5. Judges settle disputes according to the law.

6. The High Court may deal with family law.

7. The Chancery Division can issue an injunction against the losing party.

8. This business cannot meet its debt obligations.

9. The Immigration Services Commissioner brings disciplinary charges against immigration advisors.

10. The bailiff is swearing in the jury.

11. The Court and Legal Services Act lays down the minimum eligibility requirements for most judicial offices.

12. Advisory committees should seek candidates from a broad spectrum of occupations.

5 **Quantifiers. Fill in the blanks with _every_, _all_ or _each_.**

1. While that is ...... well and good, what is to happen if irreconcilable differences emerge about who should be the proposed candidate?

2. The advisory committees welcome applications from people in ...... walks of life who have the qualities and the time to serve as magistrates.

3. Case management is designed to ensure that the time and resources spent on ...... case be appropriate and proportional.

4. ...... salaried and fee-paid judicial office holders appointed for the first time after 31 March 1995 must retire on their 70th birthday.

5. The senior judges in ...... the jurisdictions of the United Kingdom have been consulted.

6. The dogs were not able to go into ...... part of the premises.

7. Equitable remedies are administered alongside common law remedies by ...... three divisions of the High Court.

8. ...... division of the High Court comprises a court of appeal called Divisional Court.

9. "I am ...... for changing the system to make it less of an old-boy network and if it gives solicitors a fair chance."

10. In case of appeal against conviction, the Crown Court judge re-hears ...... the evidence witnesses gave in the lower court, but there is no jury.

11. In five years Lord Falconer wants "......   under-represented group applying in proportion to its presence in the pool".

12. Lay magistrates are expected to sit for a maximum of 35 half days ...... year.

13. In April 2005, the administration of ...... magistrates' courts in England and Wales was centralised under the authority of Her Majesty's Courts Service (HMCS).

14. It will have a duty ...... time it meets to survey the field of ...... eligible candidates across the three jurisdictions and to focus on the most meritorious.

15. If an excellent black solicitor thinks being a judge is for "other people", then our judiciary is ...... the weaker for it.

Chapter **5**

The work of the courts

1. Fundamentals

A. Criminal trials

1. How defendants are charged with an offence

The **Crown Prosecution Service** (CPS) is the government department responsible for prosecuting cases. The role of the police in the context of criminal cases is essential. Indeed, only after specific procedures at the police station can a **defendant** be brought to court.

The provisions of the Police and Criminal Evidence Act 1984 (PACE) in relation to powers of arrest have recently been repealed and replaced by Section 110 of the Serious Organised Crime and Police Act 2005. Under that Act a police officer has the power to arrest without warrant any person whom he has reasonable grounds for suspecting to be about to commit any offence, or any person that he has reasonable grounds for suspecting to be committing an offence. In addition, if a police officer has reasonable grounds to suspect that an offence has been committed, he may arrest without warrant anyone whom he has reasonable grounds to suspect of being guilty of it.

Note, however, that a police officer is only entitled to exercise the power of arrest without warrant if the police officer *also* has reasonable grounds for believing that one or more of a number of further reasons exist, including that the arrest is required to enable the police officer to ascertain the suspect's name and address, to prevent the person causing harm to himself and/or others, to protect a child or other vulnerable person, to allow the prompt and effective investigation of the offence, or to prevent any prosecution for the offence from being hindered by the disappearance of the suspect.

At the police station, suspects are first brought before a Custody Officer who is responsible for the welfare of prisoners and the protection of their rights. Suspects are then read their rights and asked whether they wish to request the assistance of a solicitor. When the suspect is under 17 or mentally incompetent, the presence of an "appropriate adult", usually a relative, guardian or social worker, is also required. Suspects can then be held for a period of up to 24 hours, subject to a twelve-hour extension with the permission of a senior officer, i.e. a **superintendent** or a superior officer. For serious arrestable offences, magistrates can order that a suspect be detained for a maximum of 96 hours, except in cases arising under the Terrorism Act 2000, which warrant a longer police custody period.

Suspects can be questioned at the police station. Interviews are tape-recorded and usually carried out in the presence of a solicitor. Access to a solicitor may be denied in exceptional circumstances as set out in Section 58(8) of PACE 1984, i.e. if there is reason to believe that the presence of a solicitor would lead to interference with or harm to **evidence** connected with an indictable offence, or to interference with or physical injury to other persons, or lead to the alerting of other persons suspected of having committed such an offence but not yet arrested for it, or would hinder the recovery of any property obtained as a result of such an offence.

If it appears that there is enough evidence to **charge** the suspect, then the suspect must be charged straightaway . The custody officer must then decide whether to release the person on bail, or detain them in custody to be brought before the magistrates' court as soon as practicable. If released on police bail the person will be given, and must sign, a bail sheet, a document indicating when they must attend court.

In minor cases a prosecution often commences by way of a **summons** when the defendant has not been through the process described above. A Crown Prosecutor has the power to **lay an information** against a person when there are sufficient grounds to believe that a crime has been committed. A summons is then issued by a magistrates' court and served on the defendant by post. It contains details about the offence and orders the defendant to appear in court on a specified date.

2. Stages of a criminal trial

Pre-trial hearings

In a criminal case, court proceedings start with the **arraignment** of the defendant at a pre-trial hearing, during which a defendant is informed of the charges against him and is asked to enter a **plea** of **guilty** or **not guilty**. A minor case in which the defendant pleads guilty may be completed at the first hearing, especially when the offence involved is only punishable by a fine. In this instance, defendants are allowed to send their guilty plea by letter, and a ruling may be pronounced quickly and in their absence.

Cases involving other summary offences are usually adjourned to a further date for trial in the magistrates' court while indictable offences are transferred to the **Crown Court**. For either-way offences, a further hearing at the magistrates' court is necessary so that the choice of **venue** may be made. Another issue that Magistrates may have to deal with at pre-trial hearings is whether to grant or deny bail.

Summary trial (magistrates' court)

When the defendant pleads guilty, the entire procedure consists in determining the **sentence**. Accordingly, the hearing starts with the prosecutor giving a summary of the facts. If the **defence** disagrees, it may be necessary to have an additional inquiry. If, however, there is no objection, both parties have to give the court relevant information about the defendant's background, including financial situation, health, etc. The defence's final statement, which is aimed at convincing the magistrates to consider the case with leniency, is called **speech in mitigation**. The bench then retires (leaves the court room) to decide on the sentence.

When a defendant pleads not guilty, the summary trial procedure is longer. As the **burden of proof** is on the Crown, the prosecutor speaks first and introduces the **prosecution** case. In more complicated cases the defence sometimes makes an opening statement, though this is not usual. Then, the prosecution submits evidence to the court and calls its witnesses. All witnesses must take an oath before they can testify. After the prosecutor has conducted the **examination-in-chief** of a **witness**, the defence is allowed to proceed to a **cross-examination** in order to test the evidence given and to put the defence case to the witness. The court will then ask the prosecuting advocate if he wishes a **re-examination** of the witness. If the magistrates have no further questions, it then falls to the defence to present its case. The defence counsel calls witnesses who are each examined in chief, re-examined, etc. The defendant is not obliged to give evidence, nor to call any witnesses. Once the defence case is completed, the prosecutor and then the defence advocate make their submissions to the court emphasising the strengths of their respective cases and the weaknesses in their opponent's case. The bench then retires to reach its decision. Before the magistrates pronounce their decision, the defendant is asked to rise. Under the Human Rights Act 1998, magistrates are required to give the reasons for their decisions.

Trial on indictment (Crown Court)

A defendant appearing on **indictment** at the Crown Court is almost always represented by a barrister or solicitor advocate, although there is no rule prohibiting a defendant from defending himself (referred to as acting in person). In the Crown

Court the procedure is similar to a summary trial in many ways, but it is nevertheless subject to more rigorous rules. For example, under the Criminal Procedure and Investigations Act 1996, both parties are required to disclose their evidence to the other side prior to the trial.

When the defendant pleads not guilty, the first step in a Crown Court trial is the swearing in of the jury. As in the magistrates' court, the prosecution makes an **opening speech** presenting its case and stating what it intends to establish, before proceeding with a detailed presentation of its evidence and calling its witnesses to the stand. When the prosecution has finished presenting its case, the defence may argue that there is no case to answer. If the judge agrees, he may direct the jury to acquit the defendant. Otherwise, the case proceeds to the next stage. The defence gives its evidence in a similar way, calling its witnesses and introducing any relevant **exhibits**. Then, after the prosecutor and the defence lawyer have delivered their **closing statements**, the judge summarises the case and instructs the jury as to the relevant points of law. If the jury returns a guilty **verdict**, the judge may sentence the offender straight away, though usually the judge will adjourn the question of sentencing for the obtaining of reports about the defendant. If, on the contrary, the defendant is acquitted by the jury, he or she is discharged.

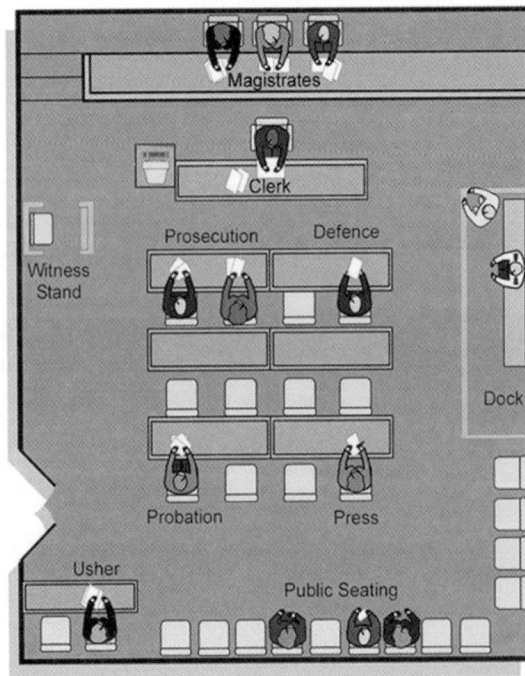

© Peter Bridge 2003

The layout of a magistrates' court.

3. How to lodge a criminal appeal...

...from magistrates' courts

In criminal cases, appeals lie from the magistrates' court to the Crown Court or exceptionally to the Administrative Court (formerly the Divisional Court of the Queen's Bench Division of the High Court), if the appeal deals with a point of law.

An appeal to the Crown Court is the usual route. Only defendants can lodge an **appeal** to the Crown Court and they need permission from the court. The entire case is then re-heard by one judge and two magistrates. The first **conviction** can be reversed, quashed or affirmed.

An application can be made by either party for a judicial review by the Administrative Court if it is believed that the magistrates have misinterpreted the law. The court can amend, affirm or reverse the decision, or remit the case to the magistrates' court. There is also a further and final appeal to the Supreme Court on points of law of public importance or interest.

Lastly, if the magistrates are uncertain as to a point of law they can seek a ruling by way of case stated from the Administrative Court.

...from the Crown Court

A defendant can appeal a decision from the Crown Court to the Criminal Division of the Court of Appeal. Defendants should be informed of the possibility of an appeal by their lawyer at the end of the trial. They need to obtain leave from the trial judge or, failing this, from the Court of Appeal. A notice of appeal (and if necessary an application for leave to appeal) must be filed with the Court of Appeal Criminal Division within 28 days after the conviction. All the rules concerning these appeals are set out in the Criminal Appeal Act 1995.

The Court of Appeal can dismiss the appeal, replace the conviction with a conviction for a lesser offence, order a new trial or allow the appeal in full. The court cannot increase a sentence.

When the prosecution wants to file for appeal, the verdict must have resulted in a conviction. The only cases when it can appeal against a not guilty verdict is when the jury in the trial is shown to have been influenced and when the Attorney-General refers a point of law to the Court of Appeal to get a ruling on the law. The appeal creates a precedent on that point of law.

...to the Supreme Court of the UK

An appeal lies from the Court of Appeal to the Supreme Court of the UK. Leave of appeal must come from the Court of Appeal or the Supreme Court and it must involve a point of law of general public importance. A certificate is issued for that purpose.

...to the Criminal Cases Review Commission

This commission is an independent public body that was set up by the Criminal Appeal Act 1995 to correct the **miscarriages of justice** not reviewed through the normal appeal system. It investigates cases where the defendant has possibly been wrongly convicted of a criminal offence or unfairly sentenced, and refers these cases back to the court which handled the appeal for another hearing. It can also help the Court of Appeal in some of its investigations. The monarch, on recommendation of the Prime Minister, appoints the members of the Commission, a third of them legally qualified and the other two with experience in the criminal justice system. Some support staff and the police are also involved in the work of the Commission.

B. Civil trials

Pursuant to the Civil Procedure Act 1997, as implemented through the Civil Procedure Rules (CPR) 1998, the procedures relating to the initiation and the resolution of a civil dispute were amended to speed up civil legal actions. The new procedure uses a computerised daily monitoring of cases which allows streamlining, the prompt setting of the date of trial for some cases and the summary disposal of others. The county courts have unlimited jurisdiction for most **claims**, including personal injury and contract claims. Personal injury claims above £50,000 and other claims above £15,000 may be issued in the county court or High Court, but claims below these thresholds *must* be issued in the county court.

In the county court, cases are allocated to one of three tracks, i.e. **small claims track**, **fast track** or **multi-track**, depending on the value and complexity of the case. After proceedings have been issued and a defence served, each party completes an allocation questionnaire to assist the court in allocating the case to the most appropriate track.

1. Before the trial

Pre-action protocol

The protocols are intended to encourage out-of-court settlements. The claimant's solicitor sends a letter of claim to the proposed defendant setting out the claim and inviting him to forward a copy to his insurer. The defendant, or his insurer if he is insured, then has a set time within which to investigate and answer the letter of claim. The two parties may then agree on a common expert. If so, it is very likely that they may come to an agreement on some aspects of the case, thereby narrowing the issues, reducing the costs of fighting the claim and increasing the chances of reaching an out-of-court settlement. Nonetheless, if the proposed defendant and/or his insurers do not comply with the protocol, or the exchange of information and other steps do not enable the parties to reach a settlement, the claimant's solicitors may have to start legal proceedings.

Pre-trial civil procedure

All claims start with the aggrieved party filling in a claim form, including the particulars of claim, that is issued in the High Court (only permitted for money only claims if the value of the claim exceeds £15,000 or for personal injury claims if the claim exceeds £50,000) or in the county court. Claimants must indicate the nature and presumed maximum value of the claim. In the county court the proceedings are then **served on** the defendant by the court (or by the claimant).

Claimants then have to file a Statement of Case which is then also served on the defendant. If he wishes to defend the claim, the defendant must set out his case in a Statement of Case called a Defence.

In the county court, once this initial exchange of pleadings is over, the court allocates the case to one of the three tracks: the small claims track (for claims below £5,000), the fast track (for claims between £5,000 and £15,000) and the multi-track (for claims above £15,000). Allocation of cases depends in part on the complexity of the issues of law and fact involved, and accordingly simple cases as well as non complex cases of small value are allocated to the small claims track.

The defendant has the right at any point during the proceedings to make a payment into court of a sum of money called "Part 36 payment", as provided by Part 36 of the CPR, in settlement of the claim. The claimant then has a limited period of time to accept the payment. If a claimant turns down the Part 36 offer but at the trial recovers the same amount as or less than the Part 36 Payment, then he will usually be required to pay both his own and the defendant's legal costs incurred from the date of his refusal of the Part 36 offer. A claimant can also make a formal offer of settlement to the defendant prior to or during the course of the proceedings. This can be a wise tactical move, as if the defendant refuses it, at the end of the trial the judge can order the defendant to pay additional interest on the claimant's **damages**.

2. The civil trial

The claimant's case

The trial starts with the claimant's case. The judge should have previously had an opportunity to read the trial bundle. This consists of the pleadings, the witness statements and other documentation that the parties have agreed should be placed before the court. The claimant's barrister, solicitor advocate or solicitor (depending on the jurisdiction) opens the case to the judge. An opening speech gives the background of the claim and the facts at issue. The judge may well restrict the claimant's opening if he feels that he already has a sufficient grasp of the case, and may instead ask him to address particular issues, or move on to calling his first witness. The judge would not be told about any payment into court under Part 36 or offer to settle by the claimant until after he has decided the issues in the case.

The claimant generally gives his evidence first, followed by the witnesses called to support his case. Each witness takes the oath prior to giving his evidence. **Evidence-in-chief** is when the claimant and witnesses narrate their account of the facts in response to questions asked by the claimant's advocate. However, statements will have been exchanged some time prior to the trial and accordingly the parties already know what the other side wishes to say. Witnesses begin their evidence by confirming that their witness statement is true, and the judge may well restrict the questions that the claimant's counsel can ask his witnesses. Cross-examination is then carried out by the defendant's advocate. The purpose of this stage is to question each witness to test his account and to put the defendant's case to the claimant's witnesses. To that aim, **leading questions** are accepted. Following the cross-examination of each witness, the claimant's barrister or solicitor can re-examine the witnesses (including the claimant) but only on points raised by the cross-examination. All the witnesses will give their evidence in the same order: evidence-in-chief, cross-examination and re-examination.

The defendant's case

Once all the claimant's witnesses have given their evidence, the court hears the defendant and the defendant's witnesses (if any) according to the same procedure. In particularly long or complex cases, the defendant's counsel is permitted to make an **opening speech** before calling his witnesses.

Both the defendant's and the claimant's advocates make **closing** submissions setting out the merits of their respective cases and highlighting the flaws in their opponent's case. They may be invited to address the judge on the question of damages (referred to as *quantum*) or other **remedies**, though the judge may prefer to leave these matters until after he has given his decision on **liability**.

The judgment

The judge sums up the facts and gives his or her view on the points at stake either at the end of the trial or at a later date if the case is more complex. If the claimant wins then the defendant will have to pay both parties' legal costs, unless there has been a Part 36 payment into court. If the claimant wins the claim, but is awarded damages at or below any payment into court, then, although the defendant will have to pay both sides' costs up to the date of the Part 36 payment, the claimant will have to pay both sides' costs thereafter.

In a fast track case, the barrister's fee and the solicitor's costs for the preparation of the trial are fixed according to the amount of the claim. In small claims cases, the judge does not normally order the losing party to pay the costs of the successful party.

3. How to lodge a civil appeal...

...from the county courts

According to the Civil Procedure Rules, appeals are heard by a judge at the next level of the judicial hierarchy both for fast track cases and small claims. Accordingly, if a fast track case or a small claim is dealt with by a circuit judge, the appeal will be heard by a High Court judge.

In multi-track cases, the right of appeal lies to the Court of Appeal by a **leapfrog** procedure. Where a first appeal is heard by a circuit judge or a High Court judge, a further appeal lies to the Court of Appeal. But it is only used when an important point of principle or practice is raised, or when the court has a compelling reason to want to hear it.

...from the High Court

Appeals generally lie from the High Court to the Court of Appeal's Civil Division. Sometimes, and only when the case involves a point of law of general public importance, a leapfrog appeal lies to the Supreme Court of the UK.

Further appeals

A further appeal lies from the Court of Appeal Civil Division to the Supreme Court of the UK with leave (permission) from either court.

If a point of European law is raised in an appeal, the case may be referred to the European Court of Justice after all domestic resorts have been exhausted.

C. Judges and juries at a trial

1. The role of juries

In England and Wales juries are used for all serious criminal offences. In civil trials, a **jury** is only required in cases of libel, malicious prosecution and false imprisonment and in certain inquests.

In criminal cases, juries listen to the evidence presented in the court case and give a verdict of guilty or not guilty. In a civil case, a jury will be asked to give answers to specific factual questions. Members of the jury must be impartial and must stand down if they know anyone involved in the case or have a personal interest in the outcome of the trial. Their verdict must be solely based on the evidence they have heard.

After the conclusion of the evidence, when the cases for both sides have been presented, the judge sums up the evidence for and against the defendant and highlights the main points that the jury needs to consider. The judge also explains the exact meaning of any specific points of law that are important in the case. The jury then retires to the jury room. They must first decide who will be their **foreman** or chairperson. They then discuss the evidence until all the members agree on the verdict. These discussions are confidential as outside influence might prevent the trial from being fair and impartial. It is an offence (contempt of court) for a jury member to tell anyone what happened in the jury room, even after the trial has ended. It is also an offence for the media to comment on a case while it is *sub judice*; they may only report the facts. The jury is asked by the judge to reach a unanimous verdict but if a jury cannot agree, the judge may decide to accept a majority verdict, agreed upon by at least 10 of the 12 jurors.

When the jury has reached a verdict, it returns to the court room and the foreman announces the verdict. If the verdict is guilty, the judge may sentence the defendant, but will normally adjourn this decision until reports have been obtained about the defendant. If the jury returns a not guilty verdict, then the judge discharges the defendant. Jurors do not give the reasons for their decision.

2. The role of judges

Judges may take little part in the trial itself. Their role is to oversee the proceedings in order to ensure that the process is fair to both parties and that the decision reached is based upon facts.

In criminal cases, the judge or magistrates must pass sentence following conviction. In a civil case, where the claimant succeeds, the court must assess the amount of damages to be awarded to the claimant.

A judge frequently has to interpret case law and legislation. The accepted view is that judges simply apply the laws as passed by Parliament or in accordance with established case law. Nonetheless, this view plays down the role of the judiciary in the law-making process, especially in relation to the doctrine of judicial precedent applied to the common law and to the interpretation of statutes.

There are two views as to the attitudes that judges should adopt when interpreting legislation:

• The literal approach. This stresses the words used in the legislation. It is the dominant approach in the English legal system.

• The purposive approach. This involves judges looking beyond the words of a statute to the intention of Parliament when making the act. It is mainly used in English courts to interpret EU legislation (civil law). However, in the common law system, when interpreting English statutes, judges may take this approach only when there is a clear statement of the intention of the law (see *Pepper v Hart*).

When interpreting legislation, judges are now required to take into account the rules of interpretation laid out in the Human Rights Act 1998.

Definitions in context and key words

arraignment: the process of calling defendants into court, reading out the charges against them, and taking their plea.

burden of proof: what a party has to prove in court.

charge *(v.)*: accuse formally of an offence.

evidence-in-chief: the evidence given by a witness on behalf of the party for whom he is called.

claim: a demand for damages or other remedy.

closing speech: the final speech by either the prosecution or the defence advocates to the jury.

conviction: the pronouncement of guilt by a court or judicial authority.

cross-examination: the interrogation of witnesses carried out by the opposing party.

Crown Court: the court of original jurisdiction that hears criminal cases involving indictable offences.

Crown Prosecution Service (CPS): a government department set up in 1985 responsible for the public prosecution of offenders.

damages: monetary compensation awarded to the successful party at a trial.

defence: the accused party.

defendant: a person against whom legal proceedings are started.

evidence: proof.

examination-in-chief: questions addressed to a witness by the prosecutor.

exhibit: an object or document submitted for the record and introduced as evidence in court.

fast track: the procedure for rapid hearing of simpler and/or lower value cases.

foreman: someone chosen by the jury from among their number to announce their decision.

guilty: responsible in law for a criminal act.

indictment: a formal written statement charging a person with an offence.

jury: in a criminal case, a group of twelve citizens assembled to judge the guilt or innocence of a person charged with a criminal offence; in a civil case, a group of ten citizens (in the High Court) or eight citizens (in the County Court) charged with determining the facts at issue between the parties.

lay *(v.)* **an information**: initiate criminal proceedings.

leading question: a question which attempts to guide the respondent's answers, by suggesting its own answer.

leapfrog procedure: a process by which an appeal is not referred to a court immediately above the trial court but to a superior court.

liability: the fact of being legally responsible for a civil wrong.

lodge *(v.)* **an appeal**: make a request – on the part of a losing party – for a review or re-hearing of a decision.

magistrates' court: court of first instance generally dealing in criminal jurisdiction (summary offences) but also some areas of civil jurisdiction (debt collection, application for licences, recovery of income tax).

miscarriage of justice: a wrongful conviction and sentencing of a person for a crime.

multi-track: the process by which cases worth over £15,000, or which are unusually complex, are dealt with under the supervision of a judge and tailored to each case.

not guilty: not responsible for a criminal act.

opening speech: a speech by the prosecution advocate in a criminal case (or by the claimant's advocate in a civil claim) before any evidence is called, setting out the issues between the parties.

plea: a defendant's formal response of guilty or not guilty to criminal charges brought against him.

prosecution: the accusing party in a criminal trial.

re-examination: a further examination of a witness by the advocate who called him, following cross-examination by the opposing party.

remedies: the options available to a court to give redress to a party that has been wronged. They include awards of damages, injunctions and declarations of rights.

sentence: sanction.

serve *(v.)* **on someone**: send or hand someone an official document.

small claims: the cases involving claims for small amounts of damages.

speech in mitigation : a speech explaining circumstances surrounding an offence, or about an offender, made with the intention of persuading a court impose a lenient sentence.

summary trial: a trial in the magistrates' court.

summons: a legal document issued by a court and addressed to a party or a witness in the course of legal proceedings.

superintendent: rank in the police force between Chief Inspector and Chief Superintendent.

venue: a place in which a certain mode of trial is conducted (the magistrates' court for summary offences or the Crown Court for indictable offences).

verdict: the pronouncement of guilt or innocence by a judge, court, or jury.

witness: a person who was at the scene of a crime and observed the events or whose participation in a trial could enlighten the court as to the facts and issues involved in the case.

Exercises

1 **Choose the appropriate ending for each sentence.**

1. Witnesses can be examined
   a. once.
   b. three times.
   c. as many times as desired by the parties.

2. Crown court trial procedure is similar to
   a. county court trial proceedings.
   b. magistrates' court trial proceedings.
   c. High Court trial proceedings.

3. The judge instructs the jury
   a. as to what the relevant law is.
   b. to convict the defendant.
   c. to acquit the defendant.
4. The pre-trial hearing of an indictable offence is dealt with
   a. by the Crown Prosecution Service.
   b. in the Crown Court.
   c. in the magistrates' court.
5. In cases where indictable offences are tried, the prosecution
   a. has detailed information on the defendant's strategy.
   b. has information as to which witnesses will be called.
   c. does not have any relevant information.
6. A prosecution can commence by
   a. an allocation questionnaire served on the claimant.
   b. a claim form served on the defendant.
   c. a summons served on the alleged offender.
7. Appeals on points of law from a magistrates' court can be heard by
   a. the Crown Court.
   b. the Court of Appeal.
   c. the Administrative Court.
8. Guilty pleas can be entered
   a. in summary trials.
   b. in trials on indictment.
   c. in civil trials.
9. Counsel start the trial with a speech aimed at informing
   a. the judge of the facts, since in most cases the judge did not have time to read the statements.
   b. the magistrate of the law, since magistrates are not legally trained.
   c. the judge of the time that the trial will last.
10. A Part 36 payment is advantageous to
   a. the claimant only.
   b. the defendant only.
   c. both.
11. The county court allocates non-personal injury claims below £5,000 to
   a. the small claims procedure.
   b. the fast track procedure.
   c. the multi-track procedure.
12. The new CPR rules aim to
   a. increase the number of people instructing counsel to appear in court.
   b. increase the number of court cases.
   c. decrease the number of hearings.

13. In a trial, the defendant's barrister
a. always starts the proceedings to ensure that the interests of justice are secured.
b. usually presents his case after the conclusion of the claimant's case to counter the accusations levelled against his client.
c. can interrupt the claimant's barrister at any time to guarantee a fair trial for the claimant.

14. Claims above £10,000 can be heard by
a. the county court.
b. the High Court.
c. the Divisional Court.

15. A statement of case by a solicitor is sent
a. after the claim form is issued and served on the defendant.
b. before the claim form is issued and served on the defendant.
c. at the same time as the claim form is issued and served on the defendant.

2 Complete the text with the words below.

Court Service	summons	small claims	multi-track
appeal	costs	cross examine	claim
writ	fast track	county court	High Court judge

A party wishing to issue proceedings must complete a ...... form (formerly called a ...... or a ......). This should be taken or sent to the court office. These forms are issued by the .... [...] Claims not exceeding £5,000 will normally be allocated to the ...... track. They will normally be heard in the ...... by a district judge, with ...... only where there is a serious irregularity affecting the proceedings, to a circuit judge unless a circuit judge hears the case when there may be an appeal to a .... A serious irregularity could exist where the district judge had, e.g. failed to allow a party to ...... a witness. Claims over £5,000 but not exceeding £15,000 will normally be allocated to the ...... where the trial will take place within 30 weeks of allocation. The length of the trial will be no more than one day and there is a cap on lawyers advocacy .... [...] Where the claim is over £15,000, it will normally be allocated to the ....

Denis Keenan in *Smith and Keenan's English Law*, 13th ed. Longman, 2001, pp. 139-143.

3 Find the words in the text corresponding to the following definitions.

1. A person making a claim.
2. The examination of a defendant by the defendant's advocate.
3. The person/company against whom a claim is made.
4. The form for starting a case.
5. The claimant's solicitor examines a witness on points raised by the cross-examination.
6. A defendant pays a sum of money to the court.

7. The long and complex proceedings for cases involving claims above £15,000.
8. The examination of a claimant's witness by the defendant's counsel.
9. Giving the defendant papers from the court.
10. The claimant's barrister presents the facts and the issue to be resolved.
11. Civil proceedings.
12. A speech made by the defence to convince magistrates to hand down a lenient sentence.
13. A group of magistrates or judges sitting in a court.

4 **Match each word (1-6) with its antonym (A-F) and write a sentence containing both terms.**

1. grant	**A.** undefended
2. plaintiff	**B.** reverse
3. acquit	**C.** defendant
4. charge	**D.** convict
5. affirm	**E.** discharge
6. defended	**F.** deny

5 **Criminal moot court.**
a. Read the facts of the case below and write a paragraph describing the likely procedure at the police station.
b. Stage a moot trial of the young man. Which court has jurisdiction here and why?

Facts

A woman reports to the police that an individual has been seen acting suspiciously around a payphone on Friday at 10 pm. The police, arriving on the scene, spot a man and follow him as he makes his way to a second nearby payphone. They see the man tampering with the machine in a way that more than strongly suggests he is breaking it to retrieve coins. The police then arrest him for causing criminal damage. At the police station, a bag full of coins (£78) is found in the inside pocket of the man's coat as well as a crowbar (i.e. a tool used to lift or open things).

Characters
The defendant: Mr Stephen Taylor, 22 years old, no prior convictions.
The defence lawyer: Lindsey Thomas.
The prosecutor: Helen Gable.
The witness: Celia Merryweather.
A police constable: Henry Adams.
A judge/judges/magistrates.
An usher.
A British Telecom expert: Philip Hassan.

Preparing the trial

You can be creative but stick to the procedure! Do not forget that the prosecution speaks first. Make sure you do not overlook important stages in the process, such as the swearing in of the witnesses by the court clerk.

Do not forget that the judge or chairman of the magistrates oversees the proceedings.

Consider the following questions and prepare your case according to your part in the proceedings: Was the act deliberate? Did it occur only once? How serious were the consequences of the act? Were there any mitigating factors?

Useful courtroom language

My friend *(solicitor to solicitor)*

My learned friend *(barrister to barrister)*

I appear for the prosecution.

"I swear by almighty God that the evidence I shall give shall be the truth, the whole truth and nothing but the truth," or "I solemnly swear that the evidence I shall give shall be the truth, the whole truth and nothing but the truth." *(the oath)*

Counsel, do you have any more questions?

I have no further questions, Sir/Madam.

This closes the evidence of the prosecution.

The Bench will retire.

6 Civil moot court.

a. Fill in and serve the claim form in this case.
b. Stage the trial in the county court.

Facts

In August 2000, Mr Jones had a 100 sq.ft. extension built to his house for £30,000 by a company called Dumont and Co., builders. Two weeks after being built, the extension collapsed, thankfully without injuring anyone, but damaging £5,000 worth of furniture that had been moved into the extension.

Mr Jones was very angry and called an expert, Mr Roger, to inspect the building and Mr Roger found that the building had been poorly built with poor quality materials.

Mr Jones then decided to sue Dumont and Co. for damages. On seeing the statement of the other party's expert, Mr Dumont, the CEO of Dumont and Co. decided to instruct their own expert, Mr Sharpee, to inspect the damage. The conclusions of

Mr Sharpee were slightly different from those of Mr Roger. The former concluded that the collapse of the building was caused by a leak from the sewage under the extension, making the ground less secure, and by a hole bored by Mrs Jones in the wall to attach the clothes-line to hang her linen on.

Since an out-of-court settlement was not reached, the case proceeded to trial.

Characters
The judge
Mr. Roger, an expert
Mr. Sharpee, an expert
Mr Dumont
Mr Lamb, Dumont's employee who built the extension
Mrs Daisy, the architect who designed the building
Mr Jones
Mrs Jones
Mr High, Mr Jones's lawyer (with or without junior counsel)
Mr Bailey, Mr Dumont's barrister or solicitor

Preparing for trial
There are a certain number of questions you should ask yourself before starting the trial:
• If you are a judge or lawyer:
– What are the facts that need to be established to determine liability or guilt?
– What are the questions you should ask?
• If you are a witness
– How are you involved in the litigation?
– What should your testimony prove?
– What should you avoid saying?

What the witnesses did but do not wish to tell
1. First expert, Mr. Roger: he is no longer a member of the body regulating his profession because of previous malpractice.
2. Second expert, Mr. Sharpee: he was paid to write a statement in favour of his client.
3. Mr Dumont: he is almost bankrupt.
4. Mr Lamb (Dumont's employee who built the extension): he was drunk when he built the foundations of the extension.
5. Mrs Daisy (the architect who designed the building): she never graduated as an architect but as an interior designer.
6. Mrs Jones: she did bore a hole in the wall and damaged a pillar holding the building together.

7 Role play and research. Choose one of the following situations.

1. A is a shop-owner who has a claim against a supplier. B is a legal advisor from the Citizen's Advice Bureau. A phones B to inquire about how to file a civil claim.

2. Log on to the Citizens Advice Bureau website. Find the helpline telephone number and the UK telephone country code as well as the helpline's opening hours. Then imagine a situation that might lead to a claim and phone the CAB to gather the required information. Take notes. Report to your peers.

8 Discuss.

1. Compare proceedings in magistrates' courts and county courts.

2. What are the safeguards that English law provides to protect criminal defendants?

2. More about...

A. The work of the courts: juries

Juries generally consist of twelve jurors. They are each randomly selected from the electoral register for the locality of the court. As stated in the Criminal Justice Act 2003, most people between the ages of 18 and 69 are eligible. However, people with certain criminal convictions, those who are on bail awaiting trial and people with severe mental problems are exempted from jury service. Before the 2003 Act, these exemptions included people who did not have a sufficient understanding of English and certain occupations such as students, teachers, the armed forces, MPs and members of closed religious orders. When summoned, jurors can defer service for up to twelve months if they have a good reason. If the trial is expected to be long, the judge will ask the jurors whether any of them would have a problem in serving on such a case. If employment-related grounds are cited, the juror must be able to argue that they are the only ones who can do a particular professional task in the time the jury service is thought to take. For example, self-employed people who might lose their business if jury duty is too long are likely to be heard sympathetically. In the course of the service, the courts reimburse some lost earnings and travel costs and also provide a catering allowance.

When a court requires a jury, a large number of potential jurors are asked to appear. Twelve names are drawn from the list in the final selection and those people are sworn in. For this, jurors can either take an oath swearing on a religious book or make a non-denominational affirmation.

At the end of the trial the jury members return to the jury assembly area and may serve in another trial. Jury service usually lasts ten working days, although members can be dismissed earlier. In the case of a long trial, members must attend the court hearings every day until the trial ends even if the trial lasts for months. Failure to attend jury service is an offence and can be punished.

The key principles

There are two main principles that jurors must bear in mind when considering evidence and reaching a verdict:

• Everyone who stands trial is innocent until proved guilty. The presumption of innocence is one of the key principles of English law and is enshrined in the Universal Declaration of Human Rights. A defendant is presumed to be innocent until a jury reaches a guilty verdict based on the evidence presented in a fair trial.

• The case against the defendant must be proved beyond reasonable doubt. The jury must be convinced that there is no alternative explanation of the evidence that would exonerate the defendant. Defendants can therefore be acquitted even if they are believed to be guilty because the jury feels that the case against them is not conclusive and has not been proved beyond reasonable doubt.

Information from the Department of Education and Skills
(http://www.teachernet.gov.uk).

B. The work of the courts: principles of statutory interpretation

1. The literal rule (the plain meaning rule)

The literal rule means taking the words of an Act in their natural, literal and ordinary meaning.

> The only rule for the construction of Acts of Parliament is that they should be construed according to the intent of the Parliament which passed the Act. If the words of the statute are in themselves precise and unambiguous, then no more can be necessary than to expound those words in their natural and ordinary sense. The words themselves alone do, in such case, best declare the intention of the lawgiver. But if any doubt arises from the terms employed by the legislature, it has always been held a safe means of collecting the intention to call in aid the ground and cause of making the statute, and to have recourse to the preamble [...].
>
> The Sussex Peerage Case [1843-60] All ER Rep 55 per Tindal CJ at 64-65.

2. The golden rule

The golden rule provides that words should be given their ordinary meaning as much as possible, but only to the extent that they do not produce an absurd or totally obnoxious result.

I have been long and deeply impressed with the wisdom of the rule, now I believe universally adopted – at least, in the courts of law in Westminster Hall, that in construing wills, and indeed statutes, and all written instruments, the grammatical and ordinary sense of the words is to be adhered to, unless that would lead to some absurdity or some repugnance or inconsistency with the rest of the instrument, in which case the grammatical and ordinary sense of the words may be modified so as to avoid that absurdity or inconsistency, but no further.

Grey and others v Pearson and others [1843-60] All ER Rep 21 *per* Lord Wensleydale at 37.

3. The mischief rule

The mischief rule is one applied by judges in order to discover what "mischief" Parliament wanted to remedy.

Heydon's Case [1584] 3 Co Rep 7a: For the sure and true interpretation of all statutes in general, be they penal or beneficial, restrictive or enlarging of the common law, four things are to be discerned and considered: (a) What was the common law before the making of the Act; (b) what was the mischief and defect for which the common law did not provide; (c) what remedy the Parliament has resolved and appointed to cure the disease of the common-wealth; and (d) the truc reason of the remedy (*per curiam*).

http://www.lexisnexis.com

Exercises

1 **Read the case summary and answer the following questions.**

In the case *Adler v George* [1964], the defendant had obstructed HM forces in a prohibited place (an army base). The Act made it an offence to obstruct HM Forces "in the vicinity of" a prohibited place.
1. Using your knowledge of rules of statutory construction, which rule would you use?
2. Did the defendant commit an offence?

2 **Read the case summary and answer the following questions.**

In the case *Whiteley v Chappell* [1868], the defendant pretended to be someone who had died recently in order to vote in that person's place. The Act regulating the area stated that it was an offence to "personate any person entitled to vote".

1. Using your knowledge of rules of statutory construction, which rule would you use?
2. In your opinion, was the defendant found guilty?

3 **Read the case summary and answer the following questions.**

It is an offence to solicit "in a street or a public place for the purpose of prostitution". In the case *Smith v Hughes* [1960], six women were charged with solicitation although one was on a balcony and the other five behind the windows of rooms on the ground floor.
1. Using your knowledge of rules of statutory construction, which rule would you use?
2. Did the defendants commit the offence of soliciting?

4. Rules of language

Ejusdem generis *(of the same kind)*

For example, where the general word "injury" follows the specific terms "shock", "burn", the word "injury" is read as applying to other items akin to electrical injuries since the items are specifically enumerated in the Act.

> The plaintiff, an electrician employed by the defendants, was instructed to install additional lighting in one of their sub-stations, which was being reconstructed. While moving through a passage between two pieces of equipment in the sub-station, to inspect certain machinery, his foot missed the edge of an open duct […], and he fell and sustained injuries. […] The plaintiff alleged that the defendants were in breach of their statutory duty under the Electricity (Factories Act) Special Regulations, 1908 and 1944, reg 26, in that the part of the premises where the accident occurred was not adequately lighted to prevent danger. The case is reported only as regards the claim for breach of statutory duty.
>
> Danger is defined in the Electricity (Factories Act) Special Regulations, 1908 and 1944, reg 26:
>
> "'Danger' means danger to health or danger to life or limb from shock, burn, or other injury [...], or from fire attendant upon the generation, transformation, distribution, or use of electrical energy."
>
> In my opinion the words "or other injury" must be read in this context strictly *ejusdem generis* with "shock or burn", viz, as, "or other injury" due to electrical energy.
>
> *Lane v London Electricity Board* [1955] 1 All ER 324 *per* Parker LJ at 325.

Noscitur a sociis *(known from associates)*

If the meaning of words or phrases in a statute is questionable or doubtful, the meaning may be ascertained by reference to the meaning of other words or phrases associated with it.

Defendants had broken s.28(1) of the Factories Act 1961, which says: "All floors [...] shall, so far as is reasonably practicable, be kept free from any obstruction... "

The plaintiff said that the reels on the floor were an obstruction, and the judge has so held. But the judge held that plaintiff was two-thirds to blame and the defendants only one-third. He apportioned the damages accordingly.

The defendant appeals to this court. The short point is whether in point of law these big reels were an "obstruction" on the floor [...]. The word "obstruction" is not capable of precise definition, and I do not think it wise to attempt it. In one sense anything that is on a floor is an obstruction. If you want to walk straight across a room, even a table or a chair may be an obstruction in your path. If you carried it thus far, you might say that a machine on a factory floor was an obstruction. Even one of these racks in this storeroom would be an obstruction. That would be absurd. In this section, an "obstruction" is something on the floor that has no business to be there, and which is a source of risk to persons ordinarily using the floor. It is the duty of the occupier to keep the floor free of it, so far as is reasonably practicable [...]. It seems to me that these reels of paper were no more an obstruction than the racks themselves. This floor was used as a place on which to store reels of paper, no matter whether in racks or on the floor itself. It cannot be said that the reels had no business to be there. Nor can it be said that they were a source of risk to persons ordinarily using the place. The floor had been used in this way for years without any mishap whatever.

Pengelley v Bell Punch Co Ltd [1964] 2 All ER 945 *per* Lord Denning at 947.

Expressio unius est exclusio alterius

This rule of statutory interpretation assumes that the legislature intentionally specifies one set of criteria as opposed to the other. Therefore, if an item is not specifically named in the statute, it must be assumed the statute does not apply to the case mentioned.

The relevant provisions of the Act, for present purposes, are contained in s 1(1) and (3) and are as follows:

(1) Where after the commencement of this Act − (a) an employee suffers personal injury in the course of his employment in consequence of a defect in

equipment provided by his employer for the purposes of the employer's business [...]

(3) In this section [...] "equipment" includes any plant and machinery, vehicle, aircraft and clothing [...]

The key word in the definition is the word "any" and it underlines, in my judgment, what I would in any event have supposed to be the case, having regard to the purpose of the Act, that is to say that it should be widely construed so as to embrace every article of whatever kind furnished by the employer for the purposes of his business. Thus it is not just particular plant and machinery or vehicles (for instance, a combine harvester) or particular types of aircraft (for instance, a crop-spraying aeroplane) which are to be regarded as "equipment" but plant and machinery, vehicles, aircraft and clothing of all types and sizes subject only to the limitation that they are provided for the purposes of the employer's business.

It is certainly curious that, having resolved to refer specifically to means of transport, the draughtsman should have omitted to refer in terms to water transport. Indeed, it is difficult to see why, after the express inclusion of "plant and machinery", it was thought necessary to refer to any further examples. [...]

It must, in the light of this, be at least doubtful whether, in the context of this Act, the expression 'plant and machinery' is properly to be construed as including ships, and I am, for my part, content to approach the problem on the footing that it is not. [...] Whatever may be embraced in the expression "plant and machinery" it quite clearly includes any machinery installed in or affixed to a ship in the absence of some compelling context to the contrary; and there is no context whatever in this Act for reading the expression as excluding maritime machinery from 'any' plant and machinery. Unless, therefore, one is to read the Act as if it contained some unexpressed limitation excluding from its operation plant or machinery which comes to be installed in a ship, the exclusion from the definition of "equipment" of a ship itself produces the absurd position that the employer is liable for injury caused by defective machinery on or in the ship but not for injury caused by anything which can properly be described as constituting the ship itself, i.e. the hull or a part of the hull. This at once raises almost insoluble problems of demarcation between those constituent parts of the ship which may properly be described as "plant"or "machinery" and those parts which are properly to be described as the hull or parts of the hull. There simply is no context in the Act which enables one to read "equipment" as including the ship's winches, derricks, generators, pumps, engine-room plant, steering gear and so on, but as excluding the structure of the ship itself.

Coltman v Bibby Tankers Ltd [1987] 3 All ER 1068 *per* Lord Oliver of Aylmerton at
1071-2 and 1074-5.

1 **Read the case summary and answer the following questions.**

It was a statutory offence to use a "house, office, room or other place for betting" as stated in s.1 of the Betting Act 1853. Tattersall's Ring, from which the defendant operated, was an outdoor area at the race course.

1. Using your knowledge of rules of language, which rule would you apply?

2. Was the defendant guilty of committing the offence?

2 **Read the case summary and answer the following questions.**

An Act required that contracts for the sale of "goods, wares and merchandises" has to be written down. In the case *Tempest v Kilner* [1846], the issue at stake was whether the statute applied to a contract for the sale of stocks and shares.

1. Using your knowledge of rules of language, which rule would you apply?

2. Did the statute apply?

3 **Read the case summary and answer the following questions.**

A statute held that all houses open at night for "public refreshment, resort and entertainment" had to be licensed. In the case *Muir v Keay* [1875] a café owner argued that his house did not need a licence because he did not provide any form of entertainment.

1. Using your knowledge of rules of language, which rule would you apply?

2. Did the defendant need to take out a licence?

4 **Research project.**

Sarah went to a nightclub. She met Peter and they had several drinks together. At the end of the evening, Peter drove her home and accompanied her to her apartment. She then asked him to leave but they had sex before Peter went back to his place. Because Sarah kissed him after asking him to leave her alone, Peter thought Sarah had consented to having sex with him. The next morning Sarah was outraged that Peter had taken advantage of the fact that she was drunk in order to have sex with her. She phoned her best friend, a trainee solicitor, to know whether she could have Peter prosecuted for rape.

1. How would you explain to Sarah:
  – the steps she has to take to have Peter prosecuted?
  – the different stages of a trial?
  – Sarah's role as a witness?

2. In your opinion, is Peter likely to be convicted of rape? Help is provided in the following extract of the Sexual Offences Act 2003.

> **Rape**
>
> (1) A person (A) commits an offence if
>
> (a) he intentionally penetrates the vagina, anus or mouth of another person (B) with his penis,
>
> (b) B does not consent to the penetration, and
>
> (c) A does not reasonably believe that B consents.
>
> (2) Whether a belief is reasonable is to be determined having regard to all the circumstances, including any steps A has taken to ascertain whether B consents.

3. Off the presses

A. Initiation of proceedings in a county court: a claim form (see pages 166-167)

`Exercise`

Research project.

Mrs Arabella Bane had her roof repaired by Repairs and Co. Two weeks later Mrs Bane's roof started leaking again. She called Repairs and Co. several times but no one answered her calls or got back to her. In despair, Mrs Bane called an independent workman, Mr Brown, to fix her roof, because the leak was threatening to damage the ceiling of her TV area. This cost her £550 + VAT on top of the £760 + VAT she had already paid to Repairs and Co. She sent the following letter to Repairs and Co.

---

2 Winter Gardens

Anytown

23rd October 2006

Dear Mrs Smith,

You came to repair my roof on September 1st, 2006. I rang you on September 14th, on September 16th and again on September 18th to tell you it was leaking again.

You did not call me back, so I had to get someone else to come and repair it on September 20th which cost £550 + VAT.

In a letter dated September 23rd, I wrote to you that I thought you ought to pay for these repairs because it was the work you should have done. You have neither paid for them nor answered my letter.
If you do not pay me by October 30th, I will issue a county court claim against you.

Yours sincerely,

A. Bone

Mrs A. Bane

1. Mrs Bane goes to see her solicitor to start civil proceedings against Repairs and Co. Can you help her fill in her claim form?
2. Access the Court Service website and determine the fees the claimant and the defendant will have to pay to the courts for these proceedings.

B. The trial of a GP

Jury clears former GP of murdering patients with morphine doses
Relatives and detective shocked by verdict. Campaigners say trial shows law's lack of clarity

A retired GP was cleared yesterday of murdering three patients with heavy overdoses of morphine painkiller.

After a long trial and a judge's summing-up which lasted almost a week, a jury decided that Howard Martin had not been "playing God" in his treatment of two men who were suffering from aggressive cancers and a third who had senile dementia.

As Dr Martin, 71, left Teesside Crown Court he described his relief at the end of "a year and a half under house arrest, and eight weeks of hell on earth". Relatives of the patients, all from the Newton Aycliffe area in County Durham, where Dr Martin practised, were visibly shocked when the jury of six women and six men gave their unanimous verdict.

The Voluntary Euthanasia Society said that the 33-day trial, the biggest investigation in Durham police's history, showed how British law "struggles to distinguish murder from mercy". The society's chief executive, Deborah Annetts, said: "It shows the lack of clarity in the law surrounding decision making at the end of life. It was all about what the doctor intended. People may be surprised to discover that it makes no difference what the patients wanted. Bad practice is not being properly exposed and good doctors are not being properly supported or protected. The sooner we move to a system that allows a patient's wishes to be respected, with proper safeguards, the better-protected patients will be."

Dr Martin, a practising Christian and former army officer, did not give evidence during the trial. The defence barrister, Anthony Arlidge, QC, called expert witnesses who said that the patients were close to death. Mr Arlidge also argued that the prosecution had failed to prove that the morphine doses were lethal or that Dr Martin knew exactly what effects his prescriptions would have.

The GP's 80-year-old wife, Theresa, burst into tears of relief as he was acquitted of murdering Frank Moss, 59, and Harry Gittins and Stanley Weldon, who were both 74, between March 2003 and January last year. Dr Martin, who retired from medicine in the north-east to live in Penmaenmawr, Gwynedd, north Wales, was accused of intending to kill the three patients after relatives of Mr Gittins complained of his treatment and forensic science tests found large traces of morphine. Exhumations were then carried out on the bodies of the other two men.

Mr Gittins' family said the verdicts had left them and the relatives of the other patients devastated. Detective Superintendent Harry Stephenson said he shared their feelings: "In my 31 years as a police officer, this is one of my most disappointing days." Police will consider whether checks should be made on a number of other deaths of patients of Dr Martin.

The GP's solicitor, Sara Mason, said afterwards: "Dr Martin has always maintained that he was doing no more than doing his best to relieve the suffering of these three patients. Being prosecuted for murder came as a particularly bitter blow as he has spent nearly 50 years of his life caring for others, at personal sacrifice."

Martin Wainwright, *The Guardian* (http://www.guardian.co.uk).

Exercises

1 **Answer the following questions on the article.**

1. What was Howard Martin charged with?

2. Using the characteristics of the trial, describe the jury's situation.

3. What was the reaction of the patients' relatives? Why?

4. Sum up the Voluntary Euthanasia Society's position.

5. Describe the legal problem this case exposes.

6. What strategy did counsel for the defendant use in the trial?

7. What initiated Dr Martin's indictment?

8. Explain the position of the police in this case.

9. How does Sara Mason's declaration fit with Anthony Arlidge's defence?

10. What general feeling does this article give? Is the journalist objective?

2 Discuss.

1. British law 'struggles to distinguish murder from mercy'. Discuss.

2. What is the real debate here? Give your own opinion on this issue.

4. Food for thought

Guildford Four released after 15 years (1989)

The Guildford Four have had their convictions quashed by the Court of Appeal following an extensive inquiry into the original police investigation. As he emerged from the court, one of the four, Gerard Conlon, announced to the waiting crowds: "I have been in prison for something I did not do. I am totally innocent."

"The Maguire seven are innocent. Let's hope the Birmingham six are freed," he added. The investigation into the case, considered to be the biggest miscarriage of justice in Britain, was carried out by Avon and Somerset Police. They found serious flaws in the way Surrey police noted the confessions of the four.

The confession of Patrick Armstrong was central to the investigation and the inquiry concluded the notes taken were not written up immediately and officers may have colluded in the wording of the statements.

Roy Amlott QC said in court: "New evidence of great significance has come to light after a police inquiry. It has thrown such doubt on the honesty and integrity of a number of Surrey police officers investigating this case [that] the Crown is now unable to say that the convictions of any of the four were safe or satisfactory," he added.

The Guildford Four – as they were dubbed – were jailed for life in 1975 for bombing pubs in Guildford. The attacks left five people dead and over 100 injured. Paul Hill and Patrick Armstrong were also wrongfully sentenced for a bomb attack in Woolwich that killed two people. They each served 15 years in prison. Gerard Conlon, Patrick Armstrong and Carole Richardson were released immediately while Paul Hill was taken to a Belfast prison. He is serving time for the murder of a British soldier, Brian Shaw, but is expected to be released soon.

Three of the police officers who conducted the original interviews have now been suspended by Surrey police. Two others have already left the force. Home Secretary Douglas Hurd has ordered an immediate judicial inquiry into the case as well as an official criminal investigation into the conduct of the officers involved.

"We must all, I believe, feel anxiety, regret and deep concern at what has occurred," he said.

http://www.bbc.co.uk

Examining injustice in the UK

Numerous miscarriages of justice have come to light in the last 15 years, but have changes to the law made fresh tragedies impossible or is there a need for a more radical and fundamental reform of the criminal justice system?

Rumblings of discontent with the British criminal justice system began to grow in the 1980s. Campaigns started to spring up around individual cases. The phrase "miscarriage of justice" was crystallised around two big cases – the Birmingham Six and the Guildford Four. Both stemmed from IRA outrages against civilian targets at the height of the bombing campaign. Police appeared to have quickly rounded up the suspects and brought them to justice. In reality the wrong men had been convicted. It was only due to the determination and investigative skills of a TV documentary team and MP Chris Mullin, himself a former journalist, that the injustice suffered by the Birmingham Six came to light. When they were released by the Court of Appeal in 1989 it seemed there was hope for dozens of prisoners who had been pleading their innocence in vain for years. Other campaigns sprung up and gradually, over the next 11 years, many of these succeeded - including the Guildford Four, Judith Ward, the Darvell brothers, the Cardiff Three, Danny McNamee, the M25 Three and the Bridgewater Four. Even cases from beyond the grave, such as Derek Bentley and Hussein Mattan, have been revisited and names cleared. But there are still many people in prison proclaiming their innocence. A miscarriage of justice can result from non-disclosure of evidence by police or prosecution, fabrication of evidence, poor identification, overestimation of the evidential value of expert testimony, unreliable confessions due to police pressure or psychological instability and misdirection by a judge during trial. Since 1984 two pieces of legislation have been introduced in an attempt to prevent further miscarriages. The Police And Criminal Evidence Act (PACE) gave detectives rigid rules on how long they could question suspects for and insisted interviews be taped to ensure there was no mistreatment or undue intimidation. The Criminal Procedure and Investigations Act was also introduced in an attempt to make sure police or the Crown Prosecution Service (CPS) disclose to the defence everything which could be relevant to their case. However a recent review of disclosure undertaken by the Crown Prosecution Service Inspectorate found the CPIA did not have the "confidence of criminal practitioners".

Adversarial system under attack

Paddy Hill, one of the Birmingham Six, is sceptical such legislation is enough. Mr Hill, who has set up his own pressure group *Miscarriages Of Justice Organisation* (MOJO), told BBC News Online: "Justice is something that is not on this government's curriculum." He said the criminal justice system needed a radical overhaul to make it "more open and accountable". Mr Hill would like to see:

    – The adversarial system replaced with a continental-style inquisitorial system, where the driving motive behind any police investigation is the search for the truth.

    – Juries forced to give their verdicts in writing, to amplify on their reasons and guard against the danger of "perverse" verdicts.

    – Judges and other judicial officials being elected, rather than chosen by "the establishment".

    – Changes in the law to ensure police officers who break the law are convicted and sent to prison.

    Kevin Christian, whose brother Derek is serving a life sentence for a murder he denies committing, is a member of the pressure group *Innocent*. He told BBC News Online: "The biggest problem seems to be the Court of Appeal and its lack of willingness to recognise and correct errors. The Guildford Four is a prime example. Even after the Balcombe Street Gang had admitted they were responsible for the Woolwich bomb, the Court of Appeal would not even entertain the possibility that the Guildford Four were innocent. The adversarial system means that the criminal justice system can easily turn into an upmarket local dramatic society with the two main protagonists being the prosecuting and defence counsel, the difference being that the defence counsel may not have had time to learn his lines before the curtain goes up." Mr Christian favours the French system of investigating magistrates or the Staatsanwalte in Germany, in which the prosecuting lawyers are involved from the outset. "A mixture of circumstantial evidence and tenuous or contentious forensic evidence can be very tempting to a jury. Many miscarriages result, ironically, from weak prosecution cases. Where there is very little in the way of a prosecution case to dismantle, it is very difficult to mount a cogent defence case," he said.

Investigating alleged miscarriages

The Criminal Cases Review Commission was set up by the last government in an attempt to investigate alleged miscarriages of justice properly. It is an independent body responsible for investigating alleged miscarriages in England, Wales and Northern Ireland. The commission has 14 members including chairman Sir Frederick Crawford, barrister Jill Gort, former chief constable Baden Gitt and journalist David Jessel, former presenter of Trial and Error and Rough Justice. Critics say it is under-funded, understaffed and not sufficiently independent. It currently has a backlog of 1,200 cases (about a third of all applications to date). Chris Mullin MP, a former journalist for TV's World In Action, said: "Miscarriages of justice can occur under any system and I have no doubt they will occur in the future." But Mr Mullin, nowadays a junior minister, told BBC News Online: "We should never be complacent. The system has improved considerably since the big miscarriages of the mid-1970s. PACE, which came in 1983, had regulated interviews and improved the treatment of suspects and just about all interrogations are now recorded. But the most important change is that people who believe they are the victims of miscarriages of justice have somewhere to go: the CCRC." He admitted the CCRC had a backlog and "could do with speeding up its handling of cases" but said it had a good track record. Mr Mullin said: "73% of cases which have been referred back to the Court of Appeal by the CCRC have resulted in quashed convictions." Mr Mullin admitted the adversarial system had flaws and said: "There is a strong case for a system which finds the truth, rather than a contest between skilled adversaries. But you should realise that the continental inquisitorial system had also led to miscarriages of justice."

Police role "exaggerated"

The Chief Constable of Kent, Sir David Phillips, is the Association of Chief Police Officers' spokesman on criminal justice and he admitted the system is not perfect. "It's not safe. Far too many guilty people are acquitted to the danger of the public. We are too often strangled by a system of rules and interpretation, which prevents us getting to the truth," he said. "While trials are contests, there is a high level of acquittals, which must mean either the police or the courts are getting it wrong. Very often the whole case is not heard. Juries are not able to put the whole picture together." Sir David does not believe the adversarial system needs replacing but he would like to see changes. He said: "The defence should have to disclose their evidence so the court can take control of it. There is no reason why the defence should be able to keep evidence secret so it can be used in an ambush." He believes there should be less of an emphasis on advocates' skills and more on the evidence. "Let the jury see the evidence. I am in favour of them seeing tapes of defendants being interviewed so they can make up their own minds," he said. As for the police's role in miscarriages of justice, Sir David believes it has been exaggerated. "In the CCRC's annual report they said that where things had gone wrong it was rarely the police's fault. It was usually the defence or the prosecution." When it comes to police officers who fabricate evidence to secure a conviction, he said ACPO was keener than anyone to see them prosecuted and convicted. "If people are going to tell lies about how they obtained evidence, you are going to have difficulties. Most cases of police corruption are discovered by the police and corrupt officers are one of our highest priorities to root out and prosecute," said Sir David.

http://www.bbc.co.uk

Exercise

Answer the following questions.

1. In your understanding, what are the mistakes at the origin of a miscarriage of justice?

2. Explain the different flaws of the justice system exposed in the two articles.
What is your opinion on the system described in this chapter?

5. Listening

Exercises

1 🔘 **Listen to an interview with a man in prison and complete the extract with the missing words. The man was convicted of murdering a young man who was attempting to burgle his home. His words, spoken by an actor, are taken from a real interview.**

TERRY MORTON: Well I haven't been exactly perfect myself. I've had speeding ...... but then I think most people have. You accept that - but when you want help from the police suddenly there isn't any help. I mean in my own particular case I've gone down a ...... over several years of giving them lots of ...... but they never do anything, so basically you are on your .... Well I'm afraid you are on your ...... aren't you? There was a meeting the other day. A Police ...... meeting, right? And the police were booing the Home Secretary. But at the end of the day there are policemen actually who are beginning to speak up. Like this Ted Houghton of the Police Federation. I read an article where he said they are talking about "oh we want another ...... policemen" – the Government is saying, but he says we want another .... But quite honestly you can have as many policemen as you like, but if you don't give them .... , it is like sending a stooge down to see you, isn't it? Isn't that right? Fill-in for what for the real thing, isn't it?

INTERVIEWER: Do the Labour Party take .... and the level of policing seriously in your opinion?

TERRY MORTON: Quite frankly both parties are suffering from ...... , aren't they? And ...... party actually has a .... All you are getting is .... It really doesn't make any difference whether the Labour Party gets in or the Conservative Party.

INTERVIEWER: So neither of them would be able to deal with rural policing?

TERRY MORTON: Well it's not just rural policing – it's all ...... , isn't it? The Law doesn't understand!

2 Answer the following questions.

1. What is Village Watch?
2. What is Terry Morton's attitude to the right to self defence?
3. What has been his relationship with the police?
4. How does he view the role of the police and what does he suggest to improve it?
5. Why does he refuse to answer the reporter's last question?
6. What is your perception of his position?

3 Discuss.

1. Do you think individuals should have an absolute right to self defence?
2. Is sending an individual to prison for killing a burglar the right form of sentence?

6. Grammar practice

Exercises

1 Prepositions. Complete each sentence with a preposition when necessary.

1. The parties reached ...... a settlement on Nov 3rd.
2. Claim forms are issued ...... the County Court.
3. Mrs Smith and Repairs and Co. have at last agreed ...... a common expert.
4. The defendant decided not to defend ...... the claim.
5. Judge Joris awarded £500 ...... damages to the claimant yesterday.

6. Repairs and Co. filled in a form setting ...... their case.

7. The parties have instructed ...... a joint expert. It is now expected that they will settle out of court.

8. Repairs and Co. paid £400 ...... the county ccourt before the start of the trial.

9. Mrs Smith's witness takes ...... the oath.

10. The burden of proof is ...... the prosecution.

11. The defence calls ...... two witnesses to establish the character of the defendant.

12. The court laid information ...... the defendant.

13. Mrs Brown accuses her neighbour ...... having broken her window pane.

14. Constable Peters charged Mrs Phillips ...... disorderly conduct.

2 **Spelling. For each word, circle the letter(s) that differ from the French spelling. Look up the words in a dictionary to check if the English meanings are different from the French ones.**

1. advantageous   **2.** levy (v.)   **3.** defer   **4.** reimburse   **5.** presumption   **6.** adhere   **7.** seize   **8.** address (verb and noun)   **9.** entertain   **10.** sum   **11.** salary   **12.** creditor   **13.** petty   **14.** exaggerate

3 **Expressing condition. Complete the sentences with the appropriate modal or verbal forms.**

1. If there is reason to believe that the presence of a solicitor ...... (cause harm to) other persons, or interfere with the enquiry or temper with evidence, access to a solicitor ...... (be denied) in exceptional circumstances detailed in the case *R v Samuel*.

2. If the trial was expected to be long, the judge ...... (ask) the jurors whether any of them ...... (have) a problem in serving on such a case.

3. If you carried it this far, you ...... (say) that a machine on a factory floor was an obstruction. Even one of these racks in this storeroom ...... (be) an obstruction. That ...... (be) absurd.

4. If the reform is approved, there ...... still (be) discretion for defendants who wish to have their cases heard by magistrates.

5. "If people are going to tell lies about how they have obtained evidence, you ...... (have) difficulties. Most cases of police corruption are discovered by the police and corrupt officers are one of our highest priorities to root out and prosecute."

6. Police will consider whether checks ...... (be made) on a number of other deaths of patients of Dr Martin.

7. Where the debt exceeds £750, bankruptcy or company insolvency proceedings ...... (consider). This ...... at least (ensure) that an insolvency practitioner – generally an accountant – ...... (be put) in charge of the debtors' assets.

4 **Indirect speech. Rewrite the following statements in indirect speech.**

1. A spokesman for the Department for Constitutional Affairs said: "Lord Falconer is a big reformer and this is the next step to make the criminal justice system more efficient."

2. "We must all, I believe, feel anxiety, regret and deep concern at what has occurred today," said Home Secretary Douglas Hurd.

3. Chris Mullin MP said: "Miscarriages of justice can occur under any system and I have no doubt they will occur in the future."

4. Mr Christian declared: "The adversarial system means that the criminal justice system can easily turn into an upmarket local dramatic society with the two main protagonists being the prosecuting and defence counsels, the difference being that the defence counsel may not have had time to learn his lines before the curtain goes up."

5. Deborah Annetts said: "It shows the lack of clarity in the law surrounding decision making at the end of life. [...] The sooner we move to a system that allows a patient's wishes to be respected, with proper safeguards, the better-protected patients will be."

6. Gerard Conlon announced to the waiting crowds: "I have been in prison for something I did not do. I am totally innocent."

5 **Have someone do something/make someone do something/get someone to do something. Look at the example, then rewrite the sentences using one of the three patterns.**

Example:
The solicitor obliged her client to confess the truth.
- The solicitor **had** her client **confess** the truth.
- The solicitor **made** her client **confess** the truth.
- The solicitor **got** her client **to confess** the truth. (strong pressure is implied)

1. After pressure from the defence, the magistrates agreed to hear the case.

2. The Court of Appeal quashed the convictions of the Guildford Four after years of lobbying.

3. You did not call me back, so I was obliged to employ another company to repair the roof.

4. Those pleading guilty to offences such as shoplifting, theft and criminal damage could have their sentence decided by a prosecutor in consultation with the police, instead of going before magistrates.

5. In order to comply with the court's decision, the defendant's employer had to deduct a specified sum from the defendant's wages.

Claim Form

In the

	for court use only
Claim No.	
Issue date	

Click here to clear your data after printing

Claimant

SEAL

Defendant(s)

Brief details of claim

Value

	£
Amount claimed	
Court fee	
Solicitor's costs	
Total amount	

Defendant's name and address

The court office at

is open between 10 am and 4 pm Monday to Friday. When corresponding with the court, please address forms or letters to the Court Manager and quote the claim number.

N1 Claim form (CPR Part 7) (01.02)   *Printed on behalf of The Court Service*

Claim No.	

Does, or will, your claim include any issues under the Human Rights Act 1998? ☐ Yes ☐ No

Particulars of Claim (attached)(to follow)

Statement of Truth
*(I believe)(The Claimant believes) that the facts stated in these particulars of claim are true.
* I am duly authorised by the claimant to sign this statement

Full name _____

Name of claimant's solicitor's firm _____

signed _____ position or office held_____
*(Claimant)(Litigation friend)(Claimant's solicitor)   (if signing on behalf of firm or company)
*delete as appropriate

Claimant's or claimant's solicitor's address to which documents or payments should be sent if different from overleaf including (if appropriate) details of DX, fax or e-mail.

http://www.hmcourts-service.gov.uk

Chapter 6

Criminal law

1. Fundamentals

Whatever their seriousness, offences against the State are called crimes. Although such offences, like theft for example, are often directed at individuals, the State has the right to prosecute and punish the perpetrators. Victims may also bring private prosecutions, which in itself does not exclude interventions from the State.

Is it a crime?

1. Definition

Part of criminal law consists in determining whether a wrongful act is a criminal offence or merely the result of an accident. Ill intentions may, however, be punished even if they have not had any harmful repercussions, such as in the case of attempted murder. To decide whether the action is criminal or not, criminal law usually looks to moral intent, which needs to be established and proved to be malicious beyond reasonable doubt. Should the **prosecution** fail to prove this or the facts be self-evident, the person whose action led to the resulting evil is not convicted. However, there are dangerous behaviours which, although they may not involve criminal intent, represent a threat for the community at large and are therefore punishable as criminal offences whether or not they have caused **injury**.

Emphasis should be laid on the fact that many crimes can be **torts** as well and vice versa. When a situation involves both a tort and a crime, the kind of legal proceeding brought against the defendant, rather than the act itself, establishes the distinction between a civil wrong and a criminal offence. A civil action, brought by the victim, aims at obtaining compensation for injury whereas a prosecution seeks to punish the perpetrator of a crime.

"As a matter of analysis we can think of a crime as being made up of three ingredients, *actus reus*, *mens rea* and (a negative element) absence of a valid defence." (D. J. Lanham, [1976] Crime LR 276).

Imposing liability in criminal law requires that the defendant be proved to have committed a guilty act with guilty intent. *Mens rea* is the Latin expression used in legal English to refer to the offender's ill-intended state of mind. *Actus reus* refers to the guilty act that must be established in a criminal case. The *actus reus* in itself helps define the **intention** behind the possible results of the action. Therefore, consequences need not always have occurred for an act to be taken into account as *actus reus*. To take an example: if someone had the intention to kill by poisoning, even if the dose of poison ingested by the victim was not sufficient to kill, the fact that poison was administered constitutes *actus reus* and is enough to prove the existence of *mens rea*. **State of affairs offences** may involve the defendant being caught preparing a crime or being in possession of illegal material. "Going equipped to steal", for example, constitutes an offence whether a theft actually occurred or not, since the defendant's preparations amount to *actus reus* and show criminal intent. In state of affairs crimes, the prosecution must prove the factual circumstances required to establish the offence.

Although a person may generally not be found criminally liable for an omission, *actus reus* may sometimes be found to exist when the defendant failed to perform a legal duty to take positive action. Such positive duties to act can be created statutorily, as under the Children and Young Persons Act 1933, which makes neglecting a child a crime.

There are cases in which providing evidence of *mens rea* is not required or in which *mens rea* is presumed by the courts, because the offence is "truly criminal in character" and represents a threat to the common good and society at large (e.g. the environment, public health, road traffic). **Liability** for such crimes may be said to be absolute. They are referred to as absolute offences of strict liability by statute. In those conditions the crime will automatically lead to penal **retribution**. Bigamy and abduction of a minor are offences of strict liability defined by statute.

2. *Valid defences*

In court, criminal defence lawyers often rely on the concept of *mens rea* to organise their defence strategy. Providing evidence that the person had little criminal responsibility in the ill he or she caused often constitutes the main purpose of the defence. The following series of "valid" defences can thus be put forward in order to prove the absence of *mens rea*:

1. Infancy

By statute, children under the age of 10 have no criminal responsibility. Above that age and until they reach 18, it is up to the prosecution to prove the child's awareness of the seriousness of the crime committed.

2. Insanity

A person proved to be suffering from severe mental illness or handicap at the time of the wrongful act will be acquitted. Insanity has to be proved on a **balance of probabilities** as opposed to "beyond reasonable doubt".

3. Diminished responsibility

This **defence** only applies to murder and allows the defendant to be found guilty of manslaughter instead of homicide. The burden of proof lies with the defence on a balance of probabilities.

4. Mistake

This term refers to an action lacking *mens rea*. However, in the case of unreasonable mistake, i.e. a deed that a reasonable man would not have done, the action amounts to negligence.

5. Intoxication

Intoxication is not valid as a sole defence and can never be an excuse for committing an act. If *mens rea* is proven, the defendant is guilty whether intoxication is voluntary or not. Involuntary intoxication and the absence of *mens rea* together lead to acquittal. The defence thus resides in proving the absence of *mens rea*. Intoxication can be found to lead to other defences such as mistake or insanity.

6. Duress and coercion

Both duress and coercion involve a person forced to commit a crime by another person using threat or violence.

7. Necessity

Necessity refers to very particular and unique situations, neither predictable nor definable, in which the defendant was bound to break the law, having to choose between two evils. The defendant was confronted with two alternatives, one involving the breaking of the law and the other causing harm to himself or to others. The defence will consist in proving that the latter outweighs the former.

8. Public and private defence

This concerns self-defence or the defence of someone else in the case of a crime against a person. It is to be understood that here the term "person" always refers to a human being and precludes organisations or corporations.

Categorisation of offences

In order for the punishment to be in adequacy with the offence, several criteria need to be taken into account in the categorisation of the offence. Distinction should be established between statutory offences and common law offences, summary offences and indictable offences, crimes against the State and crimes against public interest, crimes against property and those against the person.

The old distinction between felony and misdemeanour was abolished with the Criminal Law Act 1967. Yet these notions are still very much present in the terminology, due to the nature of the legal system based on judicial precedent. The past distinction has become one between serious and minor offences, coupled with a corresponding distinction between arrestable and non-arrestable offences. Arrestable offences include crimes as well as the attempts to commit crimes. The offenders can be apprehended without a warrant and in many cases are liable to a minimum of five years imprisonment.

The list below (by no means exhaustive) presents the main crimes and their legal terminology.

1. Homicide

1. Murder
A famous definition dates back to 1797: "Murder is when a man of sound memory, and of age of discretion, unlawfully killeth within any county of the realm any reasonable creature *in rerum natura* under the king's peace, with malice aforethought, either expressed by the party or implied by law [...]" (Coke, 3 Inst 47)

2. Manslaughter
Manslaughter includes all unlawful homicides that do not enter the category of murder. It can be voluntary (presenting the malice aforethought of murder but with some mitigating circumstances) or involuntary. Provocation must always be considered by the jury and can be part of the evidence leading to acquittal.

3. Offences ancillary to murder
Crimes in this category include solicitation, threats to kill and concealment of birth.

4. Complicity in suicide and suicide pacts
These offences are described in section 2 of the Suicide Act 1961 as such: "A person who aids, abets, counsels or procures the suicide of another or an attempt by another to commit suicide, shall be liable on conviction on indictment to imprisonment for a term not exceeding fourteen years." The murder of oneself, or suicide, ceased to be illegal with the Suicide Act.

5. Infanticide
Infanticide is the killing of a newborn baby or very young child. It is a lesser crime than murder if an infant under the age of twelve months is killed by its own mother in particular circumstances when she is considered disturbed. The Infanticide Act 1938 provides in s.1 (1): "Where a woman by any wilful act or omission causes the death of her child being a child under the age of twelve months, but at the time of

the act or omission the balance of her mind was disturbed by reason of her not having fully recovered from the effect of giving birth to the child or by reason of the effect of lactation consequent upon the birth of the child, then, notwithstanding that the circumstances were such that but for this Act the offence would have amounted to murder, shall be guilty of [an offence], to wit of infanticide, and may for such offence be dealt with and punished as if she had been guilty of the offence of manslaughter of the child."

6. Genocide
This crime covers the destruction of a national, ethnic, racial or religious group.

2. Other offences against the person

1. Assault and battery
An assault is an act in which the offender causes, intentionally or **recklessly**, what is felt as immediate and unlawful personal violence by the victim. A battery only differs from an assault in that, this time, violence includes any unlawful touching of the other, no matter how insignificant.

2. Aggravated assault
It refers to particularly heinous crimes for which severe punishment must be applied. Aggravated assault includes assault with intent to resist arrest, assault on resistance to or obstruction of constables, assault occasioning actual bodily harm and racially aggravated assault.

3. Wounding and grievous bodily harm
The Criminal Law Act 1967 provides: "Whosoever shall unlawfully and maliciously by any means whatsoever *wound* or *cause* any grievous bodily harm to any person with intent to do some grievous bodily harm to any person or with intent to resist or prevent the lawful apprehension or detainer of any person, shall be guilty of [an offence triable only on indictment], and being convicted thereof shall be liable to imprisonment of life. [...] Whosoever shall unlawfully and maliciously *wound* or *inflict* any grievous bodily harm upon any other person, either with or without any weapon or instrument shall be guilty of [an offence triable either way] and being convicted thereof shall be liable to imprisonment for five years."

4. Administering poison
The Offences against the Person Act 1861 makes it a crime to "unlawfully administer to or cause to be administered to or taken by any other person any poison or other destructive or noxious thing [...] so as thereby to endanger the life of such person, or so as thereby to inflict upon such person any grievous bodily harm."

5. False imprisonment
This crime consists in unlawfully restraining a person's freedom of movement. It includes confinement in a prison, a house (obviously even one's very own), a mine, a

vehicle, a public street or any other place. There are various types of false imprisonment, such as kidnapping, the taking of hostages and abduction of children.

6. Offensive weapons
The Firearms Act 1968 states that "any person who without lawful authority or reasonable excuse, the proof whereof shall lie on him, has with him in any public place an offensive weapon shall be guilty of an offence […]". The Public Order Act 1986 defines an offensive weapon as "any article made or adapted for use for causing injury to the person, or intended by the person having it with him for such use by him or by some other person."

7. Bomb hoaxes
Referring to a bomb hoax, the Criminal Act 1977 states that "a person who places any article in any place whatever; or dispatches any article by post, rail, or any other means whatever of sending things from one place to another, with the intention (in either case) of inducing in some other person a belief that it is likely to explode or ignite and thereby cause personal injury or damage to property is guilty of an offence."

3. Sexual offences

1. Rape
The Sexual Offences Act of 2003 defines rape as follows: "(1) A person (A) commits an offence if – (a) he intentionally penetrates the vagina, anus or mouth of another person (B) with his penis, (b) B does not consent to this penetration, and (c) A does not reasonably believe that B consents. (2) Whether a belief is reasonable is to be determined having regard to all the circumstances, including any steps A has taken to ascertain whether B consents (…). (4) A person guilty of an offence under this section is liable, on conviction of indictment, to imprisonment for life." The definition of rape includes offences committed within wedlock.

2. Other sexual offences
The Sexual Offences Act of 2003 provides criminal sanctions for a broad range of sex crimes besides rape which include assault by penetration, sexual assault and exposure. Sexual assault involves cases in which the offender intentionally touches another person in a sexual way and the person does not consent to the touching. The Act also deals with crimes perpetrated against children. Sexual activity of any kind by an adult with a young person under 16 is severely punished, and even more so if the child is under 13 years of age. People with a mental disorder impeding choice are similarly afforded protection from sexual abuse under the Act.

3. Procurement and Sexual Exploitation
Prostitution is not illegal *per se* in the UK. However, many activites surrounding prostitution do come within the scope of criminal law. Thus causing or inciting

prostitution for gain and controlling prostitution for gain in any part of the world carry a maximum term of 7 years' imprisonment. Despite recent debates on the issue, it is also still prohibited to keep, manage, or assist in the management of a brothel.

4. Road traffic offences

1. Careless driving

The Road Traffic Act 1991 states that "If a person drives a mechanically propelled vehicle on a road or other public place without due care and attention, or without reasonable consideration for other persons using the road or place, he is guilty of an offence." This offence is summary only and punishable by **fine**.

2. Dangerous driving

It is left to the court to evaluate the offence as objectively as possible according to two criteria: "[driving in a way] far below what would be expected of a competent and careful driver and [...] driving in a way that would seem dangerous [to the competent and careful driver]."

3. Causing death by dangerous or careless driving

This crime used to be likened to manslaughter, but today conviction of manslaughter is only applied in extraordinary circumstances. It is triable only on indictment and is punishable by a ten-year imprisonment sentence and/or a fine.

5. Theft

1. Theft

The Theft Act 1968 states: "A person is guilty of theft if he dishonestly appropriates property belonging to another with the intention of permanently depriving the other of it; and 'thief' and 'steal' shall be construed accordingly." The maximum sentence is seven years' imprisonment.

2. Abstracting electricity

S.13 of the Theft Act 1968 provides: "A person who dishonestly uses without due authority, or dishonestly causes to be wasted or diverted, any electricity shall on conviction on indictment be liable to imprisonment for a term not exceeding five years."

3. Robbery

Robbery refers to theft with the use of force, whether physical or not. In this respect it is considered aggravated theft.

Other types of theft include deception, cheating, making off without payment, false accounting, fraud, temporary deprivation, **blackmail**, burglary and aggravated burglary, going equipped (i.e. transporting the tools and instruments for the obvious purpose of committing those crimes) and handling stolen goods.

6. Forgery

Forgery and counterfeiting

These crimes are regulated by the Forgery and Counterfeiting Act 1981. Forgery refers to the making of a false instrument (such as official documents, stamps, recordings, banknotes etc.).

7. Criminal damage

The Criminal Damage Act 1971 provides: "a person who without lawful excuse destroys or damages any property belonging to another intending to destroy or damage any such property or being reckless as to whether any such property would be destroyed or damaged shall be guilty of an offence." The category includes the destroying or damaging of the property of another, the destroying or damaging of property with intent to endanger life, arson, racially aggravated criminal damage and threats to destroy or damage property.

8. Computer misuse

Related offences are described in the Computer Misuse Act 1990 and amendments include: unauthorised access to computer material, unauthorised access with intent to commit or facilitate further offences and unauthorised modification of computer material.

9. Criminal libels

These offences include blasphemy, defamatory libel, obscene publications and seditious words or libels.

10. Offences against public order

Within this category are **rioting**, violent disorder, **affray**, fear or provocation of violence, **harassment**, alarm or distress and public nuisance.

Punishment

Sentencing and retribution are also part of criminal law. It is considered that, in the absence of evidence, people are responsible for their acts and therefore are free not to commit any crime. Once the defendant has been proved guilty, the punishment has to fit the crime. A court may decide that the offence committed does not justify retribution and can subsequently discharge the offender totally. Still, the sentence should reflect contemporary attitudes towards the crime. It should be proportionate to the crime committed and should be compared to sentences for more serious and less serious crimes. Moreover, the sentencing is meant to act as an adequate retribution for the offence committed and as a deterrent to recidivism. When considering the sentence, courts have to assess the gravity of the crime not only through moral fault but also through the degree of harm caused, no matter whether the convict was fully aware of it at the time of the offence. They should also take into account the personality and circumstances of the defendant. Theoretically, i.e. in law, the sentence should be the same whether or not the *mens rea* led to *actus reus*. In practice, however, courts will be more lenient when the intention did not lead to completion of the crime and therefore did not cause the same amount of harm.

While there is no minimum sentence imposed, the maximum penalty for a specific crime is set by statute in Parliament. The death penalty was abolished in 1965. Most maximum sentences are regularly revised, and yet some of them have not been altered since the 19th century. In sentencing, the maximum penalty should be imposed only for the worst type of case. Nowadays, the authorities tend to avoid sending people to jail systematically and often prefer to choose from a range of non-prison sentences when imprisonment is not mandatory.

1. Fines

Fines are fixed according to the seriousness of the offence and never according to the wealth of the offender. Poverty may be a **mitigating factor**, but wealth is never an aggravating one. The maximum fine applying to a summary conviction for a triable-either-way offence is £5,000 at present.

2. Sentences

The Criminal Justice Act 1991 and its amendments provide only two possible types of sentences apart from fines: custodial sentences, which are sentences of imprisonment (being kept in **custody**), and community sentences, which are based on community orders (e.g., curfew orders, attendance sentence orders, community punishment orders, community rehabilitation orders). When both a custodial and a non-custodial sentence (a community sentence or a fine) are "justified" in a given case, it is the non-custodial one which should be favoured and applied. Sometimes, of course, a custodial sentence is mandatory, as in convictions for robbery, arson, rape, manslaughter and murder. Imprisonment may be required not only for the sake of retribution but also as a means of protecting the public from possible replication of the wrongful deed. In other circumstances, mitigating factors can lead to replacing a custodial sentence with a community one. These factors range from the good character of the defendant to remorse or a guilty plea. However, the convicted offender may at any point lose the benefit of the community sentence if he or she does not respect its rules. When a case results in conviction for more than one offence, the sentences can be combined into one.

1. Probation

Probation is the usual punishment for a first offence in the less serious cases. It is an opportunity, notably for young offenders, to pay for their crimes without being cut off from society altogether. It also enables the authorities to keep an eye on the **culprit** without using coercion too visibly. In the case of a second offence, the court is likely to apply a tougher sentence.

2. Community service orders
These orders are an alternative to imprisonment; they require the offender to perform up to 240 hours of community service, for instance, assisting the disabled or the elderly.

3. Curfew orders
Such orders make it compulsory for offenders to stay at home at certain times, in order to avoid loitering in the wrong places where they are likely to create mischief again.

4. Parole
It refers to early release from prison. Since the Crime (Sentences) Act 1997, however, parole is no longer automatic and has been reduced to a maximum of 20 per cent of the prison sentence. It will only be granted on criteria of good conduct and cooperative behaviour within prison life. Once freed, the **parolee** is placed under the supervision of a parole officer for a fixed period of time.

Definitions in context and key words

Actus reus: Latin expression used in legal English to refer to the guilty act which must be established in a criminal case.

affray: violence causing disturbance in a public place.

balance of probabilities: a standard used in most civil cases to determine whether a proposition is more likely to be true than not true.

blackmail: the threat of disclosing disreputable information and obtaining money in exchange for keeping that information secret.

coercion: the action of forcing someone to act against his or her will.

culprit: a person who is guilty of a crime.

custody: detaining of a person or a thing.

defence: the oral presentation aiming at proving someone's innocence of a crime.

duress: unlawful use or threat or force.

fine: an amount of money to be paid in retribution for a crime committed.

harassment: verbal and/or physical pressure exerted on someone resulting in annoyance and worry.

hoax: an attempt to lead someone to believe something that is not true.

injury: physical harm done to a person.

intention: the determination to do something.

liability: the legal responsibility of someone for his/her actions.

mens rea: Latin expression used in legal English; the offender's ill-intended state of mind.

mitigating factor: a factor that can lessen the responsibility of a person in committing a crime.

parolee: a person who has been released before completing the full length of their prison sentence under certain conditions.

procurement: the act of providing prostitutes to people.

prosecution: 1. in a lawsuit, the process aimed at proving someone's guilt of a crime, 2. the prosecuting party.

reckless: behaving in a way which shows clear lack of consideration for the possible dangers and repercussions of one's actions.

retribution: punishment for a crime.

rioting: violent behaviour adopted by a group of people in a public place, which may occur during a protest or in any circumstances.

state of affairs offence/crime: a crime which is based on factual circumstances (a "state of affairs"), such as possession of illegal material, and not on a positive act.

tort: a wrongdoing, misconduct.

Exercises

1 **Are the following statements true or false? Justify your answers with quotes from the text.**

1. Ill intentions are always punishable.
2. *Actus reus* refers to an evil deed.
3. Diminished responsibility only applies in cases of manslaughter.
4. A defendant acts under necessity when compelled to break the law.
5. Threats to the common good are criminal offences even if no harm was done.
6. In order to arrest someone, a police officer must have a warrant.
7. Parliament is responsible for the classification of offences and the definition of aggravating factors.
8. Punishment is determined according to a scale ranging from the least serious crimes to the most serious crimes.
9. Remorse might help the defendant receive a shorter custodial sentence.
10. A curfew order is a form of imprisonment since the convicted is confined to his home.
11. Parole is a 20% reduction of a prison sentence.

2 **Explain the following offences.**

1. murder   **2.** manslaughter   **3.** infanticide   **4.** genocide   **5.** assault and battery
6. aggravated assault   **7.** grievous bodily harm   **8.** false imprisonment   **9.** rape
10. indecent exposure   **11.** careless driving   **12.** dangerous driving   **13.** theft   **14.** robbery   **15.** forgery and counterfeiting

3 **Read the following testimonies and try to infer which crimes the defendants have been charged with.**

1. "She was asking for it, I saw it in her eyes. After all, she let me in, she told me she wanted to lie down because she was tired. The message was clear, wasn't it?"
2. "I was driving on the motorway, I didn't exceed the speed limit until I reached the

city centre when, all of a sudden, I couldn't slow the vehicle down. The accelerator seemed to be stuck. That's when I crashed into the other car, which I hadn't seen coming at all."

3. "I live with my grandmother because she is very sick. Last week she fell into a coma. I came home last night and found that she wasn't breathing. I rang for an ambulance. She was pronounced dead when we got to the hospital. The morphine vial you found by her bed had been left there by her doctor the day before."

4. "We were supposed to be working together, and she said I could use the archives on her computer while she was away for the weekend. We had a strict deadline. I knew her password and thought I was doing the right thing."

5. "He never bought drugs off us. How could we have held it against him? We never see him anyway and definitely don't know his wife's phone number."

6. "I lost my cat. I was in their house by accident. I never intended to break in; the window was open and I thought I could hear my cat, so I didn't hesitate for one moment. I went in and realised the house had been ransacked."

7. "I'm a journalist and I think people have the right to know how the people they most admire actually behave. This happened at a public event – a charity ball – and that celebrity really did act in the way that I described – in a self-important, arrogant and rude manner.

8. "I just threw my cigarette away, and it must have fallen a bit too close to the house. If I'm guilty of something, it's of being stupid. The flames looked good, though."

9. "I was only having a drink with some friends. OK, I punched him, but he started it and besides he's well-known for his very violent behaviour. He was pretty drunk himself and I wasn't the only one involved."

10. "I was driving and stopped at a petrol station. I went inside to buy some food. That was probably the moment they chose to put the axe, the crowbar and the torch in my boot."

4 Answer the following questions.

1. List the criteria that are used to distinguish between a wrongful act and a criminal offence.

2. Explain the link between *mens rea* and *actus reus*.

3. What is the main purpose of the defence in a criminal case?

4. How is insanity proved?

5. Define absolute offences.

6. Explain the concepts behind the notion of punishment.

7. What is the purpose of probation?

5 Classify the following crimes into one or more categories.

speeding, insulting, pædophilia, shoplifting, threatening someone at gunpoint, software copying, public rebellion, counterfeiting, street graffiti writing, mugging, racist attack, indecent attack, torture, euthanasia, excision, obscenity, arson, hacking, rowdiness, money laundering.

homicide	sexual offences	non-fatal offences
road traffic offences	theft	forgery
damage to property	computer misuse	criminal libels
	offences against public order	

6 Your first case.

You are a newly-qualified solicitor who has just been hired by a London criminal law firm. You are handling your first case. Make three different accounts of the case:

1. at a dinner party, with friends.

2. informally, with a fellow solicitor.

3. formally, at a staff meeting, in front of your boss.

2. More about...

A. Anti-social behaviour orders (ASBOs)
Prevention of Crime and Disorder Act 1998

> *Prevention of Crime and Disorder*
> *Chapter 1*
> *England and Wales*
> *Crime and disorder: general*
>
> 1. - (1) An application for an order under this section may be made by a relevant authority if it appears to the authority that the following conditions are fulfilled with respect to any person aged 10 or over, namely–
>
> (a) that the person has acted, since the commencement date, in an anti-social manner, that is to say, in a manner that caused or was likely to

cause harassment, alarm or distress to one or more persons not of the same household as himself; and–

(b) that such an order is necessary to protect persons in the local government area in which the harassment, alarm or distress was caused or was likely to be caused from further anti-social acts by him;

and in this section "relevant authority" means the council for the local government area or any chief officer of police any part of whose police area lies within that area.

(2) A relevant authority shall not make such an application without consulting each other relevant authority.

(3) Such an application shall be made by complaint to the magistrates' court whose commission area includes the place where it is alleged that the harassment, alarm or distress was caused or was likely to be caused.

(4) If, on such an application, it is proved that the conditions mentioned in subsection (1) above are fulfilled, the magistrates' court may make an order under this section (an "anti-social behaviour order") which prohibits the defendant from doing anything described in the order.

(5) For the purpose of determining whether the condition mentioned in subsection (1)(a) above is fulfilled, the court shall disregard any act of the defendant which he shows was reasonable in the circumstances.

(6) The prohibitions that may be imposed by an anti-social behaviour order are those necessary for the purpose of protecting from further anti-social acts by the defendant–

(a) persons in the local government area; and
(b) persons in any adjoining local government area specified in the application for the order;

and a relevant authority shall not specify an adjoining local government area in the application without consulting the council for that area and each chief officer of police any part of whose police area lies within that area.

(7) An anti-social behaviour order shall have effect for a period (not less than two years) specified in the order or until further order.

(8) Subject to subsection (9) below, the applicant or the defendant may apply by complaint to the court which made an anti-social behaviour order for it to be varied or discharged by a further order.

(9) Except with the consent of both parties, no anti-social behaviour order shall be discharged before the end of the period of two years beginning with the date of service of the order.

(10) If without reasonable excuse a person does anything which he is prohibited from doing by an anti-social behaviour order, he shall be liable–

(a) on summary conviction, to imprisonment for a term not exceeding six months or to a fine not exceeding the statutory maximum, or to both; or
(b) on conviction on indictment, to imprisonment for a term not exceeding five years or to a fine, or to both.

(11) Where a person is convicted of an offence under subsection (10) above, it shall not be open to the court by or before which he is so convicted to make an order under subsection (1)(b) (conditional discharge) of section 1A of the Powers of Criminal Courts Act 1973 ("the 1973 Act") in respect of the offence.

(12) In this section–

"the commencement date" means the date of the commencement of this section;
"local government area" means–
(a) in relation to England, a district or London borough, the City of London, the Isle of Wight and the Isles of Scilly;
(b) in relation to Wales, a county or county borough.

Crown copyright (http://www.opsi.gov.uk)

Exercise

Answer the following questions.

1. What conditions need to be fulfilled for the application of an anti-social behaviour order (ASBO) by a relevant authority?
2. John Smith, 16, tells the police that he had to increase the volume of his CD-player because his grandmother, whom he lives with, is deaf and had asked him to do so. Will this have any influence in the application of an ASBO?
3. How do you understand the expression "anti-social"?

B. Anti-terrorism Act 2000

11. - (1) A person commits an offence if he belongs or professes to belong to a proscribed organisation.

(2) It is a defence for a person charged with an offence under subsection (1) to prove–

(a) that the organisation was not proscribed on the last (or only) occasion on which he became a member or began to profess to be a member, and
(b) that he has not taken part in the activities of the organisation at any time while it was proscribed.

(3) A person guilty of an offence under this section shall be liable–

(a) on conviction on indictment, to imprisonment for a term not exceeding ten years, to a fine or to both, or
(b) on summary conviction, to imprisonment for a term not exceeding six months, to a fine not exceeding the statutory maximum or to both.

(4) In subsection (2) "proscribed" means proscribed for the purposes of any of the following–

(a) this Act;
(b) the Northern Ireland (Emergency Provisions) Act 1996;
(c) the Northern Ireland (Emergency Provisions) Act 1991;
(d) the Prevention of Terrorism (Temporary Provisions) Act 1989;
(e) the Prevention of Terrorism (Temporary Provisions) Act 1984;
(f) the Northern Ireland (Emergency Provisions) Act 1978;
(g) the Prevention of Terrorism (Temporary Provisions) Act 1976;
(h) the Prevention of Terrorism (Temporary Provisions) Act 1974;
(i) the Northern Ireland (Emergency Provisions) Act 1973.

12. - (1) A person commits an offence if–

(a) he invites support for a proscribed organisation, and
(b) the support is not, or is not restricted to, the provision of money or other property (within the meaning of section 15).

(2) A person commits an offence if he arranges, manages or assists in arranging or managing a meeting which he knows is–

(a) to support a proscribed organisation,
(b) to further the activities of a proscribed organisation, or
(c) to be addressed by a person who belongs or professes to belong to a proscribed organisation.

(3) A person commits an offence if he addresses a meeting and the purpose of his address is to encourage support for a proscribed organisation or to further its activities.

(4) Where a person is charged with an offence under subsection (2)(c) in respect of a private meeting it is a defence for him to prove that he had no rea-

sonable cause to believe that the address mentioned in subsection (2)(c) would support a proscribed organisation or further its activities.

(5) In subsections (2) to (4)–

(a) "meeting" means a meeting of three or more persons, whether or not the public are admitted, and
(b) a meeting is private if the public are not admitted.

(6) A person guilty of an offence under this section shall be liable–

(a) on conviction on indictment, to imprisonment for a term not exceeding ten years, to a fine or to both, or
(b) on summary conviction, to imprisonment for a term not exceeding six months, to a fine not exceeding the statutory maximum or to both.

13. - (1) A person in a public place commits an offence if he–

(a) wears an item of clothing, or
(b) wears, carries or displays an article,

in such a way or in such circumstances as to arouse reasonable suspicion that he is a member or supporter of a proscribed organisation.

(2) A constable in Scotland may arrest a person without a warrant if he has reasonable grounds to suspect that the person is guilty of an offence under this section.

(3) A person guilty of an offence under this section shall be liable on summary conviction to–

(a) imprisonment for a term not exceeding six months,
(b) a fine not exceeding level 5 on the standard scale, or
(c) both.

http://www.opsi.gov.uk

Exercise

Answer the following questions.

1. Describe the three different types of offences listed in the above excerpt and invent corresponding situations.

2. A young man wearing a backpack with what seem to be electrical wires sticking out is caught in the act of sending a text message on his mobile phone in the underground. As they search him, the police discover a small picture of a well-known terrorist. According to the Anti-terrorism Act, was his arrest justified?

3. In your opinion, at what point does "support" become "terrorism"?

3. Off the presses

The police

We're looking for special qualities

How would you deal with a group of binge drinkers dancing in the street?

What would you do to win the trust of housing estate residents scared to give evidence about a violent assault?

How would you handle the kids using the shopping centre for an indoor cycle speedway?

What would you do to rebuild the confidence of an elderly couple who were burgled last week?,

You can't arrest anyone. You've no handcuffs, no captor spray, no baton. All you've got is you. Your ability to get on with some of the most challegning people in some of the most difficult situations. The way you win cooperation through good-humoured persuasion. Your openness to see beneath black and white interpretations. Your understanding that the obvious solution may not be the best one. Your very presence on the streets inspiring confidence.

Do you have these qualitites? If so, you may be just who we're looking for.

How does a Police Community Support Officer (PCSO) fit into the police family?

As a PCSO, you will perform one of the most demanding roles in the modern UK police force. You will inspire confidence in your community by:

- helping reduce crime and anti-social behaviour;
- dealing with minor offences; and
- supporting front-line policing.

It is an essential role, which extends the range of activities the police are able to provide to our communities.

You will:	You will not:
• deal constantly with members of the public; • build links with employers and business and community leaders; • deal with nuisance offences such as street drinking or begging; and • be given some limited powers appropriate to your role.	• have powers of arrest; • be able to interview or process prisoners; • investigate serious crimes; or • carry out the more complex and high-risk tasks that police officers perform.

What sort of things do PCSOs do?
- go on highly visible, uniformed foot patrols;
- support Community Beat Officers and Community Action Teams in local problem-solving initiatives;
- make house visits to gather intelligence and other public reassurance following minor crimes or anti-social behaviour;
- engage with key stakeholders in the community, such as community, religious and business leaders;
- liaise with Community Watch, Business Watch, Horse Watch, Neighbourhood Watch, Pub Watch and Farm Watch schemes;
- preserve crime scenes;
- collect CCTV evidence;
- provide low-level crime prevention and personal safety advice;
- undertake low-level missing person enquiries in line with their role of increasing visible policing;
- act as professional witnesses, attending court when needed;
- undertake environmental audits to support crime prevention;
- engage with youths;
- interact with schools;
- support the Mobile Police Station;
- support Crime and Disorder Reduction Partnerships.

http://www.policecouldyou.uk

Exercise

Answer the following questions.

1. List the qualities police community support officers must have if they are to succeed in this career.

2. How does a PCSO protect the community?

4. Food for thought

Retribution, Deterrence and Rehabilitation

The judges' main concern in sentencing convicted offenders is (and always has been) stated to be 'the protection of the public' and the reflection in their sentencing policies of what they take to be the social condemnation of offence and offender concerned. The element of strong moral condemnation must not be underemphasized, for as we have seen, it occupies a central place in legal ideology: the very basis of criminal liability involves the requirement that in the majority of criminal offences there must be proof of the 'guilty mind', or *mens rea*, before conviction can ensue. This is the means whereby the moral responsibility of the offender and the voluntariness of his of her acts are written into the condition of liability within the criminal law, and the requirement of moral blame is deeply rooted in our ideas about what constitutes a criminal offender. This is one of the main reasons why there has, at various times, been reluctance on the part of judges and other lawyers to admit principles of liability based on 'strict liability' or 'liability without fault'.

Given this background, the main general objective of sentencing in our legal system has usually been presented as falling into three categories: retribution, deterrence and rehabilitation.

Retribution is straightforward punishment inflicted on the offender in response to the offence. It is sometimes called the principle of 'just deserts': it is the type of legal sanction which Durkheim called 'repressive' [...] and is perhaps the oldest type of sanction, having its Old Testament justification in the phrase 'an eye for an eye'. Examples of retributive sentences might include the Great Train Robbery case in 1965 which attracted sentences of 30 years for the participants; and the judicial comments in the 'Angry Brigade' trial and the IRA bomb trials in the 1970s reveal that retributive principles were at least partly at work in the assessment of the sentences in the sentences in these cases. Retributive principles underlie the main statute which currently governs sentencing practice, the Powers of Criminal Courts (Sentencing) Act 2000.

Until recently it was generally accepted that the principal sentencing policy of the courts tended to be not retribution, but deterrence. Deterrence is a double-edged principle. It should, of course, deter offenders themselves from committing further crimes, but also, and very importantly, it has been seen by judges as serving to inhibit the rest of the community from indulging in criminal behaviour. The message is, simply, 'if you do this, this is what you can expect'. The deterrence principle has for some years been widely used, though whether or not the policy works in these ways is somewhat debatable. [...]

To begin with, in order to be effective, a deterrent sentence must be publicised among the community, and although most crimes, serious and petty, are covered in national and local media, how many of us have any idea of the sentence we might expect if we get caught, for example, shoplifting or stealing from cars? Probably very few people have any accurate knowledge of the kind of sentences such activities might attract and it is only the sensational and unusual cases which attract much publicity. Research carried out in the aftermath of the exemplary 20-year sentence handed down to a young Birmingham man for a mugging offence in 1973 showed that, despite extensive publicity given by the media to this case, the frequency of 'mugging' offences did not appear to diminish. [...]

The third principle which may underlie criminal sanctions is that of rehabilitation. Now, whilst the principles underlying the aims of retribution and deterrence are to some extent compatible, in that in both cases the gravity of the sentence is related to the seriousness of the offence committed, the aim of rehabilitation involves consideration which are quite different, and must be regarded as an objective quite distinct from the first two. Essentially, the rehabilitative sentence is tied not to the offence and its gravity, but to the offender ad his or her 'needs': the sentencing judge must make a choice in any given case as to whether to pass a sentence linked to the offence (retributive or deterrent) or an individual rehabilitative sentence designed to reform or 'treat' the offender for an identified 'problem.

Philip Harris, *An Introduction to Law*, Cambridge University Press, 2002.

Exercises

1 Answer the following questions.

1. Explain the meanings of retribution, deterrence and rehabilitation. Give examples of each.

2. What are the arguments the writer gives in favour of or against these different sentencing principles?

2 Research tasks.

1. Find information on the Great Train Robbery case in 1965, the "Angry Brigade" case and IRA bomb trials in the 1970s.

2. Present your findings, highlighting the facts of the case, the trial and the case for miscarriage of justice.

3. Take notes on the presentation of each case.

4. Give arguments in favour and against the role of the police in each of the three cases.

5. Draft a code of conduct for policemen that would tackle the problems identified in the three cases.

3 **Essay writing.**

Write an essay on one of the following topics. You should focus your efforts on organising your ideas logically and using the right link words to express them.

1. Do you think moral blame should play a part in the sentencing of a convicted criminal?

2. Which of the three sentencing principles seems the most effective to avoid re-offending? Why, and in which cases?

3. Do you think the death penalty is an efficient deterrent for potential offenders?

5. Listening

Exercises

1 Listen to the first part of a radio interview and complete the text with the missing words. The interviewee, Daniel Culpepper, is a lawyer who works on homicide cases. The lawyer's words, spoken by an an actor, are taken from an authentic interview.

INTERVIEWER: Murder's characterised by an ...... to either kill or cause .... One of the reasons why the Law Commission is carrying out a wholesale ...... of our homicide law is the ...... surrounding it. In its ...... , the Law Commission suggests the creation of offences of first- and second-degree murder, a concept we're more familiar with in .... But do lawyers agree with this ...... ? Daniel Culpepper ...... both ...... and defends in homicide cases:

CULPEPPER: I think homicide law has been properly described as a mess and the biggest issue is that it seems to cause confusion to the .... We're talking about the most serious crime there is here, and if the criminal justice system can't get the law of homicide right, it's ...... pretty dismally.

INTERVIEWER: In your experience, do juries sometimes bring verdicts that are based on an .... of the law?

CULPEPPER: Jurors are .... but, like anybody else, they may have heard or read that when a person is convicted of murder, there is what is called a .... And that raises the issue as to whether anybody really understands, apart from the lawyers, what .... exactly means.

2 **Listen again to the end of part 1 (which begins where the previous exercise ends) and answer the following questions.**

1. What is the "licence period"?
2. In practice, do offenders who received a mandatory life sentence always die behind bars?
3. What may happen if an offender released on licence reoffends?
4. What have jurors been known to do in murder cases?

3 **Listen to part 2 of the recording. Are the following true or false?**

1. The interviewee criticises the Law Commission's report.
2. The current system divides homicides into three categories.
3. The interviewee feels the current number of categories is insufficient.
4. People convicted of first-degree murder will not incur a mandatory life sentence.
5. First-degree murder will be reserved for intentional killing.
6. "Couldn't-care-less" attitudes towards killing will be treated more leniently than under the current system.

4 **Discuss.**

1. Are the proposals made by the Law Commission likely to improve criminal justice in the UK?
2. How does the law in your country classify and punish homicides?

6. Grammar practice

Exercises

1 **Comparatives. For each pair of words, write one or two sentences comparing the gravity of the offences. Use comparative forms.**
1. assault/battery **2.** manslaughter/murder **3.** theft/robbery **4.** rape/assault
5. road traffic offences/damage to property

2 **Relative clauses. Make the two sentences into one by using a relative clause, as in the example. Make any other changes necessary.**

Example: *Mens rea* refers to the defendant's criminal intent. Defence lawyers often rely on the concept of *mens rea*. (Defence lawyers…)
Defence lawyers often rely on the concept of mens rea, *which refers to the defendant's criminal intent.*

1. The morphine vial was on the floor beside the bed. The police found a morphine vial. (The morphine vial…)

2. An assault is an act. By this act, the offender causes violence to the victim. (An assault is an act…)

3. A woman's house was robbed while she was away. She reported the crime to the police. (A woman…)

4. A weapon is being analysed by forensic experts. It is thought that a murder was committed with the weapon. (The weapon…)

5. The police are interviewing a witness. The witness's testimony will be valuable at trial. (The police…)

6. He was convicted of an offence. It is one of the most harshly punished ones. (The offence…)

7. John was found responsible for the accident. The accident caused the death of a child. (The accident…)

8. Strict liability is a statutory standard. *Mens rea* is not required to establish it. (Strict liability…)

3 **Questions. Write questions that correspond to the information in the underlined segments, as in the example.**

Example: The man was accused of <u>indecent assault</u>. *What was the man accused of.*

1. The burden of proof in criminal cases lies with <u>the defence</u>.

2. The State has the right to prosecute and punish <u>the perpetrators of criminal offences</u>.

3. <u>To decide whether an action is criminal or not</u>, criminal law usually looks to moral intent.

4. <u>The kind of legal proceedings</u> brought against the defendant allows one to distinguish between a civil wrong and a criminal offence.

5. A civil action, brought by the victim, aims at obtaining <u>compensation for injury</u>.

6. A crime is made up of <u>three</u> elements.

7. Criminal defence lawyers often rely on the concept of mens rea <u>to organise their defence strategy.</u>

8. <u>The prosecution</u> must prove the child's awareness of the seriousness of the crime committed.

9. <u>Offenders committing arrestable offences</u> can be apprehended without a warrant.

4 **Countable/uncountable.**

    A. ARE THE WORDS IN BOLD TYPE COUNTABLE OR UNCOUNTABLE NOUNS IN THE CONTEXT?

    B. COMPLETE EACH SENTENCE USING ONE OF THE ELEMENTS IN BRACKETS.

1. There wasn't …… (much, many) **evidence** to support the prosecution's case.

2. The court-appointed lawyer was given very …… (little/few) **time** to prepare the defence.

3. The police managed to dig up ...... (a, an, ø) **information** which greatly helped the investigation.

4. The whole strategy of the defence was based on establishing ...... (the, a, ø) **duress**.

5. The defendant is well aware that he faces ...... (the, a, ø) **prison sentence**.

6. However, he also knows that he will be eligible for ...... (the, a, ø) **parole** after ...... (a little, a few, few) **months**.

7. ...... (a, an, ø) **help** and ...... (a, an, ø) **advice** from a barrister are necessary in this case.

8. ...... (a, ø) **bail application** was made and the defendant was released on ...... (a, ø) **bail**.

9. There was ...... (a, an, ø) overwhelming evidence that the accused had had very ...... (little/few) **responsibility** in the affair.

Chapter 7

The law of tort

1. Fundamentals

The laws of tort and contract are branches of civil law called the law of obligations. The rules of tort law are generally judge-made although there has been some legislative intervention. Tort law covers situations in which a party, injured as a result of another party's **wrongdoing**, is entitled to a legal **remedy**.

The law of tort offers remedies mainly for four types of wrongs: negligence, nuisance, trespass and defamation. **Compensation** and **injunction** are the two remedies a claimant can be awarded in court. Although this is not the main focus of the chapter, it is important to keep in mind that certain torts may overlap with criminal law and be prosecuted as criminal cases.

Principles establishing negligence

The tort of negligence consists in the causing of foreseeable damage by unreasonable behaviour, where there is a **duty of care**, i.e. an obligation towards others. A negligence claim may arise out of a variety of contexts including for instance consumer disputes, road accidents, accidents at work and medical malpractice. If a claimant is to succeed against a defendant in a negligence suit, he must establish that (1) the defendant owed him a duty of care, (2) the defendant breached that duty and (3) the claimant suffered a loss or injury as a result of that **breach**. The standard of proof in a civil case is less stringent than in a criminal case which requires proof beyond reasonable doubt. In a civil case the burden lies with the claimant to establish each of these three requirements on a **balance of probabilities.**

1. Duty

The nature of the duty of care was set out in *Donoghue v Stevenson* [1932] AC 562, the seminal case on negligence which was decided in the 1930s. It established that a manufacturer had a duty of care to his "neighbour" and discussed the the notions of neighour and of **reasonableness**.

Ms Donoghue went to a pub with a friend. This friend bought her a bottle of ginger beer. Unfortunately, there was a dead snail in the bottle, impairing the quality of the beer and making it unfit for drinking. Ms Donoghue did not see the snail because the glass of the bottle was opaque. She drank the beer and as a consequence suffered from indigestion. Ms Donoghue could not sue the pub owner for breach of contract because there was no contract binding them, since it was a friend of hers who had bought the beer. The contractual relationship lay between this friend and the pub owner. The only remedy available to her was to sue the manufacturer in the tort of negligence.

The case reached the House of Lords and Lord Atkin created the legal concept of the duty of care. It provides that (a) you must take reasonable care to avoid acts or omissions which you can reasonably foresee will be likely to cause an injury to your neighbour and (b) you ought reasonably to have in contemplation persons who are closely and directly affected by your acts. In actions falling within the scope of defective goods and services, the claimant is usually a customer. Sellers are seldom sued for breach of the duty of care under *Donoghue v Stevenson*, since the buyer can rely on a claim for breach of contract. In many of the duty of care cases, the defendant is the manufacturer. In the 1990 ruling of *Caparo Industries v. Dickman*, Lord Bridge took the definition of a duty of care one step further by laying down additional requirements: (a) the damage must be foreseeable, (b) there must be sufficient proximity between the parties and (c) it must be fair and reasonable to impose such a duty.

Courts have defined a great number of situations in which a duty of care exists. Among them is the duty which a driver owes his passengers and other road users. Indeed, many traffic accidents lead to personal injury claims. The issue of liability in road traffic accidents is purely a matter of common law and the standard of care imposed on drivers is that of the reasonably careful motorist, even for learner drivers, as the Court of Appeal held in the case of *Nettleship v Weston* [1971].

In a negligence action, once it has been established that the defendant owed a duty to the claimant, it is necessary to prove that that duty was breached.

2. Breach and causation

When does a person's action fall short of the required standard of care? A certain number of factors are taken into account, such as **foreseeability**, risk, likelihood, gravity and cost. Foreseeability is dealt with by means of the reasonable man test, which sets the expected standard of behaviour and is based on what the "reasonable man" should have foreseen, not what the defendant actually did foresee. It is an objective test. Nonetheless, allowance is made for cases where the **tortfeasor** is a child or has special knowledge, e.g. a higher standard of care is expected of a medical specialist than a general practitioner. When establishing whether there is a breach, judges also take into account the likelihood of occurrence of harm, the gravity of the injury foreseen and the cost of overcoming the risk for the manufacturer. If the defendant is found liable, he or she will have to pay compensation to the injured party, i.e. the claimant.

The damage done must be compensable. There cannot be a claim in negligence for mere upset or inconvenience. Injuries must have been sustained or damage must have been done to property. Moreover, the damage must have been caused by the breach of duty. The claimant only needs to show that the defendant's breach of duty was an effective cause of the loss, albeit not necessarily the only cause. The damage itself must not be too remote, which means that the defendant is liable only for such consequences as should reasonably have been foreseen to arise from the breach. If the chain of events leading to an injury is too long or complex, causation may be hard to establish.

Particular cases of negligence

1. Product liability

In most civil litigation involving defective goods, the litigant may claim under the law of tort and/or the law of contract. Therefore, it is important to understand the full scope of the law of tort in order to compare claims in contract and in tort. The advantage of a claim in tort is that it is a universal legal obligation; however, the standard of proof is easier to satisfy in contract (see Chapter 8, Contract law).

When it comes to claims falling for product liability, the claimant can rely on both the "narrow rule" in *Donoghue v. Stevenson* and the Consumer Protection Act 1987.

One of the differences between these two claims is that the term "manufacturer" under the Consumer Protection Act includes repairers, installers and suppliers of goods. The manufacturer will not owe a duty of care when there is reasonable likelihood of an intermediate examination, for example in the case of a middleman assembling parts supplied by the manufacturer. The term "customer" means not only the ultimate user of the goods but anyone whom the defendant should reasonably have in mind as likely to be injured by want of care in relation to the manufacture of the product (e.g. the lorry driver transporting the goods, the workman assembling the parts, the salesman selling the article over the counter).

Pursuant to the European Council Directive of 25 July 1985, the Consumer Protection Act 1987 states that manufacturers of defective products are strictly liable for personal injury caused by the product and for non-trivial damage to personal property. In order to claim under section 2 (1) of the CPA 1987, the claimant must prove five things: (1) the claimant has suffered damage (2) which was caused by (3) a defect (4) in a product (5) and the potential defendant is covered by the Act. The damage covered by the act is death, personal injury, or loss or damage to private property exceeding £275, but not pure economic loss. This damage must have been caused by a "defect"; the product is said to have a "defect" if the safety of the product is not what people are generally entitled to expect. By "product", section 2 (1) means goods, electricity, raw material and components. Potential defendants can avoid liability by identifying their own suppliers, be they producers, own branders, importers or forgetful suppliers who did not keep track of the manufacturers of the goods they sell.

2. Vicarious liability

Employers are strictly liable for any tort committed by their employees or unpaid agents (but not independent contractors working for a fee) doing authorised work in the course of their employment. In the case *Century Insurance Co Ltd v. N. Ireland Road Transport* [1982], it was held that the employers of a petrol tanker driver were liable for the damage resulting from the negligent act of their employee, who had caused an explosion by throwing a match on the ground.

3. Contributory negligence

Contributory negligence occurs when the defendant in a negligence action can show that the claimant either contributed to the event which caused the injury or made the injury worse. In the case of a road accident where the defendant was the driver, contributory negligence would be established if the passenger claimant was not wearing a seat belt. In such a case, the claimant's damages would be reduced.

Principles establishing defamation

English law divides the tort of defamation into two categories: libel and slander. Both types of defamation concern statements which are likely to "lower [a person] in the esteem of right-thinking members of society" (*Sim v Stretch* [1936], *per* Lord Atkin). While slander consists of defamatory statements made verbally in a temporary form, libel refers to defamation made in a permanent form, which includes writing, print, electronic communication, broadcast, stage play and even waxwork. In the case of *Monson v Tussauds* (1894), the Court of Appeal ruled that the scope of libel extends beyond statements made in writing and encompasses defamatory matter conveyed in another permanent form. In that case, the famous wax museum was found liable after it displayed a waxwork figure of the plaintiff in a manner which suggested he was a murderer, although murder charges against him had recently been dismissed.

Defamation cases are handled according to common law and statutory principles. They are usually tried by a judge and jury in the High Court of Justice. One fundamental rule is that the death of either party extinguishes a claim in defamation.

A claimant filing a libel suit does not have to demonstrate any financial loss, whereas such a showing is generally required for slander except in certain instances. Slanderous statements which are **actionable** *per se* include saying that a person has committed a serious criminal offence, that he is suffering from an infectious disease, that he is incompetent to perform his job and that a woman is "unchaste". Anyone who repeats such allegations would also be liable under the law of defamation.

In a defamation action, the **onus** is on the claimant to show the three following elements:
1. the statement was indeed defamatory (damaging to the claimant's reputation),
2. it made reference to the claimant,
3. it was published, i.e. communicated to a third party.

Even when this requirement has been met by the claimant, the defendant can still prevail using one of the following defences:
1. truth or justification,
2. fair comment,
3. privilege.

Only false allegations are actionable, therefore showing that the statement involved was substantially true constitutes a defence. The defence of fair comment can be invoked when the suit concerns the expression of an opinion rather than a statement of fact. Absolute **privilege** applies to statements made in Parliament or in the course of judicial proceedings. "Fair and accurate" reports of legislative or judicial proceedings are also privileged under the Defamation Act 1996. The Act also grants a qualified privilege subject to explanation or contradiction for a "fair and accurate report" of public meetings of any local authority in the UK, general meetings of a UK public company, findings or decisions made by associations promoting the arts, science, religion, business, a profession, charity, etc.

Principles establishing nuisance

The law of tort distinguishes between two types of **nuisance**: private nuisance and public nuisance.

A private nuisance claim may arise out of a situation where a person's use or enjoyment of his land is unreasonably affected by a neighbour's activities or lifestyle. A person must take reasonable steps to prevent harm emanating from his land. In the seminal case *Rylands v Fletcher*, the defendant had a reservoir built on his land. Unfortunately, the contractors failed to secure a plug underneath the reservoir and the water flooded the claimant's adjacent mines. The court held that the defendant was liable since he had brought something to his land which had damaged his neighbour's property. This was a case of strict liability.

Public nuisance differs in that it occurs when a person acts in a way which causes annoyance to a whole class of Her Majesty's subjects. Crowds of people gathering outside a theatre on a regular basis and obstructing traffic, for example, may constitute public nuisance. It should be noted that public nuisance can be prosecuted if interference with public life is substantial enough.

Principles establishing trespass

The tort of trespass occurs when a person, by a positive act, directly invades the protected interests of another person (possession of land or goods, bodily integrity, freedom of movement and freedom from fear of attack). Trespass to the person includes the torts of **assault** and **battery**, the former being a threat of physical harm while the latter consists of any unwelcome physical contact. In the case of *Wilson v Pringle* [1987] QB 237, the claimant, a 13-year-old boy, was leaving a class when the defendant, a classmate, pulled his schoolbag. The claimant fell and suffered a hip injury. In this case, which involved a form of trespass, the law of tort was successfully invoked.

Trespass is **actionable** *per se*, which means that there is no necessity to prove damage. For example, a person who enters someone's property without permission can be sued for trespass whether he has caused damage or not.

Definitions in context and key words

actionable *per se*: a tort which is actionable even if the claimant has not suffered any damage.

assault: an act, intentional or reckless, leading a person to fear immediate personal violence.

balance of probabilities: the standard of proof required in a civil action to establish liability.

battery: offensive or harmful contact with another person.

breach: a failure to discharge an obligation, especially in the law of negligence and the law of contract.

compensation *(uncountable)*: an amount given by the wrongdoer or received by the injured party as payment or reparation for losses suffered or physical injuries sustained.

duty of care: the legal responsibility a person owes to others to act reasonably towards them, so as to avoid causing foreseeable harm.

foreseeability: a legal concept first formulated in *Donoghue v Stevenson* in relation to the notion of duty of care. Foreseeability of damage means likelihood of damage.

injunction: an equitable remedy issued by a court to forbid or to compel a party to do or continue to do a particular activity.

nuisance: act or use of something that causes inconvenience, disturbance or harm.

onus: burden.

privilege *(uncountable)*: immunity from liability enjoyed by a category of persons or under specific circumstances.

reasonableness: a legal fiction developed by the common law and used in tort and contract law as the standard by which some actions or omissions are assessed.

remedy: the resolution of a case ordered by a court. Remedies in tort can be damages, injunctions or restitution.

slander *(uncountable)*: see p. 104.

tortfeasor: a person who commits a tort.

wrongdoing *(uncountable)*: the doing of an act which amounts to a wrong.

Exercises

1 **Which item in the following list is not classified in English law as a tort?**

1. public nuisance   **2.** slander   **3.** negligence   **4.** breach of contract   **5.** trespass

2 **Choose the correct ending for each sentence.**

1. A tort can be defined as
   a. a minor criminal offence.
   b. a major criminal offence.
   c. a civil wrong.

2. The case of *Donoghue v Stevenson* laid down
   a. the principles of trespass.
   b. the principles of negligence.
   c. the principles of nuisance.

3. Slander is a form of
   a. defamation.
   b. libel.
   c. contributory liability.

4. The claimant in a negligence case has to put forward evidence of
   a. guilt.
   b. damage.
   c. having paid his solicitor's fees.

5. In a negligence suit, the claimant is required to establish the liability of the defendant
   a. as actionable *per se*.
   b. beyond a reasonable doubt.
   c. on a balance of probabilities.

3 Find the words corresponding to the following definitions.

1. When the claimant played a part in the event which caused the injury or made the injury worse.
2. Defamatory statement made in a permanent form.
3. Tort of making unwelcome physical contact.
4. The adjective applied to a tort where there is no need to prove that damage has been caused.
5. Tort of threatening someone with physical harm.

4 For each of the following cases, say if the defence can succeed and why.

1. Ms Simmons drove over a pedestrian. She claims it was not her fault as she is an old woman and growing clumsier by the day.
2. Mr Jones employs Mr Li, a truck driver, to deliver parcels. During working hours, Mr Li drove into a shop window. The shopowner sues Mr Jones for compensation. Mr Jones refuses to pay on grounds that his employee did not take the route he was told to take when delivering goods.
3. Ms Williams has a statement published in *The Sun* describing Ms Becky as a drug addict. Ms Becky sues Ms Williams on grounds of libel. Ms Williams alleges that a friend of hers, Ms Daisy, told her that Ms Becky was a heroin addict.
4. Mr Roberts says in Parliament that Ms Crook is a swindler. Ms Crook sues Mr Roberts for slander, but Mr Roberts states that what he said was a privileged statement.
5. Mr Wellington is a construction worker and he falls from some scaffolding, injuring his skull. He sues his employer, Mr Chang, on the grounds that he did not provide workers with safety helmets. Mr Chang says that providing each employee with a helmet would increase production costs and make his company less competitive.

5 Which category of tort does each of these situations fall under?

1. Acid fumes from a factory damaged the washing which was drying in a man's garden.
2. A person developed an infection after plastic surgery.
3. A man entered a person's back garden uninvited to look for his cat.
4. A man accosted a woman on the street and kissed her without her consent.
5. Splashed paint from a furniture factory damaged cars parked in the street.
6. A customer sustained serious injuries after slipping on some spilled yoghurt in a supermarket.
7. A baker started losing business when a woman told customers that the baking was carried out in unsanitary conditions.
8. A short-sighted man who was driving without his glasses had an accident in which a passer-by was hurt.
9. A little girl was bitten by an old lady's dog.

10. A man purchased a faulty television set which blew up, causing serious damage to his flat.

6 Complete the text with words from the list below.

equity	actions	liability	carelessly
wrong	thief	damages	defendant
losses	damage	omission	injury
injunction	redress	plaintiff	remedy

It is not possible to assign any one aim to the law of tort, which is not surprising when one considers that the subject comprehends situations as disparate as A ...... running down B in the street and C calling D a ...... ; or E giving bad investment advice to F and G selling H's car when he has no authority to do so. At a very general level, however, we may say that tort is concerned with the allocation of prevention of ...... , which are bound to occur in our society. It is obvious that in any society of people living together numerous conflicts of interest will arise and that the actions of one man or group of men will from time to time cause or threaten ...... to others. This damage may take many forms – ...... to the person, damage to physical property, damage to financial interests, injury to reputation and so on – and whenever a person suffers damage he is inclined to look to the law for...... . [...] This redress may take various forms. In the great majority of tort ...... coming before courts, the plaintiff is seeking monetary compensation (......) for the injury he has suffered and this fact strongly emphasises the function of tort in allocating or redistributing loss. In many cases, however, the plaintiff is seeking an ...... to prevent the occurrence of harm in the future and in this area the "preventive" function of tort predominates. [...] A tort is a ...... the victim of which is entitled to redress. It should be emphasised, however, that the law of tort, like other branches of private law, is concerned with questions of .... An action founded upon tort is an action between persons, either natural or artificial (i.e. corporations), and the outcome can only be that one of them, the ...... , is or is not liable to do or refrain from doing something at the suit of another. If there is no defendant whose liability can be established according to the principles of the law, then the ...... is left without redress so far as the law of tort is concerned. It does not follow, however, that he is without other forms of redress. The act or ...... of the other party may be some other form of wrong for which a ...... may lie in contract or restitution or according to the rules of ...... governing breach of trust [...].

From W. V. H. Rogers in *Winfield and Jolowicz on Tort*, 15th ed., Sweet & Maxwell, 1998, pp. 1-3.

7 Case study.

Emma needs a new toaster, so she goes to her local shop, 24/24 Ltd. She buys a Toast Delux manufactured by LUX Ltd and writes a cheque for £140. At the till, the cashier puts the date of purchase on LUX's guarantee leaflet and stamps it. The guarantee states that LUX Ltd will replace the toaster if it proves to be defective within the first 6 months of use.

After carefully reading the instructions, Emma uses the toaster to warm bread for her lunch. She leaves the kitchen and a few minutes later, as she re-enters the kitchen, the toaster explodes. As a result of the explosion, the toaster and the table on which it was set have been damaged beyond repair, the kitchen needs to be repainted and Emma suffers cuts and bruises. Emma takes the remains of the toaster to 24/24 Ltd, but the assistant says the store cannot help her and tells her to claim against the manufacturer since there is a guarantee. Emma asks an electrician to check the toaster and he tells her the toaster had overheated because of a defective thermostat.

1. What are the claims in tort Emma could make against 24/24 Ltd?
2. What are the claims in tort Emma could make against LUX Ltd?
3. Does Emma have any claims against anyone else?

2. More about...

A. The man on the Clapham omnibus

During the nineteenth century the judges attempted to clarify the law by inventing the notion of the reasonable man. Instead of asking, as before, whether the defendant was guilty of imprudence, the judges required the jury to consider whether the defendant had behaved like a reasonable man, or a reasonably careful man, or a reasonably prudent man.

Having invented the reasonable man, the judges had to make an effort to describe him. According to some, he was the ordinary reasonable man. This was not the same as saying that he was the ordinary man, but came rather near it. Indeed, Lord Bowen, with his gift for a phrase, equated the reasonable man with "the man on the Clapham omnibus", and this had led to the widespread supposition that the standard of care required by the common law is that of the average man. The supposition is certainly untrue.

"The ordinary reasonable man" of the judges' imagining is a meticulously careful person, so careful that very few gentlemen come up to his standard. [...] Take one obvious point. A defendant in an action for negligence would not be allowed to put the passengers of a Clapham omnibus into the witness-box to say that they would have done the same as he did. The evidence would not be listened to. One reason for this is that if ordinary standards were conclusive, the courts could not use their influence to improve these standards.

Again, ordinary people, even though normally they are circumspect in their behaviour, lapse into carelessness now and then. [...] That the judges set the standard by the nearly perfect man, rather than the average man, is lavishly illustrated in the law reports. The master of a small motor vessel, when off

Greenhithe in the Thames, fainted at the wheel as a result of eating bad tinned salmon, and a collision followed. Up to the moment of fainting the master had felt quite well, and he was obviously not negligent in fainting. A pure accident, you might say. But the judge held that the master was negligent because he had failed to foresee that he might lose consciousness, and had omitted to provide against this by having some other person on deck who might be able to get to the bridge in time to prevent an accident if fainting occurred. [...] Obviously this decision could not be applied to land vehicles without absurdity. No one would suggest that the Clapham or any other omnibus should carry a reserve driver, ready to seize the wheel in case the other driver faints.

Where, then, is our elusive standard to be found? If the reasonable man is not to be discovered on the Clapham omnibus, can he be identified with the judge or juryman who has to decide the issue? Technically, at least, the answer is again in the negative. A judge must not tell the members of the jury to determine what they would have done, because that is not the question. The individual jurors might not have acted as prudently as they now think, on reflection, they ought to have acted in the situation. Jurors are expected to follow Hume's precept that, in considering the moral character of an act, we should adopt the role of impartial spectator, seeking reactions as to what we would approve or disapprove, not as to what we ourselves would have felt or done.

Perhaps this is the key to the puzzle. The reasonable man is a phantom reflecting a certain ideal on the part of the tribunal, whether judge or jury as the case may be. He is a personification of the court's social judgment.

If this is the right conclusion, I think one is driven to admit that the device of trying to decide cases in terms of the reasonable man is not such a good idea after all. Why not address oneself directly to the problem of negligence? Values are important, but there is no point in personifying values, or attributing them to a fictitious person. In speaking of what a reasonable man does or does not do, we appear to be stating a fact, whereas in truth the question is how people ought to behave. It is merely misleading to use an expression that seems to indicate the behaviour of real people, when we are evaluating behaviour by reference to an ideal standard.

Glanville Williams, *The Listener*, 2/2/1961.

Exercises

1 Answer the following questions.

1. Explain the concept of "the man on the Clapham omnibus".

2. Explain how the notion of "the reasonable man" differs from that of "the average man".

2 **Essay question.**

2 **Essay question.**

Comment on the following statement from the article: "the device of trying to decide cases in terms of the reasonable man is not such a good idea".

B. The *ratio decidendi* in *Donoghue v Stevenson*

> If your Lordships accept the view that the appellant's pleading discloses a relevant cause of action, you will be affirming the proposition that by Scots and English law alike a manufacturer of products which he sells in such a form as to show that he intends them to reach the ultimate consumer in the form in which they left him, with no reasonable possibility of immediate examination, and with the knowledge that the absence of reasonable care in the preparation or putting up of the products will result in injury to the consumer's life or property, owes a duty to the consumer to take that reasonable care.
>
> *Per* Lord Atkin at 599, in *Donoghue v. Stevenson* [1932] AC 562.

Exercise

Answer the following questions.

1. What is the basic logical structure of this sentence?

2. Analyse the specific language used in this text.

3. Lord Atkin's statement has been interpreted as containing a narrow rule and a broad rule. Can you identify each rule and explain the difference?

C. Duty of care in *Caparo Industries v Dickman*

> What emerges is that, in addition to the foreseeability of damage, necessary ingredients in any situation giving rise to a duty of care are that there should exist between the party owing the duty and the party to whom it is owed a relationship characterised by the law as one of "proximity" or "neighbourhood" and that the situation should be one in which the court considers it fair, just and reasonable that the law should impose a duty of a given scope upon the one party for the benefit of the other.
>
> *Per* Lord Bridge in *Caparo Industries v Dickman* [1990] 1AllER 568

Answer the following questions.

1. What does this ruling make of the "neighbour principle" established in *Donoghue?*
2. Recapitulate all the "ingredients" that make up a duty of care.

D. Famous negligence cases

Duty of care

Bolton v Stone [1951] 1 All ER 1078 HL

Ms Stone, a pedestrian, was hit by a cricket ball which was shot from a cricket ground located a hundred yards away, clearing a 17-foot fence. Such a thing had only happened about six times in thirty years. Ms Stone's claim for damages was unsuccessful. The House of Lords held that the Cricket Club were not in breach of their duty of care because they had taken reasonable precautions against a highly unlikely risk.

Barrett v Ministry of Defence [1995] 3 All ER 87 CA

The plaintiff was the widow of a naval airman who became so drunk one night at his naval base that he passed out and, having received inadequate treatment there, choked to death on his own vomit. The Court of Appeal applied the test of whether it was just and reasonable to impose a duty of care in such circumstances and reversed the trial court's finding that the Navy had a duty of care to protect the deceased from intoxication. "I can see no reason," said Beldam LJ, "why it should not be fair, just and reasonable for the law to leave a responsible adult to assume responsibility for his own actions in consuming alcoholic drink. No one is better placed to judge the amount the he can safely consume or to exercise control in his own interest as well as the interest of others." However, a duty of care existed once the deceased had collapsed and could no longer look after himself and the defendant had taken responsibility for his care. It was held that the measures taken by the defendant fell short of the standard reasonably to be expected. Therefore, the defendant was in breach of a duty of care and liable in damages to the plaintiff although allowance had to be made for the deceased's own contributory negligence.

Orange v Chief Constable of West Yorkshire [2001] 3 WLR 736 CA

The claimant's husband was arrested for being drunk and disorderly and committed suicide in a police cell. The widow claimed that the custody officer in charge owed the deceased a duty of care to prevent him from committing suicide. Considering that nothing alerted the officer that the claimant's husband was a suicide risk, the Court of Appeal dismissed her claim. Latham LJ said that it would not "be fair, just and reasonable to impose upon [...] the police [...] a general obligation to treat every prisoner as if he or she were a suicide risk." A duty arises only where they should know such a risk exists.

In some cases courts are reluctant to impose a duty of care especially when the defendant is a public body for fear it might lead to undeserving claims that would impair the proper functioning of the state.

Hill v Chief Constable of West Yorkshire [1988] 2 All ER 238 HL

In spite of a massive police search, the "Yorkshire Ripper" remained free for several years and murdered a dozen young women. The mother of his last victim sued the police for negligence in failing to catch him, alleging inefficiency and errors in their handling of the investigation. The House of Lords said she could not succeed: the police owed no duty of care towards Susan Hill to protect her from Sutcliffe. Foreseeability of likely harm, said Lord Keith, is not in itself a sufficient test of liability in negligence. Some further ingredient is invariably needed to establish the requisite proximity of relationship between the plaintiff and the defendant, and all the circumstances of the case must be considered to ascertain whether such an ingredient is present. The mere investigation of a crime did not create a special relationship between the police and Sutcliffe, nor between the police and Ms Hill, who had been at no greater risk than most other members of the public.

Liability tests

Foreseeability
Haley v London Electricity Board [1964] 3 All ER 185 HL

Workmen from the Electricity Board were preparing to carry out work on underground cables. They dug a hole, and in order to give warning of the danger (before the permanent barriers arrived) they laid a long-handled hammer across the pavement. P, a blind man, walked along the pavement on his way to work. He tripped over the hammer and was injured. The House of Lords said the defendants were negligent; it was common knowledge that large numbers of blind people walked unaided along pavements, and the duty of care extended to them as well as to sighted people.

Proximity
Watson v BBBC [2001] QB 1134 CA

A boxer C suffered severe brain damage following an injury in the ring, but the evidence suggested his injuries would have been less severe had better medical attention been available at the ringside. The Court of Appeal (affirming the trial judge) said the sport's controlling body owed a duty of care to those who took part: injury was foreseeable (indeed, it was the object of the sport!), the licensing system created a proximity of relationship, and in all the circumstances it was just, fair and reasonable to impose such a duty. On the facts, the defendants had failed in their duty to ensure that those running the event had made proper arrangements for medical care, and were consequently liable for C's injuries.

The "but for" test

The "but for" test is used to determine causation in a negligence action. The test can be summarised in a simple question: in the case at issue, would the damage not have occurred but for the breach of duty committed by the defendant?

Barnett v Chelsea & Kensington Hospital **[1968] 1 All ER 1068 Nield J**

A watchman started vomiting after drinking tea. He went to the casualty department of the defendant's hospital. The doctor, who was himself unwell, refused to examine him and sent him home untreated. He died of arsenic poisoning five hours later. His family's lawsuit against the hospital failed. It was held in the QBD that the hospital's casualty officer was negligent. However, the plaintiff failed to prove that the death was caused by an act of negligence. Indeed, the medical evidence showed that the deceased would probably have died *even if* proper treatment had been given promptly.

Exercise

Case study.

A. The situation.

John Doe, who had a rare heart condition, was working on a tennis court, collecting stray tennis balls during a tennis tournament, when he was hit in the chest by a ball and passed out. He was taken to hospital. The doctors sent him home, diagnosing a temporary dizziness. He died overnight. His parents are going to see Mr Laws, a solicitor, for legal advice.

B. Research.

Find out the meaning and scope of the following tests: the *Wagon Mound* test, the *Eggshell skull* test and the "similar in type" rule.

C. Letter-writing.

Mr Laws advises Mr and Mrs Doe to institute proceedings against the tennis organisation and the hospital.

Assume the role of Mr Daws and write a letter to each defendant, stating:
1. the grounds of the claim,
2. the legal foundations of the action (highlighting relevant case law),
3. advising the defendant to settle the matter out of court.

D. Brief writing.

Now suppose you are a trainee solicitor working for Mr Laws. Browse the internet for the full text of a judicial precedent in support of John Doe's case and summarise it in the form of a case brief. Use the following headings:
1. case name and roles
2. procedural background (history of the proceedings)
3. facts
4. legal issues
5. decision (how did the court resolve the issue?)
6. reasoning (why did the court reach its decision?)
7. disposition (what happened as a result of the court's decision: affirmed, reversed...)

E. Communication skills.

1. Make a list of terms, expressions or set phrases to communicate the following notions: asking for or giving advice, agreeing, disagreeing, suggestions, doubts, regrets, apologies, making requests.
2. Stage a settlement conference between the claimants and one of the defendants. Use your language skills to negotiate efficiently.

3. Off the presses

A. Libel suit brought by pop star

Williams wins big libel damages over reports he is gay

He has joked about being an "absolute bender" and his latest album includes the raunchy track "Your Gay Friend", but yesterday Robbie Williams won a substantial libel payout over claims that he lied about his sexuality by pretending not to be gay.

A newspaper and two magazines were forced to make a public apology as part of the settlement at the High Court in London after wrongly alleging that Mr Williams had engaged in gay sex acts with strangers and then lied about his homosexuality. The singer-songwriter did not appear in court, but his counsel, Tom Shields QC, told Mr Justice Eady: "Mr Williams is not, and never has been, homosexual." The case raises the question of whether Mr Williams was more concerned about the allegation he was gay, or the implication that he lied to cover up his sexuality and was a hypocrite. He also risked alienating members of the gay community, who took a long time to forgive the former *Neighbours* star Jason Donovan when he successfully sued *The Face* magazine in 1992 over claims he was gay.

The People and two titles belonging to Richard Desmond's Northern & Shell, *Star* and *Hot Stars* magazines, made the false claims around the time of the publication of his book *Feel* in September 2004. Billed as an autobiography, the book was in fact written, with Williams's co-operation, by Chris Heath who lived alongside the singer from 2002 to 2004. Shortly before *Feel* was published, *The People* splashed with a front-page story headlined: "Robbie's secret gay lover". It suggested that Mr Williams was about to deceive the public by pretending he had sexual relations only with women, when he had engaged in casual and sordid gay encounters with strangers. [...]

None of the allegations were true, said Mr Shields, adding: "Accordingly, the book *Feel* did not lie about his sexuality." Mr Shields said the suggestion in *Star* and *Hot Stars* that Mr Williams had discussed his relationships with women in *Feel* while keeping his gay encounters secret, was also untrue.

Mark Stephens, a media law expert, said that bringing a libel case to prove someone was not gay was a dangerous strategy. "It always rebounds on them to their disadvantage. Most right-thinking people don't think the suggestion that people are gay is defamatory," Mr Stephens said. He added that it was a "common ploy" to counter allegations of homosexuality on some other ground, for example the suggestion that someone was a liar. "Where you want to complain about something that is not actually defamatory, like an allegation of being gay, they may go for the suggestion you would be thought to be a liar," he said.

Mr Williams has joked that he is gay on several occasions, telling the audience at a Paris concert that he was in a "steady sexual relationship" with his married song-writing partner Guy Chambers and announcing on Top of the Pops: "Tomorrow I will be coming out as a homosexual."

Tris Reid-Smith, editor of *The Pink Paper* said: "I don't know whether he does it for publicity or because he thinks it's funny. It's a bit rich then to turn around when someone else says you're gay and get damages out of them." He added: "It took Jason Donovan a long time to be forgiven. If people think he [Mr Williams] thinks the concept of being gay is offensive, people will be quite upset about that. The idea that he's obsessed with his sexuality to the point that he's prepared to sue over it, means he's a bit out of touch with reality. If he finds being thought a liar or promiscuous offensive, that's a different matter." [...]

The Independent, 7/12/2005.

Answer the following questions.

1. Why does Mark Stephens, a media law expert, express concern over libel cases and allegations of homosexuality?

2. In your opinion, to what extent do famous people take advantage of their visibility to access the courts?

3. Can you think of other examples of such cases?

B. Extract from a court ruling

Miller and another v Jackson and another **[1977] 3 All ER 338 Lord Denning MR**

In summer time village cricket is the delight of everyone. Nearly every village has its own cricket field where the young men play and the old men watch. In the village of Lintz in County Durham they have their own ground, where they have played these last 70 years. They tend it well. The wicket area is well rolled and mown. The outfield is kept short. It has a good club-house for the players and seats for the onlookers. The village team play there on Saturdays and Sundays. They belong to a league, competing with the neighbouring villages. On other evenings after work they practice while the light lasts. Yet now after these 70 years a judge of the High Court has ordered that they must not play there any more. He has issued an injunction to stop them. He has done it at the instance of a newcomer who is no lover of cricket. This newcomer has built, or has had built for him, a house on the edge of the cricket ground which four years ago was a field where cattle grazed. The animals did not mind the cricket. But now this adjoining field has been turned into a housing estate. The newcomer bought one of the houses on the edge of the cricket ground. No doubt the open space was a selling point. Now he complains that, when a batsman hits a six, the ball has been known to land in his garden or on or near his house. His wife has got so upset about it that they always go out at weekends. They do not go into the garden when cricket is being played. They say that this is intolerable. So they asked the judge to stop the cricket being played. And the judge, much against his will, has felt that he must order the cricket to be stopped; with the consequences, I suppose, that the Lintz Cricket Club will disappear. The cricket ground will be turned to some other use. I expect for more houses or a factory. The young men will turn to other things instead of cricket. The whole village will be much the poorer. And all this because of a newcomer who has just bought a house there next to the cricket ground. I must say that I am surprised that the developers of the housing estate were allowed to build the houses so close to the cricket ground. No doubt they wanted to make the most of their site and put up as many houses as they could for their own profit. The planning authorities ought not to have allowed it. The houses ought to have been so sited as not to interfere with the cricket. But the houses have been built and we have to reckon with the consequences. [...] Having read the evidence, I am sure that that was a most unfair complaint to make of the cricketers. They have done their very best to be polite. It must be admitted, however, that on a few occasions before 1974 a tile was broken or a window smashed. The householders made the most of this and got their rates reduced. The cricket club then did everything possible to see that no balls went over. In 1975, before the cricket season opened, they put up a very high protective fence. [...] Despite these measures, a few balls did get over. [...] No one has been hurt at all by any of these balls, either before or after the high fence was erected. There has, however, been some damage to property, even since the high fence was erected. The cricket club have offered to remedy all the damage and pay all expenses. They have offered to supply and fit unbreakable glass in the windows, and shutters or safeguards for them. They have offered to supply and fit a safety net over the garden whenever cricket is being played. In short, they have done everything possible short of stopping playing cricket on the ground at all. But Mrs Miller and her husband have remained unmoved. Every offer by the club has been rejected. They demand the closing down of the cricket club. Nothing else will satisfy them. They have obtained legal aid to sue the cricket club. In support of the case, the plaintiff relies on the dictum of Lord Reid in *Bolton v Stone* [1951] 1 All ER 1078 at 1086, [1951] AC 850 at 867): 'If cricket cannot be played on a ground without creating a substantial risk, then it should not be played there at all.' I would agree with that saying if the houses or road were there first, and the cricket ground came there second. We would not allow the garden of Lincoln's Inn to be turned into a cricket ground. It would be too dangerous for windows and people. But I do not agree with Lord Reid's dictum [1951] 1 All ER 1078 at 1086, [1951] AC 850 at 867) when the cricket ground has been there for 70 years and the houses are newly built at the very edge of it. I recognise that the cricket club are under a duty to use all reasonable care consistently with the play-ing of the game of cricket, but I do not think the cricket club can be expected to give up the game of cricket altogether. After all they have their rights in their cricket ground. They have spent money, labour and love in the making of it; and they have the right to play on it as they have done for 70 years. Is this all to be rendered useless to them by the thoughtless and selfish act of an estate developer in building right up to the edge of it? Can the developer or purchaser of a house say to the cricket club: 'Stop playing. Clear out.' I do not think so. And I will give my reasons. [...] In our present case, too, nuisance was pleaded as an alternative to negligence. The tort of nuisance in many cases overlaps the tort of negligence. The boundary lines were discussed in two adjoining cases in the Privy Council: *The Wagon Mound (No 2)* and *Goldman v Hargrave* [1966] 2 All ER 989 at 992, [1967] 1 AC 645 at 657). But there is at any rate one important distinction between them. It lies in the nature of the remedy sought. Is it damages? Or an injunction? If the plaintiff seeks a remedy in damages for injury done to him or his property, he can lay his claim either in *negligence* or in *nuisance*. But, if he seeks an injunction to stop the playing of cricket altogether, I think he must make his claim in nuisance. The books are full of cases where an injunction has been granted to restrain the continuance of a nuisance. But there is no case, so far as I know, where it has been granted so as to stop a man being negligent. At any rate in a case of this kind, where an occupier of a house or land seeks to restrain his neighbour from doing something on his own land, the only appropriate cause of action, on which to base the remedy of an injunction, is nuisance [...] It has been often said in nuisance cases that the rule is *sic utere tuo ut alienum non laedas*. But that is a most misleading maxim. Lord Wright put it in its proper place in *Sedleigh-Denfield v O'Callagan* [1940] 3 All ER 349 at 364, [1940] AC 880 at 903):' [It] is not only lacking in definiteness but is also inaccurate. An occupier may make in many ways a use of his land which causes damage to the neighbouring landowners, and yet be free from liability ... a useful test is perhaps what is reasonable according to the ordinary usages of mankind living in society, or, more correctly, in a particular society. I would, therefore, adopt this test: is the use by the cricket club of this ground for playing cricket a reasonable use of it? To my mind it is a most reasonable use. Just consider the circumstances. For over 70 years the game of cricket has been played on this ground to the great benefit of the community as a whole, and to the injury of none. No one could suggest that it was a nuisance to the neighbouring owners simply because an enthusiastic batsman occasionally hit a ball out of the ground for six to the approval of the admiring onlookers. Then I would ask: does it suddenly become a nuisance because one of the neighbours chooses to build a house on the very edge of the ground, in such a position that it may well be struck by the ball on the rare occasion when there is a hit for six? To my mind the answer is plainly No. The building of the house does not convert the playing of cricket into a nuisance when it was not so before. If and insofar as any damage is caused to the house or anyone in it, it is because of the position in which it was built. Suppose that the house had not been built by a developer, but by a private owner. He would be in much the same position as the farmer who previously put his cows in the field. He could not complain if a batsman hit a six out of the ground and, by a million to one chance, it struck a cow or even the farmer himself. He would be in no better position than a spectator at Lord's or the Oval or at a motor rally. At any rate, even if he could claim damages for the loss of the cow or the injury, he could not get an injunction to stop the cricket. If the private owner could not get an injunction, neither should a developer or a purchaser from him. […] In this case it is our task to balance the right of the cricket club to continue playing cricket on their cricket ground, as against the right of the householder not to be interfered with. On taking the balance, I would give priority to the right of the cricket club to continue playing cricket on the ground, as they have done for the last 70 years. It takes precedence over the right of the newcomer to sit in his garden undisturbed. After all he bought the house four years ago in mid-summer when the cricket season was at its height. He might have guessed that there was a risk that a hit for six might possibly land on his property. If he finds that he does not like it, he ought, when cricket is played, to sit in the other side of the house or in the front garden, or go out; or take advantage of the offers the club have made to him of fitting unbreakable glass, and so forth. Or, if he does not like that, he ought to sell his house and move elsewhere. I expect there are many who would gladly buy it in order to be near the cricket field and open space. At any rate he ought not to be allowed to stop cricket being played on this ground. This case is new. It should be approached on principles applicable to modern conditions. There is a contest here between the interest of the public at large and the interest of a private individual. The *public* interest lies in protecting the environment by preserving our playing fields in the face of mounting development, and by enabling our youth to enjoy all the benefits of outdoor games, such as cricket and football. The *private* interest lies in securing the privacy of his home and garden without intrusion or interference by anyone. In deciding between these two conflicting interests, it must be remembered that it is not a question of damages. If by a million-to-one chance a cricket ball does go out of the ground and cause damage, the cricket club will pay. There is no difficulty on that score. No, it is a question of an injunction. And in our law you will find it repeatedly affirmed that an injunction is a discretionary remedy. In a new situation like this, we have to think afresh as to how discretion should be exercised. On the one hand, Mrs Miller is a very sensitive lady who has worked herself up into such a state that she exclaimed to the judge: 'I just want to be allowed to live in peace. Have we got to wait until someone is killed before anything can be done?' If she feels like that about it, it is quite plain that, for peace in the future, one or other has to move. Either the cricket club have to move, but goodness knows where. I do not suppose for a moment there is any field in Lintz to which they could move. Or Mrs Miller must move elsewhere. As between their conflicting interests, I am of opinion that the public interest should prevail over the private interest. The cricket club should not be driven out. In my opinion the right exercise of discretion is to refuse an injunction; and, of course, to refuse damages in lieu of an injunction. Likewise as to the claim for past damages. The club were entitled to use this ground for cricket in the accustomed way. It was not a nuisance, nor was it negligence of them so to run it. Nor was the batsman negligent when he hit the ball for six. All were doing simply what they were entitled to do. So if the club had put it to the test, I would have dismissed the claim for damages also. But as the club very fairly say that they are willing to pay for any damage, I am content that there should be an award of £400 to cover any part or future damage. I would allow the appeal, accordingly.

LexisNexis Butterworths

Definitions in context

estate developer: a person or company whose business it is to buy property and make a profit by building new houses, buildings, etc.

sic utere tuo ut alienum non laedas (common law maxim): one must use one's property in such a way as not to injure that of another.

tend (v.): take care of.

wicket: a set of wooden sticks used in the game of cricket.

Exercises

1 **The extract follows several stages which are listed below. Try to identify each stage by giving line numbers.**

background
complaint
action
defence
judgment
reasons

2 **Answer the following questions and justify your answers.**

1. What do the initials MR stand for?
2. Is this a first instance decision?
3. What is another word for "plaintiff"?
4. What type of tort does the case involve?
5. Why did the plaintiff rely on *Bolton*? Is the judge of the same view?

3 **Summarise the case in three short paragraphs.**

1. Facts: "The claimants [...]"
2. Decision: "The court held that [...]"
3. Reasons: [...]

4 **Write a judgment.**

Assume you are a judge hearing a case related to one of the two situations below and write a short judgment using the three-paragraph pattern in the previous exercise. Develop the background of the case, imagine the cause of complaint, the claims of the aggrieved party, a possible line of defence and give your reasoned judgment, applying your knowledge of the law of tort.

Case 1

Claimant (owner of a house next door to defendant's factory) *v defendant* (factory owner).
Wrong: Private nuisance or negligence.
Imagine the damage done to property and the remedies claimed by the claimant and awarded by the court.

Case 2

Claimant (owner of a field) *v defendant* (cycles across the field every day).
Wrong: Trespass and/or damage to property.
Imagine the annoyance or the damage done to property and the remedies claimed by the claimant and awarded by the court.

4. Food for thought

Academic research article

Property Damage and Economic Loss: Should Claims by Property Owners Themselves be Limited?

Andrew Tettenborn

Abstract

This article takes a fresh look at the 'economic loss rule' in torts concerning damage or destruction of property: that is, the rule that while the owner of the damaged property can claim for all consequential losses subject only to remoteness limitations, claims by others for losses they suffer as a result of the damage are severely limited. The problems of anomaly and arbitrariness caused by the rule are well documented. The argument put forward here, however, is that these problems arise not so much because the non-owner has too few rights, but rather because the owner has too many. My conclusion is that the unquestioned right of the owner to claim for consequential losses needs to be substantially constricted, and that all claims for consequential loss resulting from property damage should be subject to the same searching 'duty of care' analysis, whatever the status of the claimant may be.

I. Introduction

There is a well-known story of a countryman who, when asked the way to a distant town, replied after some thought: 'Well, if I was you, I wouldn't start from here.' The object of this article is to suggest that the moral of this tale can profitably be applied to straighten out one of the more awkward anomalies in tort law: namely, the economic loss rule as it affects claims arising out of damage to property. In short, what we are dealing with is the rule that can be summarized in the following two propositions:

(a) When property is damaged or destroyed, its owner can recover damages, not only for its replacement or repair cost, but also for any other consequential losses she suffers owing to its non-availability (provided, of course, the losses claimed are not too remote)

(b) However, the right of anyone else to recover damages under either head is severely circumscribed. Effectively the plaintiff (call her, for short, an 'economic loss plaintiff') cannot obtain anything at all unless she can bring herself within one of the exceptions to the economic loss rule.

Nearly all discussions of the economic loss rule accept (a) without more ado and then go on to discuss (b) at some length, with one eye on the deficiency of the protection available to the economic loss plaintiff. The thesis of this article is that if we look at the point in this way we are in danger of putting the cart before the horse. My aim is not to re-argue the grounds on which claims for economic loss should succeed; rather, it is to suggest that whatever view we take on that question, if Anglo-American tort law is to put its house in order it is actually proposition (a) that needs some searching scrutiny. Thus what we should do in order to make our tort law coherent is not so much to extend or fine-tune the right of the non-owner to sue (though this is clearly necessary), but rather to put at least some limits on the hitherto unquestioned right of the owner to recover her own consequential loss.

II. The Economic Loss Rule

Everyone knows the classic instances of the 'economic loss' rule, and to avoid repeating what large numbers of previous writers have said we can be content with a fairly brief precis here. Imagine that a demolition contractor negligently cuts a power line, and forget for the moment about claims for the costs of repairing the cable and the like (their recovery is entirely uncontroversial, and they do not concern us, except peripherally). Quite apart from these costs, the contractor will doubtless cause a number of further money losses while the damage is repaired. If these losses are suffered by the cable owner herself, she can sue for any losses she suffers, whatever their nature. For example, if her earnings from the cable depend on its usage, or payments to her fail to be suspended while the cable is out of action, she can recover any shortfall in profits caused by the severance. But there liability stops. Nothing goes to the industrialist deprived of power and left with an idle factory, or to her workers laid off without pay; nor yet to others further down the line, such as the industrialist's customers deprived of what she produces, or motorists made late for work because the broken cable knocked out the traffic lights and caused downtown gridlock. Alternatively, take another instance. Suppose a truck driver tries to go under a bridge that is too low and bends it. The owner of the bridge can claim her economic losses over and above basic repair costs: for example, if it is a toll bridge she can claim any lost toll income. But the retail warehouse deprived of trade because its customers cannot cross the bridge, or the trucking firm put to extra expense in fuel and wages by having to divert around it, cannot claim anything. Again, imagine a ship is disabled while under time charter. If the owner is deprived of charter hire as a result (i.e. in cases where under the terms of the charter party payments are suspended while the vessel is off-hire), she has a claim for the lost hire in full. On the other hand, in so far as the charter requires the charterer in the event of damage to continue paying hire for what has become a useless and immobile mass of metal, this loss to the charterer is one she has to bear on her own. Yet again, if goods are destroyed by a third party in the course of transit, the owner has a good claim, but a buyer to whom risk has passed has none.

1. Anomalies and Criticism
The potential anomalies and arbitrarinesses arising out of a 'bright line' rule of this sort are, and always have been, fairly obvious. Break an electric cable just outside my factory, and your exposure is effectively limited to the cost of patching it up: break precisely the same cable a couple of yards away on the factory side of the fence, and while it is being fixed you face a ballooning claim for my lost manufacturing profits, and no doubt a good deal besides. Knock out the bridge leading to my luxury island hotel and golf resort: if I own the bridge, your exposure to liability for my lost profits is potentially huge, but if it is the municipality that owns it, you pay the municipality for the repairs and nothing to anybody else. Drive your truck into the front of my office building so that it cannot be used, and you open yourself to a whole congeries of claims from me for dislocated business: but hit the derelict building next door so that my office remains intact but has to be evacuated for a week for safety reasons while the mess is cleared up, and most authorities say you escape. It is cases such as these that have given rise to much of the argument on the position of the economic loss plaintiff.

The interesting thing is that most commentators who have written about the 'pure economic loss' problem have not had the property owner's peculiarly privileged position at the front of their mind when dealing with it. Instead they have tended to take the physical loss cases for granted and concentrate on discussing the policy and other issues involved in the no-property-damage cases. Arguments of this sort vary in detail, but most of them follow a pretty similar pattern of (a) accepting as a starting point the extensive rights to compensation given to the owner suffering physical damage; (b) rejecting as irrational a bar on liability based without more on the fact that the plaintiff did not suffer damage to her own property, i.e. the traditional economic loss rule; and then (c) suggesting that at least some economic loss plaintiffs should be allowed to sue and going on to look for some coherent ground for deciding which plaintiffs should be the lucky ones. The vital point, of course, and the one where all the serious argument is concentrated, is (c); and not surprisingly the variation in the solutions advocated is almost entirely due to different approaches to it. If you start – as almost everyone did until the 1970s – from the proposition that the chief difficulty with admitting economic loss claims is the pragmatic one of over-distended liability, then you are apt to conclude that the proper criterion is whether the plaintiff is uniquely foreseeable as likely to be harmed as a result of the damage (or at least foreseeable as one of a fairly small group). So, for example, if it is obvious that a damaged pipeline serves a single oil depot, which is the only entity likely to be affected, then the case for allowing the claim is strong: on the other hand, if the same pipeline serves a vast industrial complex stretching as far as the eye can see, it is much weaker. Alternatively, you might prefer to ask instead whether the plaintiff's loss could have been more easily avoided by the plaintiff herself (for example, by taking out business interruption insurance, or – in the case of electrical failure – having a generator on standby or, more abstractly, you could just look for the cheapest cost-avoider. In either of these latter cases, you will almost certainly plump for a fairly constricted liability overall. First-party insurance against business losses is normally more efficient than third-party cover against liabilities of an uncertain amount: also, if a person in business knows the kind of risks she runs, she is often in a better position to take prophylactic measures than a potential wrongdoer who does not. Yet again, you could plausibly argue that ideal tort law exists to minimize absolute losses to society, but ought to be relatively unconcerned with mere inter-personal shifts in wealth from one business to another. If so, then claims should generally fail in so far as they are likely to represent profits lost to the plaintiff but picked up incidentally by some third party (for example, where an island restaurant is marooned by the knocking out of a pontoon bridge leading to the island, but potential diners seeking a night out are likely to have shrugged their shoulders and eaten elsewhere). Or you might even take a more consequentialist view, and say that it is just as relevant to ask if the plaintiff deserves compensation, for example, because she is peculiarly vulnerable because of her status as consumer or for some other reason.

There is no doubt that arguments like these are vital in order to make tort law more logical and coherent. The blanket denial of compensation to economic loss claimants is arbitrary and unacceptable: there must be at least some cases where they should succeed. And, of course, any reduction in the ferocity of the economic loss rule has the incidental effect of making the law more consistent by narrowing the gap between economic loss and property-damage claimants. But even accepting this, it remains the fact that any treatment of the economic loss rule that does not also say something about the position of the property-damage plaintiff must leave unfinished the job of rationalizing tort law. However sophisticated or coherent our analysis of when pure economic loss should or should not be compensable, it remains the case that (for example) the viability of an industrialist's claim for profits lost through power outage due to a severed cable depends on whether she, or someone else, owned the damaged section of cable. Yet the arguments raised for or against liability to the economic loss plaintiff are, by and large, just as relevant to the plaintiff suing in respect of physical harm to her own property.

We will come back below to the argument that this is indeed a serious defect in traditional treatments of economic loss, and that we must therefore adjust the rights of the property claimant as well as the economic loss plaintiff so as to lessen the disparity between them. But before we do that, we have to deal with a preliminary point. Is it in fact true that the differentiation in treatment between property claimants and other claimants is an anomaly? Not everyone agrees that it is. Some commentators argue that there is no mismatch here: in other words, that the distinction, while apparently stark and drastic, is actually entirely coherent. We must therefore deal with this point first.

One suggestion is that the 'property – no property' distinction reflects a basic moral ordering. As one commentator pithily puts it, the discrimination exists 'because things, being capable of gratifying the senses, are more significant than wealth, just as people are more significant than things'. However, for all its homely plausibility it is submitted that this is ultimately unconvincing, for two reasons. First, most tort plaintiffs suing for losses suffered as a result of damage to property, whether the property is theirs or whether they are seeking to recover mere economic losses, are commercial or other entities rather than individuals. Whatever one's view of a mangled favourite sports car or smashed family heirloom, there is precious little sensory gratification to be had from a steelworks, a pipeline or a length of electric cable – certainly not enough to justify privileging its owner as regards the amount she can recover for damage to it. Secondly, it is also worth remembering that in any case, when we are discussing the economic loss rule, recovery of replacement or repair costs is accepted: the owner-plaintiff gets it without question, whatever the nature of the property damaged. What is in issue is compensation for further losses suffered as a result of damage to the thing concerned, such as profits foregone. Where we are talking of damages reflecting financial interests, it is suggested that the question of aesthetic or other pleasure is beside the point.

Again, it can be argued that the distinction is a necessary corollary of the whole idea of duty in negligence. A tort duty, it is said, comports a right in the plaintiff: hence the whole discussion over duties is therefore really a discussion about what rights or interests of the plaintiff the law will safeguard. Since (a) it is given that the right to physical integrity (of person and property) is almost universally protected by negligence law, but (b) nearly everyone accepts that there cannot be blanket protection of all other rights or interests, such as the interest in future profits, it follows that the 'property – no property' distinction, far from being arbitrary, is actually embedded in negligence theory. You may (and should) argue over how far there ought to be a right to recover pure economic loss in the absence of property damage: but whatever conclusion you reach, there must still be some difference between the rights of property and non-property claimants. However, this argument, while attractive, can be neatly parried. Grant that negligence law always protects interests in physical property, and hence that a claimant whose property is negligently damaged must therefore have recovery. This is clearly true: but the question remains: recovery for what? Surely, ownership as such requires compensation exclusively for loss which the owner suffers as owner: that is, loss which only she, and no one else, can suffer as a result of physical damage or destruction. Essentially, this means such matters as the value of the property destroyed, or, in the case of damage, direct repair costs and the like. What it does not require, it is suggested, is the making good of further damage, such as business or profit losses, which although suffered by the plaintiff might equally well have been suffered by a third party having an interest in profiting from the property concerned. In short, the rights argument, while it clearly mandates universal recovery of damages for direct loss suffered by property owners, does not justify differential treatment of other losses, or allowing the property owner to claim as damages consequential losses which she could not have claimed in some other capacity.

Thirdly, it can be argued that even if there is no theoretical or a priori justification for distinguishing owners' claims from others, you are likely to get a similar result if you apply some other, more acceptable, criterion. For instance, it has been suggested that in practice lost profit claims by non-owners are likely to reflect transfers of wealth rather than net social losses and hence amount to weak claims on that basis. Again, something similar lies behind the claim that claims for damage to property are more naturally in the tort field, whereas claims for relational losses should be relegated to contract. Now, arguments of this sort essentially come down to an empirical claim that where the plaintiff is a person with a contractual right to benefit from property, it is relatively easy for her to stipulate with the owner for protection of her interests if she so wishes, and hence that there is no need to give her further specific protection under the law of torts. On the other hand, the empirical underpinnings may not be as clear as is sometimes thought; and in any case they only work for some criteria for deciding between the merits of various claims, and not others.

2. A Solution: Reducing the Claim of the Property Owner

It is suggested, therefore, that whatever version of the existing economic loss rule we apply, the problem of anomaly remains. The fact that A has, and B has not, suffered physical damage to property cannot on its own justify allowing A to recover her loss as of right while B can sue only in limited circumstances. Yet that is exactly what the economic loss rule says. Now, if we want to remove this anomaly, it follows that we have to do one of three things. We could increase B's rights to correspond with A's. Or we could reduce A's rights to claim lost profits and the like to something like the level of B's. Alternatively, we could engage in a combination of the two. Of these solutions, however, the first seems clearly out of the question. Virtually no one seriously suggests that absolutely anyone foreseeably losing out through the unavailability of an item of property should be able to sue in negligence. Effectively, therefore, we are left with the necessity of reducing A's rights to sue for consequential losses, whether or not in combination with some upward adjustment of B's rights so as to make further holes in the economic loss rule.

Of course, this will seem odd to a generation of tort lawyers used to a steady increase in liability and reduction of traditional bars to suit, and indeed apparently prepared to accept that the limiting idea of duty in tort has a fairly insignificant part to play. On the other hand, for a number of reasons it might not be quite as odd an idea as it might seem.

We can begin with origins. The idea of a virtually unlimited right to sue for losses due to, and following on from, physical damage to property is largely a nineteenth-century growth. To that extent it is like the economic loss rule. But it is entirely unlike it in that, whereas in the last 50 years there has been endless discussion of the pros and cons of barring suits by a person who has not suffered physical damage, there has been almost no argument over the propriety of allowing full recovery to the owner who has. It has simply been accepted that, if a proprietor can claim the cost of repair or replacement (as she must be able to), this disposes of the question of duty, and that with that issue out of the way, it follows that she can automatically go on to recover her lost profits under the rubric of consequential loss. The point has, as it were, gone by default.

There is a second, related, reason why limiting the owner's right of recovery may be less unthinkable than it looks. Not only has the argument for privileging the owner effectively been given a walkover. It has in addition been positively bolstered by tort lawyers' peculiar habit of talking about 'physical-damage-to-person-or-property' almost as if they were one word, the issues raised by this speciously composite concept being regarded as a kind of easy starter in the legal quiz show, to be got out of the way before going on to talk about the really interesting matter of the economic loss rule. Doubtless there are straightforward historical explanations for this; nevertheless, commentators ought to have known better than to engage in this sort of myopia. If one thing is obvious, it is that injury to a person and damage to an item of property are not exact equivalents, and raise very different questions. True, as regards the legal reaction both today could be said to be mainly about lost earning power: lost earnings nearly always form a substantial part of personal injury suits, and consequential profit losses equally tend to loom large in any serious property damage claim (since if the claim is substantial what has been damaged is nearly always a commercial or income-producing asset). But it is not hard to see that there is a world of difference between a man incapacitated by a broken leg and a factory made unproductive by an explosion, both morally and in terms of what, pragmatically, the law should do about it. Quite apart from any emotional belief that people are more important than things and therefore deserve to be generously protected in their own right, there are any number of more down-to-earth reasons to allow fairly full recovery for lost earnings in personal injury cases. Individuals are unlikely to be insured against lost earnings so as to allow them to weather long-term incapacitation: they often have relatively few other opportunities to prevent incapacitation proving disastrous: an element of earnings replacement is likely to be necessary to allow full restoration (e.g. by paying medical bills); the effect of long-term loss of income on dependants is likely to be drastic; and so on. Even without engaging in laborious analysis, it seems clear that these arguments apply not at all, or at the very least cannot apply to the same extent, to claims for property damage. This is especially true − be it noted − in respect of claims by corporations and similar abstractions in respect of entirely commercial chattels or realty. It is therefore not surprising that, when writers make the point that physical harm claimants are (and should be) generously treated, nearly all the discussion centres on injury suits. (If one needs an example, take the Restatement 3d of Torts, where the vast majority of cases and examples chosen to illustrate the proposition that a defendant is presumptively liable for physical harm concern personal injury situations, with property damage claims hardly appearing at all). Yet lawyers continue to assume that the personal injury arguments carry the property-damage claimant, and thus effectively allow the latter to piggyback with no good reason whatever on the sympathy given to the injury claimant.

Thirdly, despite the general orthodoxy, in recent years courts in both England and the USA have been increasingly prepared to apply duty reasoning to deny recovery even in physical harm cases. We are not talking here about exceptional or 'public policy' situations, which have always been accepted to a greater or lesser extent to militate against a liability otherwise clear-omissions, liability to trespassers, cases of administrative discretion, immunity of social hosts to suits for the depredations of drunken guests, and so on. Rather, we are dealing with decisions to deny liability on the basis that the facts, in the round, do not justify a duty. Thus the House of Lords has held that the duty to consider whether it is just and equitable to impose a duty applies as much in physical harm as in other cases. Again, the US courts have on occasion barred even personal injury actions on the ground that to allow them would create over-extensive and indeterminate liability; have refused, on duty grounds, to allow products liability claims in respect of physical damage caused to goods by defective replacement components; and in one interesting case have exonerated a defendant who negligently severed a cable from liability to a remote industrialist even where the latter suffered foreseeable physical damage to his inventory. Admittedly none of these decisions covered the subject of this article, which is specifically concerned with claims for economic losses consequential on an incidence of physical damage: nevertheless, they do show that the rule of physical harm recovery without question is perhaps not as entrenched as it might otherwise seem.

From the argument so far, the conclusion seems inescapable. Where an owner claims for physical harm to property, recovery for the repair costs or diminished value should be forthcoming as of course, but any further claims she may have for consequential loss must be scrutinized, not only for foreseeability (which has always been the case), but also in terms of duty in negligence law. However foreseeable the further loss or damage alleged may be, the claim for it ought to be disallowed if it represents losses for which, discounting her ownership of the damaged property, the defendant would not be liable. We should, in other words, have no compunction in telling an industrialist that even if she has a claim against a negligent defendant for physical harm to her plant or inventory, her further claim for profits foregone or extra expense incurred as a result represents a loss she herself (or her insurers) ought to bear. Again, where a stretch of railroad track is knocked out, we should be no more disinclined to deny compensation to the corporation that owns it than to any other railroad that may have trackage rights over it.

3. Two Further Problems

There seem to be only two difficulties to surmount in this connection, and these we deal with now.

The first is that the solution proposed here is inconsistent with a principle often thought to run through the law of damages, which for want of anything better we can call the 'consequential loss principle'. Under this, the assumption is that no essential distinction can or should be drawn in the law of damages between direct and consequential claims: liability once established (i.e. duty problems being solved) carries with it liability for all resulting losses that are not too remote. Now, the inconsistency has to be admitted. But, on the other hand, is the consequential loss principle as all-embracing as it seems?

With respect, it is suggested that it is not. There is no necessary reason to regard the concept of duty as an all-or-nothing matter of this sort, carrying with it a simple dichotomy: no duty leading to no liability, as against duty engendering full recovery. On the contrary: there is nothing formally incoherent or illogical in the idea that a plaintiff should be able to recover for loss X resulting from the breach but not for further loss Y, even if loss Y also foreseeably resulted from that same breach of duty. Moreover, as a matter of policy there may be every reason to say just this. Suppose we believe, for some reason or other (that it promotes economic efficiency, that there is no 'floodgates' danger, that the plaintiff is vulnerable or especially deserving, or whatever other justification we choose), that a plaintiff ought to be entitled to compensation in respect of a given event. It does not follow that she necessarily ought to be able to recover all the losses, or even all the foreseeable losses, she suffers as a result of that event. On the contrary: the reasons for allowing recovery may well apply to only part of them. For example, if equipment in a factory is incapacitated owing to a defendant's negligence it is perfectly plausible to argue that the defendant is the best cost-avoider as regards the repair costs but not as regards profits lost, and hence compensate her for the first but not the second.

How does this argument come to be applied to the particular case of property damage claims? The starting point, it is suggested, is a simple fact: a plaintiff claiming damages in respect of harm to property may be seeking to be made good for two fundamentally different types of loss. The first of these comprises those losses that will inevitably be suffered by somebody as a result of the harm, and whose quantification is relatively fixed. For want of anything better, we can christen this category 'standardized loss'. It is typified by straightforward capital loss claims: suits for replacement price or market value for destroyed assets, and for repair or depreciation costs in the case of damaged ones. To these, it is suggested, should also be added claims for loss of use in so far as they are not quantified by reference to actual profits lost or expenses incurred, but rather set by some more abstract formula (we will come back to this below). Of course, standardized loss is normally down to the owner's account; but it is important to reiterate that it will not always be. Contractual or similar arrangements between the owner and a third party with no proprietary interest in the affected property may have transferred the risk or burden of such loss to the latter; if they have, it will turn what would otherwise be an (ordinary) physical harm claim into an (abnormal) economic loss suit. The case of goods in transit destroyed while owned by the seller but after the risk has passed to the buyer is an obvious example (though not of course the only one).

Standardized losses aside, there are, effectively, all other losses resulting from damage to property. In particular, this left-over category includes all situations involving further (consequential) losses, sometimes dubbed 'ricochet losses', whose incidence and amount are contingent on the facts of the case: straightforward examples are the loss to shippers and carriers forced, owing to the destruction of a bridge or blockage of a railroad track, to incur diversion expenses; loss of profits due to broken cables and pipelines, and so on. The point to note about these losses is that they are entirely contingent: they are not necessarily suffered at all (a cable leading to a factory may be cut and repaired in the course of a Sunday, when the factory is idle anyway), and where they are suffered their amount is almost wholly dependent on the specific circumstances of the person suffering them.

It is respectfully suggested that this distinction between standardized and other losses provides an intellectually coherent ground for distinguishing direct and consequential losses in property damage cases and for applying different rules to them. As regards the former, there is no difficulty in their recovery by the property owner. (Nor, for that matter, do they raise serious difficulties in connection with the economic loss rule, since their eligibility is not in question, and effectively the only issue is who should be allowed to claim them. In the classic case of destruction of goods owned by a seller but at the buyer's risk, although Anglo-American law generally applies the economic loss rule, favouring the seller and disenfranchising the buyer, it would be just as defensible to follow French law in compensating the buyer as the person actually put to expense in having to pay for goods she will not now get. But this argument does not apply to non-standardized damages, where the issue is precisely whether the defendant should be liable for them at all. Here, it is suggested, the case is overwhelming for saying that, whatever we do about the actual costs of repair, the claim for (say) lost profits should be treated in exactly the same way whether it is brought by the owner or anyone else. There is all sorts of reasoning we can use to decide which other users should and should not have a claim of this kind – the need for a manageable number of plaintiffs, the ability of the plaintiff to take her own steps to avoid the loss, the question of who might be the cheapest cost-avoider, and numberless other arguments – but whichever criterion we do use, there is no reason whatever for not applying it to the property-damage claimant in the same way as anybody else.

The second difficulty is a more homely one: at least at first sight, it seems that the results of the thesis proposed in this article are so counter-intuitive that they cannot be right. If, for example, a ship is damaged, does this really mean that its owner must ipso facto be limited to a claim for repair costs tout court, and should recover nothing at all for loss of profitable use because if the claim had been brought by a non-owner (such as a charterer deprived of the benefit of the use of the vessel) the latter could not have recovered? In fact, however, the answer is 'No'. Remember the suggested limitation on our argument in favour of cutting back lost-profit claims: it would apply only to standardized losses, and would leave non-standardized losses unaffected. And it is suggested that certain kinds of loss of use claim will come into the latter category. Although it is true that many claims of this sort are plaintiff-specific (in that their quantification effectively depends on the profits that this particular plaintiff would have made but for the damage to the property concerned), it is also possible to have a fairly standardized loss of use claim – for example, a hypothetical use charge for a bridge or section of railroad, or notional interest on the capital tied up in a ship while it is unproductive. A claim of this kind, it is suggested, falls under much the same analysis as a claim for market value, and arguably should be treated in much the same way: if there is a standardized measure of damages for loss of a thing itself based on the value of the thing, by parity of reasoning there should be one for loss of use of the thing as well quantified by the value of that use. Hence the right of the property owner to claim at least something for loss of use is preserved.

III. Conclusion

The thesis of this article can thus be simply stated. The inconsistency inherent in the economic loss rule is largely due, not to differences between different economic loss claimants, but to the privileged treatment afforded by tort law to property owners, and in particular to claims brought by property owners for consequential losses. If claims of this sort can be cut back and to some extent equalized with economic loss claims, then the law of tort will be a good deal more rational.

The Common Law World Review, June 2005 [CLWR 34.2 (128)]

Exercises

1 Analysing an academic research article.

1. Outline the document. How many parts can you divide this document into?

2. Analyse the abstract:

    a. Explain the purpose of an "Abstract".

    b. How many parts can you divide this abstract into?

    c. Write one sentence summarising each part.

    d. Identify the tenses in the abstract and comment on the effect produced.

3. Work on the article:

    a. What does Andrew Tettenborn seek to demonstrate?

    b. What arguments does he use?

    c. What conclusions does he reach?

2 Research project

1. Find a research article on a topic related to tort law, contract law or criminal law in an academic journal. Academic journals should not be confused with newspapers and magazines.

2. Read the article carefully and give a two-page outline (double-spaced, Times New Roman, 12 pt) dividing it along the following lines:

    a. issues addressed

    b. research methods used

    c. conclusions reached

3. Present your outline:

    a. Summarise what the author seeks to demonstrate.

    b. Summarise the author's conclusion in *one* sentence.

    c. Answer questions from your fellow students.

Inspired by an exercise devised by L. Thompson and J.-T. Pindi in
Anglais: Langues Appliquées, 2ᵉ éd., Montchrestien, 2005. pp. 221-233.

5. Listening

Exercises

1 🔘 **Listen to part 1 of an introductory lecture on tort law and complete the extract with the missing words.**

Let's ...... what is a tort or torts. There is ...... among ...... writers on whether we're talking about one law of tort or the law of several different torts. Winfield considered that there was just a law of tort. His ...... was that there was a .... of tortious liability, which manifested itself in slightly different ways, in slightly different areas of liability. Whereas Salmond thought there was a law of torts .... , in other words that every single tort had its own definition with different ...... which would give or refuse a ....

Whichever view you take though, the law of tort or torts is about .... The word "tort" comes from the Norman French and means ...... or crooked and Winfield defines tort liability as "that which arises from the breach of a duty primarily fixed by law". This duty is towards ...... generally, and ...... for a breach of this duty can be obtained through an action for unliquidated ....

So we're going to see that the law of tort ...... remedies to victims of certain wrongs. However not every wrong will give the victim a remedy. We will also see that a line should be drawn between different wrongs: those which .... to liability and those which do not.

Let's look at Winfield's definition in a little more detail now. First, you'll see that a tort is a civil wrong which may lead to a .... in a .... That's in contrast to criminal law where legal proceedings are referred to as ...... taking place in the criminal courts at the ...... of the State. In tort, the claimant must bring a civil action to be granted a remedy. The State doesn't get ...... in tort cases. It's up to the victim to decide whether or not to .... And it is the victim who conducts the proceedings and ...... those proceedings.

2 🔘 **Listen to Part 2 of the interview and answer the following questions.**

1. Which two terms refer to the party bringing an action in tort?
2. What is a defendant also called in this recording?
3. How is tort law distinguished from criminal law?
4. What are exemplary damages?
5. To what extent is tort law similar to contract law?
6. What is the difference between liquidated and unliquidated damages?
7. What is the aim of an action in tort?

3 **Discuss.**

1. Give examples of torts.
2. What is your opinion regarding the notion of exemplary damages? When should they be awarded?

6. Grammar practice

Exercises

1 **Link words. Complete the sentences with the following link words. In some cases, there may be more than one possible answer.**

albeit	hitherto	in spite of	hence
because	unless	although	thus
despite	therefore	actually	but
nonetheless	i.e. (id est)	since	

1. What we should do now is not so much to extend or fine-tune the right of the non-owner to sue, ... rather to put some limits on the ...... unquestioned right of the owner to recover his or her own consequential loss.

2. A tort duty comports a right in the claimant: ...... the whole discussion over duties is really a discussion about what rights or interests of the plaintiff the law will safeguard.

3. The rules of tort law are generally judge-made ...... there has been some legislative intervention.

4. Effectively the "economic loss claimant" cannot obtain anything at all ...... he or she can bring himself or herself within one of the exceptions to the economic loss rule.

5. The reasonable man test is based on what the "reasonable man" should have foreseen, not what the defendant ...... did foresee. It is an objective test. ...... , allowance is made for cases where the tortfeasor has special knowledge, ... he causes a car accident but he is a driving instructor, or where he or she is a child.

6. Ms Donoghue could not sue the pub owner for breach of contract ...... there was no contract binding them, ... it was a friend of hers who bought the beer.

7. The claimant needs only to show that the defendant's breach of duty was an effective cause of his or her loss, ... not necessarily the only cause.

8. ...... a massive police search, the "Yorkshire Ripper" remained free for several years and murdered a dozen young women.

9. The cricket club then did everything possible to see that no balls went over the householders' fence. ...... before the cricket season opened, they put up a very high protective fence. ...... these measures, a few balls did get over.

2 **Translate the following sentences into English.**

1. À peine l'avocat eut-il fini sa plaidoirie que les syndicalistes furent relâchés.

2. Il l'a dissuadée de se mettre en ménage avec le fils de Monsieur Smith car ce jeune homme n'a pas un casier judiciaire vierge.

3. Il se pourrait que le plaignant soit allé aux Antilles en avion.

4. En la soudoyant, le député travailliste amena la femme de l'aveugle à ne pas faire une déposition.

5. Il est impossible que Mrs. Donoghue ait avalé l'escargot qui se trouvait au fond de la bouteille de bière !

6. Il est important que tout le monde comprenne toute la portée du droit civil afin de pouvoir s'occuper de certaines plaintes comprenant des contrats.

7. Plus cet officier de police vieillit, plus il est distrait.

3 **Translate the following sentences into French.**

1. The case raises the question of whether Mr Williams was more concerned about the allegation that he was gay or the implication that he lied to cover up his sexuality and was a hypocrite.

2. He also risked alienating members of the gay community, who took a long time to forgive the former *Neighbours* star Jason Donovan when he successfully sued *The Face* magazine in 1992 over claims he was gay.

4 **Relative pronouns. Link the sentences in each example to make one sentence, using *who*, *whose* or *whom*.**

1. The Herstell family told *The Guardian* they hoped the action would elicit an acknowledgement of wrongdoing. The Herstell family has three daughters. The three daughters were taken away for questioning by social services.

2. One of the claimants has succeeded in his case against a defendant. The claimant had sued the defendant for negligence.

3. A property developer may be a company or an individual. A property developer's business is to make a profit from the buying and selling of houses and other buildings.

4. The importers and suppliers have been arrested. They had not kept track of the goods they had sold.

5. The claimant's property was damaged through negligence. The claimant must have recovery.

6. The employers of a petrol tanker driver were liable for the damage resulting from the negligent act of their employee. He had caused an explosion by discarding a match near a petrol tanker.

7. The customer is the ultimate user of the good. The defendant should reasonably have in mind that the customer is likely to be injured by want of care in relation to the manufacture of the product.

5 **Modals.**

a. Complete the sentences with the appropriate modal auxiliary from the list below. There may be more than one possible answer.

b. Say if the modal in each example expresses probability, obligation or ability.

may	*might*	*can*	*could*
would	*should*	*must*	

1. If the chain of events leading to an injury is too long or complex, causation ...... be hard to establish.

2. Contributory liability occurs when the defendant in a negligence action ...... show that the claimant either contributed to the event which caused the injury or made the injury worse.

3. The individual jurors ...... not have acted as prudently as they now think they ...... have acted in the situation.

4. In order to claim under section 2 (1) Consumer Protection Act 1987, the claimant ...... prove five things: (1) the claimant has suffered damage (2) which was caused by (3) a defect (4) in a product (5) and s/he wants to sue a potential defendant.

5. The judge held that the master was negligent because he had failed to foresee that he ...... lose consciousness, and had omitted to provide against this.

Contract law

1. Fundamentals

Defining the law of contract

The common law does not give any precise definition of a contract. In his introduction to *Anson's Law of Contract* (28th ed., Oxford University Press, 2002, p. 1), Sir Jack Beatson states: "The law of contract is understood to be the branch of the law which determines that a promise should be legally binding on the person making the promise."

Parties who seek redress for a breach of contract can seek an injunction for specific performance in order to have their contract enforced by the law. In most cases, however, they will claim damages as compensation for the loss suffered.

There are many different types of legally binding agreements, hence the term "laws of contracts". Buying food from the grocer's shop around the corner (a sale of goods **contract**) does not create the same type of relation as a contract between an employee and an employer (a **contract of employment**). Likewise, paying for a holiday at a licensed travel agency is not the same type of contractual relationship as buying a car on credit (a consumer **credit agreement**). There are nonetheless concepts common to all these promises which form the essence of the law of contract.

In Continental systems, academics draft codes of law and then these general principles are applied to particular commercial disputes. This way of handling cases is labelled the deductive approach. Conversely, the English or inductive approach consists of the consideration of particular cases, from which general principles of law are drawn by the judges hearing these cases. That is why the common law system is said to have a more practical approach to dispute resolution than the civil law systems.

Elements of a contract

A contract is based on three elements: **agreement, intention** and **consideration**.

1. Agreement

In order to have a legally binding promise, both parties must agree: the offeror –
i.e. the person who makes the **offer** – and the offeree – i.e. the person who accepts
the offer. In some cases, it is not easy to determine whether there is a contract.
There are three essential steps in the formation of a contract: an offer, the acceptance of the offer and the communication of the acceptance.

Offer

Prior to an agreement, an offer of the goods or services must be made. This is to be
distinguished from an **invitation to treat**. Goods on display in a shop window are
an invitation to treat (see *Fisher v Bell* [1961] 1 QB 394) since the seller should be
able to refuse to sell his goods to a prospective buyer, or offeror. Advertisements are
considered as invitations to treat (see *Partridge v Crittenden* [1968] 2 All ER 421),
unless there is the offer of a reward (see *Carlill v Carbolic Smoke Ball Co.* [1893] 1
QB 256 CA).

   If the offeree responds to an offer by a counter offer made up of different
terms, the original offer is revoked. The party who made the initial offer may then
either accept or reject this counter offer.

Acceptance

The offer must be accepted and acceptance notified. A mere request for information about an offer does not constitute acceptance of an offer (see *Stevenson v
McLean* [1880] 3 Beav. 334).

Communication

Once the offer has been made and accepted, the offeror must be informed that the
offeree has agreed to the offer. The postal rule, however, states that a contract is
complete and binding on transmission of the acceptance through the post, if it was
the medium of communication chosen by both parties, and not on reception of the
notice of acceptance (see *Household Fire Insurance Co. v Grant* [1879] 4 ExD 216).

Revocation of a contract

An offer can be revoked by the offeror at any time before acceptance unless the
offeree has already provided consideration (see *Mountford v Scott* [1975] Ch 258).

2. Intention to create legal relations

A contract has been defined as a legally binding promise. What is the difference between a father promising he will buy his son a sports car if he succeeds in his A-level
exams and a woman walking into a car dealer's showroom and ordering a yellow

mini-van which is not on display but which will have to be custom made? The first promise is not legally enforceable whereas the second is. Generally speaking, if the agreement is a commercial one, the presumption is that there is an intention to create legal relations, but if the agreement is a domestic one, the presumption is that there is no such intention. As might be expected, in the latter case the presumption is strongest between husband and wife (see *Balfour v Balfour* [1919] 2 KB 571) and between parent and child (*Jones v Padavatton* [1969] 1 WLR 328). In some cases the line is not easily drawn between the two types of promise. In *Simkins v Pays* [1955] 3 All ER 10, a domestic agreement between three people to take turns to enter a newspaper competition and to share the winnings if one of them won, was considered contractually binding.

3. Consideration

What makes a promise binding is that the promise to do something (to pay for goods, for example) is made *in return* for another promise (to give the goods to the person paying for them) as defined in *Currie v Misa* (1875) LR 10 Ex 153. There is always a bargain element in a contract. This consideration is mainly in the form of money, but can take other forms. The case of *Bret v JS* (1600) Cro Elis 756 made it clear that love and affection are not of themselves sufficient consideration. The consideration for a promise must be given *in return* for the promise. If what is alleged to be consideration has already been done before and independently of the giving of the promise, then the consideration is said to be *past consideration*. Thus if goods are guaranteed by the seller *after* they have been sold, the buyer cannot rely on the guarantee as the consideration for the guarantee is past (see *Roscorla v Thomas* [1842] 3 QB 234). As a general rule, past consideration can never be effective. Consideration does not have to be sufficient but it has to be adequate, which means that although the payment given in consideration need not be the exact money equivalent to the good or service purchased, it nonetheless cannot be completely out of proportion.

Statutory contractual provisions

Even if contract is a field mainly dominated by case law, the influence of parliamentary legislation and European Union law in certain areas of contract law cannot be underestimated.

1. Privity of contract

Under the common law rule of privity of contract, only parties to a contract are normally entitled to make a claim based on that contract. However, under the Contracts (Rights of Third Parties) Act 1999, it is possible for a third party to claim under the contract in certain specific cases, e.g. if the buyer made it clear to the supplier that he was buying the goods for a third party, as in the case of a present.

2. Sale of Goods Act 1979

This Act may be invoked for any purchase of goods by description or by sample. Straightforward situations fall within the ambit of the law, for example when a consumer buys a woollen jersey in a department store. When a customer has a contract with a business for the sale of goods, terms will be implied into his contract by the Sale of Goods Act 1979. These terms include s.14(2) relating to defective goods:

> (2) Where the seller sells goods in the course of a business, there is an implied term that the goods supplied under the contract are of satisfactory quality.

S.14(3), relating to goods sold for a particular purpose, provides that:

> (3) Where the seller sells goods in the course of a business and the buyer, expressly or by implication, makes known – to the seller, [...] any particular purpose for which the goods are being bought, there is an implied [term] that the goods supplied under the contract are reasonably fit for that purpose, whether or not that is a purpose for which such goods are commonly supplied, except where the circumstances show that the buyer does not rely, or that it is unreasonable for him to rely, on the skill or judgment of the seller or credit-broker.

If there is evidence of a breach of s.14(2) or s.14(3) and if the consumer used the goods correctly so that he did not contribute to the defect, then the consumer may claim damages for breach of contract. The consumer's solicitor or barrister will have to show that:
   – the breach of contract caused the loss suffered, and
   – the loss which was suffered is not too remote.

The aim of contractual damage is to put the victim into the position he would have been in had the contract been properly performed. The victim will therefore be able to claim for loss which flows directly from the breach and for the loss which may reasonably have been in contemplation of both parties at the time the contract was made (*Hadley v Baxendale* [1854] 9 Exch 341).

3. Supply of Goods and Services Act 1982

This Act applies to any purchase of goods and services, such as when a consumer pays for both a boiler and the installation of the boiler from the same supplier. When a customer has a contract with a company for the sale of goods and services, terms will be implied into his contract by the Supply of Goods and Services Act

1982. These terms include that the service has to be provided with reasonable skill and care (s.13) and that the goods must be of satisfactory quality and reasonably fit for their purpose (s.4).

Classification of contracts

There are different ways of classifying contracts:

1. Deeds and simple contracts

A **deed**, also known as **contract under seal** or **covenant**, is a written promise which derives its validity from being intended, witnessed and signed (see the Law of Property [Miscellaneous Provisions] Act 1989). Deeds are to be distinguished from contracts, also known as **simple contracts** or **parol contracts**, since a deed is valid on being delivered. Consideration can be a gratuitous promise and is often used to lend added formality to an agreement without being legally binding, for example in the case of charities raising funds.

2. Bilateral and unilateral contracts

A **bilateral contract** binds both parties to the contract, as, for example, in the case of a contract for sale. A unilateral contract binds only one party, the promisor, but subject to some condition. An estate agent receives a commission for the sale of property. He is not compelled to find a buyer for the house, but if he does and if the sale is made, then the seller has a contractual obligation to pay a commission.

3. Express, implied and quasi-contracts

An **express contract** is clearly one specifically agreed by the parties, whereas an **implied contract** can be inferred from the conduct of the promisor and the promisee or from the circumstances of their promises. A **quasi-contract** is a fiction and the act giving rise to a quasi-contract is considered as a contract only in order to avoid the **unjust enrichment** of a party.

4. Valid, void, voidable and illegal contracts

A contract which gives rise to the full force and effect of the promise is a **valid contract**. A contract is **void** when either the requirements of acceptance and consideration necessary for the formation of a valid contract are absent or when, although these requirements are present, the law forbids the purpose for which the contractual relationship was formed A **voidable contract** is a contract which is capable of producing the results of a valid contract but which can be avoided (i.e. rendered void) by one of the parties, as for example in case of fraud. **Illegal contracts** are not only those which contravene criminal law, but also those which are contrary to public interest (e.g. prostitution).

5. Executed and executory contracts

An **executed contract** is completely carried out whereas an **executory contract** is either partially performed or totally unperformed.

Vitiation of contract

A party to a contract can have it vitiated, i.e. ended because of actions of the other party, especially when those actions affected the circumstances of consent. A contract can be made voidable in this way if any one of the following vitiating factors is established: misrepresentation, duress, mistake, undue influence or illegality.

1. Misrepresentation

Misrepresentation in the context of contract law occurs when the innocent party was deceived by the other party, usually into believing that the object of the transaction was other than it actually was. If that can be established, the innocent party may claim damages and/or seek **rescission** of the contract.

A false assertion of fact can enable the innocent party to challenge the validity of a contract on grounds of misrepresentation. The misleading representation does not have to have been in writing, or indeed oral. For example, concealing dry rot under a coat of paint prior to sale of property was considered a fraudulent misrepresentation in the case of *Gordon v Selico Ltd* (1986) 278 EG 53.

To succeed in a claim based on misrepresentation, claimants also have to show that they were induced to enter into the contract by the misrepresentation; that they would not have entered into the contract if it had not been for the misrepresentation. If a person bought an object in which a defect was concealed but did not look at the object prior to purchase, that person would not be able to bring a claim for misrepresentation.

Duress
When a party was coerced into entering a contractual relationship, consent may have been vitiated by duress and the contract may be voidable. Duress assumes various guises although threats and physical brutality are the most common.

Mistake
Mistake in the context of the formation of a contract can be of two kinds. Not all mistakes are operative, i.e. capable of affecting the validity of a contract. A mistake can either be a common mistake, where both parties make the same mistake, or a unilateral mistake.

Unilateral mistakes may be mistakes made by only one of the parties or they can occur in cases where both parties have made mistakes, but different and conflicting ones. The latter category is operative.

Common mistakes may arise when both parties mistakenly believe that the seller owns the goods involved in the transaction or that the goods exist when they do not. Such circumstances make a contract void. A common mistake related to the quality of goods, on the contrary, is usually not enough to render a contract void.

In the category of unilateral mistakes, mistake as to identity arises when one of the parties believes the other one to be someone else, e.g. when a false name is given. Mistake as to the identity of one of the parties does not necessarily invalidate a contract, inasmuch as the intention to create a binding agreement still exists. However such a contract may be void where the intention of the mistaken party had been to enter into that contract with a specific person.

Another example of unilateral mistake is mistake as to the terms of the contract, but a mere error of judgment would not be considered as an operative mistake by the courts.

In cases of mistake, courts may order rescission of the contract or refuse specific performance, depending on which party is the claimant.

2. Illegality

Although some transactions, such as drug dealing or prostitution, are easily identifiable as illegal, there are more difficult areas where illegality is harder to define.

Any contract whose object is the deliberate commission of a criminal offence or a civil wrong is void. A contract which was lawful in its formation but performed in an illegal manner becomes unlawful. Other examples of contracts which are rendered void on grounds of illegality are contracts prejudicial to the administration of justice, contracts likely to lead to corruption in public life, contracts promoting sexual immorality etc.

3. Undue influence

Undue influence is another way acceptance can be vitiated, but it differs from the other vitiating factors in that it is a matter of equity and, as such, not as precisely defined as the others. Using a position of authority or greater experience to extract consent from a party to enter into a contract has been found by the courts to constitute undue influence.

Definitions in context and key words

agreement for sale: a legal contract between a seller and a purchaser stating the sale price, the settlement date and terms and conditions of sale.

bilateral contract: a contract which binds both parties to the contract.

consideration: a promise of money, goods or service given by one party to another to induce them to enter into a contract.

contract : an agreement that is legally binding upon the contracting parties.

contract of agency: an agreement between principal and agent.

contract of employment: a contract for work binding upon the employer and the employee.

contract under seal: (see deed).

covenant: (see deed).

credit agreements: agreements between borrowers and credit providers, forming an essential part of consumer law.

deed: a written promise which derives its validity from being intended, witnessed and signed.

executed contract: a contract which is completely carried out.

executory contract: a contract which is either partially performed or totally unperformed.

express contract: a contract which is clearly mentioned as such by both parties.

implied contract: a contract can be inferred from the conduct of the promisor and the promisee or from the circumstances of the promise.

illegal contract: a contract which not only contravenes criminal law, but which is also contrary to public interest.

intention: presumed purpose or goal.

invitation to treat: a situation, such as the display of goods, which may lead to the formation of a contract but which is distinguished from an offer in that it does not show specific intention to enter into legal relations.

misrepresentation: in contract, a false representation of fact made by a party prior to the formation of the contract and that may entitle the innocent party to rescission of a contract if he relied on the deceptive representation when deciding to enter into the contract.

offer: a specific proposal to enter into a contract, which can be oral, written or by conduct.

parol contract: (see contract).

quasi-contract: a contract which is a fiction and the act giving rise to it is considered as a contract, whose purpose is to avoid the unjust enrichment of a party.

rescission: the cancelling of a contract which may be ordered by a court when there has been a breach or when a vitiating factor such as misrepresentation affected the formation of the contract.

revocation of a contract: the abrogation of a contract.

revocation of an offer: the cancelling of an offer which can be made by the offeror as long as acceptance has not been communicated to the offeror.

simple contract: (see contract).

term: a condition in a contract that limits or defines its scope. A term can be either implied or express.

unilateral mistake: a mistake made by only one of the parties which can occur in cases where both parties have made mistakes, but different and conflicting ones.

common mistake: a mistake which may arise when both parties mistakenly believe that the seller owns the goods involved in the transaction or that the goods exist when they do not.

unjust enrichment: the fact of benefiting from another party without giving proper compensation.

unilateral contract: a contract which binds only the promisor, but is subject to some condition.

valid contract: a contract which gives rise to the full force and effect of the promise.

void contract (*void ab initio*): an agreement that is not legally binding, as in the case of common mistake, illegality, etc.

voidable contract: a contract which comes into existence but which can be avoided because of the actions of one of the parties.

Exercises

1 **Choose the correct answer or correct ending for each sentence.**

1. A contract is an agreement
    a. enforced by the law.
    b. which is legally binding.
    c. implemented by a law.

2. The English approach to contract law is
    a. theoretical.
    b. deductive.
    c. inductive.

3. An offer may be preceded by
    a. an intention to treat.
    b. a contract.
    c. an agreement.

4. The display of goods in a shop window is considered to be
    a. an invitation to treat.
    b. an offer.
    c. an agreement.

5. The offer is binding only
    a. on reception of an acceptance.
    b. on sending an acceptance.
    c. when made verbally over the phone.

6. If the offeree has provided consideration, the offer can be revoked
    a. before the acceptance.
    b. after the acceptance.
    c. at any time.

7. A promise which creates a legal relation is made between
    a. ward and guardian.
    b. parent and child.
    c. husband and wife.

8. In no case can affection be considered as
    a. love.
    b. consideration.
    c. a consignment.

9. Which of the following are deeds?
    a. Covenants.
    b. Unilateral contracts.
    c. Voidable contracts.

10. A parol contract is
    a. an executory contract.

b. a quasi-contract.

c. a verbal contract.

11. Misrepresentation occurs when a deceptive representation is made

a. verbally only.

b. in written form only.

c. in any form whatsoever.

12. In cases of misrepresentation in contract, the remedies that can be granted by a court are

a. rescission only.

b. damages only.

c. both rescission and damages.

13. Which of the following render a contract void?

a. An operative mistake.

b. Duress.

c. A lie.

14. Mistake as to identity

a. always renders a contract void.

b. renders a contract void in some circumstances.

c. has no impact on the legality of a contact.

15. A common mistake occurs when

a. both parties to a contract have made a mistake, whether it is the same one or not.

b. both parties to a contract have made the same mistake.

c. both parties make a unilateral mistake.

---

2 **Find the key word corresponding to the following definitions.**

1. The person who makes an offer.

2. Agree to an offer.

3. Branch of the law which determines that a promise should be legally binding on the person who makes the promise.

4. Approach consisting in deriving principles of law from particular court cases.

5. The bargain element in the contract.

6. A contract is enforceable because of the relationship between the parties to it.

7. A contract is binding on the transmission of the acceptance through the post.

8. The person who accepts an offer.

9. A legally binding promise.

10. Approach consisting in applying principles of law to particular court cases.

11. Contract binding both parties to the contract.

12. Contract binding only one party.

13. Contract which is capable of producing the results of a valid contract but can be avoided (i.e. rendered void) by one of the parties.

14. Contract which contravenes the criminal law or goes against the public interest.

15. Contract which is partially performed or totally unperformed.
16. Contract implied from the conduct of both parties.
17. Contract expressed in so many terms.
18. Contract completely carried out.
19. Contract that can be avoided.
20. Contract which is not valid.
21. Contract which gives rise to the full force and effect of the promise.
22. Contract which is a fiction.

3 **Find the corresponding words, as the example suggests.**

Example: *employer = employee.*
1. offeror **2.** promisor **3.** contractor **4.** seller **5.** donor **6.** trainer **7.** detainer
8. protector **9.** bailor **10.** lessor **12.** grantor **13.** assignor **14.** guarantor
15. patentor

4 **Complete the text with words from the list below.**

promise	revoked	binds	terminated
obligations	rejected	expiry	acceptance
performance	revocation	offeror	
revocable	offeree		

The formation of a contract is the process which creates legal .... Until acceptance there is nothing but a ...... offer which binds nobody. After acceptance there is a completed contract which ...... both parties. The acceptance, like the offer, contains within it two ideas, namely (1) the ...... of the offeror's proposal, and (2) either the ...... requested by the offeror or the ...... of the act required. [...] If an offer is not turned into a contract by acceptance, it may be ...... , that is lose its ability to be converted into a contract, in a number of ways. First, an offer may be .... This destroys its efficacy in so far as the particular offeree is concerned. The result is that it is no longer open to the ...... to change his mind and accept the offer after all, unless indeed the ...... renews his offer. [...] The second way in which an offer may be terminated is by .... An offer may be ...... , i.e. withdrawn, at any time before it is accepted, even if the offeror has promised to keep the offer open for a specified time. [...] The third method by which an offer may be terminated is simply by ....

P. S. Atiyah in *An Introduction to the Law of Contract*, 5th ed., Clarendon, 1995, pp. 56-79.

5 **Say whether, in legal terms, there is a contract in each of the following situations.**

1. Stephen has agreed to buy Helen's horse but has not paid for it yet.
2. Ruth sees a nice top in a shop window. She enters the shop and says she wants to buy it.

3. Ashley's grandfather says he will inherit all his fortune if his grandson loves him.

4. Rachel buys a shirt for Brandon but she does not specify to the shopowner that it is a gift.

5. The accountant of the Fish and Salmon company sends the signed contract back to Tank and Co. agreeing to the purchase of 50 salmon tanks. Due to a national post office strike, Tank and Co. never receive the signed contract.

6. Russell agrees to sell Simon his bicycle in exchange for work that the latter did in his garden last year.

6 Case studies.

1. John has a skin disease and as a consequence cannot wear clothing made of wool. One cold winter's day, John needs a jumper. He goes to a local department store and sees a pile of red turtle-neck pullovers advertised as 100% acrylic. He asks a saleswoman if the they are free of any woollen content, explaining to her the reason why. The saleswoman checks the label and phones the sales manager to confirm that the jumpers are wool free. Some days later, when John wears his new pullover, he gets a rash. It turns out that the fibre contains wool.
Explain what remedies John has in tort and contract.

2. Sarah buys an automatic garage door. She has it fitted by the company from which she buys it. A couple of days later, the garage door collapses, thankfully injuring no one. Sarah calls in a buildings inspector and it turns out that not only was the manufacture of the door defective but the bolts had not been properly secured.
Explain what remedies Sarah has.

7 Can the following contracts be voided? Justify your answers.

1. A farmer bought a cow after the seller told him what a good breeder the animal was. During a subsequent examination by a veterinary surgeon, the cow was found to be infertile.

2. Two brothers owned and operated a restaurant together. The older brother managed to buy his brother's shares after repeated pressure and threats.

3. A woman who was in urgent need of a car bought a second-hand vehicle in a rush. The next day, she noticed that there was rust all over the bonnet covered by a thin coat of paint.

4. A highly religious young man was persuaded by the leader of a charitable organisation to do a good deed by buying dozens of books from the organisation.

5. A man bought a painting from an art gallery where it was displayed as a work by Pablo Picasso. An expert friend of his noticed that the signature was a fake. It turned out that the gallery owner had known about it all along.

6. The owner of a small furniture company hired a delivery man. The vehicle concerned was not insured, but the employee was obliged to drive it anyway.

7. A man promised to sell his old car to a neighbour's young cousin. A young woman came to buy the car introducing herself as the neighbour's cousin. In fact she was only a friend of that person but the transaction took place.

8. A man purchased a manuscript which both he and the seller believed to be by Charles Dickens. It was later found out that it had been written by some unknown author.

8 Writing.

1. In a few sentences, explain the difference between undue influence and duress in contract.

2. Write a short paragraph presenting a situation in which a contract could be voided on grounds of duress or undue influence.

9 Case study.

Contract for sale of goods

Agreement made and entered into this [date], by and between [name of seller], of [address], [city], [country], herein referred to as "Seller", and [name of buyer], of [address], [city], [country], herein referred to as "Buyer".

Seller hereby agrees to transfer and deliver to buyer, on or before[date], the following goods: ....
....

Buyer agrees to accept the goods and pay for them in accordance with the terms of the contract.

Buyer and Seller agree that identification shall not be deemed to have been made until both parties have agreed that the goods in question are to be appropriated and fulfill the requirements of performance of said contract with the buyer.

Buyer agrees to pay for the goods at the time they are delivered and at the place where he receives said goods. Goods shall be deemed received by buyer when delivered to address of buyer as herein described. Until such time as said goods have been received by buyer, all risk of loss from any casualty to said goods shall be on seller.

Seller warrants that the goods are now free from any security interest or other lien or encumbrance, that they shall be free from same at the time of delivery, and that he neither knows nor has reason to know of any outstanding title or claim of title hostile to his rights in the goods.

Buyer has the right to examine the goods on arrival and has [number] of days to notify seller of any claim for damages on account of the condition, grade or quality of the goods. That said notice must specifically set forth the basis of his claim, and that his failure to either notice seller within the stipulated period of time or to set forth specifically the basis of his claim will constitute irrevocable acceptance of the goods.

This agreement has been executed in duplicate, whereby both buyer and seller have retained one copy each, on .... [date].

....
[Signatures]

Mr Jones buys a sofa and two armchairs from ARI FURNITURE. The above standard contract form is used, with the following TERMS AND CONDITIONS appearing at the end:

1. If the suite is defective and causes you injury, ARI FURNITURE will not be liable to you in any way. ARI FURNITURE in fact accepts no liability at all for any defects in the product.
2. The price of the suite is £1,500, but ARI FURNITURE reserves the right to increase this price when sending you the invoice for the suite.
3. ARI FURNITURE will be the sole judge of whether the suite actually delivered is in accordance with the terms of the contract.
4. If you have any complaint against ARI FURNITURE, you must refer it to the Furniture Manufacturers' Association for arbitration, rather than go to court.

When the sofa and the two armchairs are delivered, Mr Jones is presented with an invoice for £2,000. The suite is green, not red as ordered, and when Mr Jones sits on one of the armchairs, it collapses and he is injured. He contacts ARI FURNITURE about these problems but is told that terms and conditions 1 to 4 mean that he has no grounds for complaint.

Using your knowledge of unfair contract terms and on the basis of Directive 93/13, do you think Mr Jones would be able to make a claim against ARI FURNITURE? Explain.

10 Discuss.

1. What is the difference between a contract and a promise?
2. What makes a valid contract?

2. More about…

A. Famous contract cases

1. Offer and acceptance

Fisher v Bell **[1961] 1 QB 394**

A shopkeeper displayed a flick-knife with a price tag in his shop window. He was charged with offering it for sale in violation of the Restriction of Offensive Weapons Act 1959. The magistrates construed the words "offer for sale" in the Act as under the general law of contract. The display of the flick-knife in the window was only an invitation to treat and the knife had not been offered for sale.

Carlill v Carbolic Smoke Ball Co **[1893] 1QB 256 CA**

The defendants placed an advert for "smoke balls" claiming that they prevented influenza. The advert offered to pay £100 to anyone who contracted influenza despite using the ball as prescribed. The company made a £1,000 deposit with the Alliance Bank as evidence of their sincerity. Mrs Carlill purchased a smoke ball but contracted influenza. The company refused to pay the £100 claimed by Mrs Carlill. It was held that she was entitled to receive the £100 as advertised. The Court of Appeal reasoned that:

(1) the deposit of money showed an intention to contract, therefore the advert constituted a genuine offer and not mere advertising "puff";

(2) an offer to the world at large is nevertheless a valid offer, which is accepted by whoever buys a smokeball;

(3) the offer of protection from influenza would cover the period of use; and

(4) the purchase and use of the smokeball constituted acceptance.

The postal rule

Special rules have been created to cover acceptance by post because of the period of uncertainty inherent in this form of acceptance. Although the rule is normally that acceptance is only effective when it is received by the offeror, acceptance by post is considered as complete when the letter of acceptance is posted.

Adams v Lindsell **[1818] 106 ER 250, Lord Ellenborough**

The defendant wrote to the plaintiff, offering to sell some wool, and required a reply "in course of post". Because this offer was delayed two days in the post, the plaintiff's acceptance was late in coming back. On the day before the defendant received the acceptance letter (but after it had been expected), he sold the wool to a third party. The court held that the plaintiff was entitled to damages: his acceptance was complete as soon as his letter was posted, which happened before the wool was sold to the third party.

2. Consideration

Chappell v Nestlé [1959] 2 All ER 701, HL

The plaintiffs owned copyright in a piece of music which the defendants used as part of a promotion offering records featuring this copyrighted material in exchange for 1s 6d [7 1/2p] and three chocolate wrappers. In an action to recover royalties, the question arose whether the wrappers were part of the sale price. The House of Lords said they were; a contracting party (*per* Lord Somervell) may stipulate for what consideration he chooses, and a peppercorn does not cease to be valuable consideration just because the promisee intends to throw it away.

3. Breach

Frost v Aylesbury Dairies [1905] 1 KB 608, CA

A woman died of typhoid after drinking infected milk supplied by the defendants. Her husband sued for breach of contract, relying on a term implied by s.14(1) of the Sale of Goods Act 1893, equivalent to that in s.14(3) of the 1979 Act. The Court of Appeal affirmed the decision of the trial judge in favour of the plaintiff: although the defendants had not explicitly stated that the milk they produced was intended to be consumed by the plaintiff's family, the advertising statements issued by the defendants, laying emphasis on quality, should be construed as expressing such intention. Therefore the defendants were in breach.

4. Illegality

Archbolds (Freightage) v Spanglett [1961] 1 All ER 417, CA

The plaintiffs contracted with the defendant for the transport of a load of whisky. The defendant did not have a license allowing him to carry such a load, which made the contract illegal. However, the plaintiffs were able to sue on the terms of the contract because they had had no knowledge of the illegality, nor any reason to know of it. The contract was *prima facie* legal when it was made, and only the manner of its performance was illegal (*prima facie* is the Latin expression for "on the face of it"), meaning that the relationship is presumed to be true, unless other evidence disproves it.)

Exercise

Answer the following questions.

1. In your opinion, would the reasoning which gave rise to the postal rule apply to acceptance by voicemail?

2. Could the facts of *Frost v Aylesbury Dairies* have generated another cause of action?

B. Law of contract and national sovereignty

1. Towards a European law of contract?

EU contract law plan under attack

Lord Falconer, the Lord Chancellor, will spell out today the government's opposition to harmonising contract law across the European Union, telling lawyers and business leaders that it would be inefficient and counter-productive.

He is expected to say that the "common frame of reference" - the European Commission's proposal for a code of European contract law - should be used to encourage judicial recognition and co-operation between different jurisdictions, rather than create a back-door route to harmonisation.

The Lord Chancellor is due to make his remarks in a speech at the Mansion House, in the City of London, at a conference being co-hosted by the European Commission and the UK presidency.

In principle, many European businesses would welcome a single form of contract law because the current plethora of national laws adds to costs. A survey by Clifford Chance, the world's largest law firm, of 175 European companies found more than 80 per cent in favour of harmonisation.

However, these businesses were sceptical that a single European contract law could be achieved. In addition, there was little support for a compulsory single law across the EU; the majority of those canvassed thought they should be able to choose other laws if they preferred.

Big City law firms, meanwhile, argue that even attempting to draw up a uniform European contract law would lead to protracted debates. The ensuing uncertainty would drive international companies away from using the popular English law for commercial business.

That, it is argued, could seriously undermine Britain's legal industry where the combined annual turn-over of the top 100 firms tops £9bn.

In his speech, Lord Falconer is expected to warn that any weakening of the attractiveness of English common law to commercial business would be a loss for Europe - and an opportunity that would be seized on by rival jurisdictions, such as New York and Geneva.

He will tell his audience that proposals to create a "code of contract law" in Europe would be a waste of resources. Instead, he will suggest that the common frame of reference should be used as a tool for encouraging co-operation between different legal jurisdictions.

Nikki Tait, *The Financial Times*, 26/9/2005.

2. The primacy of English law of contract in the global market

Commercial & Chancery: **Vive la chancery**

The Chancery Court may be no more, but the Chancery Division is still providing a world-leading service in business disputes.

[...] Chancery practitioners are undertaking a vast and increasing amount of international work. Due to start next week in the Chancery Division is a huge case between two Russian businesses about a joint venture. Because many companies and trusts are set up for various purposes on islands which are common law jurisdictions such as the Cayman Islands, the British Virgin Islands, Bermuda, the Channel Islands or Hong Kong, when problems arise they look to the English chancery practitioners for advice.

What does the future hold?

[...] The Lord Chancellor (the *fons et origo* of the Court of Chancery) recently gave a speech to the Commercial Bar Association about the primacy of English commercial law, the importance of maintaining its standing (including improving the facilities of the Commercial Court and its IT facilities) and the quality of its judges. He justified this by reference to the fact that the English law of contract is the international law of choice over a wide range of areas. All of which is quite true.

Everything he said applies equally, if not more so, to the Chancery Division and much of its work. Not only is English law the international law of choice in contracts, but it (or its offsprings, such as the Commonwealth, the Eastern European bloc and developing jurisdictions that base their law on

English law) is often the compulsory law of the problem - the law of the place of the company's incorporation, or the law governing the trust that frequently underpins the commercial entity which enters into the contractual arrangement. It is just as important that the court hearing trust, fraud, IP and company work has the same standing and judges as the Lord Chancellor is advocating for the Commercial Court.

Unless the Department of Constitutional Affairs and the Government can be made to realise that the Chancery Division and its work are a mainstay of the reputation of English law, then life "in chancery" may be in a bleak house* indeed.

Carolyn Walton, *The Lawyer*, 24/10/2005.

* A reference to *Bleak House*, by Charles Dickens, a novel dealing largely with legal problems, bankruptcy and the Court of Chancery.

Exercise

Answer the following questions:
1. Describe the project of an EU law of contract.
2. Why is English law the international law of choice in contracts?
3. In your opinion, why would the UK be reluctant to adopt an EU law of contract?

C. Meanings (citations, acronyms...)

(1) **Primary legislation: Act of Parliament**
e.g. Guard Dogs Act 1975

(2) **Secondary legislation: statutory instrument**
e.g. SI 1975 No. 1767

(3) **Case law**
e.g. *Punch v Judy* [1978] 1 All ER 945

Exercises

1 Answer the following questions.

In (1):
1. What is the date of the Act?
2. What is the Act about?

In (2):
1. What does SI stand for?
2. What is the year of the statutory instrument?
3. What does 1767 refer to?

In (3):
1. Who is Punch?
2. Who is Judy?
3. What does 'All ER' stand for?
4. What does the figure 1 refer to?
5. What does the figure 945 refer to?
6. What does the date between brackets refer to?

2 **Research project. Using textbooks or the legal resources on the internet, find the meaning of the following acronyms which refer to a law report.**

1. AC   2. Ch   3. Fam   4. QB   5. KB   6. WLR   7. IRLR   8. LGR   9. Lloyd's Rep
10. Tax Cas   11. Cr App R   12. ECR   13. CMLR   14. EHRR

3 **Read the following text and find out what the advantages of a neutral citation are.**

Neutral citation

In line with the ongoing modernisation of the whole legal system, the way in which cases are to be cited has been changed. Thus, from January 2001, following Practice Direction (Judgments: Form and Citation) [2001] 1 WLR 194, a new neutral system was introduced and extended the following year in a further Practice Direction in April 2002. Cases in various courts are now cited as follows:

House of Lords [year] UKHL case no
Court of Appeal (Civil Division) [year] EWCA Civ case no
Court of Appeal (Criminal Division) [year] EWCA Crim case no

High Court

Queen's Bench Division [year] EWHC case no (QB)
Chancery Division [year] EWHC case no (Ch)
Patents Court [year] EWHC case no (Pat)
Administrative Court [year] EWHC case no (Admin)
Commercial Court [year] EWHC case no (Comm)
Admiralty Court [year] EWHC case no (Admlty)
Technology and Construction Court [year] EWHC case no (TCC)
Family Division [year] EWHC case no (Fam)

Slapper and Kelly, *The English Legal System*, Cavendish, 2004.

---

4 **What information do the following citations give?**

1. *Lister v Forth Dry Dock and Engineering Co. Ltd* [1989] 2 WLR 634
2. SI 1998 No.1833
3. Sale of Goods Act 1979
4. *P v S and Cornwall County Council* [1996] IRLR 347
5. The Sale and Supply of Goods to Consumers Regulations 2002 (SI 2002 No.3045)
6. *Hobson v Gledhill* [1978] 1 All ER 945
7. *Jane v Crown Drinks and Co* [2007] UKHL 34
8. Consumer Protection Act 1987
9. *Webb v EMO Air Cargo* [1994] ECR I-3567
10. *Brown v Jones* [2001] EWCA Civ 12

5 **Research project.**

1. Using textbooks or the legal resources on the internet, find the meaning of the term "estoppel" and read the following explanation.

> If A owes B £10 and if B agrees to take £9, as he must before there can be any question of discharging the obligation of A to pay £10, why should B be allowed afterwards to break his promise to take £9 and succeed in action against A simply because A gave him no consideration? [...] The doctrine of estoppel is basically a rule of evidence under which the court, surprisingly enough, is not prepared to listen to the truth. It occurs at common law out of *physical conduct*. Suppose A and B go into a wholesaler's premises and A asks for goods on credit. The wholesaler who knows B is credit-worthy, but has no knowledge of A, is not prepared to give credit until A says "Don't worry, you will be paid, B is my partner". If B says nothing and A receives the goods on credit and does not pay, then B could be sued for the price, even though he can produce evidence that he was not in fact A's partner. This evidence will not be admitted because the wholesaler relied on a situation of partnership created by B's conduct and the statement is concerned with *existing fact* which is essential at common law. Promissory estoppel in equity is very little different except that the equitable estoppel arises from a *promise* [...].
>
> Denis Keenan, *Smith and Keenan's English Law*, Longman, 2001. pp. 252-253.

2. Describe a situation which would fall within the scope of equitable promissory estoppel.
3. Using textbooks or legal resources on the internet, find the case below. What are the facts of the case and what is the point of law you should remember?
Central London Property Trust Ltd v High Trees House Ltd. [1947] KB 130

D. Discharge of contracts

1 Research project. Using textbooks or law resources on the internet, find the cases in the list below. What are the facts of the case and what is the point of law you should remember?

Bolton v Mahadeva [1972] 2 All ER 1322, *Sumpter v Hedges* [1898] 1 QB 673, *Chas Rickards Ltd v Oppenhaim* [1950] 1 KB 616, *Storey v Fulham Steel Works* (1970) 24 TLR 89, *Taylor v Cadwell* (1863) 3 B & S 826, *Krell v Heny* [1903] 2 KB 740, *Jackson v Union Marine Insurance Co* (1874) LR 10 CP 125, *Omnium D'Entreprises and Others v Sutherland* [1919] 1 KB 618.

2 Case study.

1. Circus and Co., a family-operated circus, signed a first contract with Builders and Co. for setting up the tent in which the circus performance was to take place on the occasion of the wedding of Arthur and Olivia, members of the royal family.

They paid £1,000 for the services of Builders and Co., but the work was poorly done and the tent threatened to collapse. Builders and Co agreed to strengthen the structure of the building for an extra £500. *Would they be entitled to make an extra charge?*

2. Circus and Co. agreed to pay for the extras and the second contract stipulated that the work had to be completed by the Friday preceding the wedding day (which was on a Saturday). On the Friday, Builders and Co. had not completed the work and Circus and Co. refused to pay the £500. *Would they be entitled to do this?*

3. On Saturday morning, the wedding was cancelled. Circus and Co. refused to pay for both contracts, arguing that the contract was frustrated. *Would they have to pay for the work?*

4. Builders and Co. went out of business on the following Monday and left their tools on the site. Circus and Co. decided to finish the setting of the tent themselves and held their circus performance on the following week. Builders and Co. heard about it and wanted Circus and Co. to fulfil their obligations under the contracts. *Did Builders and Co. have a claim?*

E. Remedies

1 Research project. Using textbooks or legal resources on the internet, find the cases in the list below. What are the facts of the case and what is the point of law you should remember?

Beach v Reed Corrugated Cases Ltd [1956] 2 All ER 652, *Jarvis v Swans Tours Ltd* [1973] 1 All ER 71, *Victoria Laundry Ltd v Newman Industries Ltd* [1949] 2 KB 528, *Brace v Calder* [1895] 2 QB 253, *Lynn v Bamber* [1930] 2 KB 72.

2 Case study.

Joshua buys a microwave oven, which costs him £600, from Magor, an electrical retailer. Joshua uses his microwave oven in his small apartment for a week or so; however, one day, he switches it on and it explodes. The oven and an antique table next to which it was set (worth £1,000) are destroyed, and Joshua's fitted carpet and wallpaper are so badly damaged that they will have to be replaced. Joshua takes the opportunity to fully redecorate his apartment. Joshua himself suffers minor but painful cuts from the blast. However, he suffers intense trauma as a consequence and it is many months before he can get himself to use another kitchen appliance. As a consequence, he cannot properly perform his duties as the husband of a successful career wife. His wife has to stay at home to help him and she is passed over for promotion. *What are the damages Joshua is entitled to?*

Use the following expressions in your answer:
the Article/ Article... gives...
Article... indicates...
according to Article...
Article...
see Article... of...
as required by Article...
under English/EU law...
be a product under Article...
the provisions of Article...
the requirement of... is contained in Article...
satisfy the test in Article...
suffer damage as contemplated by Article...
satisfy the... criteria
imply the words into...
be legislation in this area
the... reflects the directive correctly/incorrectly on this point
a... brings a directive into effect.

3 Case study.

You bought a computer online from a company called Electronics Ltd. Once you get home you try to turn it on but it does not work.
1. Write an e-mail to the company explaining your problem.
2. The reply e-mail you receive a couple of days later is as follows:

From: Electronics Ltd., Consumer Services
To: Student
Re: Defective TV set
Dear Mr Student,
We are sorry to inform you that, under the provisions of our warranty coverage policy, your claim regarding a computer purchased from our online store cannot be covered.
Sincerely yours,
Mr. X
Head of Consumer Services, Electronics Ltd

3. Imagine the e-mails you should now write in an attempt to solve the problem, and the answers you would receive.

3. Off the presses

Law report

Vitol SA v Norelf Ltd; *House of Lords (Lord Mackay of Clashfern, Lord Chancellor, Lord Griffiths, Lord Nolan, Lord Steyn, Lord Hoffmann) 20 June 1996.*

An aggrieved party could as a matter of law accept a repudiation of a contract merely by himself failing to perform the contract. Whether in any particular case he had done so must depend on the circumstances.

The House of Lords allowed an appeal by the sellers, Norelf Ltd, reversed the decision of the Court of Appeal (1996 QB 108) and restored the decision of Mr Justice Phillips (1994 1 WLR 1390) affirming an arbitration ruling against the buyers, Vitol SA.

The dispute arose out of a contract of 11 February 1991, by which Norelf sold to Vitol a cargo of propane c.i.f. north-west Europe to be shipped from the United States. Delivery of the cargo to the ship was to take place from 1 to 7 March. The sellers were to tender the bill of lading to the buyers promptly after loading. On 8 March the buyers telexed the sellers as follows:

It was a condition of the contract that delivery would be effected 1-7 March 1991... We are advised that the vessel is not likely to complete loading now until some time on 9 March, well outside the agreed contractual period. In view of the breach of this condition we must reject the cargo and repudiate the contract.

The buyers never retracted nor attempted to retract their repudiation of the contract. The sellers did nothing to affirm or perform the contract. Instead they resold the cargo at a loss. They then claimed against the buyers US$ 950,000 in damages, being the difference between the original contract price and the resale price. The premise of the claim was that they had accepted the buyers' repudiation.

The arbitrator held that the tenor of the rejection telex was such that the failure of the sellers to take any further step to perform the contract which was apparent to the buyers constituted sufficient communication of acceptance of the buyers' repudiation.

Jeremy Cooke QC and Andrew Wales (Clyde & Co) for the buyers; Andrew Popplewell and Miss N. Davis (Holman Fenwick & Willan) for the sellers.

Lord Steyn said it was established law that where a party had repudiated a contract the aggrieved party had an election to accept the repudiation or to reaffirm the contract. Acceptance of a repudiation required no particular form; it was sufficient that the communication or conduct clearly and unequivocally conveyed to the repudiating party that the aggrieved party was treating the contract as at an end. The aggrieved party need not notify the repudiating party of his election to treat the contract as at an end; it was sufficient that the fact of the election came to the repudiating party's attention.

The issue here was whether non-performance of an obligation was ever as a matter of law capable of constituting an act of acceptance. One could not generalise on the point. It all depended on the particular contractual relationship and the particular circumstances of the case. Like Phillips J, his Lordship was satisfied that a failure to perform might sometimes signify to a repudiating party an election by the aggrieved party to treat the contract as at an end.

The Court of Appeal had been strongly influenced by an obiter dictum of Kerr LJ in *State Trading Corp of India Ltd v Golodetz Ltd* 1989 2 Lloyd's Rep 277 at 286, that saying and doing nothing at all, other than a continuing failure to perform, cannot constitute an acceptance of a repudiation even if the grounds for such an acceptance then exist.

In his Lordship's opinion that passage, if intended to enunciate a general rule, went too far. A continuing failure to perform would necessarily be equivocal; but his Lordship disagreed with the view of Nourse LJ in the Court of Appeal (1996 QB 106 at 116-117) that failure to perform a contractual obligation was necessarily and always equivocal.

Sometimes in the practical world of businessmen an omission to act might be as pregnant with meaning as a positive declaration.

Paul Magrath, in *Vitol SA v Norelf Ltd* (Law Report, *The Independent*, 28/6/1996).

Exercise

Answer the following questions.

1. What are the facts of the case?
2. What is the point of law at issue?
3. What is Lord Steyn's opinion?

4. Food for thought

Terms and conditions of a warranty

1. Definitions and keywords

In this policy, words that appear in bold have the following special meaning: "accidental damage" means any sudden and unforeseen damage occurring to the insured product not otherwise excluded under the terms of this policy; "authorized repairer" means a service provider we approve and instruct to repair the insured product; "commencement date" means the date you purchase this extended warranty as shown in the schedule; "insured product" means the domestic goods shown in the schedule; "period of insurance" means the period from the commencement date to the termination date; "policy" means this policy numbered [number]; "premium" means the single payment paid by you for cover under this policy; "schedule" means the document setting out the details of your cover under this policy which has been issued to you together with this policy document; "termination date" means the earliest of the following dates: (i) the date on which the period of insurance expires; or (ii) the date you cancel this insurance cover under Clause 7; or (iii) the date we advise you that this insurance cover is terminated under Clause 8; or (iv) in respect of each insured product, the date we compensate you for the total loss of the insured product; "total loss" means a repair we consider to be impossible or uneconomic; "we" "us" "our" means Pinnacle Insurance plc; "you" "your" means the individual named in the schedule. The singular shall include the plural and vice versa.

2. Benefits

We will indemnify you against:

(i) Mechanical/Electrical Breakdown outside the manufacturer's Guarantee Period. The cost of repair (or replacement if the repair is considered a total loss) of the insured product due to a breakdown in normal use as a result of technical or electrical failure resulting in the insured product ceasing to operate in accordance with the manufacturer's specification.

(ii) Accidental Damage*

The cost of repair (or replacement if the repair is considered a total loss) of the insured product due to accidental damage to the insured product.

*Please note: No cover available for Plasma Screen televisions.

(iii) Frozen Food Loss – If applicable to the insured product. Accidental loss of frozen food stored in the insured product in the event of a Mechanical Breakdown as set out in Clause 2 (i) above.

3. Limits of indemnity

(i) The maximum payment for any one claim under Mechanical/Electrical Breakdown or Accidental Damage, as set out in Clause 2 (i) and (ii) above, shall not exceed the original purchase price of the insured product. The maximum payment in aggregate for all claims for Mechanical/Electrical Breakdown or Accidental Damage during the period of insurance of this policy shall not exceed the original purchase price of the insured product, or £5,000, whichever is less.

(ii) The maximum payment for any one claim under Frozen Food Loss, as set out in Clause 2 (iii) above, shall not exceed £300. The maximum payment in aggregate for all claims for Frozen Food Loss during the period of insurance of this policy shall not exceed £600.

(iii) This insurance is limited to the United Kingdom, the Channel Islands and the Isle of Man only.

4. When will you not be covered?

We shall not be liable for:

(i) any loss, damage, malfunction or breakdown resulting from or as a consequence of:

(a) fire, lightning, explosion or flood;
(b) theft or any attempt thereat;

(c) the variation and/or failure of electrical supplies for any reason including adverse weather conditions;

(d) any wilful act or neglect;

(e) rusting, corrosion, denting or scratching;

(f) damage caused by sand, sea water, the action of sunlight, wind, weather or other natural elements;

(g) the insured product not being installed or operated in accordance with the manufacturer's instructions;

(h) use other than domestic use by you or your family permanently living with you;

(i) use of unapproved accessories; or

(j) any repairs carried out outside the United Kingdom, the Channel Islands and the Isle of Man.

(ii) the cost of:

(a) routine cleaning, service, inspection and maintenance;

(b) rectifying cosmetic damage not affecting the safe use of the insured product, or the replacement of or adjustment to plastic, metal trim badges or insignia;

(c) repair or replacement of taps;

(d) consumable items requiring routine replacement such as any projection lamps, light bulbs, disposable bags, oven liners, batteries or styli;

(e) materials or labour charges for which the manufacturer, supplier, installer or repairer may be responsible for under any guarantee or warranty;

(f) work covered by manufacturer's recall of the product;

(g) adjustment of aerial sockets and re-alignment of satellite antennae;

(h) unblocking drainage channels on refrigeration equipment;

(i) repairing or replacing scratched photographic and camcorder lenses;

(j) call out charges where no fault is found;

(k) frozen food loss where proof of purchase is unavailable;

(l) medication or vaccines stored in the insured product under a frozen food loss claim;

(m) modifying the insured product in any way;

(n) changing from analogue to digital broadcasting, including the termination of any type of analogue transmission; or

(o) installing a replacement item if the insured product is considered a total loss; or

(iii) loss of use of the insured product or any consequential loss; or

(iv) any accidental damage claims for plasma screen televisions.

5. Claims

(i) In the event of mechanical/electrical breakdown or accidental damage to the insured product, you should contact us on [telephone number] to obtain a claim reference number. You will be given details of the authorised repairer, who will undertake repairs covered by this policy and charge the cost of a valid claim directly to us. The authorised repairer will require you to pay for any repairs falling outside the scope of this policy.

(ii) If a repair is considered to be a total loss, we will at our discretion, replace the insured product with a product of similar or equivalent specification. The damaged insured product shall become our property.

(iii) In the event of a claim for Frozen Food Loss, you should contact us on [telephone number] to obtain a claim form. Simply complete the claim form and return it to us at [address].

Alternatively, you may fax the claim form to [telephone number]. In the event that an inspection is required, you will be advised within 48 hours (normally immediately).

Please note: All spoiled food must be kept for at least 48 hours and any loss adjusters we appoint must be given access to the insured product in the event that an inspection is required.

6. Cool off period

You may cancel this policy within 14 days of the date you purchased the insured product and receive a refund of premium provided you have not made a claim. Thereafter, you may cancel your policy at any time, however, no refund of premium shall be payable. To cancel, simply contact [telephone number].

7. Invalid payments

In the event that any payments are made which are found to have been made as a result of your fraud, recklessness or negligence, we may terminate this policy and we reserve the right to demand that any such benefits are repaid by you and/or take the appropriate legal action against you. We may demand that you reimburse us for any investigation costs reasonably incurred.

8. General conditions

(i) This policy document, together with the schedule and any endorsement hereon will contain all the terms and conditions relating to cover of your insured product. The provisions of this policy are, where their nature permits, conditions precedent to our liability under this policy.

(ii) You cannot assign or charge the policy in any manner whatsoever.

(iii) This policy shall not acquire a surrender value.

(iv) The parties to this policy are free to choose the law applicable to it. Without agreement to the contrary, English Law will apply. If you live in Scotland, Wales, Northern Ireland, the Channel Islands or the Isle of Man, you will be entitled to commence legal proceedings in your local courts.

(v) Insurers share information with each other to prevent fraudulent claims via a register of claims. A list of participants is available on request. In the event of a claim, any information you have supplied relevant to this insurance and on the claim form, together with other information relating to the claim, will be provided to the register.

(vi) We are covered by the Financial Services Compensation Scheme (the "Scheme"). You may be entitled to compensation from the Scheme if we cannot meet our obligations. The amount of compensation depends on the type of business. Most types of insurance business are covered for 100% of the first £2,000 of a valid claim and 90% of the remaining amount of the loss. Further information about compensation arrangements is available from the Financial Services Compensation Scheme.

(vii) To improve the quality of our service, we will be monitoring and recording some telephone calls.

Enquiries and complaints

While it is always our intention to provide a first class standard of service, if you do have any concerns regarding your insurance cover, please address them to [address].

Should you remain dissatisfied with the outcome of any internal enquiries, you have the right to refer your complaint to:

The Financial Ombudsman Service (FOS)

South Quay Plaza, 183 Marsh Wall, London E14 9SR

This procedure will not prejudice your right to take legal proceedings. However, please note that there are some instances when the FOS cannot consider complaints.

A leaflet detailing our full complaints/appeals process is available from us on request.

Exercise

Case study.

Mary buys a £500 waterproof radio to pick up the weather reports when she is sailing. She is careful to buy one advertised as seaworthy. Nonetheless, in less than a year, seawater damages her radio. She is outraged and calls the Customer Relations Manager to get her money back. *Will she be covered by the supplier's warranty?*

5. Listening

1 💿 **Listen to an introductory lecture on contract law and complete the following extract with the missing words.**

There were two .... in the context of contract law: firstly the notion of .... of contract and secondly a ...... of contract. The sanctity of contract means that nobody can ...... the contract once it has been agreed. Well that's the ..... . Going back to the first element, freedom of contract, it essentially means that anybody can .... any contract. How true is that? How true was it ever? Well of course it isn't entirely true. One aspect of this .... any contract is the converse, i.e. that people are free not to contract if they choose not to. We can ...... that this was probably truer in the 19th century than it is today. I suppose it was true in the sense that the .... going on at the time generally provided more freedom of choice. There were fewer ...... for example. Freedom of contract meant in a ...... sense, in a third sense, that any contract could be entered into on any term. And again this was more true than it is today. But it was never totally true. You couldn't always enter into any contract on any term. There have always been ...... and one would be .... A person certainly could not enter into a contract to ...... someone for instance or to commit any other crime. That would be ....

2 **Answer the following questions.**

1. Explain the differences between the Continental approach to contract and the common law approach.
2. Define the "deductive" approach. What is it set in opposition to?
3. What are the two fundamental characteristics of contract law inherited from the 19th century laissez-faire philosophy?
4. Explain the meaning of the concept of sanctity of contract.
5. Explain the meaning of the concept of freedom of contract.

3 **Discuss.**

1. Do you think that contract law should provide freedom for individuals to agree to any contractual term?
2. What can you say about the notion of freedom of contract today?

6. Grammar practice

Exercises

1 **Expressing condition. Transform the sentences, following the pattern of the example.**

Example: If the offeree provides consideration, the offer can be revoked. *Had the offeree provided consideration, the offer could have been revoked.*

1. A father promises he will buy his son a sports car if he passes his A-level exams.

2. According to the domestic agreement, if one of them wins, the three people will share the winnings.

3. If the agreement is a commercial one, the presumption is that there is an intention to create legal relations.

4. If there is evidence of a breach of s.14 (2) and if the consumer uses the goods correctly so that he does not contribute to the defect, then he may claim damage for breach of contract.

5. If an estate agent does not receive a commission for the sale of property and if the sale is made, then the seller has a contractual obligation to pay a commission.

6. If any of the following vitiating factors is established (misrepresentation, duress, mistake, undue influence or illegality), the contract can be avoided.

7. If misrepresentation can be established, the innocent party may claim damages and/or seek rescission of the contract.

8. If the suite is defective and causes you injury, ARI FURNITURE will not be liable to you in any way.

2 **"Any" or "some"? Complete the sentences.**

1. The common law does not give ...... precise definition of what a contract is.

2. An offer can be revoked at ...... time before acceptance unless the offeree has already provided consideration.

3. We are advised that the vessel is not likely to complete loading now until ...... time on March 9th.

4. To improve the quality of our service, we will be monitoring and recording ...... telephone calls.

5. This act may be invoked for ...... purchase of goods by description or by sample.

6. A contract can be made voidable in this way if ...... one of the following vitiating factors is established: misrepresentation, duress, mistake, undue influence or illegality.

7. The plaintiff asked a saleswoman if the tops were free of ...... woollen component and explained the reason for her question.

8. Please note that there are ...... instances when the FOS cannot consider complaints.

9. The seller or supplier to alter unilaterally without a valid reason ...... characteristics of the product or service to be provided.

10. The defendant wrote to the plaintiff, offering to sell …… wool, and required a reply "in course of post".

11. In …… cases, it is not easy to determine whether there is a contract.

3 **Expressing the future. Rephrase the sentences using other means of expressing the future, as in the example. You may use other expressions, such as "is expected to", "is due to", etc. Explain the difference between the meanings of each form.**

Example: The seller will be the sole judge of whether the suite actually delivered is in accordance with the terms of the contract.

*The seller **is going to** be the sole judge of whether the suite actually delivered is in accordance with the terms of the contract.*

*The seller **is to** be the sole judge of whether the suite actually delivered is in accordance with the terms of the contract.*

1. They will claim damages to compensate for the loss suffered.

2. The consumer's solicitor or barrister will have to show that the breach of contract caused the loss suffered.

3. The victim will therefore be able to claim for loss which flows directly from the breach of contract.

4. Ashley will inherit his grandfather's fortune if the old man is convinced of Ashley's love for him.

5. Today, the Lord Chancellor will spell out the government's opposition to harmonising contract law across the European Union.

6. He will say that the European Commission's proposal for a code of European contract law should be used to encourage judicial recognition.

7. The Lord Chancellor will make his remarks in a speech at the Mansion House, in the City of London.

4 **Concession vs opposition. Complete the sentences with one of the following words or expressions. There may be more than one possiblity in each case.**

even if	*although*	*nonetheless*
while	*whereas*	*even though*

1. …… paying for a holiday at a licensed travel agency is not the same contractual relationship as buying a car on credit, there are …… concepts common to all these promises.

2. The first promise is not legally enforceable …… the second is.

3. …… Mary was careful to buy a £500 waterproof radio advertised as seaworthy, seawater …… damaged her radio in less than a year.

4. Saying and doing nothing at all, other than a continuing failure to perform, cannot constitute an acceptance of a repudiation …… the grounds for such an acceptance then exist.

5. Duress assumes various guises ...... threats and physical brutality are the most common ones.

6. An express contract is clearly mentioned as such by both parties, ... an implied contract can be inferred from the conduct of the promisor and the promisee or from the circumstances of the promise.

7. An executed contract is completely carried out ...... an executory contract is either partially performed or totally unperformed.

8. If B says nothing and A receives the goods on credit and does not pay, then B could be sued for the price, ... he can produce evidence that he was not in fact A's partner.

9. ...... the payment given in consideration need not be the exact money equivalent to the good or service purchased, it cannot ...... be completely out of proportion.

10. ...... the rule is normally that acceptance is only effective when it is received by the offeror, acceptance by post is considered as complete when the letter of acceptance is posted.

5 Translate the following document into French.

The Annex of Directive 93/13 contains an indicative and non-exhaustive list of the terms which may be regarded as unfair. Terms which have the object or effect of:

1. excluding or limiting the legal liability of a seller or supplier in the event of the death of a consumer or personal injury to the latter resulting from an act or omission of that seller or supplier;

2. inappropriately excluding or limiting the legal rights of the consumer vis-à-vis the seller or supplier or another party in the event of total or partial non-performance or inadequate performance by the seller or supplier of any of the contractual obligations, including the option of offsetting a debt owed to the seller or supplier against any claim which the consumer may have against him;

3. making an agreement binding on the consumer whereas provision of services by the seller or supplier is subject to a condition whose realisation depends on his own will alone;

4. permitting the seller or supplier to retain sums paid by the consumer where the latter decides not to conclude or perform the contract, without providing for the consumer to receive compensation of an equivalent amount from the seller or supplier where the latter is the party cancelling the contract;

5. requiring any consumer who fails to fulfil his obligation to pay a disproportionately high sum in compensation;

6. authorizing the seller or supplier to dissolve the contract on a discretionary basis where the same facility is not granted to the consumer, or permitting the seller or supplier to retain the sums paid for services not yet supplied by him where it is the seller or supplier himself who dissolves the contract;

7. enabling the seller or supplier to terminate a contract of indeterminate duration without reasonable notice except where there are serious grounds for doing so;

8. automatically extending a contract of fixed duration where the consumer does not indicate otherwise, when the deadline fixed for the consumer to express this desire not to extend the contract is unreasonably early;

9. irrevocably binding the consumer to terms with which he had no real opportunity of becoming acquainted before the conclusion of the contract; [...]

Chapter 9

Employment law

1. Fundamentals

Employees and independent contractors

1. Different status

Students starting their study of employment law should be aware that the term "worker" is of no legal relevance. The terms used for the parties to an employment contract are "employee", i.e. a person working for an employer for wages, and "employer", i.e. a person employing an employee. It is vital to distinguish "employees" from "independent contractors" or "self-employed individuals", since a different legal and economic status flows from this distinction. The differences are summarised in the table below:

	EMPLOYEE Contract of service	SELF-EMPLOYED PERSON Contract for services
Contract		
Unemployment benefit	Yes	No
Sick pay	Yes	No
Industrial injury benefit	Yes	Sometimes
State retirement pension	Yes	Yes, but lower rate of pension
Maternity leave	Yes	No

Contract	EMPLOYEE **Contract of service**	SELF-EMPLOYED PERSON **Contract for services**
Security of employment after maternity leave	Yes	No
Time-off rights	Yes	No
Right to belong to a union	Yes	No
Vicarious liability for employers	Yes	No
Sex Discrimination Act 1975 implied in the contract	Yes	Yes
Race Relations Act 1976 implied in the contract	Yes	Yes
PAYE (Pay-As-You-Earn) (Income Tax)	Deducted at the source by the employer	Paid by the self-employed
Salary received by the worker	Net wages	Gross wages

2. Tests for determining status

Determining whether a person is an employee or an independent contractor is not always obvious, as in the case of home workers. Over the decades, the courts, deciding vicarious liability cases, have created a series of tests to ascertain the status of the employee.

The first test, known as the control test, was established in the case *Performing Rights Society v Mitchell and Booker* [1924] 1 KB 762. It states that the degree of control the employer has over the work performed by the employee determines his status. However, technological changes have made it increasingly difficult to use the concept of control as a defining criterion of the employment relationship between the employee and the employer.

A second test was developed in the case *Stevenson, Jordan & Harrison Ltd v McDonnel and Evans* [1952] 1 TLR 101. It is called the organisation test and Denning LJ defines it as follows: "Under a contract of service, a man is employed as part of the business and his work is done as an integral part of the business, but under a contract for services his work, although done for the business, is not integrated into it but only accessory to it."

Over the years, the courts have become more aware that only a multiplicity of factors could assess the nature of the employment relationship. The multiple test was devised with the case *Ready Mixed Concrete (South East) Ltd v MPNI* [1968] 2 QB 497. The whole point of this test is to balance a host of factors indicating whether the person falls under the category of self-employed or of employed. These factors include investment and ownership of tools, as well as the questions of who bears the risk and who stands to make a profit.

A contractual relationship

An employment contract is only a particular form of contract, it must therefore comply with the basic elements of an enforceable contract, i.e. an offer made by the employer. It is then accepted expressly or implicitly by the employee and the consideration is the wage that the employer promises to pay the employee in exchange for services. Nevertheless, an employment contract is to be considered as a particular form of contract in that the parties to the contract have not negotiated each term. Indeed, employment contracts are regulated by different sources, in particular UK and EU statutory provisions. Terms may also be incorporated into the contract by the conduct of the parties or as a result of collective agreements.

The terms of the contract

1. Express terms

The terms agreed upon by both parties, i.e. the express terms, include salary, hours of work and details of the job. If an employee refuses to perform a material part of the contract, as part of an industrial action for example, he will be considered as having committed a **repudiatory breach** of contract. In such a case the employer has several options. He can either decide to **terminate** the contract or to **waive** the breach. If the employer does not act upon the breach and if the employee continues working, it will be assumed that the employer has waived the breach and **affirmed** the contract. The employer can also deduct an appropriate portion of the employee's pay, in order to compensate for the non-fulfilment of the employee's contractual duties.

There are some express terms that the parties cannot include in the employment contract. Liability in case of death or personal injury of the employee and in some cases, damage to his property, caused by the negligence of the employer cannot be excluded. Moreover, the terms have to comply with the Equal Pay Act 1970, the Sex Discrimination Acts 1975 and 1986, the Race Relations Act 1976 and also the more recent disability and age discrimination legislation. Lastly, no term can prevent an employee from taking an action in court or in an employment tribunal against his employer.

In any case, an express term in a contract should be clear and cannot be over-ridden by an implied term.

The terms of the contract can be altered as long as the amendments are agreed upon by both parties. Some minor changes affecting the working conditions of employees are possible within the terms of an existing contract, especially in cases where adapting the job of the employee to new methods and technologies is necessary. The courts have been prepared to read implied terrms as to adaptability into **contracts of employment** as long as the tasks performed are still within the scope of the employee's contractual duties.

2. Collective agreements

The enforceability of agreements resulting from negotiations between a union and an employer, i.e. a collective agreement, will depend on whether the agreement is incorporated impliedly or expressly into the individual employee's contract of employment. The contractual principle of privity of contract applies as it does to any contract. As the parties to the collective agreement are the union and the employer the employee cannot directly enforce the agreement.

There are three ways around this legal problem. The most common is implied incorporation, if it is clear that the parties considered the agreement as binding. In the case of *Joel v Cammel Laird* [1969] ITR 206, the courts defined the criteria to determine whether an employee can be bound by a collective agreement: he must know of the agreement, he must show by his conduct that he accepts the agreement and there must be some form of incorporation into the contract. The limits of implied incorporation are that it only applies to union members.

The second means is by express incorporation, where the agreement of the individual employee is evidenced by a statement in his employment contract. Once the statement has been incorporated, it is part of the employee's contract and governed by the rules of contract, i.e. legally enforceable.

The third method is agency and is based on the argument that the union representative acted as an agent of its members when he negotiated the collective agreement. This is a way of solving the problem of the non-enforceability of collective agreements. However, it raises several issues such as: does the agreement apply only to the persons working in the company at the time when it was made, how can the union act as an agent of its members and what is the basis of the negotiator's agency?

When there are conflicting collective agreements, *Gascol Conversion Ltd v Mercer* [1974] IRLR 155 establishes that a national agreement takes precedence over a later local one.

3. Implied terms

These are terms which are not stated in the agreement but which are read into the contract by the courts. The courts will imply terms into the contract when the contract is silent on a matter in order to give the contract "business efficacy" (*The Moorcock* [1889] 14 PD 64) or when a term is blatantly absent (*Shirlaw v Southern Foundries Ltd* [1939] 2 KB 206). Implied terms may be implied by statute, obligation, fact or custom (see below).

4. Other elements

Other documents, such as staff handbooks, work rules, disciplinary and grievance procedures, statutory statements and customs, can be construed as express terms of the contract, if they are incorporated in the contract. Otherwise they are no better than a gentleman's agreement. It is of note that courts have tended to interpret work regulations as orders, and therefore as part of the employee's job duties. Failure to comply with a given rule can be read by the employer as a breach of contract by the employer, although in determining, for example, whether a dismissal was fair, the courts will consider the reasonableness of the rule and whether dismissal for the breach was a sanction that a reasonable employer might impose. Custom and practices of a particular industry can also be the basis of a contractual term. Deducting a proportion of wages on account of bad workmanship (*Sagar v Ridehalgh* [1931] 1 Ch 310) constituted such a practice.

Implied duties in the contract of employment

1. Personal nature of the contract

It has long been recognised that the employment relationship is imbalanced and bargaining power is in favour of the employer. Nonetheless, the courts interpret an employment contract as a personal contract whereby both parties agree to provide personal services to each other. The principle which flows from this basic assumption is that an employee cannot be forced to continue the contract if he does not wish to do so. That is why injunctions for specific performance are normally not granted by the courts (see *City & Hackney Health Authority v National Union of Public Employees* [1985] IRLR 252 and *Powell v Brent London Borough Council* [1988] ICR 176).

2. Duties of the employer

The employer-employee relationship has moved away from the traditional concept of master-servant to one where the employer owes a duty of respect to his employee. The courts can consider the consequences of the breach of that respect on the contractual relationship and in *Bliss v South East Thames Regional Health Authority* [1987] ICR 700 decided that the refusal by the Health Authority to permit a doctor to return to work because he refused to submit to a psychiatric examination constituted a repudiatory breach of contract. Courts have repeatedly refused to imply a duty on the employer to provide work, except in some cases where work is needed to maintain the reputation of the employee (e.g. an actor in a play), to enable the employee to earn his bread (e.g. a piece-worker), to develop the employee's skill, etc. However, the employer has a duty to pay wages to his employees. The National Minimum Wage (NMW) Act 1998 sets a statutory **minimum wage** for all eligible workers above 21 years of age. It applies to a worker's **gross pay**, not including tips, premium payments, company car, private health insurance, etc. Working time, for the purpose of calculating the minimum wage, is defined according to the provisions set out in the EU Working Time Directive (No 93/104) and implemented in Working Time Regulations 1998. The employer also has the duty to indemnify the employee for expenses incurred in the course of his employment.

The main duty of the employer is to ensure his safety. This area is regulated by the common law of negligence and the Health and Safety at Work Act 1974. The law of negligence provides for a safe place of work, safe plant and equipment, a safe system of work and reasonably competent fellow employees. Section 2(1) of the Health and Safety at Work Act 1974 states: "It shall be the duty of every employer to ensure, so far as is reasonably practicable, the health, the safety and welfare of all of his employees."

It is up to the courts to determine what is to be considered as "reasonable" in the circumstances of a particular case. In addition, it is generally accepted that employers are vicariously liable for the torts of their employees committed in the course of their employment. Therefore, if an employee is injured as a result of a co-worker's incompetence, the injured party may have a multiple cause of action. He may sue his co-worker in his own right and his employer along two lines: first for failing to provide reasonably competent co-workers and, vicariously, for the co-worker's negligence.

3. Duties of the employee

Employees owe a duty of obedience, loyalty, care and skill to their employers. This means that they are expected to cooperate with their employers, obey reasonable lawful orders, carry out their work with reasonable care and skill, refuse bribes, refrain from disclosing confidential information, and decline working for a competing company.

Rights and protection of employees

Numerous measures have been taken to protect employees and promote a discrimination-free workplace in the UK. Legislation has been passed to bridge the pay gap between men and women (Equal Pay Act 1975) and to prevent discrimination against women. Similarly, efforts to limit racial discrimination have been undertaken, both statutorily and in the form of awareness campaigns and other incentives. Recent legislation, such as the amendments to the Disability Discrimination Act 1995, the Employment Equality (Sexual Orientation) Regulations 2003 and the Employment Equality (Religion or Belief) Regulations 2003, emerged in the European context to comply with European Directives. Indeed, the Employment Directive outlaws discrimination on grounds of sexual orientation, religion or belief, disability and age in employment and vocational training. In addition, the Race Directive outlaws discrimination on grounds of racial or ethnic origin in the areas of employment, vocational training, goods and services, social protection, education and housing. Changes to the Race Relations Act 1976 were made to implement the Directive which came into force in July 2003.

1. Part-time employees

The Part-Time Workers (Prevention of Less Favourable Treatment) Regulations 2000, which implement the EC Directive on part-time work provide that part-time employees should not be treated less favourably than full-time employees. This protection applies to the following aspects of their employment (taking account of the proportionate number of hours worked):
- hourly rates of pay,
- statutory annual leave,
- maternity leave and parental leave,
- contractual sick pay and maternity pay,
- overtime pay,
- selection of employees for redundancy,
- access to pension schemes.

2. Maternity leave and rights of working parents

A pregnant employee is entitled to a 26-week maternity leave (increased to nine months from October 2006). This applies irrespective of how long the employee has worked for her employer, though she must have worked for 26 continuous weeks with her employer and earn at least a certain amount defined statutorily to qualify for Statutory Maternity Pay, which is paid for a maximum of 26 weeks by the employer (nine months from October 2006) but partly (or, for small firms wholly) reimbursed by the state. For the first six weeks she is paid 90 per cent of her average weekly earnings and is paid at a flat rate for the time remaining. The pregnant employee is required to notify her employer of her intention to take maternity leave before the end of the fifteenth week prior to the expected week of childbirth, unless exceptional circumstances prevent her from complying with that requirement. The employer must reply in writing, indicating the date on which the employee is due back.

Since 2003, a series of family-friendly measures have been developed, such as paid paternity leave, which is available to fathers for up to two weeks. Under the

Flexible Working Regulations 2002, parents of children under six years old and parents of disabled children under eighteen have the right to request flexible working arrangements if they have worked for their employer for at least 26 continuous weeks. The employer has a duty to consider such applications seriously and the Regulations provide a right to appeal against an employer's decision by referring their case to ACAS, to an employment tribunal, or through another mode of dispute resolution. ACAS (Advisory, Conciliation and Arbitration Service) is a publicly funded independent organisation whose aim is to help improve employment relations and life in the workplace. Employees who have worked a minimum of one year with their employer may take up to thirteen weeks' unpaid parental leave. Leave is also available for adoptive parents.

3. Racial discrimination

The Race Relations Act 1976 outlaws both direct and indirect discrimination in all stages of employment and a Commission for Racial Equality (CRE) was set up to oversee its implementation. The Act covers arrangements made for deciding who is offered a job; the terms on which the job is offered, opportunities for promotion, training and transfer, the benefits and services granted to employees, and job termination or other unfavourable treatment of employees. The Act provides for specific exemptions where there may be a genuine occupational qualification (GOQ) justifying the hiring of a member of a particular race, ethnic group, etc. The list of genuine occupational qualifications includes actors, models, personal welfare offices and certain jobs in places like restaurants where "for reasons of authenticity" a person of a particular racial group is required, for example an Indian restaurant.

Nothing in the legislation requires discrimination in favour of ethnic minorities but there is very limited provision for positive action. For example, training may be provided to equip people from an under-represented group to apply for posts. However, no positive discrimination is allowed at the point of selection. The Race Relations Act applies to discrimination by employers, trade unions, professional associations, employment offices and similar bodies, and redress may be sought against an individual and their organisation.

In 2001, the Race Relations Act was amended to give public authorities new duties regarding the promotion of racial equality. One of the aims of the amended legislation is to improve equal opportunities in employment. Public authorities are bound by a racial equality duty which requires them to eliminate unlawful racial discrimination and to promote equality of opportunity and good race relations.

4. Gender discrimination

At the end of 1975 the Sex Discrimination Act was passed, the Equal Pay Act came into force and the Equal Opportunities Commission (EOC), an independent public body, was set up to promote equality between men and women. Sex discrimination may concern, among other things, hiring practices, wages, or it may take the form of sexual **harassment**. Under the Equal Pay Act 1975, a female employee has a right to equal pay for like work, i.e. similar work, and for work of equal value within the same organisation regardless of the type of employment contract. Equal pay covers basic pay, bonuses, overtime, holiday pay, sick pay and **pension**. An equal pay claim which has not been resolved out of court may be taken to an employment tribunal.

The Equality Act 2006 places public bodies under a gender equality duty mirroring the racial equality duty mandated by the Race Relations Amendment Act 2001 and under a disability duty as provided by the Disability Act. The Equality Act also contains provision for the establishment of a Commission for Equality and Human Rights to fulfil the missions carried out by the EOC and the CRE.

5. Discrimination on grounds of religion and belief

Discrimination on those grounds is outlawed by the Employment Equality (Religion or Belief) Regulations 2003. The law protects people against discrimination on the grounds of their religion and belief in all aspects of employment and vocational training. This form of discrimination was not explicitly covered by English law before. The Regulations prohibit direct and indirect discrimination, harassment and **victimisation**. Anyone who has been treated less favourably because they have been assumed – correctly or incorrectly – to have a particular religion or belief, may thus invoke the protection of the law.

6. Discrimination on grounds of sexual orientation

Discrimination on grounds of sexual orientation has been made unlawful under the Employment Equality (Sexual Orientation) Regulations 2003, which apply to employment and vocational training. Like the Religion and Belief Regulations, the Sexual Orientation Regulations offer protection against discrimination, harassment and victimisation. They safeguard the rights of homosexual men and women, bisexuals and heterosexuals. Amendments to the Regulations, taking account of the introduction of civil partnership in the UK, were approved by Parliament and took effect on 5 December 2005 (the date on which the Civil Partnership Act came into force). The amended regulations provide that an employer must not treat a civil partner less favourably than he would treat a spouse in similar circumstances unless he can show that being heterosexual or gay, as the case may be, was a genuine occupational requirement (GOR) of the job (regulation 7(2)). This exception concerns employment in the context of an organised religion, where an employer may have just cause to consider matters "related to sexual orientation". A narrow range of employers in relation to a very limited number of posts, may therefore require that an employee be married (rather than having a civil partner) but only where such a requirement is necessary.

7. Age discrimination

The Employment Equality (Age) Regulations 2006 translate a European directive into domestic law and prohibit less favourable treatment or prejudice on grounds of age at all stages of an individual's employment. In addition, the Regulations set a national default retirement age of 65 and impose on all employers a "duty to consider" any employee's request to work beyond the default retirement age.

Termination, redundancy and dismissal

These three notions are by no means synonymous although they may be relevant in the same context.

Redundancy involves one of the following situations: closure (whether temporary or permanent) of a business as a whole, closure of a particular workplace where the employee was employed or a reduction in the size of the workforce. The employer must use a fair and consistent procedure in deciding who is going to be made redundant and pay the terminated employee a redundancy payment, either based on the legal minimum or (if higher) on the terms of the employment contract. If fairness is overlooked, the employer may be sued for unfair dismissal. Redundancy may also raise a case of wrongful dismissal. Unfair dismissal differs from wrongful dismissal in that the latter occurs when terms of the employment contract are violated by the employer in the course of dismissal.

Unfair dismissal claims are tested against two parameters. The first part of the test is whether there was a fair reason to dismiss the employee. The second part of the test looks to the way the dismissal was handled and consists in determining whether it was dealt with fairly. Legitimate grounds for dismissal include fair redundancy, job qualification, ability and conduct. Theft or drunkenness are examples of types of conduct which justify dismissal.

Definitions in context and key words

affirm *(v.)*: where an innocent party is entitled to accept a repudiation of the contract by the other party and treat himself as discharged from further obligation, but chooses instead to treat the contract as continuing.

contract for services: a contract which is used for appointing a self-employed individual (or company) to perform services for another party where the relationship between the parties is not that of employer and employee.

contract of service/contract of employment: a contract between an employer and an employee regarding service or apprenticeship, either express or implied and, if express, either oral or in writing.

gross pay: salary before deduction of income tax and national insurance contributions.

harassment: unwanted conduct which violates the dignity of a person or creates a hostile, intimidating, degrading or offensive environment.

maternity leave: the right to take paid or unpaid time off work prior to and after giving birth.

minimum wage: a rate of pay established by statute as the lowest wage which employers may legally pay employees.

PAYE: Pay-As-You-Earn system; the system by which employers deduct income tax from the salaries of their employees on behalf of the Her Majesty's Revenue and Customs.

pension: a sum of money paid on a regular basis as a retirement benefit.

redundancy: dismissal occurring when a company reduces the size of its workforce or closes down a workplace.

repudiatory breach: a breach of contract by one party which entitles the other party to regard the contract as terminated with immediate effect and sue for damages for breach of contract.

sick pay: a sum of money paid to an employee who is on sick leave.

State retirement pension: a sum of money paid on a regular basis to a person by the State after they retire.

terminate: cancel a contract on the relationship between the employee and the employer.

vicarious liability: the liability of an employer who is held responsible for the damages caused by his employee in the course of the employment.

victimisation: the less favourable treatment of a person because they have raised a grievance or supported someone else in raising a grievance, or because they are or are not a member of a trade union, or because of their sex, religion, race, sexual orientation, disability, etc.

unemployment benefit: a sum of money paid on a regular basis to the unemployed by the government.

waive *(v.)*: to voluntarily forfeit (one's rights under a contract).

Exercises

1 Answer the following questions.

1. Explain the difference between an employee and an employer.

2. Explain the difference between an employee and a self-employed person.

3. In order to determine the status of the employed, explain what the control test is.

4. Explain the significance of the organisation test in determining whether there is a relationship of employer/employee.

5. Explain how the multiple test is used to determine whether there is an employee/employer relationship.

6. What are the ways in which a collective agreement is enforceable? Explain what implied incorporation, express incorporation and agency are.

7. What are the duties of the employer?

8. What are the duties of the employee?

9. How does maternity leave work in the UK?

10. What are the provisions of the Race Relations Act 1976?

11. What are the provisions of the Employment Equality (Religion or Belief) Regulations 2003?

12. What are the provisions of the Employment Equality (Sexual Orientation) Regulations 2003?

13. Explain what termination means.

14. Explain what redundancy means.

15. Explain the difference between unfair dismissal and wrongful dismissal.

2   **Complete each sentence with the appropriate word from the list below.**

wage	*implied*	*dismissal(s)* (x 2)	*practices*
union	*repudiatory*	*statutory*	*action*
express	*unfair*	*redundant*	*waive*
collective	*breach* (x 2)		

1. An employee who has failed to carry out his contractual duties has committed a .... of contract. The employer may then either bring an ...... against the employee or ...... the ....

2. A company which has suffered major losses may have to make some of its employees .... If the ...... are not handled fairly, however, the discharged employee may have a case for ....

3. A ...... agreement is the product of the bargaining between an employer and a trade ....

4. An employer's duties include paying his employees the minimum ...... , which is a ...... obligation.

5. The terms of the employment contract may be ...... or .... The latter category is sometimes considered as covering trade customs or ....

3   **Research project.**

1. Search the website of ACAS and write a summary of the different steps of the arbitration and conciliation services that the organisation provides.

2. Find on their website two different examples of employment disputes which may be resolved through the ACAS conciliation scheme.

2. More about…

A. Case law

Poussard v Spiers & Pond [1876] LR 1 QBD 410, DC

An actress agreed to play the leading role in an opera to be produced by the defendants. Owing to illness she could neither attend the last rehearsal, nor the first four performances and when she offered to take her part in the fifth performance, the defendants refused. She sued for wrongful dismissal. The court said the plaintiff's participation in the first four performances was a condition fundamental to the contract. She had breached the contract, which entitled the defendants to treat the contract as terminated.

Ready Mixed Concrete Southeast Ltd v Minister of Pensions and National Insurance **[1968] 2 QB 497; [1968] 1 All ER 433; Mackenna J.**

The claimant employed a lorry-driver who was required by his contract to follow the employer's instructions, wear a uniform and use the lorry exclusively for the employer's business. The driver paid for the hire-purchase of the lorry and for its maintenance.

   The case raised the issue as to whether the driver was self-employed or an employee. The court looked to whether the employer exercised "control" over the worker. The driver's contract would have been considered a "contract of service" if he had not borne the costs of the vehicle. In this case, therefore, the driver was not a servant.

   "A contract of service exists if these three conditions are fulfilled. (i) The servant agrees that, in consideration of a wage or other remuneration, he will provide his own work and skill in the performance of some service for his master. (ii) He agrees, expressly or impliedly, that in the performance of that service he will be subject to the other's control in a sufficient degree to make that other master. (iii) The other provisions of the contract are consistent with its being a contract of service." Regarding mutual obligations, it was held that: "There must be a wage or other remuneration. Otherwise there will be no consideration and, without consideration, no contract of any kind. The servant must be obliged to provide his own work and skill".

Stevenson Jordan Harrison v McDonnel & Evans [1952] 1 TLR 101 (CA)

The question was raised whether the defendant employer could be held vicariously liable for copyright violations of trade secrets committed by one of its employees, who was also self-employed. The courts had to determine whether the master-servant relationship between the two parties was sufficiently established to engage the employer's vicarious liability. It was held that the traditional "control test" used to determine whether there was a contract of service or a contract for services was inadequate in this case and that a better test was necessary. The relevant test was to determine whether the tortfeasor was performing duties which constituted an "integral part of the business" or tasks which were only accessory to the employer's business. In the former situation, the employer would be vicariously liable.

Answer the following questions.

1. What modern terms can be used instead of "master" and "servant"?
2. Determine which area of employment law each ruling deals with.
3. Summarise the rule established by each decision in one sentence.

B. Commission for racial equality

*Does the Race Relations Act provide for exceptions
to the ban on discrimination in the workplace?*

There are some particular circumstances where racial discrimination will not be unlawful. Positive action by employers is one example; another is where it can be shown that discriminating on racial grounds in employment is a genuine occupational requirement, or that a person being of a particular racial group is a genuine occupational qualification for a job. There may also be an exception on the grounds of national security (see below).

Genuine occupational requirements (GOR)

This exception relates to amendments to the Race Relations Act introduced by the Race Relations Act 1976 (Amendment) Regulations 2003. It is lawful for an employer to discriminate on racial grounds in recruiting, promoting or transferring people for jobs, dismissing them from a post and in training for a job where being from a particular race or ethnic or national origin is a genuine occupational requirement (GOR). Employers must however show that it is proportionate to apply the GOR in the particular case.

Genuine occupational qualifications (GOQ)

The genuine occupational requirement exception may not be used to discriminate on grounds of colour or nationality. Discrimination on grounds of colour

or nationality will be lawful however where being of a particular racial group is a genuine occupational qualification for a job:
• to achieve authenticity in a dramatic performance or similar entertainment or in modelling or photographic or artistic work (for example, a theatre director may decide that only a black person can convincingly play the part of Dr Martin Luther King);
• to achieve authenticity in bars or restaurants;
• to provide personal services to people from a particular racial group, defined by colour or nationality, in connection with their welfare, which a person of the same colour or nationality can do most effectively.

National security

An act of discrimination on racial grounds in fields such as employment, education, by public authorities, in the provision of goods, facilities or services may be permitted if it is done to safeguard national security and it can be justified.

Commission for Racial Equality, 2006.

Exercise

Answer the following questions.

1. Define the notions of GOQ and GOR.

2. Examine the following hypothetical situations and discuss whether there was a GOQ or GOR in each case:

   a. An Asian women's refuge seeking to recruit an Asian woman for the post of staff manager.

   b. A Chinese restaurant seeking to hire a Chinese waiter.

   c. A stage production company seeking a white blonde actress for the part of a small-town middle-class housewife in the 1930s and rejecting the application of a coloured actress.

   d. A model agency organising a menswear fashion show seeking to recruit only black models.

C. Replying to a job advertisement

Wanted: a trainee solicitor

One Trainee Solicitor required for a successful London-based property firm. We offer a practical, skills-based training programme, extensive client base and access to the database. We require, in return, candidates with a 2.1 from a British University or similar, with drive and ambition. CVs to recruitmentoffice@litigation.co.uk.

Job title: trainee solicitor
Sector: private law firm
Duration: temporary (9 months)
Area of Law: Conveyancing
Region: Greater London
Contact: Mr Law, senior lawyer at Litigation and Co.

1. How to write a CV

• Your CV should be typed and printed on good quality white paper using a standard black typeface. Avoid using boxes, shading or fancy typefaces as they add very little if nothing to your CV.
• Make sure the type is spaced evenly and aligned.
• Try to limit your CV to two pages if at all possible; three is acceptable if you have a longer career history.
• Do not include a photograph.
• Avoid including a personal summary as it serves little purpose and may be using up valuable space.
• Begin your CV with personal details such as your name, address, date of birth, etc. You do not need to include information such as marital status, state of health, number of children... These are all irrelevant and of no interest to a recruiter.
• List your educational achievements in chronological order (beginning with the most recent) stating results clearly, highlighting particularly good grades. It is not necessary to list every exam taken as part of your course. It may be helpful, however, to include subjects chosen as electives (on the Legal Practice Course for instance).
• List your work experience in chronological order, providing all relevant information. You should place this before education if you have significant job experience. Using bullet points can make a CV easier to read and direct the reader to the salient points.
• Make sure it is clear to the reader what your job involved and highlight any achievements.
• Always include months and years in your CV and explain any gaps.
• Place greater emphasis on your most recent jobs and summarise older positions.
• Remember to include your competence in foreign languages (basic, intermediate, fluent) but be honest as you could be tested.
• Also make sure you include any other skills which may be of interest to employers.

2. The cover letter

(your address)

Mrs Jane Selection
Human Resources Director
Smith and Co. Law Firm
5, Rumpole Road
London

(date)

Dear Mrs Selection,

With reference to your advertisement in the *Law Journal* of January 20th 2006, I wish to apply for the position of international business trainee in your law firm.

I am currently completing my *Master 2* degree (LLM) in European Business Law at the renowned (*name your university and city in France*). This second-year postgraduate programme covers all aspects of business law in the context of EU trade, and I have become particularly interested in tax law as applied to EU firms. In my first three years at university I obtained a second-class *Licence en droit* (LLB).

EITHER: I have job experience in the legal field, having worked for two successive summers as a trainee with a senior partner in the small French law firm Delamare & Associés, specialising in international business. During my placement, I carried out background research on cases, drafted briefs, organised meetings between the team of lawyers and their clients and attended hearings. Because of my knowledge of the English language and of common law, I was often asked to work on matters involving businesses in the UK.

OR: Although I do not have any work experience in the legal field, I have learnt communication and negotiating skills in various summer jobs and internships, including a two-month job in an import/export company. My advanced level in English and my sound knowledge of the common law system would make it easy, I am sure, for me to adapt to the London working environment.

It is especially important for me to have two years of legal practice experience in the UK, because I may eventually want to qualify as a solicitor and settle permanently in London. If not, the experience should enable me to move on to a prominent international law firm in Paris.

I believe I could successfully apply my knowledge and experience of ......
to this post and therefore I enclose my curriculum vitae for your consideration.
Please do not hesitate to contact me if you require further details. I am available
for interview at any time.

(*or...*)

In the hope that my application will interest you, I enclose my curriculum
vitae for your consideration. Please do not hesitate to contact me if you require
further details. I am available for interview at any time.

I look forward to hearing from you,

Yours faithfully,

S. Cordelier

Stéphane Cordelier

3. Attending an interview

• Dress smartly and conservatively, unless you know that the dress code of the
firm is different. Be aware of your body language. These are obvious points but
if overlooked, they can be extremely detrimental to your chances.

• Arrive in good time for the interview and, if you are early, take the time to sit
in the reception area and get a feel for the firm. Ensure you are polite to everyone you meet – the secretary's/receptionist's opinion may be as important as
that of a partner. If the meeting is delayed, try to stay calm and relaxed. If you
show visible irritation the firm will pick up on this and this may make them
reconsider whether you would be suitable for the post.

• Be prepared for anything. Although psychometric testing and other tests
involving your legal skills are not the norm at the first interview, they do happen. Your ability not to be phased by this and adapt quickly is as much a part of
the interview process as the test itself.

• Listen carefully to the questions and make sure you answer each specific question put to you. If this naturally leads into another area you want to talk about,
don't launch straight into this area and forget about the initial question. Answer
the initial question first and then move on.

• As well as being asked about your technical legal skills, you may be asked
about your business development/marketing skills and increasingly about your
IT experience. For many firms, business skills are as crucial as technical skills.

If the firm is looking to recruit a future partner you will need to show genuine interest in the future development of the firm.

• It may be that the person interviewing you is from the Human Resources department, in which case they have been trained to handle interviews and control them. However, you may be interviewed by your prospective immediate superior, or by a departmental head, who may have had no such training. In this case, you may find it necessary to gently guide the interviewer and concentrate on the areas you want to talk about. Try not to give long, detailed answers to questions. Short concise answers have a greater impact. If there are silences, do not try to fill them by "waffling"; simply wait for the next question.

• Do ask questions, usually at the end of the interview. This is your opportunity to find out whether this job is for you. Remember: this is a two-way process and this is your chance to interview your potential new employers.

• Be yourself. Both you and your prospective employer need to know if your personality fits in with the firm's ethos and "chemistry".

• Finally, if you have gone through an agency or a consultant, don't forget to report back to them. The firm will usually ask them for your views and if you have not told them you are interested, this may give the firm the impression you are not that keen to get the job.

4. Filling in an employment contract

Exercises

1 Research project.

1. Read the previous documents and write a CV and letter of application for the position of trainee solicitor at Litigation and Co.

2. Pair up with another student and stage a mock interview for the position.

3. Fill in the employment contract above.

2 Research project.

Mr Laws is a senior lawyer at Litigation and Co. He wishes to employ Jane Smith as a trainee solicitor for one year, but he does not wish to give her employment conditions that would be too advantageous.

Go to the Law Society website and find what the standard conditions for a trainee solicitor are.

THIS CONTRACT is made on

....

BETWEEN "X" .... [the training establishment] and

.... [the trainee solicitor]

1. The purpose of this contract is to set out the principal duties and responsibilities of the training establishment and the trainee solicitor in accordance with the Training Regulations 1990 and "Training trainee solicitors: The Law Society requirements".

2. "X" is the training establishment for the purpose of the Training Regulations 1990.

3. [The training establishment] is authorised by the Law Society and has agreed to provide training for the trainee solicitor according to the rules of the Law Society as set out in "Training trainee solicitors: The Law Society requirements".

4. The trainee solicitor agrees to be trained by [the training establishment].

5. [The training establishment] has appointed .... to be its training principal who will ensure that training is given in accordance with the requirements of the Training Regulations 1990 and "Training trainee solicitors: The Law Society requirements".

DATE OF COMMENCEMENT AND FIXED TERM

6. This contract begins on .... and continues for two years, subject to the provisions for earlier termination.

COVENANTS OF [THE TRAINING ESTABLISHMENT]

Salary
7. [The training establishment] will:
   a) pay the trainee solicitor a yearly salary of not less than £............ payable by equal monthly instalments;
   b) ensure that the Trainee Solicitor's salary is never less than the minimum prescribed for trainee solicitors in the local law society area where the trainee solicitor is based.

Training Principal
8.   a) The training principal is the individual responsible for [the training establishment's] obligations under this contract.
   b) The training principal may delegate those responsibilities to others but where this is done the name of the person or persons appointed must be given to the trainee solicitor.

Terms and Conditions
9. The trainee solicitor is employed by [the training establishment] under the terms and conditions of employment which have been supplied but if there is any conflict between those terms and this contract then the terms of this contract prevail.

Basic Skills

10. [The training establishment] will:

a) provide the trainee solicitor with the opportunity to practise:
   - i) client care and practice support skills;
   - ii) communication skills;
   - iii) drafting;
   - iv) interviewing and advising;
   - v) legal research;

b) provide the trainee solicitor with the opportunity to gain experience of the practice of:
   - i) advocacy and oral presentation skills;
   - ii) case and transaction management;
   - iii) dispute resolution;
   - iv) negotiation.

Legal Topics

11.　　a) [The training establishment] will provide the trainee solicitor with proper training and experience in at least three distinct substantive areas of English law. The following examples are for information only; this list is not exhaustive:

Banking;	Family;
Civil Litigation;	Immigration;
Commercial Law;	Insolvency;
Company Law;	Insurance and Reinsurance;
Construction;	Intellectual Property;
Criminal Litigation;	Local Government;
Employment;	Magisterial;
Environmental Law;	Personal Injury;
European Community;	Planning;
Property (including	Trusts;
Landlord and Tenant);	Welfare;
Shipping and Airways;	Wills and Probate.
Tax and Financial Planning;	

If [the training establishment] is not able to provide proper training and experience in at least three distinct substantive areas of law it must make suitable arrangements for the trainee solicitor to be seconded to an office of another solicitor or elsewhere as agreed by the Law Society to acquire the appropriate experience.

b) [The training establishment] must ensure that during the term of the training contract the trainee solicitor gains experience of both contentious and non-contentious work in accordance with the Training Contracts Skills Standards.

Review of Experience and Appraisal of Performance

12. [The training establishment] will:

a) provide the trainee solicitor with the means to maintain a record of the trainee solicitor's training;

b) ensure adequate arrangements for guidance, including access to a supervising solicitor, on a day to day basis;

c) make suitable arrangements to regularly monitor the trainee solicitor's progress and that in accordance with "Training trainee solicitors: The Law Society requirements" a minimum of three appropriately timed compulsory appraisals take place during the two years;

d) make prompt and adequate arrangements to deal with any personnel concerns in respect of the trainee solicitor.

Law Society Requirements

13. [The training establishment] will:

    a)   i) permit the trainee solicitor to have paid leave to attend courses and interviews as required by the Law Society;

        ii) pay all the fees and reasonable expenses in connection with such courses and interviews.

    b) inform the trainee solicitor of any change:

        i) in the Law Society's requirements relating to this training contract;

        ii) of the training principal;

    c) permit the trainee solicitor to have 20 working days paid holiday in each yearof employment in addition to public holidays;

    d) complete a certificate of training at the end of this contract.

COVENANTS OF THE TRAINEE SOLICITOR

Duties

14. The trainee solicitor will:

    a) carry out the duties given by partners or employees of [the training establishment] faithfully and diligently and follow all reasonable instructions;

    b) treat all information about [the training establishment] and its clients and their business as wholly confidential;

    c) deal properly with any money or property entrusted to the trainee solicitor;

    d) keep a proper record of all work done and training received;

    e) comply with all requirements of the Law Society;

    f) attend courses and interviews as required by the Law Society and the training principal.

Disputes

15.   a) Any dispute about this contract or the conduct of either party in relation to it may be referred to the training principal (or to another appropriate person within [the training establishment] if the dispute concerns the training principal), who must deal with it within four weeks of referral.

    b) If the dispute is not resolved within four weeks the issue may be referred by either party to the Law Society or such person as it may appoint.

    c) The trainee solicitor may also use [the training establishment's] grievance procedure.

Applicable Law

16. This contract is subject to English law.

Notices

17. Any notices must be in writing and given:
     a) personally; or
     b) by post addressed to the other party at:
          i) the address set out in this contract; or
          ii) any other address given by one party to the other for the purpose of this clause.

18. Any notice to be given to [the training establishment] must be addressed to the training principal.

19. Notices will be deemed served two working days after posting.

Termination

20. This contract may be terminated by:
     a) agreement between [the training establishment] and the trainee solicitor
     b) the Law Society
          i) with or without an application for that purpose by either party;
          ii) following an application by [the training establishment] in the event of poor performance by the trainee solicitor.

21. This contract would not normally be terminated by:
     a) the resignation or appointment of any partner of [the training establishment]; or
     b) the merger of [the training establishment] with another body, firm, company or individual.

22. If the trainee solicitor:
     a) has completed a Legal Practice Course, Integrated Course or an Exempting Law Degree Course
     b) commenced this contract prior to the publication of the results of that course or examination;
either party may end this contract within four weeks of the results being published if the trainee solicitor does not reach the required standard as set out in the letter of offer.

Signed by:
....
on behalf of [the training establishment]

Signed:
....
Trainee solicitor

http://www.lawsociety.org.uk

3. Off the presses

A. Equal pay between men and women

One in five firms break law over women's pay

The following correction was printed in the Guardian's Corrections and clarifications column, Tuesday January 31st 2006.

The above headline was a case of statistical simplification leading to exaggeration. In the report below we said that 16% of women are paid less than men in equivalent jobs: 16% of a **sample** is fewer than one in six.

Almost one in five of the country's biggest employers are breaking the law by paying women significantly lower wages than their male colleagues, according to research by the Equal Opportunities Commission. A study by the commission of 870 employers, all of whom have reviewed their pay structures to check if they are paying equally, found that 16% are unlawfully discriminating against their female workers by paying them less than men to do the same job.

The EOC said that the true proportion was likely to be higher as these **organisations** were among the more enlightened employers, having voluntarily undertaken pay reviews. Jenny Watson, **chair** of the commission, told the *Guardian*: "It's bad enough that 16% have found a pay gap that could be the subject of legal challenge following their equal pay review – but even these figures mask the true extent of the problem".

The 16% of companies which were breaking the law were found to have a gap between men and women's salaries which could only be explained by the workers' **gender**. In some cases, women were routinely being paid less for doing the same job as their male colleagues.

The survey also revealed that women were routinely missing out on senior jobs, starting on lower salaries and taking longer to get promoted, largely because they were more likely to take career breaks to have children.

A review of Lloyds TSB's wage bill revealed deep divisions in pay, with high-flying men reaping rewards in bonuses because the bank feared it might lose them. Men were also more likely to negotiate higher starting salaries when they joined the bank. Lloyds TSB has since overhauled its pay structures.

The new figures come as the government prepares to announce the full findings of the Women and Work Commission, which was charged by the prime minister with making recommendations on narrowing the gender pay gap. Tony Blair is expected to launch its report next month. Equality campaigners are waiting to see whether experts who have been working for 18 months on a plan to tackle unfair pay for women will recommend making pay reviews compulsory – something which is opposed by many employers.

The EOC's survey also reveals that the government is likely to miss a 2008 target designed to tackle discriminatory pay against women because employers are dragging their feet in conducting internal reviews of the pay gap between male and female workers. Only 34% of large employers have conducted a review of salaries. The government's target is for 45% of large organisations to have reviewed pay by 2008.

Last year the pay gap between men and women was 17% for full-time workers and 38% for part-time workers, compared with 20% and 41% respectively five years ago in 2000.

Much of this is explained by women choosing to take career breaks to have families or opting for lower paid jobs – so-called occupational segregation. But a proportion of the gap is still attributed to employers discriminating against women.

Susan Henderson, head of human resources policy at the Confederation of British Industry, said that their own internal research revealed a different picture. She said that 40% of large employers had so far undertaken reviews and found little evidence of widespread discrimination. "Of course there are some issues but it is not as great as the EOC suggests," she said.

"Firms are stepping up to the issue. They are talking about flexible working, encouraging women back to work after having children and how we get young girls to consider different careers. Pay audits will not solve those problems."

Ms Watson said the EOC was calling for employers to carry out "equality checks", a lighter touch audit which would prompt a full pay review if discrepancies were found. Other causes of the pay gap such as job segregation and a lack of family-friendly policies would be identified and employers would have an "amnesty" period in which to change pay systems.

A spokeswoman for the Department for Trade and Industry said: "We continue to make good progress on encouraging organisations to do equal pay reviews. The government has set challenging targets and the EOC data shows we are on our way to meeting these."

Polly Curtis, *The Guardian*, 27/1/2006 (http://www.guardian.co.uk)

Definitions in context

sample: a selection of people intended to be representative of the population being studied.

organisation: a formal group of people working together, such as in a company or in another entity (government body).

chair: the name given to the officer who presides at the meetings of an organisation or committee.

gender: the sex of an individual.

1 Answer the following questions.

1. Is the title accurate?
2. What are the proposals made by Equality campaigners?
3. Has the pay gap widened over the past five years?
4. What are the causes of the pay gap?
5. What are equal pay reviews?

2 Research project.

Find information on the work of the Equal Opportunities Commission.

3 Finding legal documents.

Find documents about European Union provisions for men and women in terms of pay: go to the Europa website and find the following pieces of legislation (1) and cases (2):

1. What are the rights which are guaranteed in EC law? (Article 141 EC)
2. What are the facts of the cases and what are the issues at stake?

– Macarthys v Smith (Case 129/79) [1980] ECR 1275,
– Garland v British Rail Engineering (Case 12/81) [1982] ECR 359,
– Barber v Guardian Royal Exchange Assurance Group (Case C-262/88) [1991] 1 QB 344,
– Directive 76/207,
– Ministère Public v Stoeckel (case C-345/89) [1991] ECR I-4047,
– Johnston v Chief Constable of the Royal Ulster Constabulary (Case 222/84) [1986] ECR 1651,
– Kalanke v Freie Hansestadt Bremen (Case C-450/93) [1996] 1 CMLR 175,
– Jenkins v Kingsgate (Clothing Productions) Ltd (Case 96/80) [1981] ECR 911.

4 Case study.

Andrew runs a small business, which was set up a few months ago. He expects it to grow quickly and to be successful, but at the moment, his business is struggling to survive.

All his employees are full-time, but he pays a higher hourly rate to employees who are prepared to work their hours flexibly (night and weekend work). He has two male (John and Peter) and two female (Jane and Elizabeth) employees. The men both work flexible hours, but the women have opted for fixed hours because of their duties at home. His justification for paying the lower rate to fixed-hours employees is that such workers are less profitable for the business. In order to motivate his employees, Andrew decides to enroll his employees in a contracted-out pension scheme, by which pension payments are made to retired men over 65 and retired women over 60. Andrew dismisses Jane for "persistent lateness" and advertises her job. He has five candidates for the job, four women (Charlotte, Ruth, Daisy and Pauline) and one man (Stephen). All four women are qualified for that kind of work, since they have held similar positions, but two of them are married with children and two are single mothers. Andrew needs an employee willing to work extra hours. He therefore decides to hire the man, who is neither qualified nor experienced in the field.

Jane, Elizabeth, Charlotte, Ruth, Daisy and Pauline decide to sue Andrew collectively for sexual discrimination. Where can they seek advice? Guide them.

4. Food for thought

Exercises

1 Research activity: reading an Act of Parliament.

Find the Act of Parliament called Employment Rights Act 1996 on the UK Government's official website. Read it and say whether the following statements are true or false. Give reasons for your answers.

1. The company's name and address should appear on the contract but the employee's name only, not his or her address.

2. The date when the contract is to begin should be mentioned in the contract.

3. No information is given as to the method of calculating pay, so that the employer can change it at will.

4. The contract should state the intervals of pay (weekly, monthly or other).

5. The contract can state the normal number of hours worked and the holiday entitlement, but need say nothing about the possibility of overtime.

6. The job title is written in the contract of employment.

7. The contract provides a brief description of the tasks the employee is expected to carry out.

8. Nothing is said about where the employee is to work.

9. A contract includes terms defining the scope and the provisions of sick pay.

10. The employer does not have to mention whether the job is part-time or full-time, temporary or permanent.

11. No mention is made of a pension scheme since the State takes care of that.

12. A contract provides a code of conduct.

13. A contract of employment states the length of notice that has to be given in order to terminate the employment.

14. An employer is not bound to mention the collective agreement that might affect the contract.

2 Write an employment contract.

Use the following information to write John Smith's contract of employment.

Hannah Goodwin, owner of a sock factory in Oxfordshire, situated at 7 Factory Rd, Oxford, recruits Anthony Bingham, living at Tower Flats, to be a shop floor manager, supervising a line of 15 workers working on sock-sewing machines. He is to work in the factory 45 hours a week, and overtime will be paid at twice the hourly wage rate, which is £5. All workers are entitled to 4 weeks' holiday a year and the company pays a fixed amount (10% of the salary) into a contracted-out pension scheme. Employees are allowed 15 days a year of justified sick pay at full rate and another 15 days at 50% of their salary. Since most of the workers are female, the company is attentive to any problems concerning sexual harassment. The trade unions managed to get a compulsory ten-minute break every four hours so that employees can stretch their legs. If Anthony Bingham wishes to terminate his 3-year contract of employment before the end of the contract, he has to give three weeks' notice.

5. Listening

Exercises

1 🔘 Listen to Part 1 of the recording and complete the extract with the missing words.

INTERVIEWER: Women now make up nearly half of the British ...... , but you won't be too surprised to hear that over thirty years since the .... and the .... , there is still a big difference between men's and women's wages. If we examine average .... , the .... is .... for full-time female workers and .... for women working part-time. So what would it take to make equal pay happen?

We asked the .... of the TUC.

INTERVIEWEE: Equal pay can become a reality if the following three measures are adopted. The first would be to allow ...... to take group cases. Over the last thirty years, unions have conducted and won many equal pay cases, but the cases have to be handled .... If they could be grouped together, then a shop worker in ...... would ...... automatically from the victory of a shop worker in .... Secondly, ... should be introduced to compel employers to publish pay rates within an ...... so that women could ...... what they do earn with what men are paid. .... are kept a secret by too many British bosses.

2 🔘 Now listen to both Parts 1 and 2 and say if the following statements are true or false. Give reasons for your answers.

1. The TUC is a labour organisation.
2. The person interviewed in Part 1 thinks the statutory minimum wage is too low.
3. He blames some bosses for being too greedy.
3. The person interviewed in Part 2 works for the Government.
4. She agrees with the first interviewee's views on equal pay.
5. She thinks employment discrimination does not explain the pay gap.
6. Her view is that nothing can be done to help close the gap.
7. Girls cannot be encouraged to study IT or engineering, in her opinion.

3 Discuss.

1. Briefly recapitulate the opinions and proposals presented here.
2. Do they reflect a specific kind of ideology or political orientation?
3. Do you agree with these views?
4. In your opinion, is there a way to close the equal pay gap?

6. Grammar practice

Exercises

1 Modals. Rewrite the following sentences using a modal expressing possibility, permission, prohibition, necessity or obligation.

1. Some minor changes affecting the working conditions of employees are possible within the terms of an existing contract, especially in cases where adapting the job of the employee to new methods and technologies is necessary.
2. The employer owes a duty of respect to his employee as well as a duty to pay wages to him or her.
3. A pregnant employee is entitled to a 26-week maternity leave irrespective of how long she has worked for her employer.
4. The pregnant employee is required to notify her employer of her intention to take maternity leave before the end of the 15th week prior to the expected week of childbirth.
5. Discrimination on grounds of racial or ethnic origin in the areas of employment is outlawed by the Race Directive.
6. Employees who have worked a minimum of one year with their employer usually take up to 13 weeks unpaid parental leave.

7. The Part-Time Workers Regulations 2000 prohibit employers from treating part-time employees less favourably than full-time employees.

8. The Regulations prohibit direct and indirect discrimination, harassment and victimisation.

9. Employment contracts are regulated by different sources and terms are normally implied into the contract by the parties.

10. Every employer has the duty to ensure the health, the safety and welfare of all his employees.

11. No positive discrimination is allowed at the point of selection.

12. There are circumstances where racial discrimination is not unlawful.

2 Negation. The following sentences all express the opposite of what is true. Transform them to make true sentences and use the negative infinitive.

1. Employees are expected to accept bribes, to disclose information and to work for a competing company.

2. Try to fill long silences by waffling and try to give long detailed answers to questions.

3. An equal pay claim which has been resolved out of court may be taken to an employment tribunal.

4. To report back to your consultant would be a mistake.

5. It is recommended that an employer should treat a civil partner less favourably than he would treat a spouse in similar circumstances.

6. Implied terms are terms which are known to appear explicitly in a contract.

7. It is illegal for employers to pay employees a minimum wage.

8. To gain experience in the practice of case and transaction management is unwise.

9. To include your skills in foreign languages on your CV would be regrettable.

3 Comparatives/superlatives. Complete the sentences with comparative or superlative forms (that express superiority, equality or inferiority).

1. The common law system is said to have a ...... practical approach to dispute resolution ...... the civil law system.

2. Statutory statements and customs can be construed as express terms of the contract if they are incorporated into the contract; otherwise they are no .... a gentleman's agreement.

3. Under the Equal Pay Act 1975, a female employee has a right to be paid .... a male employee for like work and for work of equal value within the same organisation.

4. 16% of women are paid .... men in equivalent jobs: 16% of a sample is .... one in six.

5. The survey also revealed that women were routinely missing out on senior jobs, starting on ...... salaries and taking ...... to get promoted, largely because they were ...... likely than their partners to take career breaks to have children.

6. A pregnant employee is entitled to 26 weeks maternity leave only if she has worked for 26 continuous weeks with her employer and earns £1,000 at the ....

7. The Part-Time Workers Regulations 2000 provide that part-time employees should not be treated ...... favourably ...... full-time employees.

8. Almost one in five of the country's ...... employers are breaking the law by paying women significantly ...... wages ...... their male colleagues.

9. When attending an interview, ensure you are polite to everyone you meet – the secretary's/receptionist's opinion may be ...... important ...... a partner's.

10. The employee complained that her company was treating her ...... favourably than other employees because of her disability. Her legal advisor agreed and thought it was one of the ...... cases of discrimination he had ever encountered.

4 **"Since" or "for"? Complete each sentence with "since" or "for" and the correct form of the verbs in brackets. Give reasons for your choice of "since" or "for".**

1. ...... 2003, a series of family-friendly measures ...... (be developed), such as paid paternity leave which ...... (be) available to fathers ...... up to two weeks.

2. ...... the Flexible Working Regulations ...... (be introduced) in 2002, parents of children under six years old and parents of disabled children under eighteen ...... (have) the right to request flexible working arrangements if they ...... (work) for their employer ...... at least 26 continuous weeks.

3. She ...... (work) there ...... Christmas which meant she only had three months seniority.

4. If you get the job, you ...... (work) with this firm ...... five days a week so make sure your personality ...... (fit in with) the firm's ethos.

5. He starts his new job next week. He ...... (work) in the factory ...... 45 hours a week .

6. ...... decades, the courts, deciding upon vicarious liability cases, ... (create) tests to ascertain the status of the employee.

7. When she was just a trainee she ...... (work) there ...... a few months. She ...... (come) a long way ...... !

8. The pay gap between men and women ...... (widen) ...... decades when the Equal Pay Act ...... (be voted) in 1975.

5 **Prepositions. Complete the text with the appropriate prepositions.**

Firms are making progress ...... encouraging women back to work ...... having children, as well as ...... promoting equal pay reviews. Still, the pregnant employee is required to notify her employer of her intention to take maternity leave ...... leaving work, on the 15th week prior ...... the expected week of childbirth at the latest, unless of course exceptional circumstances prevent her ...... complying with that requirement. If she should leave ...... doing so, she might not benefit from the same advantages. That is exactly what happened recently to Kathy who, instead ...... informing her employer about her pregnancy, left ...... saying a word. At the time, she was ...... pressure because her husband had taken up drinking and she was no longer sure she wanted to stay with him. She was fed up ...... him coming back late every night. Her employer complained ...... her not giving the required 15-weeks' notice and threatened not to take her back, so Kathy appealed against the employer's decision ...... referring the case to ACAS.

Property law

1. Fundamentals

Property law refers to the complex laws and legal relationships between and among persons with respect to things. Property rights are rights that are enforceable against other persons in regard to these things. Property may be tangible, such as land, structures or goods, or intangible. Intellectual property, which includes patents, copyrights or trademarks, is an example of intangible property.

Property law governs the various forms of ownership in real property and personal property, within the common law system. In many European Union and civil law systems, this division is between movable and immovable property. **Movable property** law corresponds to the associated rights and obligations regarding personal property, while **immovable property** corresponds to real estate or real property. This legal area is also referred to as Land Law.

In the common law system, **personal property** may also be called **chattels** and refers to any property that can be moved from one location or another, or in other words, to any property except for land. It should be noted that this exception does not include leases, which are considered personal property. Personal property may be classified in a variety of ways, such as money, animals, furniture, merchandise, contracts and stocks and bonds.

Modern English property law provides for the ownership of practically all things that have or may have value. The origins of this terminology, and to a great extent the substance of modern property law, are traceable to feudal times. The fundamental distinction between realty (real estate or real property or land) and personalty (personal property or chattels) was the basis of early feudal society.

Property rights refer to the enjoyment of things of economic value, whether the enjoyment is exclusive or shared, present or future. This rightful or legal possession of such rights is called ownership. Ownership is essentially the right to exclude others from enjoyment of property. Therefore, the person who holds **title** to a house, an automobile or a patent, even though there maybe a lien attached (debt), can still claim it as their property. Unlawful appropriation of someone's personal property, generally known as theft, is mostly dealt with under the Theft Act 1968 (see Chapter 6, Criminal law).

Real property

Real property is principally land and the structures built on it. It can be owned in various ways. The interest which a person has in land is called an **estate**. An important area of real property is the definition of the various types of estates in land. These are interests that may limit the ownership rights that one has over the land.

The most common interest or right in real estate is known as fee simple or freehold. This estate provides the owners with the right to use their real estate for any lawful purpose, to leave it to heirs and to lease or sell their interest to whoever and whenever they want to. The right to possess and use real estate pursuant to the terms of a lease or a rental agreement is called **leasehold**.

Estates may also be held jointly by joint tenants with rights of survivorship or by tenants in common. The difference between these two types of joint ownership is principally in the passing on of the interest on death. In a joint tenancy, the surviving tenant becomes the sole owner of the estate. Nothing passes to the heirs of the deceased tenant. Tenants in common may, however, pass their share of the estate on to their heirs (children, grandchildren, descendants).

1. Conveyancing

Transferring ownership of property from one person to another is called **conveyancing**. It is important that buyers make sure that they receive good title to the property. The proper conveyance of a title to a purchaser should ensure that the land is transferred with all the rights that go with it (save for those which a vendor has expressly retained) and that the buyer is informed of any restrictions.

A **deed** is a legal instrument which is used to grant these rights. The deed of transfer is most commonly used to convey title of real estate. Common law establishes two conditions for an instrument to be a valid deed. The grantor must have the legal capacity to grant the estate and the party receiving the estate must have the legal capacity to receive it. In the past, a seal had to be affixed to the deed, but today, it is usually no longer required and it has been replaced by the signature of the grantor. However, most jurisdictions still require that the deed be attested to, before a notary public, with at least one witness present.

A typical conveyancing transaction consists of a deed of transfer, delivery of the land, the acceptance of title and payment of an agreed price. Completion is facilitated by a system of land registration.

Under the Land Registration Act 2002, registration of an estate in land is compulsory when the freehold is transferred, that is when real property is sold or is given as a gift. In England and Wales these formalities are usually prepared by a solicitor. However, it is possible to carry out one's own conveyancing in order to save expense. The standard practice is for the buyer and seller to negotiate an agreed price, organise a survey and have the solicitor prepare the contract. The conveyancing process normally takes several weeks from start to finish, but it can be completed within a matter of days.

2. Mortgage

A **mortgage** is a legal instrument for protecting creditors by transferring an estate or interest in land in order to secure the payment of the debt. English law regards mortgages as liens on property. If the mortgagor defaults on payment of the debt, the creditor may seek a court judgment which would order a sale of the property called **foreclosure**. This would be done at an auction and the debt would be satisfied from the proceeds of the public sale.

3. Modern law of landlord and tenant

Over the centuries, leases have served many purposes, but the originally leaseholds were used primarily for rural or agricultural purposes. In the early 19th century, with the advent of the industrial revolution and the growth of cities, leasehold became an important form of landholding in urban areas.

A **landlord** or **landlady** is the owner or lessor of a house, flat, farm or apartment, which is rented or leased to an individual or business, who is called the **tenant** or lessee. Registration under the Land Registration Act 2002 is compulsory if a legal lease for more than seven years is granted.

A written **lease** or **rental agreement** sets out the amount of **rent** due each week or month, any penalties for late payments, the duration of the lease, and the amount of notice required before the landlord or tenant may cancel the agreement. As a general rule, a lease states that the landlord is responsible for substantial repairs and maintenance, and the tenant is responsible for keeping the property clean and safe and for carrying out minor repairs. There are a limited number of reasons for which a landlord might lawfully terminate the lease and evict the tenant before the expiration of the tenancy. Failure to pay the rent when due or disturbance to neighbours would be considered breaches of the lease and may justify possession proceedings.

Many landlords engage a property management company to take care of all the details of renting their property out to a tenant. This typically includes advertising the property, presenting it to prospective tenants, negotiating the terms of the lease and, once rented, collecting the rent payments from the tenant and maintaining repairs on the premises as needed.

4. Non-possessory interests

A **non-possessory interest in land** is a term used to describe a category of rights held by a person to use land that is in the possession of another. Such rights are created either by an agreement between the owner of the land and the party who seeks to own the interest or by a court order. It is also possible for a property deed to further restrict general ownership rights with conditions or **covenants**, which are attached to the deed. Examples of such rights include easements, restrictive covenants, and licences. An **easement** is an interest in land which entitles a person to use land possessed by another. Unlike a lease, an easement does not give the holder a "right of possession" of the property, only a "right of use". Typical examples of easements might include electrical, cable or telephone lines, common areas in buildings, or advertising signs.

A **licence**, as distinguished from an easement, only gives a personal privilege to do something on the land of another and is not an interest in land. For example, a licence may grant a person the right to park a car in a car park with the consent of the car park owner or the right given to the post office to deliver a package on private property.

A **restrictive covenant** is a legal obligation imposed in a deed by the seller upon the buyer of real estate to do or not to do something. These restrictions often "run with the land" and are enforceable on subsequent buyers of the property. Examples include maintaining the property in a reasonable state of repair, preserving rules on height, gardens, or the "sight-line" for a neighbouring property, not operating a business from a residence, or not building on certain parts of the property. Restrictive covenants are very simple and are intended merely to protect a neighbourhood from homeowners destroying trees or historical structures or just indirectly harming property values. A restrictive covenant may state what a homeowner can or cannot do to the exterior, such as restrictions on the colour that the exterior may be painted, or impose a limitation on the number of occupants.

5. Adverse possession

There is a way of acquiring title to real property without compensation by appropriating it in a manner that conflicts with the rights of the true owner. This is called **adverse possession** (otherwise commonly referred to as "squatting") and it means that the person attempting to claim the property is occupying it openly as if it were their own. Adverse possession is related to the law of statute of limitations. When trespass of real estate occurs, there is only a certain number of years in which legal action can be taken by the owner. Once this period of time has expired, the **trespasser** can no longer be evicted from the property.

6. Compulsory purchase

Compulsory purchase is the power of the State to expropriate private property without the consent of the owner. The term originated in English law as a natural inherent power of the sovereign. Governments use this power to acquire real property when it is necessary for the completion of a public project such as a road and where the owner of the property involved is averse to negotiating a price for its sale. Compulsory purchase is limited to public purpose and just compensation must be paid to the owner for the appropriation. Today it is implemented in accordance with statutory law, and disputes may be heard by the High Court.

Intellectual property

At the origin of intellectual property legislation is the fact that society wants to reward and protect inventors, artists, designers and developers of businesses and their reputations. Inventors are given control over their creativity and innovation, and also an incentive to create. Intellectual property (often referred to as **IP**) can be compared to physical property in the sense that inventors own the product of their creativity. IP creates a type of monopoly and is therefore an exception to competition law, which protects against the unlawful restraint of trade. IP covers the creation of a name or brand, inventions, art, music, literature, designs, images, processes or knowledge. Ideas are sometimes given protection but most of the time they require elaboration before protection can be guaranteed. IP protection and rights must be applied for by the inventor and those rights have to be granted to be effective. Only copyright is automatically protected and there is no need for registration, as simple evidence of the creation is sufficient.

The four main categories of intellectual property are patents, trademarks, designs and copyright, but the same invention or creation can often be in more than one category. There are also other categories of IP:

– a trade secret, which is a formula, practice, process, design, instrument, or compilation of information used by a business to obtain an advantage over competitors within the same industry or profession, such as recipes or soft drink formulas. One of the most significant differences between a trade secret and a trademark or a patent is that a trade secret is protected without **disclosure** of the secret;

– plant breeders' rights, which give protection for the creation of new plant varieties.

"Passing-off" law is another type of IP legislation which protects against unfair competition and reputation abuse.

The principal legislation on copyright can be found in the Copyright, Designs and Patents Act 1988, which amended the Patents Act 1977. The procedural details of the patents system are contained in the Patents Rules 1995. The legislation on trademarks appears in the Trademark Act 1994 and its amendments.

1. Patents

A **patent** gives an inventor rights for a limited period, i.e. rights to stop others from making, using or selling an invention without the permission of the inventor. As described by the Patent Office, a patent can be seen as a **bargain** between the State and the inventor. The State offers a short-term monopoly of up to 20 years in return for allowing the invention to be made public and for a full description of the invention, which is published by the Patent Office.

Patents protect products and processes and their functional and technical aspects. This includes all types of inventions, formulas, mechanical components, and new and improved products and processes used in industrial application. The areas mostly concerned today are information technology, telecommunications and pharmaceuticals. There is no requirement for an inventor to seek a patent in order to put an invention into practice, but once the invention is published, there will be no protection against others using the invention.

Specific conditions must be satisfied to get a patent. First and most importantly the invention must be new and not form part of the "state of the art". The state of the art comprises all patents that have been made available to the public before the application date for the new patent. Another condition is that the invention must truly be inventive, i.e. it must not be obvious from the state of the art; this obviousness is assessed from the perspective of a person skilled in the technical area of the invention.

A patented invention is first recorded and then published by the Patent Office. A patent document, sometimes drafted with the help of a patent agent or a patent attorney, must consist of a description of the invention, with drawings and enough detail for a person skilled in the area of technology to perform the invention. Patent rights are territorial and a UK patent does not include rights outside of the UK. Patent rights last for a maximum of 20 years. Some patents, e.g. for medicinal products, may be granted an additional five-years' protection with a Supplementary Protection Certificate.

As well as protecting the inventor's business, patents can be sold, bought, licensed, or mortgaged to others. They also benefit others since information can be obtained from other patents. Once the term of the patent expires, it enters the **public domain** and can be used by anyone. Furthermore, a patent empowers the owner, or "proprietor", of an invention to take legal action against others who might be **infringing** the patent, to claim damages and to prevent the unlicensed use, sale, manufacture or importation of the patented invention. An invention may be exploited by another person or company under a licensing agreement and in exchange for payment of royalties. The European Patent Convention (EPC) governs the European patent system. The EPC presents articles setting out the general principles for the grant of European Patents and Rules which are similar to the UK Acts and Rules.

2. Trademarks

A **trademark** is a sign which can take the form of words, slogans, colours, logos, three-dimensional shapes and sometimes sounds and gestures. It distinguishes the goods and services of one trader from those of another and is used as a marketing tool so that customers can recognise the product of a particular trader.

Trademarks have to be registered; mark registration establishes the trademark and its ownership. Registration gives the owner the exclusive right of use for the goods and/or services for which it is registered. The owner must apply to the UK Patent Office. For protection throughout the entire European Union, the owner must go to the Office for Harmonization in the Internal Market (OHIM) and apply for a Community Trade Mark. Owners may use the ™ symbol: the word or logo referred to then functions as a trademark but is not necessarily registered as such. The © symbol shows that the creation referred to is a registered trademark.

After registration, the owner has the right to pursue an infringement action against anyone who unlawfully uses their registered trademark. **Infringement** occurs when a **third party** uses a sign identical or similar to a registered mark. A Registered Trade Mark is property which owners can sell or rent out by mortgaging or licensing. When the mark is not registered, owners have to rely on the common law tort action of passing off. For this they need considerable evidence that they used the mark sufficiently to claim ownership, and then additional evidence that the public was under the impression that they were purchasing the owner's goods rather than the infringer's.

3. Designs

Designs surround us in every aspect of our daily life and cover such diverse areas as furniture, kitchen implements, medical instruments and clothes. Design legislation covers the appearance of the whole or a part of a product resulting from features such as contours, lines, shape, colours, materials or texture of the product itself or its ornamentation. The three types of legal rights which protect designs in the UK are registered designs, unregistered design rights and artistic copyright.

Design registration gives the owners a monopoly on their product design, i.e. the right for a limited period to stop others from using, making or selling a product to which the design has been applied, or in which it has been incorporated, without their permission. The design of a product can become indistinguishable from the brand and image of a company and may become an asset with increasing monetary value. Registration provides the right to take legal action against others who might be infringing the design. It also allows the owner to claim damages. Moreover, it brings the exclusive right to offer, make, use, market, import, export, or stock any product to which the design has been applied or is incorporated. It gives the right for others to use the design under the terms of an agreement with the registered owner.

Design right applies to original, non-commonplace designs of the shape or configuration of products. It is not a monopoly right but a right to prevent deliberate copying, and it expires 10 years after the first marketing of articles made to the design and 15 years maximum after the creation of the design. A design right is property which may be bought, sold or licensed, and unlike design registration, it does not have to be registered.

4. Copyright

Copyright covers material, i.e. literary and artistic material, music, films, sound recordings and broadcasts. It also includes software and multimedia multimedia products. Copyright gives the creators economic rights enabling them to control the use of their material in a number of ways, such as the making of copies, issuing copies to the public, public performance, broadcasting and its use **on-line**. It also gives moral rights to the inventor to be identified as the creator of certain kinds of material, and to object to distortion or mutilation of it. Material protected by copyright is termed a **work**. However, copyright does not protect ideas, names or titles.

In the case of a dramatic, literary or musical work, the author is the person who creates the work and the first owner of the economic rights under copyright. This also applies to commissioned works. However, when the work is created during employment, the employer is the first owner of these economic rights, unless an agreement to the contrary has been made with the author. In contrast to economic rights under copyright, moral rights are concerned with protecting the reputation and personality of authors.

Like physical property, copyright can be bought, sold, inherited or transferred, wholly or in part. Therefore, these economic rights may subsequently belong to someone other than the first owner. On the other hand, moral rights granted to authors of dramatic, literary and musical works and to film directors remain with the author or director or will pass to their heirs.

Copyright owners generally have the right to authorise or prohibit any of the following in relation to their works:

– copying the work,

– issuing copies to the public,

– lending or renting copies to the public (though the Public Lending Right scheme allows for some lending of copyright works which does not infringe copyright),

– showing, performing or playing the work in public,

– broadcasting the work or other communication by electronic transmission to the public (this includes putting the material on-line),

– adapting the work, such as translating a literary or dramatic work, converting a computer program into a different code or computer language, and transcribing a musical work.

Infringement of copyright occurs when any of these acts are done without authorisation, either directly or indirectly, and whether a "substantial part" or the whole of a work was used. Protection prevents others from very easily exploiting material without paying the creator. Therefore, most uses of copyright material require the permission of the copyright owner. Nevertheless, there are exceptions to copyright and some minor uses may not infringe copyright. Protection is automatic as soon as there is a record, in any form, of the material that has been created. There is no official registration, form or fee. When copyrighted material is published, i.e. reproduced in printed or other form and put on sale to the general public, owners can mark their material with the international copyright symbol ©, followed by the year of publication and the name of the copyright owner. It is not essential but may be useful to the creator in infringement proceedings.

Some exceptions to copyright allow limited use of copyright works without the authorisation of the copyright owner. Examples include the use of a copyright work for criticism, review or news reporting. A limited use of works can also be allowed for teaching in schools and other educational institutions, for the playing of sound recordings without profit and to help visually-impaired people. Some of these exceptions are limited by "fair dealing". Fair dealing with a dramatic, literary, musical or more generally any artistic work for the purposes of private study or non-commercial research does not infringe any copyright. Fair dealing has been interpreted by the courts by taking the economic impact of the use of the material into consideration. If this impact is not significant, the use may count as fair dealing.

Definitions in context and key words

adverse possession: a means of acquiring title to the real property of another without compensation, by possessing it in a manner that conflicts with the rights of the true owner.

bargain: a negotiation between two or more parties leading to an agreement.

chattels: (see personal property).

compulsory purchase: the power of the State to expropriate private property without the consent of the owner.

conveyancing: transferring ownership of a property from one person to another.

copyright: the economic rights enabling creators to control the use of their material in a number of ways, such as the making of copies, issuing copies to the public, public performance, broadcasting and use on-line.

covenant: a condition attached to the performance of a contract.

deed: a legal document, often an agreement, showing someone's ownership of a piece of property.

design registration: a registration which gives the owner the right for a limited period to stop others from using, making or selling a product to which the design has been applied, or in which it has been incorporated, without their permission.

design right: a right which applies to original designs of the shape or configuration of articles to prevent deliberate copying.

disclosure: the revelation of something which was not known to others.

easement: a right over someone else's land, such as the right to have pipes running under a neighbour's land.

estate: the interest which a person has in land; the property, goods and monies that are inherited after a death.

foreclosure: a situation in which the mortgagor defaults on the payment of the debt and the creditor ultimately obtains a court order for the sale of the property.

immovable property: real estate or real property.

infringe *(v.)*: act illegally against someone's rights.

infringement: an action taken when a third party uses a sign identical or similar to a registered mark.

IP: intellectual property.

landlord, landlady: the owner of a rented property.

lease: a legal document setting out an agreement for the use of a property under specific terms including terms as to the length of the agreement and the amount of the rent.

leasehold: the right to possess and use real estate pursuant to the terms of a lease or rental agreement.

licence: a legal document presenting the authorisation for a party to own, use, or do something.

mortgage: a legal document by which a financial institution such as a bank lends someone money in order to buy property and in return receives regular repayments by way of interest (and usually capital also) and takes a lien over the property.

movable property: (see personal property).

non-possessory interest in land: a category of rights held by a person to use land that is in the possession of another.

on-line: on the internet.

patent: a right granted by a government for a limited period, allowing an inventor to own his/her invention and control its use.

personal property: property that can be moved from one location or another as opposed to immovable or real property.

public domain: the status of what is available to everyone for use and possession.

rent: the amount of money regularly given by the tenant to the landlord or landlady in exchange for living in a property.

rental agreement: (see lease).

restrictive covenant: a legal obligation imposed in a deed by the seller upon the buyer of real estate to do or not to do something.

tenant: someone who lives on or uses the land or property belonging to a landlord in exchange for regular payments called rent.

third party: a person who is involved in a situation other than the two main persons, also called parties.

title: a legal document and right proving someone's ownership of a piece of property.

trademark: a distinctive sign used so that customers may recognise the products of a particular trader.

trespasser: a person who enters or lives on someone else's land or property without legal or proper authorisation.

work *(countable)*: a piece of copyright material.

1 **Answer the following questions on the previous text.**

1. What are the distinctions used in the description of property? Give a short definition of each.

2. What is the difference between property and ownership?

3. Are joint tenants, tenants in common and tenants in possession of a lease similar? If not, explain how they differ.

4. How are deeds transferred?

5. How are mortgages liens on property? Give a concrete example of a mortgage, identifying the mortgagor and the mortgagee.

6. What is the use of leaseholds?

7. Why are management companies used by many landlords?

8. Why are non-possessory interests necessary?

9. How is adverse possession limited? What is the common word used to refer to this interest?

10. When is the power of compulsory purchase used? Who holds it?

11. Why was intellectual property legislation created?

12. Precisely describe the areas covered by the four main types of IP.

13. What can patents be compared to?

14. Why does IP need protection? How is that protection acquired?

15. Which type of trademarks are protected without registration?

16. Give the requirements necessary for the application of design rights. How does the application of design rights differ from design registration?

17. Do works have to be registered to be protected by copyright legislation?

18. What is the idea behind the use of an expression such as "substantial part"?

19. What do the exceptions to copyright have in common? What is the particularity of fair dealing? How does it differ from the use of copyright material in reviews for example?

20. Search for several precise examples for all four types of IP.

2 **Are the following statements true or false? Give reasons for your answers.**

1. The distinction between movable and immovable property is unique to the British system.

2. Animals can be referred to as movable property.

3. Non-possessory interests limit the ownership that proprietors have over their land.

4. Registration is necessary in the transfer of freeholds but never in the case of a lease of the property.

5. By the terms of a lease, the tenant is responsible for keeping the smoke alarm in good working order and must replace it when necessary.

6. Protection is automatic for musical and literary works.

7. Anyone can manufacture, produce and market any product already under patent after a period of 20 years.

8. Passing off law offers protection against trademark violations.

9. All types of intellectual property can be bought, sold or licensed.

10. For official registration, copyright material has to be presented to the UK Patent Office.

3 What types of intellectual property are involved or protected in the following situations?

1. Two domain names were registered for internet websites without the consent or permission of the concerned parties. One name was registered as www.johnlennon.com, and the site had no connection with the musician other than to reserve and sell domain names; the other domain name was registered under www.princessdiana.com and the owner claimed to be running the site as a fan club for her.

2. Two recipes for an identical dish were offered simultaneously in the restaurants of two famous chefs, one in trendy Soho in London and the other in Birmingham. One chef, it seemed, had knowingly duplicated the other's recipe without crediting the innovator.

3. University students make regular use of a software program to share files from peer to peer, which involves downloading thousands of songs for free, without paying any compensation or royalties to the recording artists.

4. An author has written a best-selling novel which uses the same central themes as have appeared in previous non-fictional works by other authors. He does not, however, quote verbatim from these works. The ideas and events that figure in his novel are historical conjecture and, although they have been used before, no one has ever assembled, developed or expressed them in the same way.

5. A famous fashion designer is complaining that many of her very expensive and well-made garments are constantly being copied by a chain of retail outlets in Britain that mass-produce and market low-priced garments. Another designer, in a similar position, has decided not to complain as he believes the copies provide him with free advertising and develop a desire for the "real thing".

4 Are the following interests licences, easements or restrictive covenants?

1. British Rail needs to expand and build new tracks for the Eurostar passing through the countryside.

2. There is a city ordinance stating that certain houses in the community cannot be over a certain height.

3. Agreement is given to allow a company to erect large advertising displays at prominent sites in Manchester.

4. A British energy company needs to build pylons to carry electrical power lines.

5. The purchase of a ticket gives right of entry to a theatre, cinema or stadium.

6. A provision is made in a real estate agreement between a seller and purchaser that no business or trade shall be conducted on that land.

7. Vending machines are installed in the university student lounge and cafeteria.

8. A provision is made in a real estate contract to prevent another party from blocking sunlight or a view.

9. Homeowners cannot paint the exterior of their houses a certain colour or have outdoor radio or television aerials.

10. Permission is required to hunt or fish on another person's property.

2. More about...

A. Private leases: a tenancy agreement

An Assured Shorthold Tenancy Agreement for a residential property sets out the duties and responsibilities of the (non resident) landlord and tenant. The property or any part of it can be furnished or unfurnished and the tenant or tenants must be an individual or individuals (i.e. not a company or partnership). It gives special rights to the landlord to repossess the property at the end of the term and special rights to the tenant to apply to a rent assessment committee for a rent determination in certain circumstances.

An Assured Shorthold Tenancy can be for any length of time. Prior to 1997 the initial tenancy had to be for a fixed period of at least 6 months. It is recommended that this Agreement is not used for terms exceeding 3 years, in which case a solicitor should be consulted.

It is recommended that the Tenancy Agreement be prepared in duplicate and both copies should be signed by all parties, with both the landlord and tenant retaining a copy. An inventory should also be prepared of the furnishings or equipment included in the letting.

Clauses in this Agreement include:

– the amount of rent and deposit payable and the term of the tenancy,

– the landlord's obligation to insure the property and keep it wind and water-tight,

– the right of the landlord to charge interest on late rent payments,

– the tenant's obligation to

• pay bills and council tax,

• keep the property and any garden in good order and repair,

• use the property for residential purposes only,

• not to cause nuisance or annoyance to others,

• not to keep pets without written permission,

• not to leave property unattended for more than 21 days without informing the landlord.

Group work.

Work with another student – one being the landlord and the other the tenant – and draft a tenancy agreement for a furnished property. The agreement must include:
- names,
- addresses,
- terms,
- an inventory,
- the amount of the rent (weekly or monthly),
- the list of clauses which should be included in such an agreement.

B. Law of Property Act 1989

Law of Property (Miscellaneous Provisions) Act 1989 (c.34)

An Act to make new provision with respect to deeds and their execution and contracts for the sale or other disposition of interests in land; and to abolish the rule of law known as the rule in *Bain v Fothergill*. [27th July 1989]

Be it enacted by the Queen's most Excellent Majesty, by and with the advice and consent of the Lords Spiritual and Temporal, and Commons, in this present Parliament assembled, and by the authority of the same, as follows:–

Deeds and their execution.

1. [...] (2) An instrument shall not be a deed unless (a) it makes it clear on its face that it is intended to be a deed by the person making it or, as the case may be, by the parties to it (whether by describing itself as a deed or expressing itself to be executed or signed as a deed or otherwise); and (b) it is validly executed as a deed by that person or, as the case may be, one or more of those parties.

(3) An instrument is validly executed as a deed by an individual if, and only if (a) it is signed (i) by him in the presence of a witness who attests the signature; or (ii) at his direction and in his presence and the presence of two witnesses who each attest the signature; and (b) it is delivered as a deed by him or a person authorised to do so on his behalf.

(4) In subsections (2) and (3) above "sign", in relation to an instrument, includes making one's mark on the instrument and "signature" is to be construed accordingly.

(5) Where a solicitor or licensed conveyancer, or an agent or employee of a solicitor or licensed conveyancer, in the course of or in connection with a transaction involving the disposition or creation of an interest in land, purports to

deliver an instrument as a deed on behalf of a party to the instrument, it shall be conclusively presumed in favour of a purchaser that he is authorised so to deliver the instrument.[…]

Contracts for sale etc. of land to be made by signed writing.
2. (1) A contract for the sale or other disposition of an interest in land can only be made in writing and only by incorporating all the terms which the parties have expressly agreed in one document or, where contracts are exchanged, in each.

(2) The terms may be incorporated in a document either by being set out in it or by reference to some other document.

(3) The document incorporating the terms or, where contracts are exchanged, one of the documents incorporating them (but not necessarily the same one) must be signed by or on behalf of each party to the contract.

(4) Where a contract for the sale or other disposition of an interest in land satisfies the conditions of this section by reason only of the rectification of one or more documents in pursuance of an order of a court, the contract shall come into being, or be deemed to have come into being, at such time as may be specified in the order.

Exercise

Answer the following questions.

1. Make a list of all the conditions required for an instrument to be considered a deed.

2. Giving examples of your choice, describe what terms need to appear in a contract for the sale of land and what is required for it to be valid. Can such a contract be changed easily?

C. Case study: *McAlpine v McAlpine* [2004]

Sir Robert McAlpine Limited v Alfred McAlpine Plc
High Court, Mr Justice Mann, 31/03/04

Facts:
The Defendant and Claimant were well known construction companies. Both were offshoots of the same family business started by Sir Robert McAlpine in 1869 and both used "McAlpine" in their names. Whilst not identical in every respect, the two businesses had overlapping areas of trade within civil engineering and construction.

For some 70 years, co-existence was possible by use of the prefixes "Richard" and "Alfred" as identifiers. However, in 2001, the Defendant commenced a "rebranding" exercise to drop the "Alfred" from its name. The Defendant (or its brand consultants) believed that the inclusion of "Alfred" in the name contributed to a "muddy boots" image, which the Defendant was keen to leave behind. Without any warning to the Claimant, the Defendant began to describe itself as "McAlpine" in October 2003. Although the Defendant retained its company name, "Alfred" was dropped from its logo and domain name and there was also evidence, in the form of guides prepared by the Defendant's brand consultants, that the Defendant's employees were instructed to refer to the firm as "McAlpine" in written and oral communications.

The Claimant sued for damages in passing off, on the basis that the Defendant's use of "McAlpine" without an identifier, such as "Alfred", amounts to a misrepresentation to the effect that the services being provided or offered are those of or associated with the Claimant.

Held:

Mann J found for the Claimant:

Both the Claimant and Defendant were joint owners of goodwill in the name "McAlpine". Whilst neither party could prevent the other using the name, both had a policy (until the Defendant rebranded), of using the name in conjunction with an identifier. There was evidence that the name "McAlpine" is capable of referring to the Claimant in the absence of an identifier. Sometimes it can also refer to both businesses and in this sense the name can give either business an illusion of greater size. The evidence suggests that this may have been another reason why the Defendant chose to use "McAlpine" without the identifier.

Goodwill can be damaged by a co-owner using the name in circumstances where the use amounts to a misrepresentation and a partial ouster of the Claimant. It is sufficient, for the purposes of passing off, if there is a misrepresentation that one business is associated with another. The Defendant's use of "McAlpine" minus the identifier to refer to itself amounts to a misrepresentation and passing off in respect of those areas of trade where the Claimant and Defendant had overlapping interests.

The Judge accepted the Claimant's argument that goodwill attaches to the name "McAlpine" in relation to "the commercial area of the provision of construction, civil engineering, Private Finance Initiative, property development and capital projects services and services ancillary and/or complementary thereto". Therefore, passing off was established in relation to these activities.

Although the Court recognised that damages would be difficult to quantify, it awarded damages because the risk of harm to the Claimant's goodwill was real.

Answer the following questions.

1. Identify the different reasons for the claim, including those implied in the text.
2. How would you define "goodwill"?
3. Explain how the court came to its decision and what type of legislation it used.

3. Off the presses

A. Real property

> ### *Travellers lose landmark eviction appeal*
>
> A family of Travellers today lost an appeal to the House of Lords that their eviction from a public park near Leeds breached their human rights.
>
> In a ruling that will allow councils to continue the practice of planned evictions of Gypsies and Travellers, the seven-strong bench unanimously dismissed an appeal from the Maloney family.
>
> They had claimed that Leeds City Council infringed their Human Rights under article eight of the European Convention by evicting them from land at Spinkwell Lane, Tingley, West Yorkshire, in June 2004.
>
> But the Law Lords rejected the appeal. They ruled that the family had no links to the land, which is legally necessary under the European Convention's definition of a home.
>
> Lord Bingham ruled: "There is nothing to suggest they could show continuous links with the land, as would be necessary if it were to be regarded as their home. It is plain that their eviction was in accordance with domestic property law, which had the legitimate end of enabling public authorities to evict unlawful squatters from public land and restore it to public use. I can see no ground on which such action could be stigmatised as disproportionate, despite the personal afflictions to which these appellants were unfortunately subject."
>
> Lord Hope of Craighead noted that the Maloneys had been at the recreation ground for just two days when evictions proceedings against them began.
>
> The family, who have been evicted from 50 sites, have received legal aid, which is understood to have already cost about £300,000.
>
> The court of appeal dismissed the case in March last year, but took the unusual step of referring it to the Law Lords because of conflict between national and European rulings.

Possession proceedings over the land began at Leeds County Court, but were transferred to the High Court where a deputy judge ruled that human rights were not infringed.

Leeds City Council welcomed the ruling but called for local authorities to be given stronger powers to move unauthorised encampments.

Les Carter, the Council's executive board member responsible for Travellers' issues, said the problem cost the council around £250,000 every year.

He said: "Every year in Leeds we have to deal with around 60 unautho-rised encampments which cost the council £250,000 in legal, cleansing and other costs as well as creating significant problems in the communities where they are located. Today's ruling is extremely good news since it upholds our right to take swift and effective action to regain possession of our land. The problem of unauthorised encampments will continue until stronger powers are given to local authorities to allow unauthorised encampments to be moved more effectively than exists at the moment."

The Guardian (Press Association) 8/3/2006.

Exercises

1 Are the following statements true or false? Give reasons for your answers.

1. The Travellers' appeal was dismissed because the Court ruled that their human rights did not have to be respected in this issue.

2. By rule, city councils are allowed to forbid unauthorised encampments on their land.

3. The European Convention allows land appropriation if the occupiers can prove that they think of the land as their home.

4. Domestic property law allows the authorities to claim land back only if they need it for a particular public use.

5. Lord Hope of Craighead justified his decision by noting that the Travellers had not been on the site long enough for them to be allowed to stay permanently.

6. The Travellers have already tried to settle on 50 different sites and have therefore cost the state a large amount of money.

7. The case was transferred from the county court to the High Court and then to the House of Lords because it was a human rights case.

8. In Leeds, the authorities feel that their powers in this matter are too limited.

9. In spite of many problems, the city council still welcomes unauthorised encamp-ments on their public land.

10. The means available to the authorities for the removal of unauthorised encamp-ments are judged insufficient and ineffective.

2 Discuss.

1. Why was the case not considered as an infringement of the family's human rights?

2. Using information from the text and your knowledge on public property law, can you think of situations in which Travellers or Gypsies might have a case against the authorities and obtain permission to permanently camp on public land?

4. Food for thought

An agreement of purchase and sale of real property

1. ...... ("Seller") of (address) ...... and ...... ("Purchaser") of (address) ......

2. INTERPRETATION.
In this Agreement, unless the context indicates otherwise, the following expressions shall have the meanings assigned to them hereunder:
    2.1 the Property. no. ...... measuring ...... in the city of ...... and situated at (street address) ...... together with all buildings and structures thereon and all fixtures and fittings of a permanent nature pertaining thereto;
    2.2 the Estate Agent. The firm ...... of (address) ......
    2.3 the Conveyancer. The transferring solicitors appointed by the Seller/Purchaser, namely ...... of (address) ......

3. SALE AND PURCHASE.
Subject to the hereinafter mentioned terms and conditions, the Seller hereby sells to the Purchaser, who hereby purchases the Property. Included in the sale of the Property are the following movables:

4. PURCHASE PRICE AND GUARANTEES.
    4.1 The purchase price is ...... (British Pound Sterling) and is payable as follows:
        4.1.1 immediately after the Seller has signed this Agreement, the Purchaser shall pay ...... (British Pound Sterling) in trust to the Estate Agent who shall as soon as possible thereafter invest same in an interest bearing trust account, the interest accruing to the Purchaser;
        4.1.2 the balance of the purchase price shall be paid to the Seller against registration of transfer of the Property into the name of the Purchaser;
        4.1.3 immediately after registration of transfer of the Property into the name of the Purchaser, the Estate Agent shall pay to the Seller the payment referred to above, less the commission due to the Estate Agent in

terms of 11 hereunder, and to the Purchaser all the interest which has accrued on such payment.

4.2 The Purchaser shall within ...... days after fulfilment of all suspensive conditions contained in this Agreement lodge with the Conveyancer, a guarantee which shall:

4.2.1 be issued by an Financial Institution, the terms and conditions of which, shall be reasonably acceptable to the Seller (or the Conveyancer on his behalf); and

4.2.2 secure payment of the said balance to the Seller on registration of transfer of the Property into the name of the Purchaser and registration of a mortgage bond.

5. ACKNOWLEDGEMENTS BY PURCHASER.

The Purchaser acknowledges that:

5.1 they have acquainted themselves with the nature, condition, extent and locality of the Property; and

5.2 they will have no claim whatsoever against the Seller for any deficiency in the size of the Property which may be revealed on any re-survey nor shall the Seller benefit from any possible excess; and

5.3 the Property is sold:

5.3.1 to the extent as it now lies, without any warranties whether express or implied and the Seller shall not be liable for any defects whether latent or otherwise in the Property nor for any damages suffered by the Purchaser by reason of such defects; and

5.3.2 subject to all conditions, easements, licenses and restrictive covenants mentioned or referred to in the current and/or prior title deeds of the city planning scheme applicable thereto.

6. RISK AND OWNERSHIP.

With effect from the date of registration of transfer:

6.1 all the benefits and risks of ownership of the Property shall pass to the Purchaser; and

6.2 the Purchaser shall be entitled to the rents (if any) payable in respect of the Property and shall be liable for all rates and taxes levied thereon; and

6.3 the Seller shall become liable for and forthwith refund to the Purchaser the rents (if any) paid in respect of any period after the said date and the Purchaser shall similarly become liable for and forthwith refund to the Seller any rates and taxes and other imposts paid by the Seller in respect of any period after the said date.

7. TRANSFER.

7.1 The Purchaser is liable for payment of the fees of the Conveyancer in respect of the registration of transfer of the Property in the Purchaser's name, such fees being payable on demand by the Conveyancer. The Purchaser shall on demand pay all other expenses of and incidental to the registration of transfer of the Property into the name of the Purchaser, including transfer and stamp duty and survey and diagram fees (if any), as well as the costs of registration in this Agreement.

7.2 The Seller and the Purchaser undertake immediately, upon being requested to do so, to sign all documents in connection with the transfer, the cancellation of all bonds at present registered over the Property and the registration of any mortgage bond to be registered in terms of this Agreement.

7.3 Transfer of the Property shall be effected by the Conveyancer within a reasonable time after the provisions of this agreement, have been complied with.

8. BREACH.

8.1 In the event of:

8.1.1 the Purchaser failing to pay the payment referred to above and persisting in such failure for a period of 3 (three) days after receipt of a written notice from the Seller calling upon him to make such payment; or

8.1.2 either one of the parties ("the defaulting party") committing a breach of any of the other terms of this Agreement and failing to remedy such breach within a period of 14 (fourteen) days after receipt of a written notice from the other party ("the aggrieved party") calling upon the defaulting party to remedy the breach complained of, then the aggrieved party shall be entitled at his sole discretion and without prejudice to any of his other rights in law, either to claim specific performance of the terms of this Agreement or to cancel this Agreement forthwith and without further notice claim and recover damages from the defaulting party.

8.2 In the event that the defaulting party is:

8.2.1 the Purchaser, the Estate Agent will be entitled immediately upon cancellation of this Agreement to receive payment of the commission out of the payment referred to above. The balance of such payment, together with all the interest that has accrued thereon, shall be forfeited and paid to the Seller subject, however, to any remedies in that regard which are available to the Purchaser at law;

8.2.2 the Seller, the Purchaser shall immediately upon cancellation of this Agreement receive from the Estate Agent the payment made by the Purchaser above, together with all the interest that has accrued thereon.

8.3 Should there be a dispute as to the determination of the defaulting party, the Estate Agent shall retain in trust under his control, the payment referred to above until such dispute is resolved either by agreement between the Purchaser and the Seller or by order of a competent Court.

9. CAPACITY OF PARTIES.

9.1 If the Purchaser signs this Agreement as trustee or agent for a company the Purchaser in his personal capacity shall be regarded as purchaser in terms of this Agreement unless the said company duly adopts and ratifies this Agreement within 30 (thirty) days after the date upon which the Seller signs this Agreement, in which event the Purchaser by his signature hereto hereby interposes and binds himself in favour of the Seller as surety for and co-principal debtor with such company for the due and timeless performance by it of all of its obligations as purchaser in terms of this Agreement.

9.2 If any of the parties to this Agreement is a company, the person who signs the Agreement in the name of such company warrants that the company or is registered in terms of the applicable legislation. Such person shall be personally liable as Purchaser or Seller in terms of this Agreement, if such company legally does not exist, or for whatever reason is not bound to this Agreement or fails to comply with the provisions thereof.

10. GENERAL.

10.1 The parties undertake to do all such things as may be necessary, incidental or conducive to the implementation of the terms, conditions and import of this Agreement.

10.2 This Agreement constitutes the sole and entire agreement between the parties and no warranties, representations, guarantees or other terms and conditions of whatsoever nature not contained or recorded herein shall be of any force or effect.

10.3 No variation of the terms and conditions of this Agreement or any consensual cancellation thereof shall be of any force or effect unless reduced to writing and signed by the parties or their duly authorised representatives.

10.4 The Seller warrants that the amount referred above is the true purchase price in respect of the Property and that no other consideration is involved between the parties, directly or indirectly, in respect of the acquisition of the Property.

11. ESTATE AGENT'S COMMISSION.

11.1 Commission in the amount of …… (British Pound Sterling) shall be paid by the Seller to the Estate Agent.

11.2 The said commission will be earned upon the signature of this Agreement by both the Purchaser and the Seller and the fulfilment of all suspensive conditions contained herein and is payable upon registration of transfer of the Property into the name of the Purchaser.

11.3 As a result of a breach on the part of either the Purchaser or the Seller, the Estate Agent will immediately be entitled to payment of the commission from the party at fault;

11.4 It is recorded that the Purchaser warrants to the Seller that he was not introduced to the Property or the Seller by any person other than the Estate Agent.

11.5 By their signature hereto, the Estate Agent hereby accepts all benefits and obligations conferred upon them in terms hereof.

12. SUSPENSIVE CONDITIONS.

This Agreement is subject to the following condition(s):

12.1 Approval of Mortgage bond. The Purchaser (or the Estate Agent on behalf of the Purchaser) obtains approval, by not later than ...... for the granting of a loan by a Financial Institution of not less than ...... (British Pound Sterling) upon the security of a first mortgage bond to be registered over the Property at such rates of interest and on such conditions as are stipulated by the Institution to which application for the loan is made. This suspensive condition shall be deemed to have been fulfilled if such loan is approved.

AND

12.2 Sale of Purchaser's property

12.2.1 It is recorded that the Purchaser is currently the owner of certain Property .... ("*the Second Property*") which has been or is to be sold to a third party. The Seller acknowledges that the Purchaser requires the proceeds of the sale by him of the Second Property in order to meet his commitments under this Agreement. It is accordingly agreed that this Agreement is subject to the following additional suspensive condition consisting of four parts:

12.2.1.1 if the Purchaser has not yet signed an agreement of sale in respect of the Second Property, he shall by not later than .... have concluded an agreement for the sale of the Second Property for purchase price of not less than £......................... (pounds); and

12.2.1.2 all suspensive conditions contained in that agreement for the sale of the Second Property shall be fulfilled by not later than ....; and

12.2.1.3 the Purchaser shall be furnished with a guarantee securing payment to the Purchaser of the purchase price (or part thereof) of the Second

Property and a copy of such guarantee is to be furnished by the Purchaser to the Seller by not later than .... ; and

12.2.1.4 transfer of the Second Property shall be registered into the name of the purchaser thereof within 90 (ninety) days after the date referred to in clause 14.2.1.3 above.

12.2.2 The Purchaser shall within 30 (thirty) days after compliance with his obligation in terms of clause 12.2.1.3 above and (if applicable) fulfillment of the condition referred to in clause 14.1 above, whichever occurs last, lodge with the Conveyancer a guarantee or guarantees which shall:

12.2.2.1 be issued by an Institution or Institutions, the terms and conditions whereof shall be reasonably acceptable to the Seller or the Conveyancer on his behalf; and

12.2.2.2 secure payment of the balance of the purchase price of the Property to the Seller and/or his nominee/s on registration of transfer of the Property into the name of the Purchaser and registration of a mortgage bond, if applicable.

12.2.3 The Purchaser and the Seller undertake to cooperate with each other to procure as far as possible that the transfer of the Property and the Second Property shall be linked in the conveyancing and financing processes, it being their intention that the transfers and payments shall take place simultaneously. The Purchaser and the Seller hereby authorize their respective conveyancers to take such steps as may be necessary or conducive for the implementation of their aforesaid intention.

12.2.4 Pending fulfilment of the condition referred to above, the Seller may continue to market the Property through any estate agent, subject to any sole mandate granted to the Estate Agent, and which is still in force. Should they prior to fulfilment of the said condition receive a further bona fide written offer to purchase the Property, the following provisions shall apply:

12.2.4.1 a copy of the said offer shall be delivered to the Purchaser who shall be given an opportunity for 48 hours from such delivery to waive in writing all the provisions of clause 14.2; and

12.2.4.2 should the Purchaser not timelessly avail themselves of the opportunity as aforesaid, the Seller may accept the said further offer whereupon this Agreement between the Seller and the Purchaser shall immediately lapse and be of no further force or effect.

12.2.5 Upon non-fulfillment of this condition, or the lapse of the Agreement in terms of clause 12.2.4.2, the provisions of clause 13 shall apply.

13. WAIVER OF CONDITIONS AND LAPSE OF AGREEMENT.

Should any suspensive condition contained in this Agreement not be timelessly fulfilled, the entire Agreement shall automatically lapse and be of no further force or effect. In such event all amounts paid by the Purchaser shall be refunded plus any interest accrued.

14. SIGNATURE.

14.1 It is recorded that this document is intended to be signed firstly by the Purchaser and thereafter by the Seller.

14.2 The Purchaser acknowledges that their signature hereto constitutes an offer by them to purchase the Property on the terms and conditions set out herein which offer shall remain irrevocable until ...... (time) on the ...... (date) and available for acceptance by the Seller at any time prior thereto.

14.3 This Agreement shall be duly concluded upon timeless signature by the Seller and its validity will in no way be dependent upon the fact of such signature being communicated to the Purchaser.

THUS DONE AND SIGNED BY THE PARTIES ON THE DATES AND AT THE PLACES STATED HEREUNDER:

PURCHASER (OR DULY AUTHORISED REPRESENTATIVE)
I, the Purchaser, hereby consent to the aforegoing and confirm all of the terms and conditions herein contained.

SELLER (OR DULY AUTHORISED REPRESENTATIVE)
I, the Seller, hereby consent to the aforegoing and confirm all the terms and conditions herein contained.

WITNESS ESTATE AGENT (OR DULY AUTHORISED REPRESEN-TATIVE)

Signature

Exercises

1 **Answer the following questions.**

1. What are the obligations, liabilities and rights of each of the parties to this contract?

2. What factors could result in the default or breach of the agreement?

3. Explain in what situations the contract might be rescinded or voided and the performances of the parties excused.

2 Role play.

Pair up with another student to play the roles of the purchaser and the estate agent. The former, who has just signed the agreement, finds clauses in it that worry him or her, and the latter provides reassurance point by point.

C. Intellectual property

Beatles sue Apple over trademark

The Beatles' record company Apple Corps today accused Apple Computer of breaching a trademark agreement by selling music online.

The charge was levelled as the latest round of a 25-year dispute between the two companies over the brand name and fruit logo got under way in the High Court.

The argument centres on Apple Computer's iTunes service, which allows users to download and save pre-recorded songs through the Internet. There have been more than 1bn downloads through the iTunes Music Store, with 3.7m tracks available worldwide.

London-based Apple Corps, owned by Sir Paul McCartney, Ringo Starr and the widows of John Lennon and George Harrison, is suing over the alleged breach of a 1991 agreement between the two companies.

The agreement forbids Apple Computer from using the trademark for any application "whose principal content is music."

Geoffrey Vos QC, representing Apple Corps, told the court that Apple Computer had violated that agreement by selling music on-line.

He said the computer company's argument that it uses the fruit logo only in connection with a delivery system was "plainly wrong".

He said Apple Computer founder Steve Jobs had said that downloading music from the Internet was exactly the same as buying an LP.

The Beatles, through Apple Corps, have so far refused to license any of their recordings for sale through on-line music services.

Their record company is seeking court orders to stop Apple Computer using the apple logo in connection with the iTunes Music Store.

It is also seeking damages after an investigation into the computer firm's profits.

Apple Computer has transformed the way people listen to music, through iTunes and the sale of some 14m iPods around the world. Mr Justice Mann, who is hearing the case, confessed in a preliminary hearing that he owns an iPod.

The High Court case will centre on the meaning of a 15-year-old agreement arguably designed to cover only CDs and tapes, but not envisaging ground-breaking developments such as iTunes.

The legal wrangle between the two companies goes back to 1981, when an original agreement allowed the Californian company to use the name only for the sale of computers.

But Apple Computer later used the logo for computers to edit and record music, prompting the Beatles' company to file its first lawsuit against the hardware giant in 1989.

The companies settled their dispute in 1991 following a high court trial lasting more than 100 days. Apple Computer is believed to have paid out around 16.3m British pounds and the two sides also signed a new trademark agreement replacing the earlier contracts.

The contract stipulated Apple Computer could use the logo for computers, data processing and telecommunications, while the Beatles could retain it for music.

But in September 2003 Apple Corps said Apple Computer had entered the entertainment business with iTunes and breached their trademark agreement.

At the time, Apple Computer responded: "Unfortunately, Apple and Apple Corps now have differing interpretations of this agreement."

The Guardian, 29/3/2006.

Exercises

1 Answer the following questions.

1. Who are the parties involved in this case?
2. What kind of dispute is this?
3. What is the record company seeking through this legal action?
4. Explain the argument put forward by the computer company.
5. Who is Geoffrey Vos? What does he hold against Apple Computer?
6. Explain what the court case is expected to centre on.
7. Why does Apple Corps object to iTunes?
8. How does this case fit into trademark laws described at the beginning of this chapter?
9. How does the evolution of the music industry play an important role in this case?

2 Research project.

1. Find out what the verdict was in the case mentioned in the article.
2. Look up what the present legislation concerning internet downloads in the UK is. Find out whether there are current campaigns in favour of or against free downloading and who the different groups involved in those campaigns are.

5. Listening

1 🔘 Listen to part of a radio programme – *Money Does Matter* – in which an interviewer asks Emily West, the Information Commissioner, about banks processing personal information outside the EU. Complete the extract with the missing words.

INTERVIEWER: And those contract terms themselves – like the Three-Cities ...... ones – are you happy with them?

WEST: I think we're all learning that there are different ways of ...... the information so as to be as straightforward as possible with ...... without creating unnecessary alarm. At the beginning of the programme, you said this was to reduce ...... and to be able to apply weaker or less onerous rules on data .... I think that may be unfair in this context. Yes, it is to make processing less expensive, but all the ...... you've referred to are talking about situations where processing's being done on their behalf. In those circumstances, the bank remains the "data ......", to use a legal term, which means it is responsible for your ...... throughout. They are therefore liable if anything goes wrong, so they take the matter very seriously. And the law requires a ...... that makes that perfectly clear to the processor ...... and places a duty of ...... on that processor overseas.

INTERVIEWER: Yes, but it's very difficult, isn't it? Enforcing a contract on the other side of the globe is different from finding someone ...... the law in the UK. Can you really ...... contracts with companies in China or India?

WEST: No, I can't, but the ...... is in fact on a data controller within the European Union. It's not at all the situation your original ...... described where he felt his bank would ...... his personal information, selling it abroad for others to market. That isn't what's happening here. That would require much stricter tests and would need the ...... of the individual.

INTERVIEWER: So there's no danger people's personal ...... will be on sale for $10 on a CD-ROM in Hong Kong?

WEST: Well, I'd rather not say "no danger": there are always people who seek to break the .... But the purpose of the law and the intention of banks is to ensure that the banks keep ...... of the data. It's not in the banks' ...... for there to be any problems with that. What we can do is make certain they've got good contracts, that they've ...... customers properly, and then we have to keep an eye on what follows. But I think it's an important thing for your customers to remember that ...... rests with the banks, so there's somebody they can get hold of in the UK.

2 **Answer the following questions.**

1. Why do banks have their customer data processed abroad?

2. What are the dangers of having information on customers processed abroad?

3 **Discuss.**

Highlight the link between data protection and property law. Does information on an individual belong to the individual himself or to the person who collected and processed it?

6. Grammar practice

1 **Complete the sentences with *a, an,* or ø.**

1. He is ...... honest estate agent.
2. The company made ...... U-turn and agreed to change the name of the website.
3. Can you get ...... B.A. in Property Law?
4. The landlord is of ...... American origin but is resident in the UK.
5. Those Travellers have ...... history of illegal occupation of public land.
6. He paid ...... eight-figure sum for the house.
7. Do you spell "lease" with ...... "s" or ...... "z"?
8. This is ...... one-way street.
9. This property shows how British architecture was affected by ...... Italian influence in the late 16th century.
10. Your action constitutes ...... infringement of my copyright.

2 **Complete the sentences with the article "the" if necessary.**

1. In general terms, what exactly is ...... relationship between ...... landlord and ...... tenant?
2. He told me on ...... phone that he hadn't signed ...... deed yet.
3. Real estate owners in ...... Germany and ...... United Kingdom pay fewer taxes than owners of property in ...... USA and ...... Netherlands.
4. There are many magnificent castles in ...... Loire Valley, but very few in ...... north of France.
5. She doesn't like ...... people interfering in her negotiations with ...... estate agent.
6. He spends all day thinking up ...... inventions. Just the other day, he designed ...... first automatic toothbrush.
7. He is very nice to ...... landlady, and hopes to get out of paying ...... rent this month.
8. Copyright gives creators ...... right to control ...... use of their material.
9. Throughout the world, French and Italian fashions are considered ...... most elegant.
10. Compared to mine, ... rent set by your landlord is extremely high.

3 **Translate the following sentences into English.**

1. Je n'ai pas encore vu sa nouvelle maison. Moi, si. Elle m'a invité chez elle la semaine dernière.

2. C'est la première fois que j'achète cette marque.

3. Nous avons déjà signé le bail et nous avons aussi rencontré le propriétaire.

4. Quand va-t-il va augmenter le loyer ? La loi ne l'autorise pas à le faire avant trois ans.

5. Elle a écrit le livre il y a dix ans, et Hollywood veut maintenant lui acheter les droits pour en faire un film.

6. Regardez ! Il est en train de déchirer le contrat de prêt bancaire ! Arrêtez-le !

7. Nous étions deux à inventer le premier ordinateur parlant, par conséquent le brevet est à nos deux noms.

8. As-tu lu les petites annonces aujourd'hui ? Ils ont enfin publié l'annonce de la mise en vente de notre appartement.

9. Beaucoup de gens téléchargent de la musique sur des sites *peer-to-peer*, ce qui peut constituer une menace pour la propriété intellectuelle.

10. Il est en panne d'idées ; cela fait longtemps qu'il n'arrive plus à écrire un mot de son roman.

4 **Translate the following sentences into French.**

1. Property law governs the various forms of ownership in real property and personal property within the common law system.

2. In many European Union and civil law systems, this division is between movable and immovable property.

3. Conveyancing is the act of transferring the ownership of a property from one person to another.

4. A deed is a legal instrument which is used to grant a buyer of land all the rights that go with this purchase.

5. A landlord is the owner or lessor of a house, flat, farm, or apartment which is rented or leased to an individual or business, called the tenant or lessee.

6. Society wants to reward and protect inventors, artists, designers, and developers of businesses and their reputation.

7. In order to obtain a patent for an invention, first and foremost, it must be new and not form part of the "state of the art".

8. A trademark distinguishes the goods and services of one trader from another and is used as a marketing tool so that customers can recognise the product of a particular trader.

9. A design right is property which may be bought, sold or licensed and, unlike design registration, it does not have to be registered.

10. Like physical property, copyright can be bought, sold, inherited or transferred, wholly or in part.

Chapter 11

European Union law

I. Fundamentals

The building of the European Union (EU): a brief history

The European Union as such was created on November 1st 1993, when the Treaty of Maastricht came into effect. The numerous stages leading up to this important event resulted from the significant efforts and willpower on the part of European leaders. Though the hope for a unified Europe had been expressed since the time of Charlemagne, it was only following World War II that the European Union's symbolic **forefathers**, Jean Monnet and Robert Schuman, laid the groundwork towards ending violence and bloodshed among Europeans once and for all.*

Their proposal, that of first allying Europe's major steel and coal industries, was to become reality with the 1951 European Coal and Steel Treaty (ECSC), otherwise known as the Treaty of Paris. This Treaty joined together the coal and steel industries of France, Germany, Italy and the Benelux countries under the auspices of the High Authority, presided over by Jean Monnet.

Following this initial endeavour, the most fervent advocates of a united Europe called for the next step, i.e. increased cooperation in the area of defence, and the creation of institutions that would lead to stronger political union. Though this has yet to be fully accomplished*, significant strides have nonetheless been taken towards this goal. The majority of them have centred on expanding and improving economic cooperation between Member States.

Though essentially economic in nature, the Treaty of Rome, signed in 1957 and establishing the European Economic Community and Euratom (the

---

* This asterisk and subsequent ones indicate that the information provided is true at the time of writing, in 2006.

European Atomic Energy Community), led to the parallel creation of four political and juridical institutions: the European Council, now called the Council of the European Union, the Assembly, now known as the European Parliament, the European Commission and the European Court of Justice.

Since the late 1950s, the European Union has undergone successive **enlargements** due mostly to the success of common policies in trade and agriculture as well as the abolition of customs duties between EU member countries. The most striking accomplishment to date of these shared policies, and the most tangible for European people at large, was the creation of the common currency – the euro – an ambitious project launched in the early 1970s by European Community leaders and finally implemented on January 1st 2002. The steps preceding this distinctive economic event are contained in the 1986 Single European Act, which laid the ground for the free circulation of goods, services, capital and workers. Political foundations were also reinforced during this period with the 1992 Treaty on European Union (Treaty of Maastricht), the 1997 Treaty of Amsterdam, and the 2001 Treaty of Nice. Many advocates of reinforced political union within the European Community have also called for the drafting and approbation of a European Constitution; however, this still remains to be achieved*.

Despite obstacles and setbacks, the initial six-member group has now grown* to a union of 25 members – by order of accession: Belgium, France, Italy, Luxembourg, the Netherlands, West Germany, Denmark, Ireland, the United Kingdom, Greece, Portugal, Spain, Austria, Finland, Sweden, Cyprus, the Czech Republic, Estonia, Hungary, Latvia, Lithuania, Malta, Poland, Slovakia, and Slovenia. Two additional countries, Bulgaria and Romania, have completed accession negotiations and are awaiting their integration in 2007 or 2008; and Croatia, the Republic of Macedonia and Turkey are in various stages of accession discussions. The remaining states in the Balkans (Albania, Bosnia and Herzegovina, Serbia and Montenegro) are defined as "potential candidates" and aspire to join the European Union. Georgia, Moldova, and Ukraine expressed the same desire, but have met with little response on the part of EU institutional leaders*.

How the European Union's institutions work

Treaties signed by European Union Member States, also known as primary legislation, have established what is to be decided at the EU level and how these decisions are to be taken. Three major institutions were created toward this end, and they simultaneously represent the interests of individual Member States (the Council of the European Union), the citizens of all EU countries (the European Parliament), and the EU as a whole (the European Commission). Article 249 of the Treaty of Maastricht defines the interaction between these three institutions as follows: "In order to carry out their task and in accordance with the provisions of this Treaty, the European Parliament acting jointly with the Council and the Commission shall make regulations and issue directives, take decisions, make recommendations or deliver opinions."

The Council of the European Union (or the Council of Ministers, or simply the Council) is the EU's highest decision-making body. It represents the governments of the individual Member States and is made up of one minister from each country. The agenda of Council meetings determines which minister from a Member State will attend; for example, if the Council's agenda focuses on environmental issues, each Member State will send its own Minister for the Environment.

The Council is required by treaty to take its decisions either unanimously or by a majority or "qualified majority vote" (a specified minimum number of votes cast in favour). This raises the issue of "weighted votes", i.e. countries with larger populations having more votes than less-populated countries, as in the case of "qualified majority decisions". For example, Germany, France, Italy and the United Kingdom each have 29 votes and Spain and Poland each have 27 votes, while Cyprus and Luxembourg have 4 and Malta has 3.

In addition to the aforementioned Council, there is also the European Council, the highest policy-making body. It comprises the Member States' heads of state or government and the President of the European Commission (see below). The European Council's task is to take initiatives and provide guidelines for EU development. However, it does not take any formal decisions. It is easy to confuse the European Council with the Council of Ministers (the Council) as their composition is sometimes similar. However, their tasks are entirely separate, the former acting as a policy inventor, the latter as the law-maker.

The European Parliament is a fully-fledged participant in the EU's legislative process and also monitors the Commission. Members of the European Parliament are elected directly by the citizens of Member States every five years. Elections were last held in 2004 and the Parliament has 732 members.

One of the most important tasks of the European Parliament involves sharing legislative responsibility with the Council. This is carried out through several procedures provided for by the 1986 Single European Act (**cooperation procedure** and **assent procedure**), and the 1992 Treaty of Maastricht (**co-decision procedure**). The Treaty of Amsterdam and the Treaty of Nice expanded to 30 the number of areas wherein Parliament and the Council legislate, using the confines of the co-decision procedure.

Other important tasks of the European Parliament include approving the EU budget (together with the Council), approving the Commission as a whole and monitoring its work. The latter task gives to Parliament a genuine democratic control over the Union, as it has the power to dismiss the Commission by adopting a **motion of censure** (with a two-thirds majority).

Number of Members of Parliament (MEPs) by Member State

Austria:	18	Greece:	24	Poland:	54
Belgium:	24	Hungary:	24	Portugal:	24
Cyprus:	6	Ireland:	13	Slovakia:	14
Czech Republic:	24	Italy:	78	Slovenia:	7
Denmark:	14	Latvia:	9	Spain:	54
Estonia:	6	Lithuania:	13	Sweden:	19
Finland:	14	Luxembourg:	6	United Kingdom:	78
France:	78	Malta:	5		
Germany: 99		Netherlands:	27	**Total**	732

The European Commission (the Commission) is the third key institution and carries out many of the day-to-day tasks of the EU. Among other things, it is the only institution that has the right to propose new EU legislation. It also monitors the application of EU decisions and compliance with regulations. Its members are meant to represent the European Union as a whole, not their respective native countries, and therefore must act with complete independence.

The Commission consists of 25 members, one from each Member State. Each **Commissioner** is responsible for a different area of EU policy. As "Guardians of the Treaties", the Commissioners have to make sure that the regulations and directives adopted by the Council and the European Parliament are implemented. If not, the Commission can take the offending party to the European Court of Justice.

The President of the Commission is nominated by the Council of the heads of state at government level. Commission Members are nominated by individual Member States. Parliament then takes a vote on whether to approve the Commission as a whole. The Commission is appointed for a period of five years.

Several other important European Union institutions should also be mentioned, in particular the Court of Justice, the European Economic and Social Committee, the European Central Bank, and the Court of Auditors.

As EU law must be applied in the same way throughout the Union, the European Court of Justice (ECJ) has the task of interpreting EU regulations when they are unclear and of providing rulings in litigation. National courts may turn to the European Court of Justice for explanations on how a particular provision is to be interpreted. The Court of Justice can also handle matters of dispute between Member States, the EU institutions, and in certain cases individuals affected by EU legislation.

The Court has one judge from each Member State, and judges are appointed by joint agreement of the governments of the Member States for a period of six years. The Court of First Instance, established in 1989 and made up of one judge per EU country, hands down rulings on cases that deal more particularly with litigation involving firms and/or private individuals and cases linked to competition law.

EU law: general principles

Traditionally, legislation is divided into two types: primary and secondary legislation. EU primary legislation is found in the treaties. Secondary legislation, made up of regulations and directives, is legislation made by the Community under the authority of a treaty. Regulations and directives do not have the same status as Treaty Articles, which means that they do not give rise to the same rights for individuals. The provisions of EU legislation are either directly effective or indirectly effective.

There are five EU treaties: the Treaty of Rome, the Single European Act, the Treaty on European Union, the Treaty of Amsterdam and the Treaty of Nice. Their provisions are directly effective, which means they give rise to rights or obligations which individuals may enforce before their national courts. Nevertheless, in order to be directly effective, certain conditions, called the *Van Gend* criteria, must be satisfied: the article giving rise to a right or an obligation must be clear, precise and unconditional, and it must leave no room for discretion in its implementation by a Member State.

A provision is said to have either vertical direct effect or horizontal direct effect. A provision has vertical direct effect when an individual has the right to bring an action against a public body, such as in the case of *Van Gend en Loos,* where a company sued the Dutch customs authority. A provision is said to have horizontal direct effect when an individual has the right to bring a claim against another individual, as in the case *Defrenne v Sabena.*

Apart from Treaty Articles, EU law falls into one of four categories : regulations, directives, decisions, and recommendations and opinions.

1. Regulations

Regulations are defined in Article 249 EC: "A regulation shall give a general application. It shall be binding in its entirety and directly applicable in all Member States." Where the *Van Gend* criteria are satisfied, a regulation is directly effective. It is both horizontally and vertically effective, as the case of *Leonesio v Italian Minister of Agriculture* established. Regulations are the most important and binding form of legislation. They tend to be initiated by the European Commission and are passed, of course, at the European level.

2. Directives

Directives are defined as follows: "A directive shall be binding in its entirety, as to the result to be achieved, upon each Member State to which it is addressed, but shall leave to the national authorities the choice of form and methods." In *Van Duyn*, the ECJ ruled that if directives were not capable of direct effect, this would weaken the useful effect of directives. In order for directives to be directly effective, the *Van Gend* criteria must be satisfied, the date for implementation should have expired and, in cases where the provision is unclear, the provision should be referred to the ECJ for interpretation under Article 234 EC. At home, the UK government has sometimes been accused of over-implementing directives by enacting laws that go further than the minimum requirements of the directives (a process called "gold plating"). Paradoxically, in a few of those same cases, the ECJ has ruled against the UK for inadequate implementation of directives, as there can be different interpretations of the objectives involved and how to achieve them.

Directives have a vertical direct effect against public bodies. However, it is important to note that a directive cannot have a horizontal direct effect, as *Marshall v Southampton and South West Hampshire Area Health Authority* established. The ECJ applies the principle of fairness, since it is unlikely that a private body would know about the many existing directives, and the rule that a private body should not suffer from a government's lack of action in applying a directive.

The fact that a directive cannot give rise to horizontal direct effect creates problems for individuals and the correct implementation of EC laws. Over the years, the ECJ has developed the concepts of state liability and indirect effect to guarantee redress to European citizens.

State liability was established by the *Francovich* case in which the ECJ ruled that a State was liable for its failure to implement a directive and would have to compensate individuals for damage suffered as a result of that failure. A directive must satisfy three tests to enable a claim against the State to succeed: it must give rights to individuals, these rights must be identified from the directive and there must be a causal link between the State's failure to implement it and the damage suffered by the individual.

Indirect effect allows someone to obtain a remedy under EC law in national courts if there is a relevant national law that a court may interpret purposefully in the light of an EU directive. This is derived from an interpretation of Article 10 EC which states that "Member States shall take all appropriate measures, whether general or particular, to ensure fulfilment of the obligations arising out of this Treaty or resulting from action taken by the institutions of the Community." In the case of *Van Colson*, the ECJ concluded that the national courts must ensure that they interpret national law in such a way as to ensure that the objective of a directive is fulfilled. And in the *Marleasing* case, the ECJ extended this principle and stated that national courts should apply a purposive approach even to non-implementing legislation. However, the principle of indirect effect cannot work where there is no relevant national law.

3. Decisions

Decisions can be addressed to a country, a company, or even an individual and are binding upon them.

4. Recommendations and opinions

These are not legally binding.

EU competition law

One of the essential tenets of the common market is to allow competition to develop freely. The government and businesses in the UK must abide by European rules on fair trade practices. EU competition policy applies to the following areas: **antitrust law** and **cartels**, **merger** control, liberalisation and the way state aids may be granted to businesses. The European Commission is empowered to investigate cases and propose appropriate measures to end infringements of EU competition law. It may sanction companies and states which violate the European competition rules. The decisions of the Commission to enforce EU competition rules are subject to judicial review by the European Court of Justice.

Article 81 of the Treaty establishing the European Community prohibits "all agreements between undertakings, decisions by associations of undertakings and concerted practices which may affect trade between Member States and which have as their object or effect the prevention, restriction or distortion of competition within the common market." These practices include colluding to fix prices or carve up markets and limiting production. The Article provides an exception for agreements between undertakings which "contribute to improving the production or distribution of goods or to promoting technical or economic progress, while allowing consumers a fair share of the resulting benefit, and which does not [...] afford such undertakings the possibility of eliminating competition in respect of a substantial part of the products in question." Article 82 bans "any abuse by one or more undertakings of a dominant position within the common market or in a substantial part of it [...] as incompatible with the common market in so far as it may affect trade between Member States."

The European Commission has power to oversee mergers and **takeovers** of one company by another to preserve competition within the Union. It may thus ban a merger which would result in a single company having a **dominant position** in a given market.

The EU has been committed to eliminating **monopolies**, whether state-operated or private, based on the notion that they tend to stifle innovation and drive prices up. The liberalisation of goods and services is already effective in the areas of transportation and telecommunications, for instance. However, an exception exists for inherently uneconomic services which may be regarded as a public service, like postal services in underpopulated areas.

An important part of part of EU competition law concerns the issue of State aid to businesses, over which the European Commission exercises very strict supervision. Article 87 of the Treaty states that "any aid granted by a Member State or through State resources in any form whatsoever which distorts or threatens to distort competition by favouring certain undertakings or the production of certain goods shall, in so far as it affects trade between Member States, be incompatible with the common market." This clause, however, does not apply to: "(a) aid having a social character, granted to individual consumers, provided that such aid is granted without discrimination related to the origin of the products concerned; (b) aid to make good the damage caused by natural disasters or exceptional occurrences; (c) aid granted to the economy of certain areas of the Federal Republic of Germany affected by the division of Germany, in so far as such aid is required in order to compensate for the economic disadvantages caused by that division."

Aid may also be considered as compatible with the principles laid down by the Treaty. "Aid to promote the execution of an important project of common European interest or to remedy a serious disturbance in the economy of a Member State" and aid aimed at promoting regional development, research, culture or certain activities without being contrary to the common interest. The tests for determining if State aid complies with European law consist in determining first whether the aid is likely to benefit the whole Union and second whether the aid is granted to a business that would have otherwise received private sponsorship. No State funds may be allocated to undertakings which would not serve the Union's interest or do not appear financially viable.

Finally, it is worth noting that the UK also comes under the authority of the World Trade Organisation in matters related to competition.

UK *v* EC legislation

Membership of the European Union has created many legal problems for the UK courts, among which are the issue of the supremacy of the UK Parliament and the literal tradition of statutory interpretation.

Is the UK Parliament still supreme?

In its present form, EC law is supreme over all other forms of conflicting national law, no matter when the national law was passed. The Treaty of Rome does not mention anything about the supremacy of EC law. This principle was established in each member State by rulings from the ECJ and from national courts.

Four years after the UK Parliament passed the European Communities Act 1972, which incorporated EU law into the body of UK law, the English courts still considered that UK law should prevail over EU legislation, on account of the supremacy of the British Parliament. In the case of *Felixstowe Dock and Railway Co. and European Ferries Ltd. v British Transport Docks Board* [1976] 2 Lloyd's Rep 656, Lord Denning, sitting in the Court of Appeal, stated that a Statute should override the Treaty of Rome. The courts should apply the Statute without any reference to the fact that its provisions might conflict with Article 82 EC (ex 86 of the Treaty of Rome). He wrote: "It seems to me that once the Bill is passed by Parliament and becomes a Statute, that will dispose of all this discussion about the Treaty. These Courts will then have to abide by the Statute without regard to the Treaty at all." This is quite a striking comment considering the way the courts subsequently applied the principle of the supremacy of EU law over UK law.

Four years later, a new decision overturned the principle that EU law was not supreme. In *Macarthys Ltd v Smith* [1979] 3 All ER at 329, the same Lord Denning ruled that when legislation seemed deficient or inconsistent with EU law, the courts should interpret the national law as much as possible in the light of the EU legislation. He stated at 329: "In construing our statute, we are entitled to look at the Treaty as an aid to its construction [...]." If that was not possible, because it would induce a construction of the English statute that would be too far fetched, then the courts should give **precedence** to the EU law, and apply it to the case at hand, notwithstanding conflict with an Act passed by the British Parliament. He also stated at 329: "If on close investigation it should appear that our legislation is deficient or inconsistent with Community law by some oversight of our draughtsmen then it is our bounden duty to give priority to Community law." The reason given was that Parliament passed the European Communities Act in 1972 (ECA). As a consequence, Parliament and the courts were bound to implement and apply laws in accordance with EU legislation and, even if the EU provision was not implemented in a statute, it was nonetheless directly effective in national courts. Moreover, one of the bases of EU law (and of the functioning of EU institutions) was that it takes precedence over any national law in case of conflict or inconsistency. Lord Denning stated further at 329: "Under s 2(1) and (4) of the European Communities Act 1972 the principles laid down in the Treaty are 'without further enactment' to be given legal effect in the United Kingdom; and have priority over 'any enactment passed or to be passed' by our Parliament." As long as in subsequent legislation the supreme British Parliament did not expressly state that it wished to **repeal** ECA 1972 or to override a part of EU law, then judges should consider that any Act passed by any subsequent Parliament were intended to comply with the provisions of EU law. Any inconsistency was considered as an unwilling oversight of the legislator and was to be set right by the judge. Lord Denning added: "I have assumed that our Parliament, whenever it passes legislation, intends to fulfil its obligations under the Treaty."

In 1979, case law established the supremacy of EU law over any Act of Parliament, unless a subsequent Act of Parliament expressly repelled ECA 1972. This principle still stands today. The courts interpret s2(4) of ECA 1972 as allowing the UK courts to give priority to EU law. The same conclusion was reached by a string of decisions emanating from the ECJ. In *Van Gend*, the ECJ stated that the Treaty of Rome created a new legal order and as a consequence EU provisions prevailed over national laws. This statement was easy to make since the contentious legislation was earlier than the EU law. This point was further developed in the *Costa v ENEL* case, where the ECJ decided that EU law was supreme over later national legislation. One further question was to know whether all legislation had to bow down to EU law, since some countries distinguish laws from entrenched legislation, which is often associated with constitutions. The case of *International Handelgesellschaft* established the supremacy of EU law over national constitutions. The power of EU law was taken one step further when, in *Simmenthal*, it was decided that national courts should apply EU law when there was a conflict with national law.

The most notable cases in the development of UK domestic law on the supremacy of EU law are the *Factortame* cases (*R v Secretary of State for Transport, ex parte Factortame* [1991]). The House of Lords had to acknowledge that EU law forced them to grant a remedy (an injunction against the Crown) which was beyond their power under national law.

Interpretative tradition

Chapter 5, "The work of the courts", developed the British principles of statutory interpretation. They apply only to UK law, since with EU legislation the national courts adopt a purposive approach, which is common in Continental legal systems but foreign to the English tradition.

In *Macarthys Ltd v Smith* [1980] 3 All ER at 329, Lord Denning, as quoted above, stated: "In construing [the statute in the case], we are entitled to look at the Treaty as an aid to [the] construction [of the UK statute]." Nevertheless, when interpreting a piece of UK legislation in the light of EU law induced a construction of the statute that was too far-fetched, then the UK courts declined to do so, as in the *Duke* case in 1988, when the Law Lords felt unable to construe s6(4) of the Sex Discrimination Act 1975 to comply with the Equal Treatment Directive, which they deemed unfair and opaque. This position had to be reversed the following year in the *Lister* case, when the House of Lords recognised that courts must take a purposive approach when interpreting and applying EU implementing legislation. In many respects, this was a totally new approach to statutory interpretation by the courts, but it still only applies to EU implementing legislation.

Definitions in context and key words

antitrust law: a body of laws or regulations against monopolies and restraints on competition.

assent procedure: the procedure by which the Council obtains Parliament's approval before a decision (accession of a new Member State, association agreement or other fundamental agreement with a non-EU country, or appointment of the Commission President) is finalised. The European Parliament may accept or reject a proposal but cannot amend it. The decision cannot be adopted without the assent of Parliament.

cartel (also called a trust): a group of suppliers who enter into a collusive arrangement to limit output in order to regulate pricing and production.

co-decision procedure: the procedure according to which Parliament issues an Opinion on a Commission proposal. The Council, acting by a qualified majority, draws up a common position, which Parliament examines at a second reading and should adopt, amend or reject. Ministers in the Council need to approve a rejected proposition unanimously for it to go forward.

Commissioner: an executive member of the European Commission.

cooperation procedure: the procedure whereby legislation is adopted jointly with the Council. The two bodies must agree on the same text for it to go forward.

dominant position: the market power held by one or more companies with a large share of a relevant market.

enlargement: the expansion of the EU which takes in new Member States.

forefather: the founder of a family, a concern, a body or a tradition.

MEP: a Member of the European Parliament.

merger: the combination of two or more companies into one.

monopoly: the exclusive control of the production, distribution or marketing of a good.

motion of censure: a parliamentary motion put before and voted upon by a parliament in the hope of defeating a government.

precedence: priority.

repeal *(v.)*: do away with (a law).

takeover: the acquisition by one business of another.

Exercises

1 Say whether the following statements are true or false:

1. The European Union was created on November 1st 1995 when the Treaty of Maastricht came into effect.

2. It was only following World War I that the European Union's forefathers laid the groundwork towards ending violence and bloodshed among Europeans once and for all.

3. Their proposal, that of first allying Europe's major steel and coal industries, was to become reality with the 1953 European Coal and Steel Treaty.

4. The Treaty of Rome was signed in 1957.

5. The common currency – the euro – an ambitious project launched in the early 1970s by European Community leaders, was finally implemented on January 1st 2001.

6. The Treaty on the European Union (Maastricht Treaty) was signed in 1995.

7. The Treaty of Amsterdam was signed in 1999.

8. The Treaty of Nice was signed in 2002.

9. Treaty articles, directives and regulations have the same status and applicability.

10. A provision is said to have a horizontal direct effect when it gives one individual the possibility of taking legal action against another.

11. State aid to companies is encouraged by the European Commission.

12. There is no appeal from a decision of the European Commission.

13. It is illegal for a company to squeeze competitors out of the common market.

2 **Explain the role of each of the following institutions.**

1. the Council of Ministers

2. the European Council

3. the European Parliament

4. the European Commission

5. the European Court of Justice

3 **Define the following words.**

1. directive   **2.** directly applicable   **3.** horizontal direct effect   **4.** indirect effect   **5.** primary legislation   **6.** public body   **7.** purposive approach   **8.** regulation   **9.** secondary legislation   **10.** state liability   **11.** treaty   **12.** *Van Gend* criteria   **13.** vertical direct effect

4 **In the text, what information is given about the following cases?**

1. the *Costa v ENEL* case   **2.** the *Duke* case   **3.** the *Factortame* case   **4.** the *Felixstowe* case   **5.** the *International Handelsgesellschaft* case   **6.** the *Lister* case   **7.** the *Macarthys* case   **8.** the *Simmenthal* case   **9.** the *Van Gend* case

5 **Reading figures and acronyms. Practice reading these sentences aloud, paying particular attention to what is in bold type.**

1. The Treaty of Rome was signed in **1957**.

2. Under Article **226 EC** (ex **169**) the Commission may bring proceedings in the **ECJ** against a member state for failure to observe **EU** law.

3. The **ECHR** was written in the **1950s**.

4. The United Kingdom became a member of the then **EEC** in **1972**.

5. The European Communities Act was passed in **1972**.

6. In *Defrenne v SABENA* (**No 2**) (case **43/75**) **[1976] ECR 455**, the **ECJ** ruled that Treaty Articles could have direct effect.

7. According to Article **10 EC** the Court's decisions are binding on all national courts.

8. The Single European Act was signed in **1982**.

9. The effect of the launch of the **EMU** on references to **ECU** in **EU** legislation is that those references are now read as if they were references to the **euro**.

10. The Maastricht Treaty was signed in **1992**.

11. In the case *Leonesio v Italian Minister of Agriculture* (case **93/71**) **[1972] ECR 287**, an individual wished to rely on a regulation to bring an action against a public body.

12. Under Article **234 EC** (ex **117**) the **ECJ** has power to give preliminary rulings on interim references from courts of Member States.

13. The Treaty of Amsterdam was signed in **1997** and came into force in **1999**.

14. Until **1 January 1999**, the **ECU** (European Currency Unit) was the Community's unit of account.

15. The definition of a public body is to be found in *Foster v British Gas* (case **C-188/89**) **[1990] ECR I-3133**.

16. The Treaty of Nice was signed in **2000**.

17. In *Marshall v Southampton and SW Hampshire Area Health Authority* (case **152/84**) **[1986] ECR 723** the ECJ ruled that a directive could not have a horizontal direct effect.

18. According to **Article 4 of Directive 68/360**, a worker is entitled to a five-year residence permit.

19. Article 39(3) EC (ex 48[3]) permits derogations from the principle of free movement of workers on grounds of public security, public policy and public health.

20. The **EEA** consists of the Member States of the EC, as well as Norway, Iceland and Liechtenstein.

6 **Understanding citations. Answer the questions about the following citations.**
A. Secondary legislation

Regulations: Reg (EEC) No. 139/2004
1. What is the year of issue?
2. What is the number of the Regulation within that year?
3. What is the name of the relevant Community it derives from?

B. Directives

Dir 77/249/EEC
1. What is the year of issue?
2. What is the number of the Directive within that year?
3. What is the name of the relevant Community it derives from?

C. Case law

Punch v Judy (case C–12/2004) [2005] ECR 365 and [2005] CMLR 143
1. What is the case number?
2. When was the case filed?
3. What does "C" stand for?
4. What would "T" stand for?
5. What does ECR stand for?
6. What does CMLR stand for?
7. What does the date between brackets refer to?

7 **Nationalities. For each country associated with the EU, give the corresponding noun and adjective designating its people, as in the example.**

Example : France: *a Frenchman, a Frenchwoman (a French person); French.*

A. Member States
1. France 2. Belgium 3. the Netherlands 4. Luxembourg 5. Italy 6. Germany 7. Greece 8. Spain 9. Portugal 10. the Republic of Ireland 11. the United Kingdom 12. Denmark 13. Sweden 14. Finland 15. Austria 16. Malta 17. Cyprus 18. Poland 19. Hungary 20. the Czech Republic 21. Slovakia 22. Slovenia 23. Latvia 24. Lithuania 25. Estonia 26. (01/01/2007) Bulgaria 27. (01/01/2007) Romania

B. Official candidates for membership
1. Croatia 2. Turkey 3. Macedonia

C. Potential candidates
1. Albania 2. Bosnia and Herzegovina 3. Serbia 4. Montenegro

D. Members of the European Economic Area (EEA)
1. Iceland 2. Norway 3. Liechtenstein

2. More about European Union law

A. Where to find information on EU law.

INFORMATION ON	PAPER DATABASE	ELECTRONIC DATABASE
Treaties of European Union Law: Constitutional Texts	Encyclopedia NB. A fee-paying database (e.g. Lexis) may also be used.	http://www.europa.eu.int
Regulations, directives Community Secondary Legislation	Encyclopedia of European Union Law: (e.g. Lexis) may also be used.	http://www.europa.eu.int NB. A fee-paying database

INFORMATION ON	PAPER DATABASE	ELECTRONIC DATABASE
EU cases (ECJ and CFI)	Current Law Case Citator	http://www.europa.eu.int NB. A fee-paying database (e.g. Lexis) may also be used.
EctHR cases	Current Law Case Citator	http://www.europa.eu.int http://www.echr.coe.int, NB. A fee-paying database (e.g. Lexis) may also be used.

Exercises

1 **Research project. Find the relevant cases and explain how you retrieved the information.**

1. A man lives in a religious community in the Netherlands. He does some plumbing work for them for free. The case is heard in 1988.

2. A man named Bettray is carrying out a job as part of a drug-rehabilitation programme. The case number is C-413/99. The woman involved is a French divorcee living in the UK.

2 **What information does each citation give?**

1. *Union Royal Belge des Sociétés de Football Association (ASBL) v Bosman* (case C-415/93) [1995] ECR I-4921.

2. *Kalanke v Freie Hansestadt Bremen* (case C-450/93) [1996] 1 CMLR 175.

3. *UK v Council* (case C-84/94) [1996] ECR I-5757.

4. *Lister v Forth Dry Dock and Engineering Co. Ltd* [1989] 2 WLR 634.

5. Working Time Regulations 1998 (SI 1998 No.1833).

6. Article 251 EC (ex 189b).

7. Sale of Goods Act 1979.

8. *P v S and Cornwall County Council* [1996] IRLR 347.

9. Article 39 EC (ex 48).

10. Regulation 1612/68.

11. The Sale and Supply of Goods to Consumers Regulations 2002 (SI 2002 No.3045).

12. Directive 68/360.

13. *Grant v South-West Trains* (case C-249/96) [1998] All ER (EC) 193.

14. Consumer Protection Act 1987.

15. *Webb v EMO Air Cargo* (case C-32/93) [1994] ECR I-3567.

3 **Research project on consumer protection. Go to the Europa website and find Directive 85/374 and Directive 93/13. Read them and solve the following two cases.**

Case A

Jennifer buys a microwave oven, which costs her £600, from EDEN, an electrical retailer. The microwave oven was manufactured by Magor, which sold it directly to EDEN. Magor is a company set up by the government to provide skilled work in electronic manufacturing as part of a job-creation scheme. Jennifer uses her microwave oven in her small bedsit for a week or so; however, one day, she switches it on and it explodes. The oven and an antique table next to which it was set (worth £1,000) are destroyed, and Jennifer's fitted carpet and wallpaper are so badly damaged that they will have to be replaced. Jennifer herself suffers minor but painful cuts from the blast.

---

1. Team 1 represents the interests of Jennifer: on the basis of Directive 85/374, would Jennifer be able to make a claim either against EDEN or Magor?

2. Team 2 represents the interests of EDEN: how can they defend themselves against the claim made by Jennifer?

3. Team 3 represents the interests of Magor: how can they defend themselves against the claim made by Jennifer?

Case B

Mrs Jones buys a sofa and two armchairs from MABI. The terms of the contract for the purchase from MABI are set out in a standard contract form, which Mrs Jones signs without reading. The following terms appear on the contract:

"If the suite is defective and cause you injury, MABI will not be liable to you in any way. MABI in fact accepts no liability at all for any defects in the product. The price of the suite is £1,500, but MABI reserves the right to increase this price when sending you the invoice of the suite.

MABI will be the sole judge of whether the suite actually delivered is in accordance with the terms of the contract.

If you have any complaint against MABI, you must refer it to the Furniture Manufacturers' Association for arbitration, rather than going to court."

When the sofa and the two armchairs are delivered, Mrs Jones is presented with an invoice of £2,000. The suite is dark pink, not red as ordered, and when Mrs Jones sits on one of armchairs, it collapses and she is injured. She contacts MABI about the problems but is told that according to the terms of the contract she has no grounds to complain.

---

1. Team 1 represents the interests of Mrs Jones. On the basis of Directive 93/13, would Mrs Jones be able to make a claim either against MABI?

2. Team 2 represents the interests of MABI. How can they defend themselves against the claim made by Mrs Jones?

3. Team 3 represents the interests of the *Furniture Manufacturers' Association*. How can they back MABI's terms of contract?

4 **Research project on equal treatment of men and women. Read the following information and present your case before the ECJ.**

1. Procedures in direct actions

> **Initiation of proceedings before the Court**
> The action must be brought before the Court by written application addressed to the Registry. As soon as it is received, the application is entered in the Court register. The Registrar publishes a notice of the action and of the applicant's claims in the Official Journal of the European Union. A Judge-Rapporteur and an Advocate-General, whose duty it is to follow the progress of the case, are then appointed. The application is served at the same time on the other party, who has one month within which to lodge a defence. The applicant may submit a reply and the defendant a rejoinder, the time allowed being one month in each case. The time-limits for lodging these documents must be adhered to unless an extension is specifically authorised by the President.
>
> **Preparatory inquiries and the Report for the Hearing**
> Once the written procedure is completed, the parties are asked to state, within one month, whether they wish for a hearing to be arranged. The Court decides, upon reading the report of the Judge-Rapporteur and hearing the views of the Advocate-General, whether any preparatory inquiry is necessary and to what type of bench the case should be assigned to. The President sets the date for the public hearing. In a Report for the Hearing, the Judge-Rapporteur summarises the facts alleged and the arguments of the parties and the interveners, if any. The report is made public in the language of the case at the hearing.
>
> **The public hearing and the Opinion of the Advocate General**
> The case is argued at public hearing before the appropriate bench and the Advocate-General, unless the case is decided without an Opinion by the Advocate-General. The Judges and the Advocate-General may put to the parties any questions they consider appropriate. Some weeks later, again in open court, the Advocate-General delivers his Opinion before the Court of Justice. He or she analyses in detail the legal aspects of the case and independently proposes a solution to the problem. This marks the end of the oral procedure.

> **Deliberation and judgment**
> Next, the Judges deliberate solely among themselves on the basis of a draft judgment drawn up by the Judge-Rapporteur. Each of the Judges may propose changes. When a final text has been agreed upon, judgment is given in open court.

2. The facts of the case

Andrew runs a small business, which was set up a few months ago. He expects it to grow quickly and to be successful, but at the moment, his business is struggling to survive.

All his employees are full-time, but he pays a higher hourly rate to employees who are prepared to work their hours flexibly (night and weekend work). He has two male employees (John and Peter) and two female (Jane and Elizabeth). The men both work flexible hours, but the women have opted for fixed hours because of their duties at home. His justification for paying the lower rate to fixed-hours employees is that such workers are less profitable for the business. In order to motivate his employees, Andrew decides to enroll them in a contracted-out pension scheme, by which pension payments are made to retired men over 65 and retired women over 60. Andrew dismisses Jane for "persistent lateness" and advertises her job. He has five candidates for the job, four women (Charlotte, Ruth, Daisy and Pauline) and one man (Stephen). All four women are qualified for that kind of work, since they have held similar positions, but two of them are married with children and two are single mothers. Andrew needs an employee willing to work extra hours. He therefore decides to hire the man, who is neither qualified nor experienced in the field.

3. The claim

Jane, Elizabeth, Charlotte, Ruth, Daisy and Pauline decide to sue Andrew collectively for sexual discrimination. Their case is taken to the ECJ because they cannot be granted a remedy in their national courts (this is in the early days of the EU).

4. The parties to the case

1. applicants' lawyers
2. head lawyer: Mrs Gribben
3. Jane's lawyer: Mrs J.
4. Elizabeth's lawyer: Mrs E.
5. Charlotte's lawyer: Mrs C.
6. Ruth's lawyer: Mrs R.
7. Daisy's lawyer: Mrs D.
8. Pauline's lawyer: Mrs P.
9. defendant's lawyer: Mr Crawford

10. interveners: Women's Lib' lawyer (Mrs W.), an NGO which supports equality between males and females in the workplace
11. Judge-Rapporteur: Mr J.
12. Advocate-General: Mr A.
13. Judges: Mrs B. and Mrs F.

5. The procedure
1. written procedure
2. claim (applicants' lawyers)
3. defence (defendant's lawyers)
4. reply (applicants' lawyers)
5. rejoinder (defendant's lawyers)
6. oral procedure
7. report (Judge-Rapporteur)
8. opinion (Advocate-General)
9. judgment
10. draft judgment (Judge-Rapporteur)
11. changes to the draft (judges)

5 **Research project on personal mobility. You are a team of lawyers and you are asked to advise Justine on her EU rights. Use your knowledge of EU personal mobility rights.**

1. Justine is a French national and she would like to work in the UK. She applies for two jobs in London. The first company turns her down, stating it only employs British citizens and the second company, Lovells, offers her a job, subject to the successful completion of a short vocational test to check her suitability for the job. Justine passes the test and accepts the post, but she discovers that her British colleagues working in similar positions are paid £100 per month more than she is and that she works one hour more per day.
What are Justine's remedies under EU Law?
2. Justine would now like to have her family with her in London: her two French children (Matteo, 13 years old, and Theo, 23), her mother (who is Albanian, lives with her in France and is physically dependent), her ex-husband (who is French, with whom she is close) and her (female) partner, who is Italian. She plans to buy a large house in Hammersmith.
Can she have all these family members with her?
3. At the border, her family is stopped at the British customs. Justine, her mother and her two children have passports. However, the British authorities refuse entry to her mother, because she is a non-EU national.
Are they entitled to do so?
4. On a closer check, the British authorities discover that Justine is part of the Church of Scientology, an organisation which, although not banned in the UK, the government

does not wish to promote, and that she was convicted of a bank robbery ten years ago. They want to deny her access to British territory.

Are they entitled to do this?

5. To celebrate the purchase of their home, Justine and her family have a house-warming party. She ends up drunk and is arrested by the police for anti-social behaviour. The British authorities threaten to deport her for not having a residence permit.

Are they entitled to do this?

6 **Research project on business mobility. Using your knowledge of the provisions protecting business mobility, help your law firm advise Kevin.**

1. Kevin has a successful business in the UK and wishes to expand his business into France. He provides luxury plumbing services 24hrs a day and has 25 employees. He decides to set up a branch office in Paris that he will run himself to test the market there, and he goes to the *Chambre de Commerce* to find out the requirements to set up a business in France. They tell him he should deposit 500,000 euros to guarantee customers against deficient services, and that he should have local referees that guarantee the quality of his plumbing service.

Can the French Chambre du Commerce *impose these requirements?*

2. Kevin goes bankrupt in Paris, but he likes the French lifestyle and decides to stay in France and look for a job. The problem is that he cannot find a post as a senior manager because he only has a BA in Business Administration, which has no equivalent in French universities.

What can he do?

3. Off the presses

An EU Commission press release

Mergers: Commission clears BT's acquisition of Infonet

Brussels, 25th January 2005

The European Commission has approved under the EU Merger Regulation the acquisition by British Telecommunications of Infonet Services Corporation, a US operator providing global telecommunications services to large multinational corporations. As the incremental share of the target company in these services is limited, the Commission considers that the operation will not significantly impede effective competition in the European Economic Area (EEA) or any substantial part of it.

With its acquisition of all issued and outstanding shares in Infonet Services Corporation ("Infonet"), British Telecommunications ("BT") acquires control of the whole of Infonet.

The Commission investigated the competitive effects of the proposed transaction on the possible markets for global telecommunications services ("GTS") that are provided to multinational corporations ("MNCs"). It found that the transaction would not change significantly the market conditions either on a global or on a European scale as Infonet brings only a minimal incremental market share to BT. The combined BT/Infonet will continue to face a number of competitors that are present in these markets. In addition, customers have indicated that they will still have the possibility to switch competitively to alternative GTS suppliers.

BT, a company organised under the laws of England and Wales, is a provider of telecommunications services on a worldwide basis. Its principal activities include local, national and international telecommunications services, internet products and services and IT solutions. Among other things, BT provides global telecommunications services to MNCs with global operations.

Infonet is a Delaware (US) company and its shares are listed on the New York Stock Exchange. Infonet's main shareholders are Swisscom, TeliaSonera, KDDI, KPN, Telefonica and Telstra, which together hold approximately 97% of the voting rights. The rest of the shares is held by other, smaller shareholders. Infonet provides GTS to a range of MNCs on a global basis and (unlike BT) has a comparatively strong presence in the Americas and in the Asia Pacific region. Infonet provides its services through its worldwide network, including broadband, wired and wireless services, IP Video VPN, and integrated security services.

Ref: IP/5/88, http://europa.eu.int

Definitions in context

corporation: company

incremental: additional or increased

Exercises

1 Answer the following questions.

1. Note the terms which belong to the field of economics.
2. Which company in this case was the target company?

3. Why did the Commission authorise the merger?
4. Describe the interactions between the three levels involved here: national, European and global.

Research project.

Search the Europa website for another example of a merger involving a UK-based company and write a paragraph to present it.

4. Food for thought

Exercise

Written and oral presentations.

Choose a case on one of the themes listed below, find it and read it on the Europa website. Write a two-page summary of the case, including relevant information. Present your findings to the rest of the group. Listen to your fellow students' oral presentations and write down (a) the facts of each of their cases, and (b) the findings.

1. Direct and indirect effect
– *Van Gend en Loos v Nederlandse Administratie der Belastingen* (Case 26/62) [1963] ECR 1
– *Defrenne v SABENA* (Case 43/75) [1976] ECR 455
– *Leonesio v Italian Minister of the Agriculture* (Case 39/72) [1973] ECR 101
– *Marshall v Southampton and SWH AHA* (Case 152/84) [1986] ECR 723
– *Foster v British Gas* (Case C-188/89) [1990] ECR I-3313
– *Pubblico Ministerio v Ratti* (Case 148/78) [1979] ECR 1629
– *Francovich and Others v Italian State* (Cases 6/90 and 9/90) [1991] ECR I-5357
– *Van Colson and Kamann v Land NordrheinWestfalen* (Case 14/83) [1984] ECR 1891
– *Marleasing SA v La Comercial Internacional de Alimentation SA* (Case C-106/89) [1990] ECR I-4135

2. Working time
– *UK v Council* (Case C-84/94) [1996] ECR I-5757
– *Lister v Forth Dry Dock and Engineering Co. Ltd* [1989] 2 WLR 634

3. Equal treatment for men and women
– *Macarthys v Smith* (Case 129/79) [1980] ECR 1275

– *Garland v British Rail Engineering* (Case 12/81) [1982] ECR 359
– *Barber v Guardian Royal Exchange Assurance Group* (Case C-262/88) [1991] 1 QB 344
– *Ministère Public v Stoeckel* (case C-345/89) [1991] ECR I-4047
– *Johnston v Chief Constable of the Royal Ulster Constabulary* (Case 222/84) [1986] ECR 1651
– *Kalanke v Freie Hansestadt Bremen* (Case C-450/93) [1996] 1 CMLR 175
– *Jenkins v Kingsgate (Clothing Productions) Ltd* (Case 96/80) [1981] ECR 911
– *P v S and Cornwall City Council* [1996] IRLR 347

4. Personal mobility

– *Levin v Staatsecretaris van Justitie* (Case 55/81) [1982] ECR 1035
– *Kempf v Staatsecretaris van Justitie* (Case 139/85) [1986] ECR 1741
– *Steyman v Staatsecretaris van Justitie* (Case 196/87) [1988] ECR 6159
– *Bettray v Staatsecretaris van Justitie* (Case 344/87) [1989] ECR 1621
– *R v Immigration Appeal Tribunal, ex parte Antonissen* (Case C-292/89) [1991] ECR I-745
– *Rewe-Zentral AG v Bundesmonopolverwantlung für Branntwein (Cassis de Dijon)* (Case 120/78) [1979] ECR 649
– *Baumbast and R v Secretary of State for the Home Department* (Case C-413/99) [2002] ECR I-7091
– *Cristini v SNCF* (Case 32/75) [1975] ECR 1085
– *Netherlands v Reeds* (Case 59/85) [1985] ECR 1285
– *R v Pieck* (Case 157/79) [1980] ECR 2171
– *R v Bouchereau* (Case 30/77) [1977] ECR 1999
– *Adoui and Cornouaille v Belgian State* (Cases 115 and 116/81) [1982] ECR 1665

5. Business mobility

– *Reyners v Belgium* (Case 2/74) [1974] ECR 631
– *Commisson v Italy* (Case 3/88) [1989] ECR 4035
– *Gebhard v Consiglio dell'Ordine degli Avvocati e Procuratori di Milano* (Case C-55/94) [1995] ECR I-4165
– *SPUC v Grogan* (Case C-159/90) [1991] ECR I-4685
– *Cowan v Le Trésor Public* (case 186/87) [1986] ECR 195
– *R v Human Fertilisation and Embryology Authority, ex parte Blood* [1997] 2 All ER 687
– *Groener v Irish Republic* [1989] ECR 3967
– *Vlassopoulou v Ministerium für Justiz, Bundes-und-Europaangelegenheiten Baden-Württemberg* (Case 222/86) [1990] ECR1-2327

5. Listening

Exercises

1 💿 **Listen to Part 1 of a radio programme put together by the radio station's political editor, Rachel Hughes, and complete the extract with the missing words.**

HUGHES: All across Europe, people think the European Parliament is a ...... institution. ...... % think their own national governments have a big effect on them, while only ...... % think the Parliament of the EU does. So what is the role of ......? The European Commission civil servants propose laws. Their duty is to act in the interest of the European Union as a whole. The legislation then must be approved by the ...... of Ministers, the individual countries, and the European Parliament. This is called a " ...... ". Half of all British laws now come from the EU. ...... MPs have the power to amend most of the laws. To make these rather abstract relationships clearer, you could perhaps focus on something closer to home.

NICHOLAS COLE MEP: Let's take your fridge: for a start, the fridge itself would now have to be manufactured according to European .... It will later be ...... , according to a recent European law. And everything in the fridge is affected by European laws, ... and standards.

HUGHES: That includes ...... on foods, the kinds of bananas we import and the transportation of meat. The Parliament's passed ...... laws in its last five-year term, with particular focus on consumer and environmental protection, introducing labelling for ...... foods and a ban on using animals to test cosmetics. MEPs set tougher environmental targets for lead-free petrol and strengthened the law to cut lorry drivers' working hours. Not everybody sees the European Parliament as being dynamic. The generous travel ...... of MEPs have often been criticised—allowances for air fares regardless of the cost; office and secretarial allowances are £ ...... a year; and then, one week a month, the whole Parliament travels from Brussels to Strasbourg, which costs £135 million a year. That's ...... % of its total budget. The MEPs point out that all that is decided by the Member States, and not the European Parliament, but it serves as ...... for those who want us to ...... from the Union altogether.

2 💿 **Listen to the complete recording (Parts 1 and 2) and answer the following questions.**

1. What is the role of the European Parliament?
2. How do EU laws affect our every day lives?
3. Which British party is the most pro-European?
4. How is European legislation viewed by citizens of the EU?
5. What could the EU Parliament do to improve its image?

3 **Discuss.**

Is the European Parliament a democratic institution?

6. Grammar practice

1 **Purpose and consequence.**

A. Each example consists of two sentences. Are they linked by "purpose" or by "consequence"?

B. Rewrite each pair of sentences as one sentence, using "to + infinitive", "in order to", "so as to", "so that"... Make any other changes that may be necessary.

1. The European Union brought together nations that were formerly at war. Violence and bloodshed in Europe ended once and for all.

2. The EU's forefathers thought of allying Europe's major steel and coal industries. The idea was the development of the economy.

3. Since the late 1950s, the EU has undergone successive enlargements. The idea is to avoid leaving out essential parts of the Continent.

4. The Single European Act was drafted in 1986. The drafters wanted to establish freedom of movement within the Union.

5. The decision to adopt the common currency was left to the Member States. The UK was able to keep the pound.

6. A treaty article giving rise to a right or an obligation must be clear, precise and unconditional. The idea is to avoid room for discretion in implementation.

7. The European Court of Justice interprets regulations when they are unclear. In this way, Member States know how to apply them.

8. The ECJ has developed the concepts of state liability and indirect effect. European citizens can now seek redress when a government fails to apply a directive.

2 **Purpose. Write complete true sentences using the elements supplied but without changing their order. Put the verbs into their correct forms and add any other words that may be necessary.**

1. The Treaty/draft/people and goods/move freely within the Union

2. Article 81 of the Treaty/write/ prohibit agreements which may affect trade

3. The common currency/adopt/European citizens/travel around Europe

4. The European Commission/have power to oversee mergers/competition/preserve/among Member States /more easily

5. State aids to business/supervise/the European Commission/not impede fair exchanges and development

6. UK courts/bind/interpret/domestic legislation/not conflict with EU law

3 **Consequence. Link the sentences using (1) so ... that, and (2) such ... that. Make any other changes that are necessary.**

1. WWII created a deep trauma in Europe. The need for cooperation and solidarity became pressing.

2. Campaigning against a European Constitution was very efficient in France. Voters rejected the proposal.

3. There was much reluctance among British judges to recognise EU law as supreme. It took several years for case law to establish this supremacy once and for all.

4. Enlargement is a very long and arduous process. It has not been completed yet.

5. Free circulation of goods and people has completely changed the nature of exchanges within the Union. There have been negative responses from fringes of the population.

4 "Whether" and "if". In each of the following sentences, can you replace "if" by "whether" and vice versa? What is the difference between the two?

1. To determine *if* State aid is compatible with European standards, the two litmus tests are to inquire first *whether* the aid is in the interest of the European Union as a whole and, second, *whether* a private investor would be likely to venture money in the same circumstances.

2. Aid to low-cost airlines can be accepted *if* the revenues they generate offset the cost to the taxpayer of existing under-utilised infrastructure at secondary airports.

3. "*If* on close examination it should appear that our legislation is deficient or inconsistent with Community law [...] then it is our bounden duty to give priority to Community law." Per Lord Denning.

4. *If* the Council's agenda focuses on environmental issues, each Member State will send their own Minister for the Environment.

5. After Member States have proposed Commission Members, Parliament takes a vote on *whether* to approve the Commission as a whole.

5 Complete the sentences using "whether" when it is possible to do so. If it is not possible, use "if".

1. In order to determine ...... an undertaking has a dominant position, the Commission defines the relevant market.

2. ...... an undertaking produces bananas, it is for the European authorities to decide ...... the relevant market is bananas or fruits in general.

3. ...... a merger contravenes EU regulations, the Commission may take the measures necessary to restore effective competition.

4. The Commission has to check ...... regulations and directives adopted by the Council and the Parliament are implemented. ...... not, the Commission can take the offending party to court.

5. ...... Turkey will join the Union remains doubtful.

6 Tenses. Make a sentence using either the preterite or the present perfect to state when or since when the following states became or have been part of the EC.

1. Austria and Sweden/1995, **2.** Cyprus/2004, **3.** Denmark/1973, **4.** France/1957, **5.** Greece/1981, **6.** Spain and Portugal/1986

Annexes

1. Index of UK statutes and regulations, EU legislation and directives and cases

UK statutes and regulations

EU legislation and directives

Cases

2. Index of language points (Grammar section)

3. Index of key words

Crédits

All texts protected by copyright are appropriately credited on the pages on which they appear.

Those under Crown Copyright (pp. 53-57, pp. 78-79, p. 82, pp. 114-117, pp. 148-149, pp. 181-185, p. 186) are reproduced either by permission or under Parliamentary Licence n° P2006000281.

We extend our special thanks to the following for their permission to reproduce material: The Law Society (pp. 76-78, p. 84, pp. 286-289), The Bar Council (pp. 76-77), The Adam Smith Institute (pp. 85-88), The Magistrates' Association (pp. 111-113), The Commission for Racial Equality (pp. 280-281) and LexisNexis Butterworth's (pp. 121-125, p. 150, pp. 210-214).

Photographs p. 69 by Yvonne-Marie Rogez.

Remerciements

Les auteurs tiennent à remercier Anaig Fenby pour son travail de relecture.

The tracks on your CD

IMPRIM'VERT®

Imprimé en France par SEPEC à Péronnas
N° d'imprimeur : 01662140904 - Dépôt légal : septembre 2006
N° d'édition : 70114414-06/sep2014